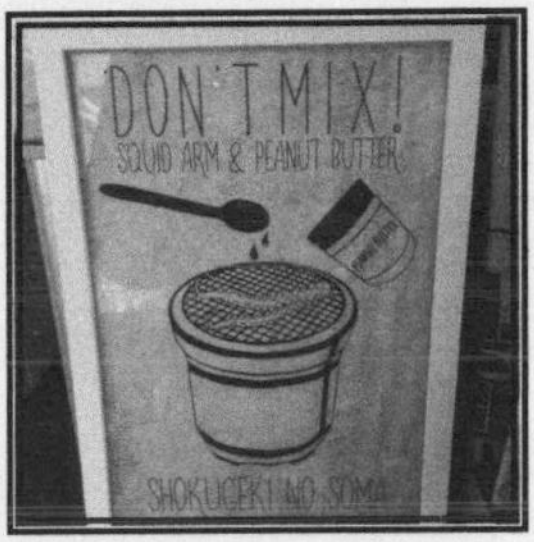
DON'T MIX!
SQUID ARM & PEANUT BUTTER
SHOKUGEKI NO SOMA

Yuto Tsukuda

A lot of earthshaking news happened in 2016. Wherever you happen to be, I hope you have a happy New Year!

Shun Saeki

We got a Pomeranian! A really energetic boy!

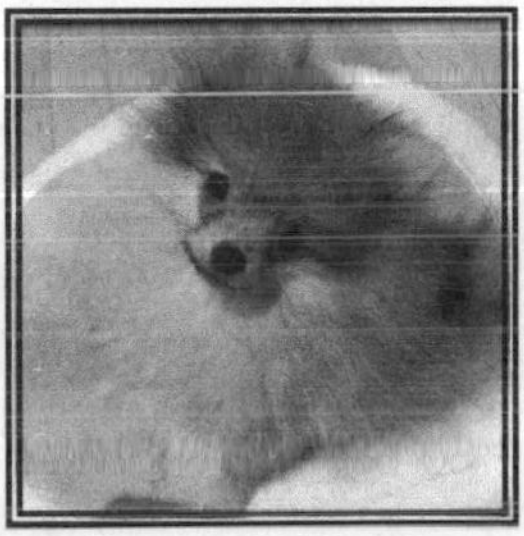

About the authors

Yuto Tsukuda won the 34th Jump Juniketsu Newcomers' Manga Award for his one-shot story *Kiba ni Naru*. He made his *Weekly Shonen Jump* debut in 2010 with the series *Shonen Shikku*. His follow-up series, *Food Wars!: Shokugeki no Soma*, is his first English-language release.

Shun Saeki made his *Jump NEXT!* debut in 2011 with the one-shot story *Kimi to Watashi no Renai Soudan*. *Food Wars!: Shokugeki no Soma* is his first *Shonen Jump* series.

Food Wars!
SHOKUGEKI NO SOMA

Volume 22
Shonen Jump Advanced Manga Edition
Story by Yuto Tsukuda, Art by Shun Saeki
Contributor Yuki Morisaki

Translation: Adrienne Beck
Touch-Up Art & Lettering: James Gaubatz, Mara Coman
Design: Alice Lewis
Editor: Jennifer LeBlanc

Published by VIZ Media, LLC
P.O. Box 77010
San Francisco, CA 94107

10 9 8 7 6 5 4 3 2 1
First printing, February 2018

www.viz.com

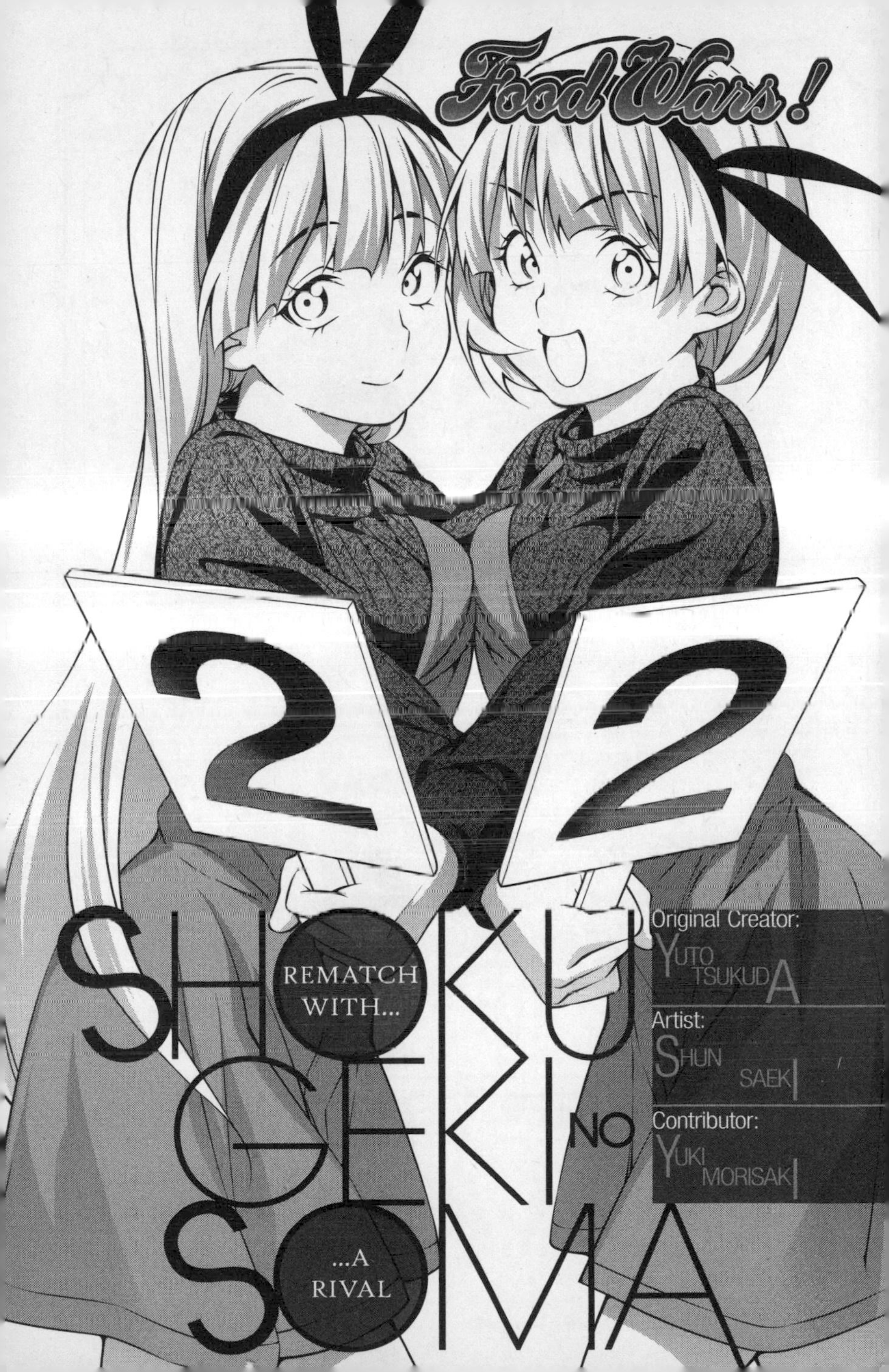
Food Wars!
22
SHOKUGEKI NO SOMA
REMATCH WITH...
...A RIVAL
Original Creator: YUTO TSUKUDA
Artist: SHUN SAEKI
Contributor: YUKI MORISAKI

CHARACTERS

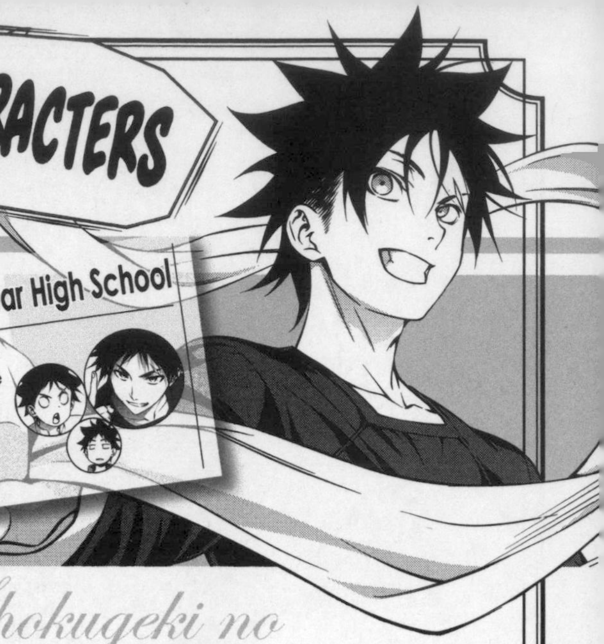

SOMA YUKIHIRA First Year High School

Helping out at his family's restaurant since he was little, Soma trained as a chef with the goal of someday surpassing his father. Out of junior high, he's suddenly sent off to culinary school. He's skilled, but sometimes invents questionable new recipes.

Shokugeki no SOMA

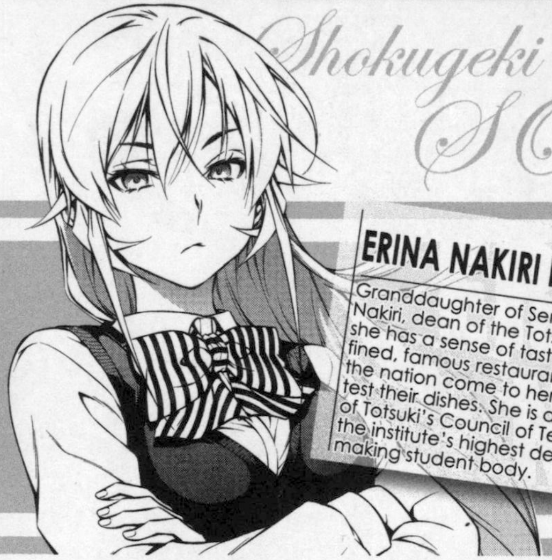

ERINA NAKIRI First Year High School

Granddaughter of Senzaemon Nakiri, dean of the Totsuki Institute, she has a sense of taste so refined, famous restaurants across the nation come to her to taste test their dishes. She is a member of Totsuki's Council of Ten Masters, the institute's highest decision-making student body.

STORY

Soma grew up helping to cook at his family's restaurant, Yukihira. But one day his father enrolls him in Japan's premier culinary school, the Totsuki Institute. Having met other students as skilled as he is and with similar goals, Soma has grown a little as a chef.

Soma and the rest of the resistance have traveled to Hokkaido for the advancement exams and are immediately faced with trouble! The proctors of the first and second stages give them blatantly unfair tests, but everyone bands together and manages to pass. After that, Central ups the ante. For stage three, every resistance member is required to win a one-on-one face-off against a Council of Ten member! Backed into a corner, Soma has no choice but to go up against the newly appointed ninth seat—Akira Hayama!

Shokugeki no SOMA

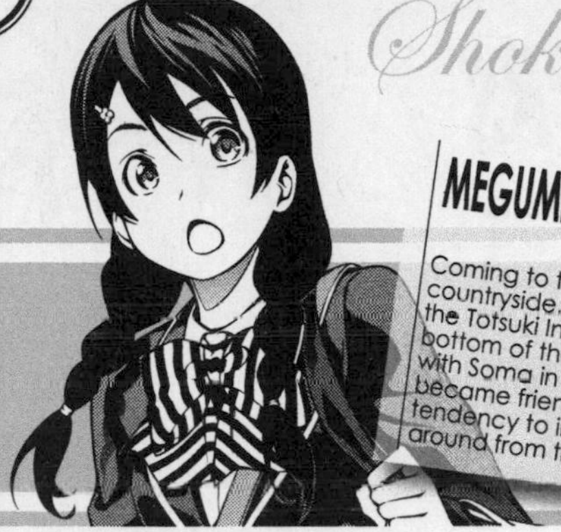

MEGUMI TADOKORO First Year High School

Coming to the big city from the countryside, Megumi made it into the Totsuki Institute at the very bottom of the rankings. Partnered with Soma in their first class, the two became friends. However, he has a tendency to inadvertently yank her around from time to time.

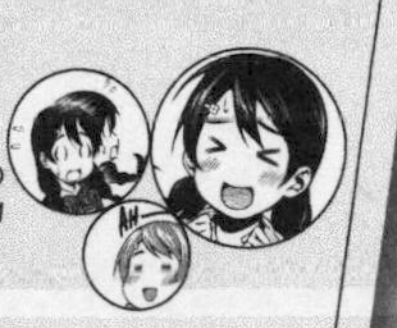
AH

ALICE NAKIRI First Year High School

Erina's cousin, she has spent much of her life overseas with her parents learning cooking from a scientific perspective through molecular gastronomy.

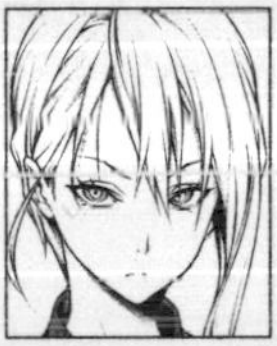

RYO KUROKIBA First Year High School

Alice's aide, he specializes in powerful, savory seafood dishes. His personality changes drastically when he puts on his bandanna.

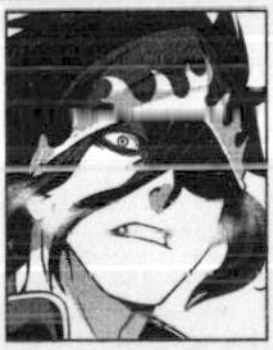

TAKUMI ALDINI First Year High School

Working at his family's trattoria in Italy from a young age, he transferred into the Totsuki Institute in junior high. Isami is his younger twin brother.

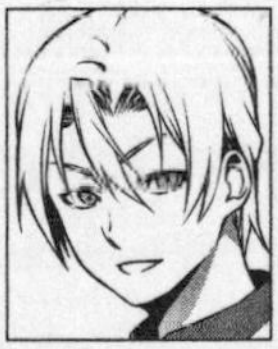

TERUNORI KUGA Second Year High School

The former eighth seat, he lost his spot on the council after opposing the Azami administration. He's captain of the Chinese-Cooking Research Society.

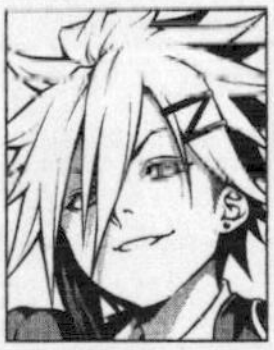

AKIRA HAYAMA First Year High School

With his inhumanly sharp sense of smell, he's a master of manipulating fragrance. After joining Central, he was given the ninth seat on the Council of Ten.

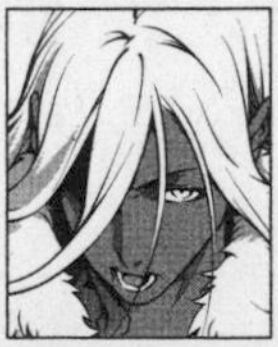

AZAMI NAKIRI

Erina's father, he convinced over half the Council of Ten to back him in staging a coup for taking control of the institute, forcing former dean Senzaemon Nakiri into retirement.

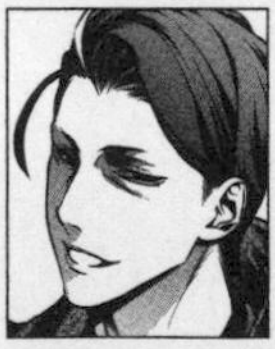

Food Wars! SHOKUGEKI NO SOMA!

22

Table of Contents

182 THE BIRTH OF THE NEW COUNCIL

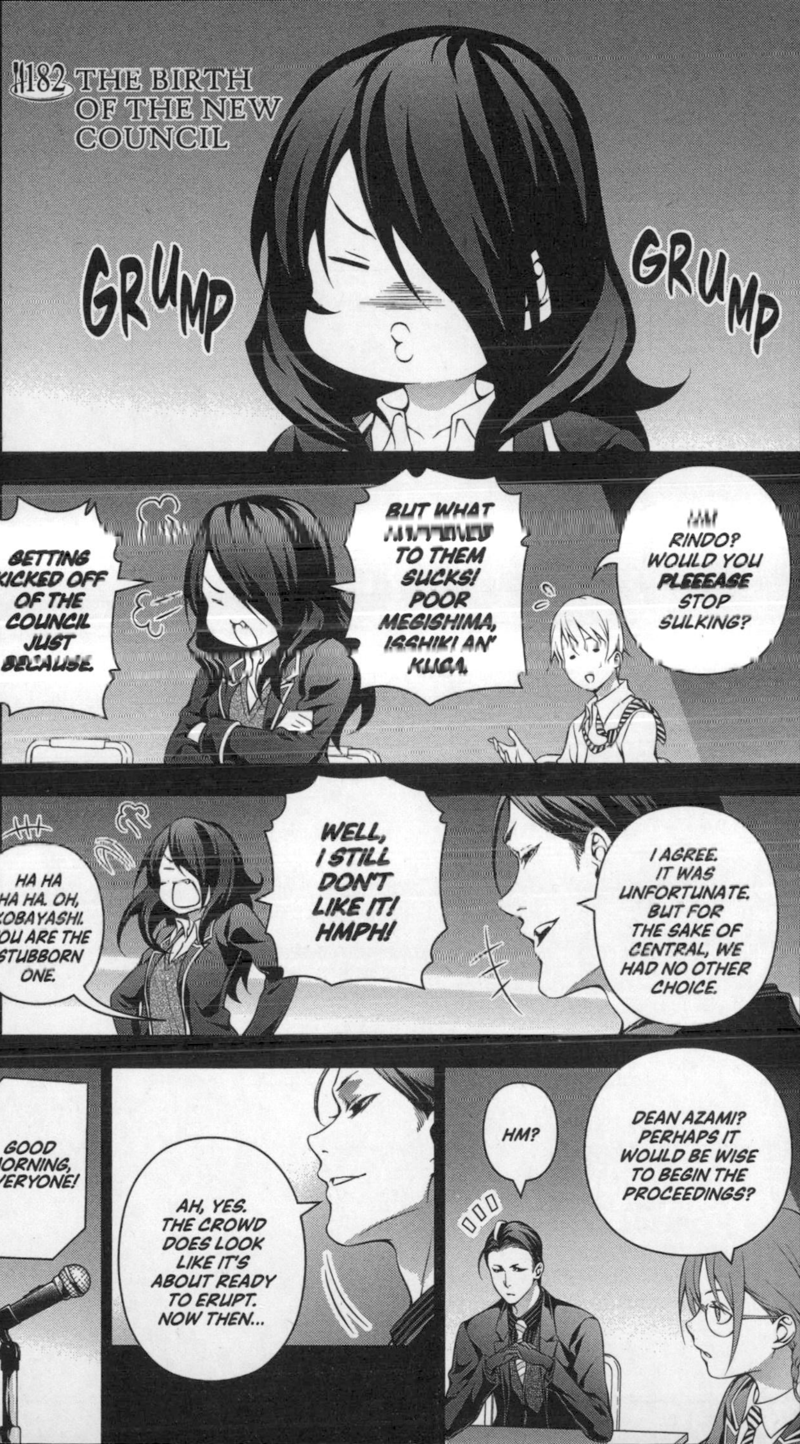
GRUMP
GRUMP
RINDO? WOULD YOU PLEEEASE STOP SULKING?
BUT WHAT TO THEM SUCKS! POOR MEGISHIMA, ISSHIKI AN' KUGA.
GETTING KICKED OFF OF THE COUNCIL JUST BECAUSE.
I AGREE. IT WAS UNFORTUNATE. BUT FOR THE SAKE OF CENTRAL, WE HAD NO OTHER CHOICE.
WELL, I STILL DON'T LIKE IT! HMPH!
HA HA HA HA. OH, KOBAYASHI. YOU ARE THE STUBBORN ONE.
DEAN AZAMI? PERHAPS IT WOULD BE WISE TO BEGIN THE PROCEEDINGS?
HM?
AH, YES. THE CROWD DOES LOOK LIKE IT'S ABOUT READY TO ERUPT. NOW THEN...
GOOD MORNING, EVERYONE!

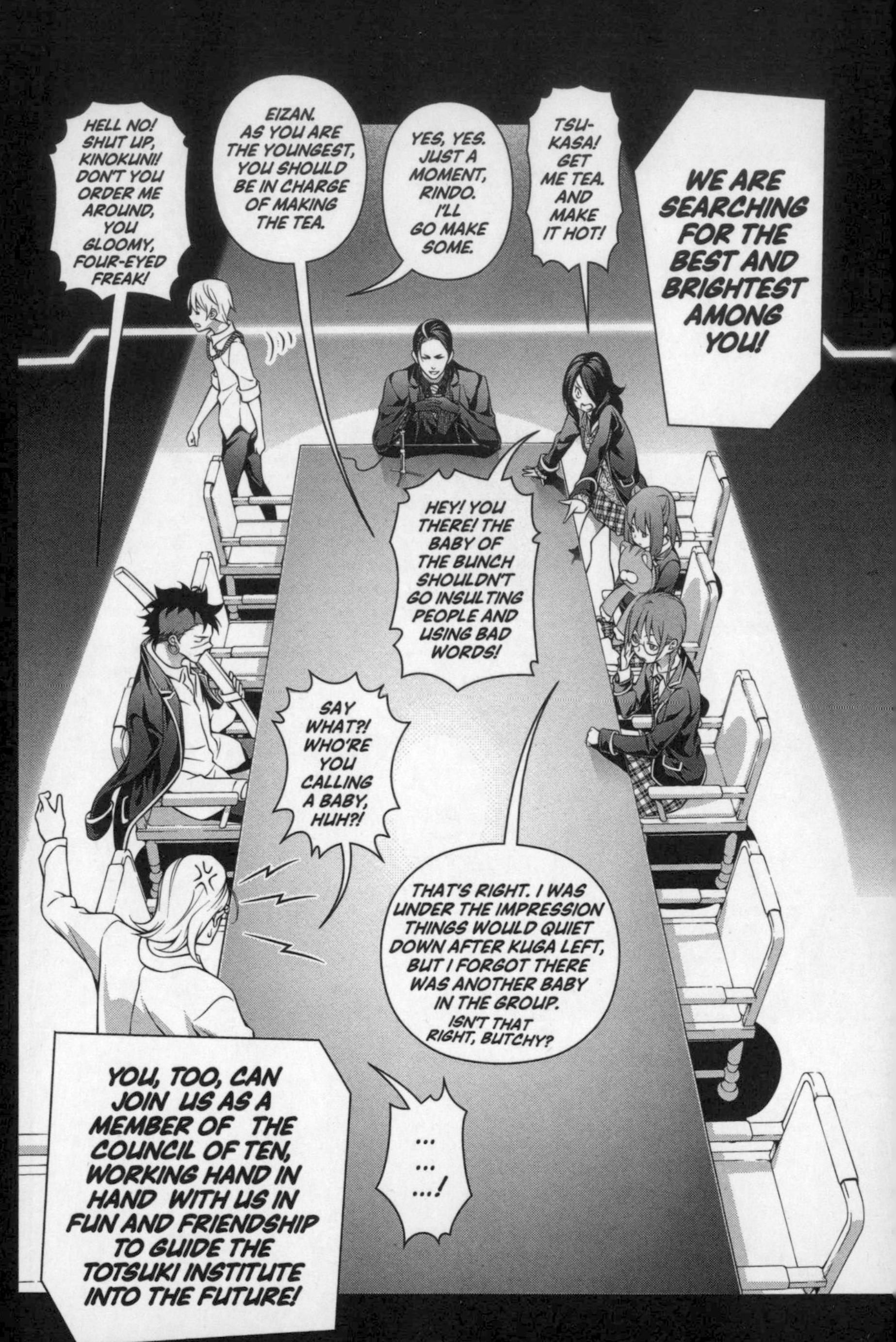
WE ARE SEARCHING FOR THE BEST AND BRIGHTEST AMONG YOU!
TSU-KASA! GET ME TEA. AND MAKE IT HOT!
YES, YES. JUST A MOMENT, RINDO. I'LL GO MAKE SOME.
EIZAN. AS YOU ARE THE YOUNGEST, YOU SHOULD BE IN CHARGE OF MAKING THE TEA.
HELL NO! SHUT UP, KINOKUNI! DON'T YOU ORDER ME AROUND, YOU GLOOMY, FOUR-EYED FREAK!
HEY! YOU THERE! THE BABY OF THE BUNCH SHOULDN'T GO INSULTING PEOPLE AND USING BAD WORDS!
SAY WHAT?! WHO'RE YOU CALLING A BABY, HUH?!
THAT'S RIGHT. I WAS UNDER THE IMPRESSION THINGS WOULD QUIET DOWN AFTER KUGA LEFT, BUT I FORGOT THERE WAS ANOTHER BABY IN THE GROUP. ISN'T THAT RIGHT, BUTCHY?
... ...!
YOU, TOO, CAN JOIN US AS A MEMBER OF THE COUNCIL OF TEN, WORKING HAND IN HAND WITH US IN FUN AND FRIENDSHIP TO GUIDE THE TOTSUKI INSTITUTE INTO THE FUTURE!

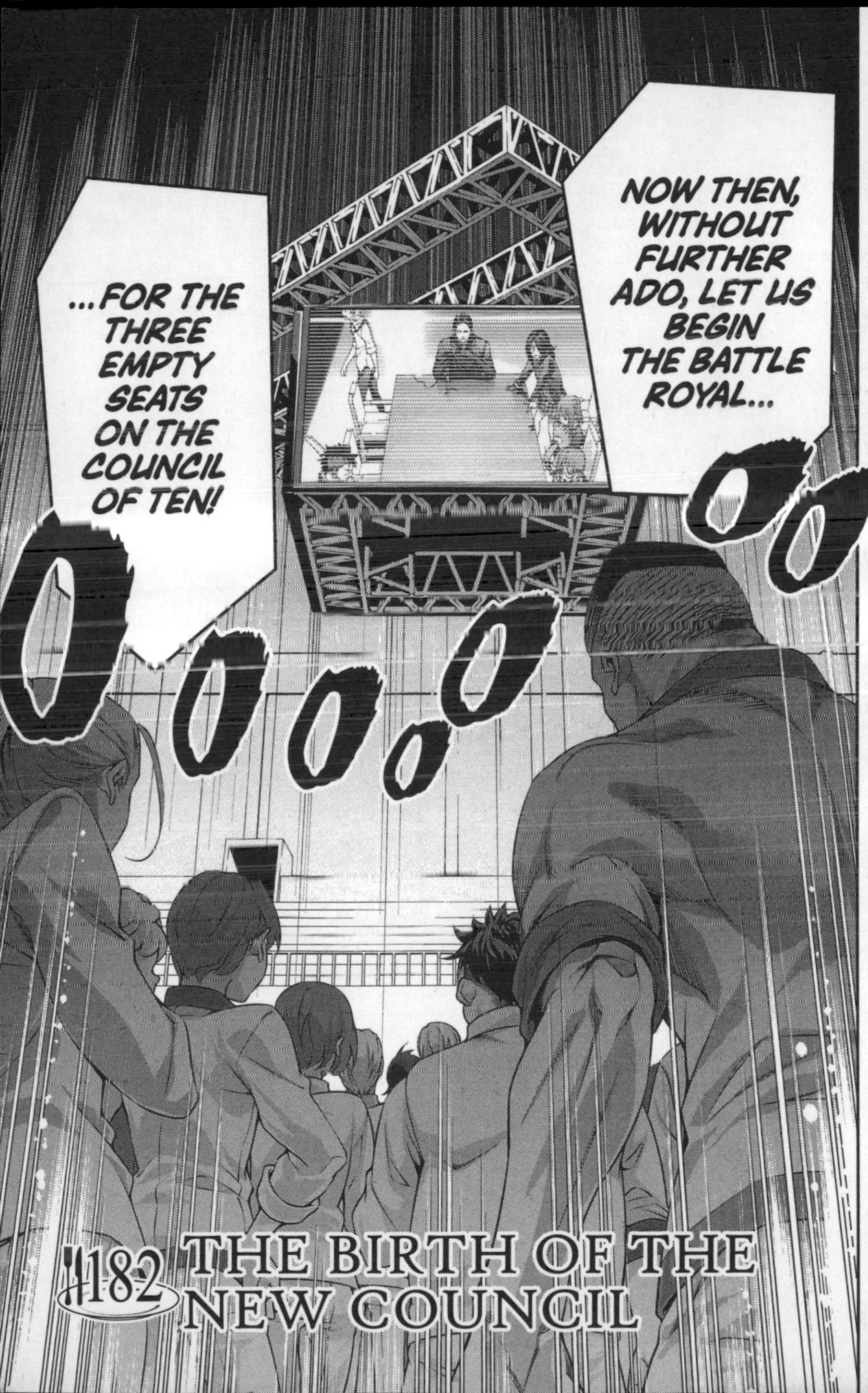
NOW THEN, WITHOUT FURTHER ADO, LET US BEGIN THE BATTLE ROYAL...
...FOR THE THREE EMPTY SEATS ON THE COUNCIL OF TEN!
OOOOOOO
182 THE BIRTH OF THE NEW COUNCIL

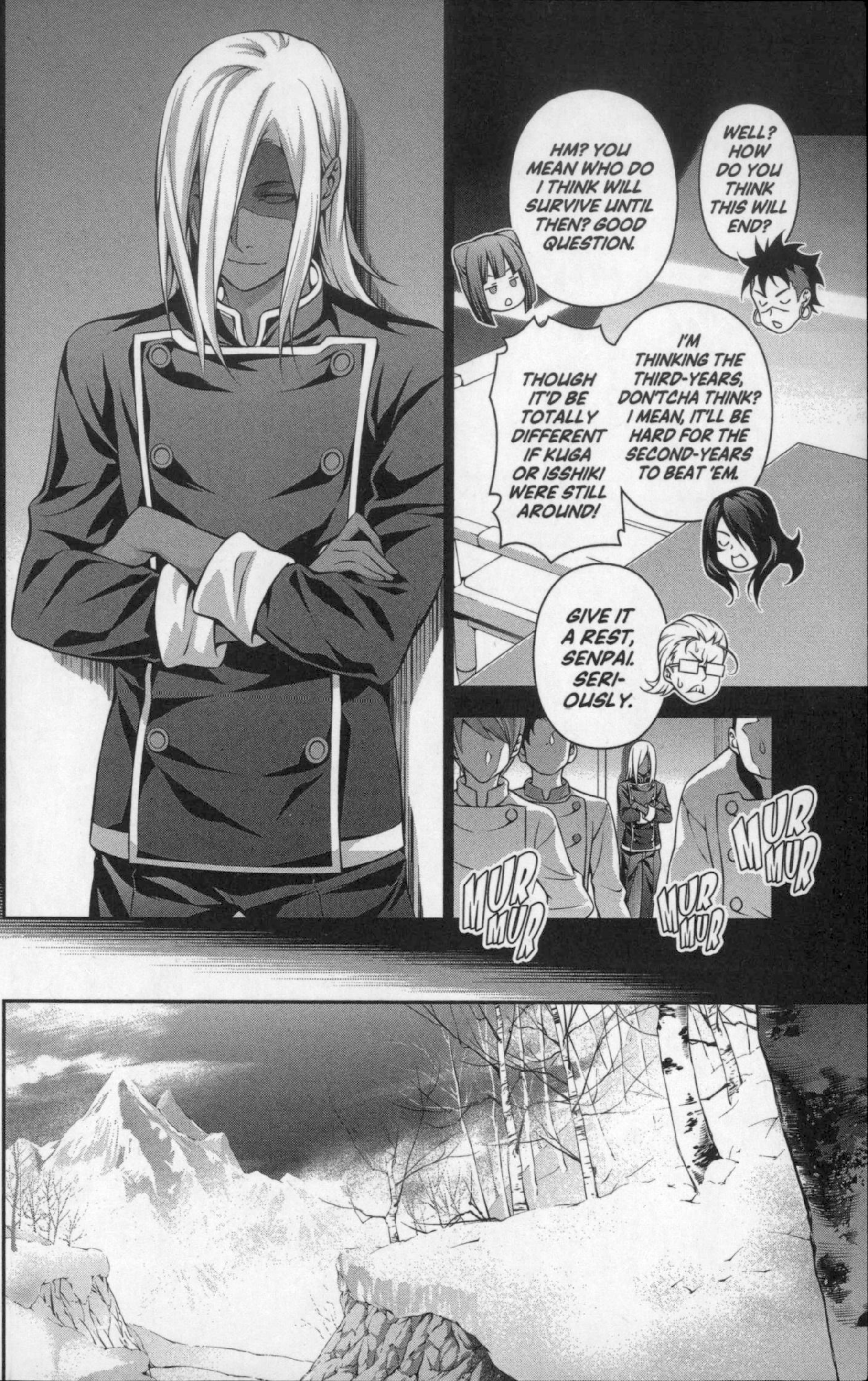
WELL? HOW DO YOU THINK THIS WILL END?
HM? YOU MEAN WHO DO I THINK WILL SURVIVE UNTIL THEN? GOOD QUESTION.
I'M THINKING THE THIRD-YEARS, DON'TCHA THINK? I MEAN, IT'LL BE HARD FOR THE SECOND-YEARS TO BEAT 'EM.
THOUGH IT'D BE TOTALLY DIFFERENT IF KUGA OR ISSHIKI WERE STILL AROUND!
GIVE IT A REST, SENPAI. SERI-OUSLY.
MUR MUR
MUR MUR
MUR MUR

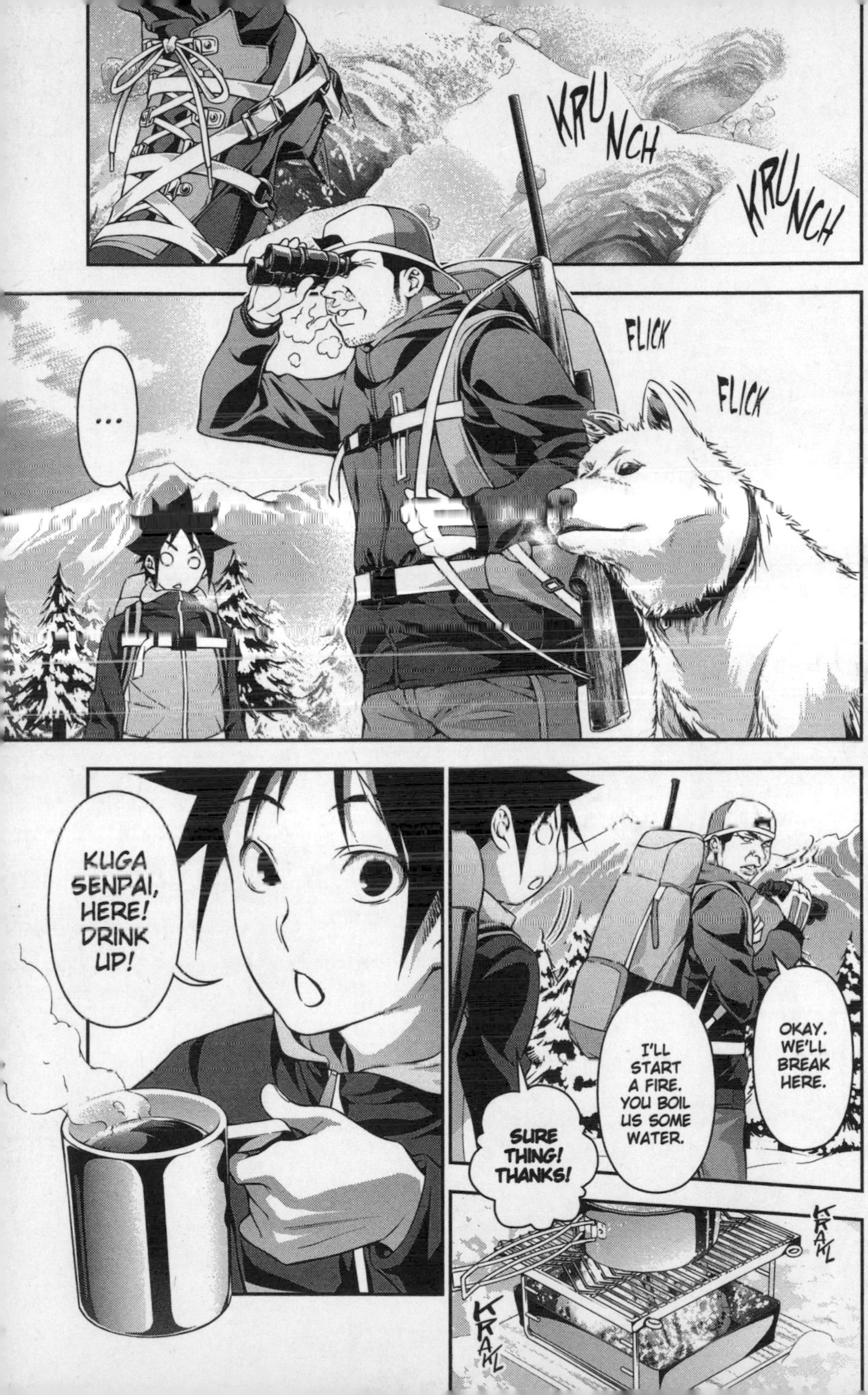
KRUNCH
KRUNCH
FLICK
FLICK
...
OKAY. WE'LL BREAK HERE.
I'LL START A FIRE. YOU BOIL US SOME WATER.
SURE THING! THANKS!
KRAK
KRAK
KUGA SENPAI, HERE! DRINK UP!

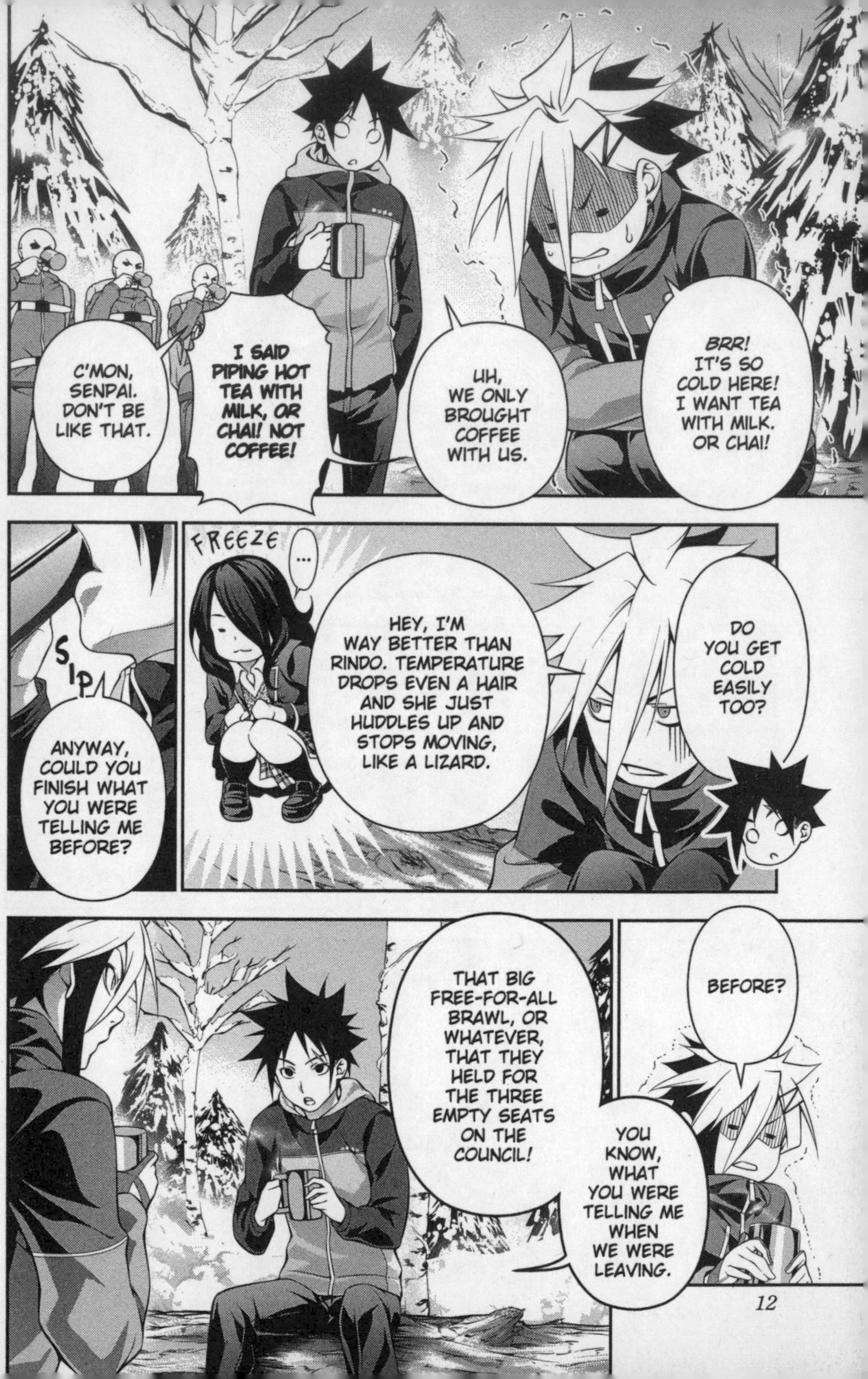
BRR! IT'S SO COLD HERE! I WANT TEA WITH MILK. OR CHAI!
UH, WE ONLY BROUGHT COFFEE WITH US.
I SAID PIPING HOT TEA WITH MILK, OR CHAI! NOT COFFEE!
C'MON, SENPAI. DON'T BE LIKE THAT.
DO YOU GET COLD EASILY TOO?
HEY, I'M WAY BETTER THAN RINDO. TEMPERATURE DROPS EVEN A HAIR AND SHE JUST HUDDLES UP AND STOPS MOVING, LIKE A LIZARD.
FREEZE
...
SIP
ANYWAY, COULD YOU FINISH WHAT YOU WERE TELLING ME BEFORE?
BEFORE?
YOU KNOW, WHAT YOU WERE TELLING ME WHEN WE WERE LEAVING.
THAT BIG FREE-FOR-ALL BRAWL, OR WHATEVER, THAT THEY HELD FOR THE THREE EMPTY SEATS ON THE COUNCIL!

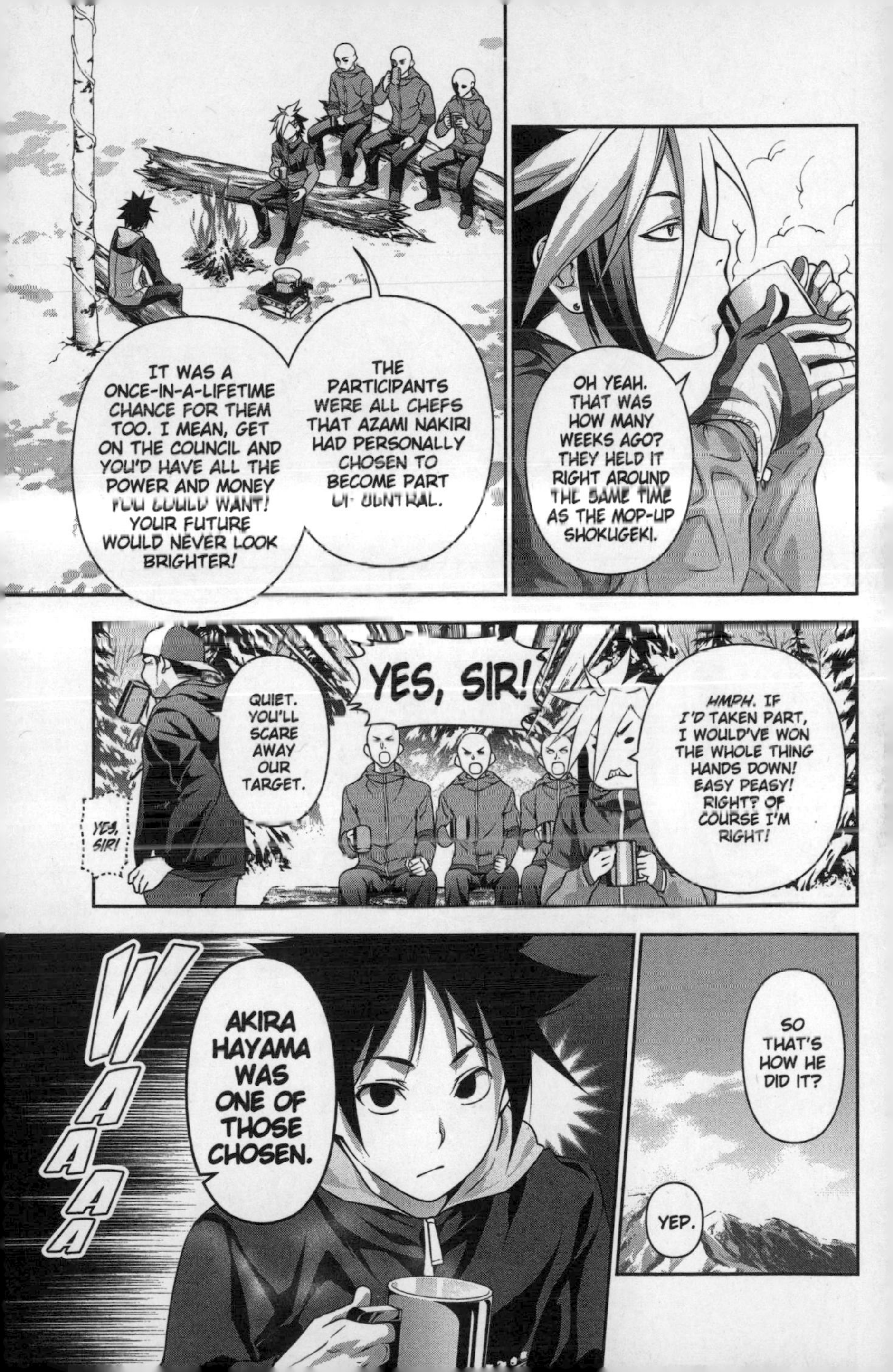
OH YEAH. THAT WAS HOW MANY WEEKS AGO? THEY HELD IT RIGHT AROUND THE SAME TIME AS THE MOP-UP SHOKUGEKI.
THE PARTICIPANTS WERE ALL CHEFS THAT AZAMI NAKIRI HAD PERSONALLY CHOSEN TO BECOME PART OF CENTRAL.
IT WAS A ONCE-IN-A-LIFETIME CHANCE FOR THEM TOO. I MEAN, GET ON THE COUNCIL AND YOU'D HAVE ALL THE POWER AND MONEY YOU COULD WANT! YOUR FUTURE WOULD NEVER LOOK BRIGHTER!
HMPH. IF I'D TAKEN PART, I WOULD'VE WON THE WHOLE THING HANDS DOWN! EASY PEASY! RIGHT? OF COURSE I'M RIGHT!
YES, SIR!
QUIET. YOU'LL SCARE AWAY OUR TARGET.
YES, SIR!
SO THAT'S HOW HE DID IT?
YEP.
AKIRA HAYAMA WAS ONE OF THOSE CHOSEN.
WAAAAA

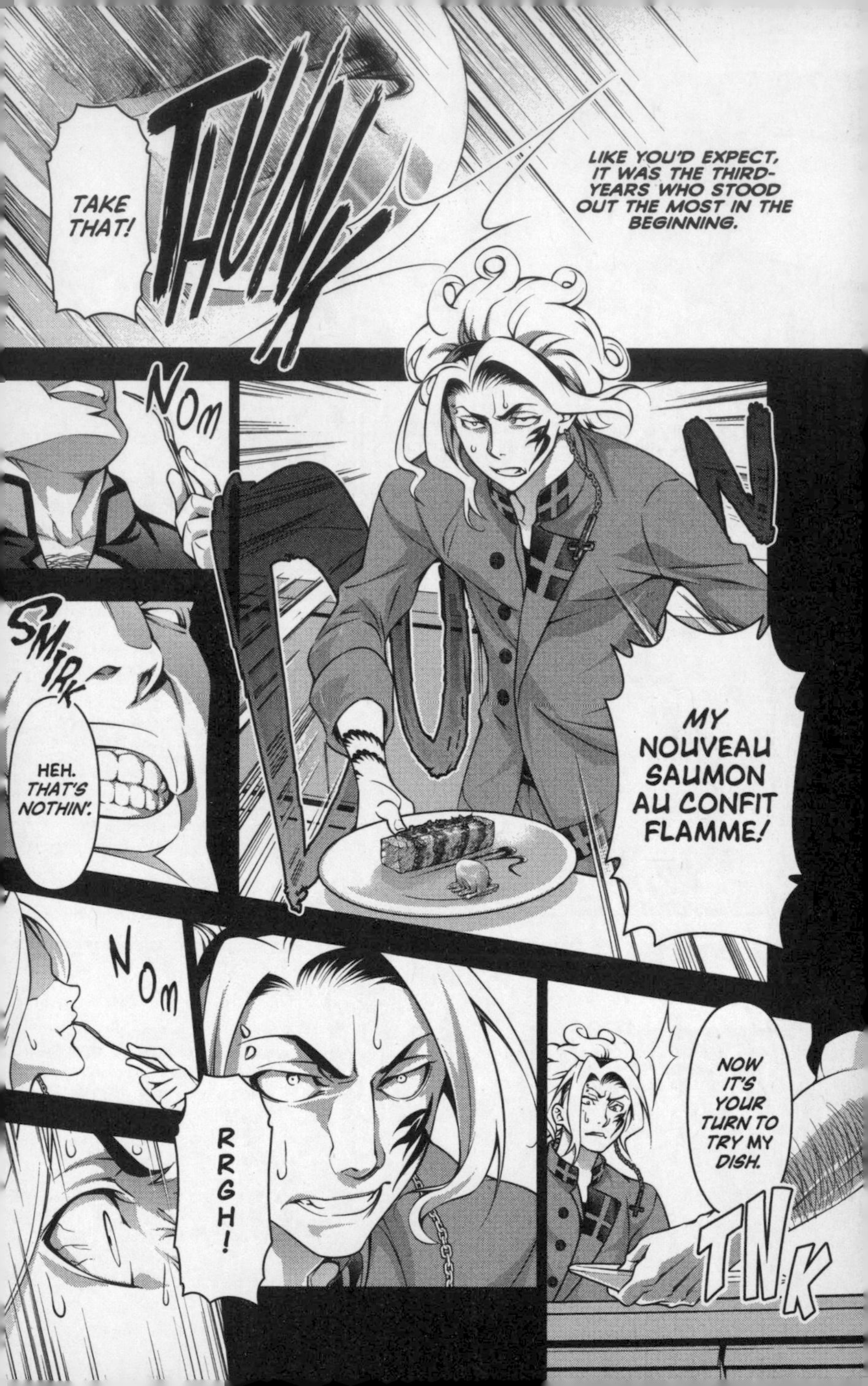
LIKE YOU'D EXPECT, IT WAS THE THIRD-YEARS WHO STOOD OUT THE MOST IN THE BEGINNING.
THUNK
TAKE THAT!
MY NOUVEAU SAUMON AU CONFIT FLAMME!
NOM
SMIRK
HEH. THAT'S NOTHIN'.
NOW IT'S YOUR TURN TO TRY MY DISH.
TNK
RRGH!
NOM

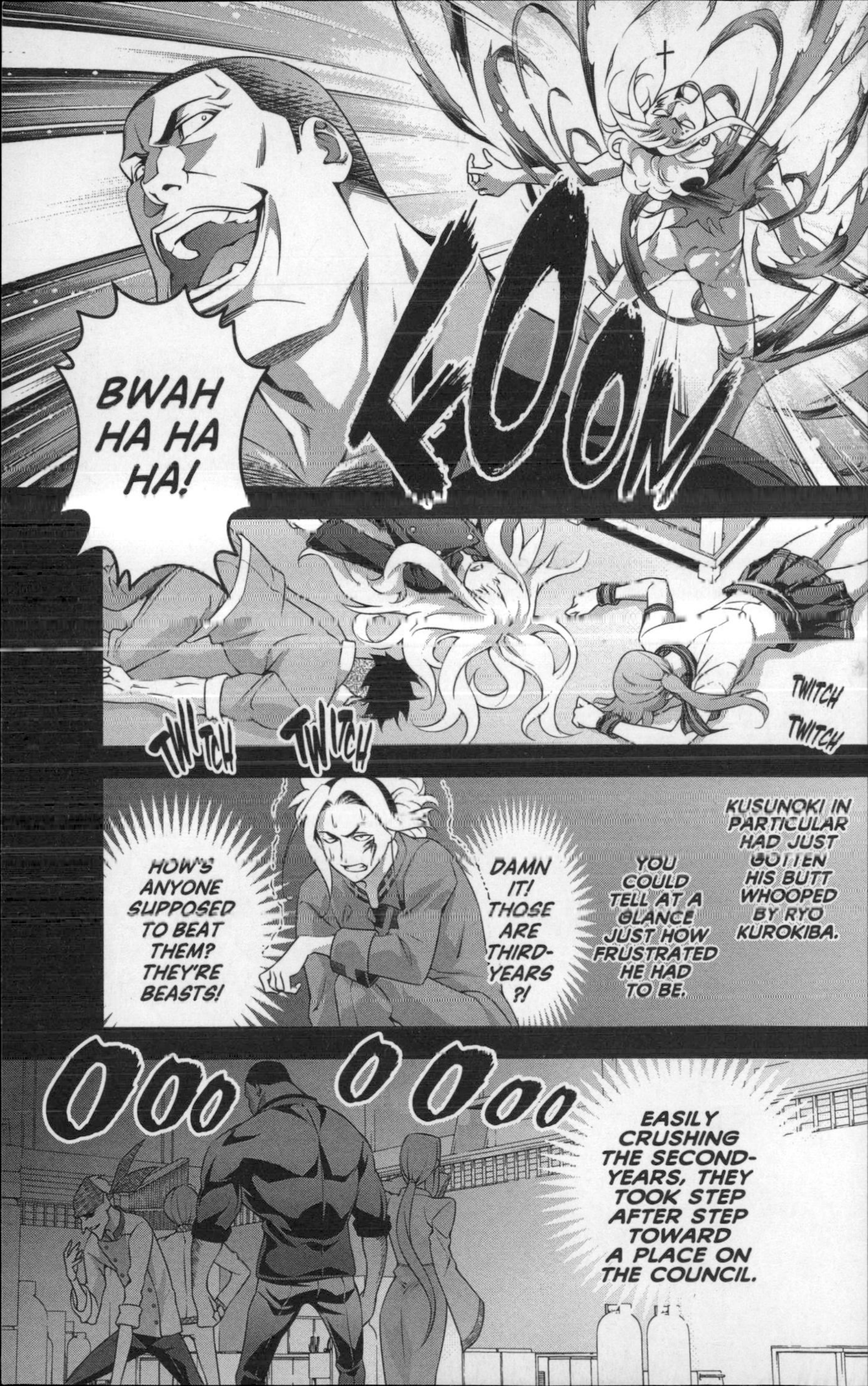
BOOM
BWAH HA HA HA!
TWITCH TWITCH
TWITCH
TWITCH
KUSUNOKI IN PARTICULAR HAD JUST GOTTEN HIS BUTT WHOOPED BY RYO KUROKIBA.
YOU COULD TELL AT A GLANCE JUST HOW FRUSTRATED HE HAD TO BE.
DAMN IT! THOSE ARE THIRD-YEARS?!
HOW'S ANYONE SUPPOSED TO BEAT THEM? THEY'RE BEASTS!
EASILY CRUSHING THE SECOND-YEARS, THEY TOOK STEP AFTER STEP TOWARD A PLACE ON THE COUNCIL.
OOO OOO

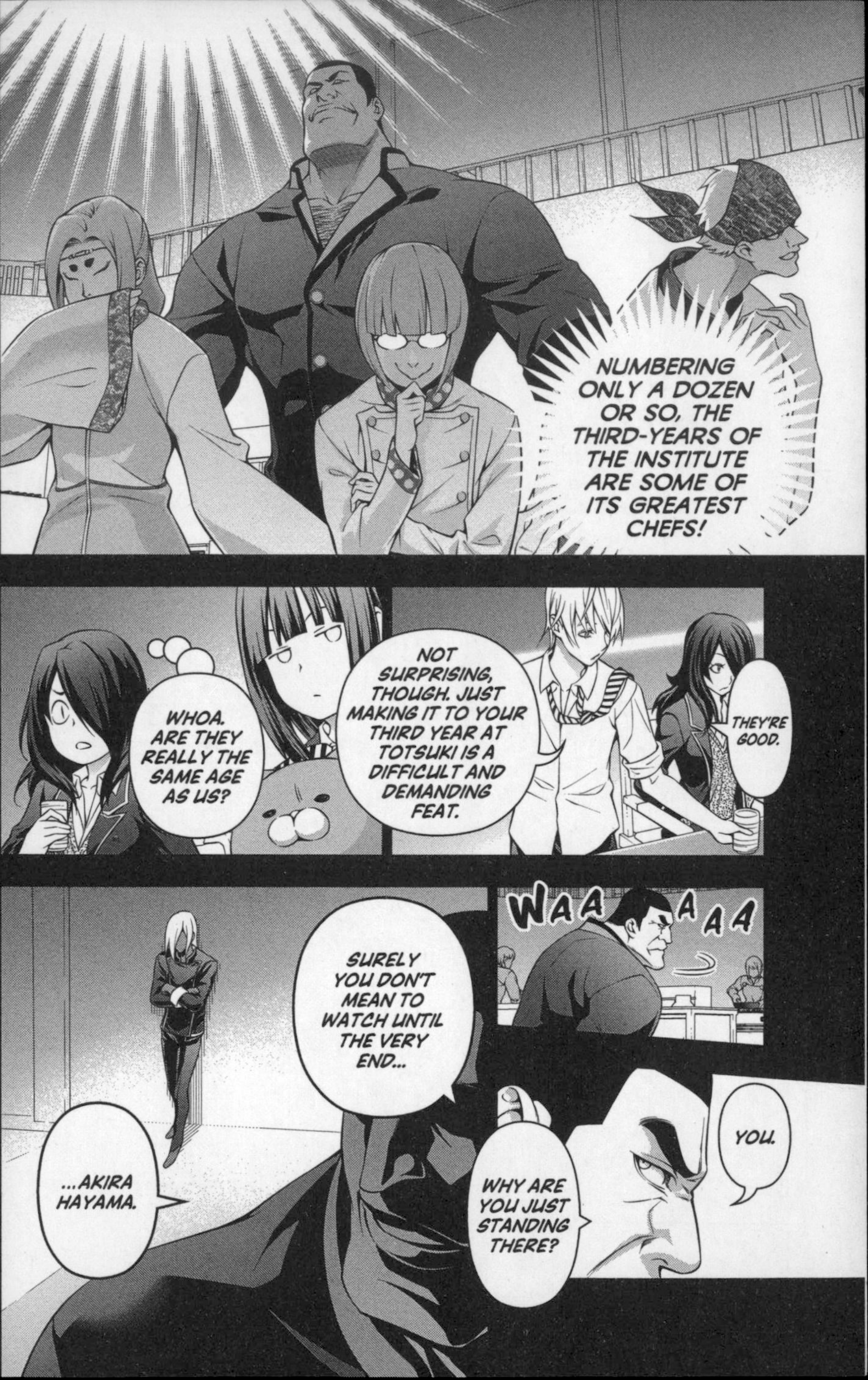
NUMBERING ONLY A DOZEN OR SO, THE THIRD-YEARS OF THE INSTITUTE ARE SOME OF ITS GREATEST CHEFS!
THEY'RE GOOD.
NOT SURPRISING, THOUGH. JUST MAKING IT TO YOUR THIRD YEAR AT TOTSUKI IS A DIFFICULT AND DEMANDING FEAT.
WHOA. ARE THEY REALLY THE SAME AGE AS US?
WAAAAAA
YOU.
WHY ARE YOU JUST STANDING THERE?
SURELY YOU DON'T MEAN TO WATCH UNTIL THE VERY END...
...AKIRA HAYAMA.

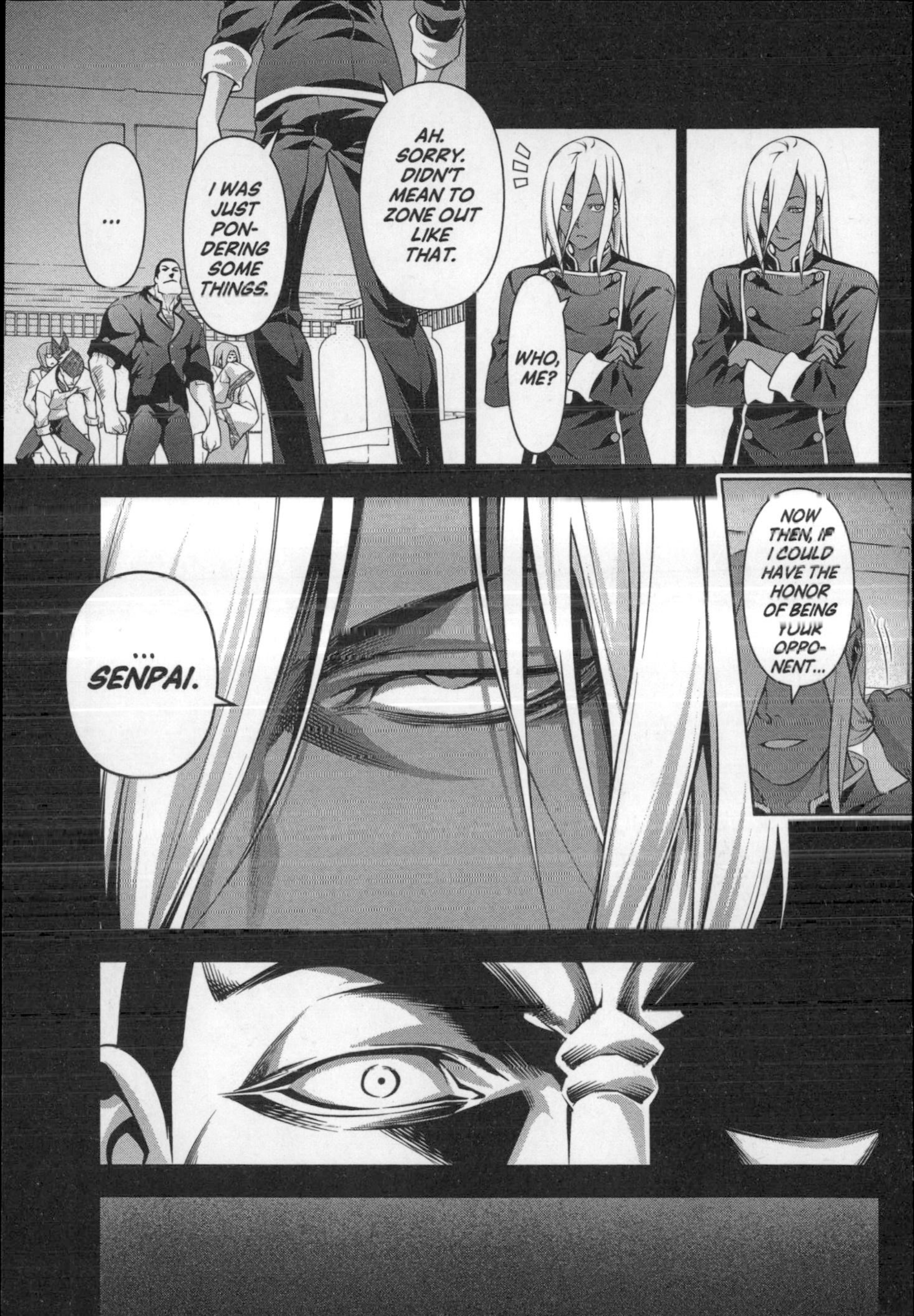
WHO, ME?
AH. SORRY. DIDN'T MEAN TO ZONE OUT LIKE THAT.
I WAS JUST PON-DERING SOME THINGS.
...
NOW THEN, IF I COULD HAVE THE HONOR OF BEING YOUR OPPO-NENT...
... SENPAI.

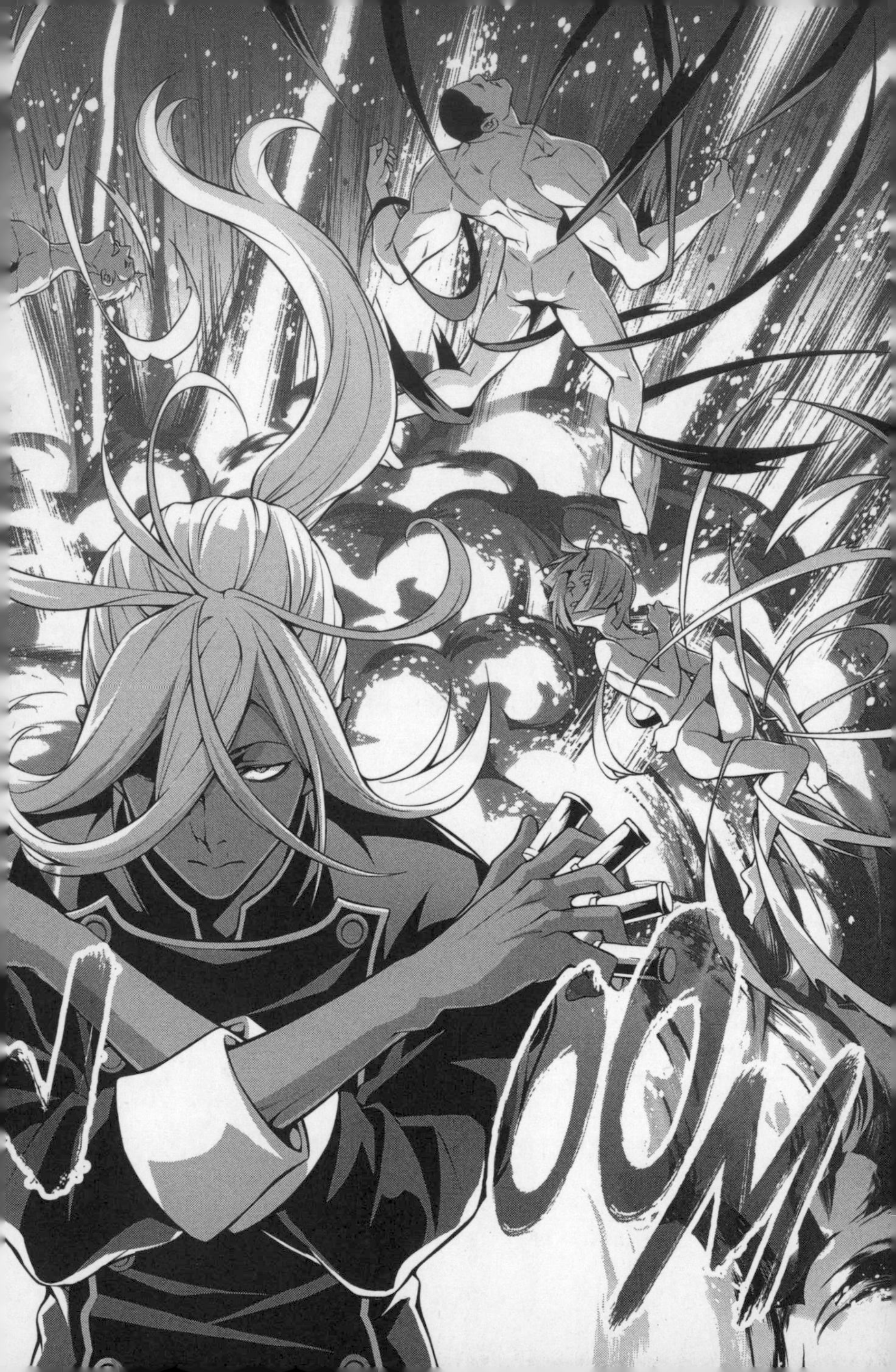
VOOM

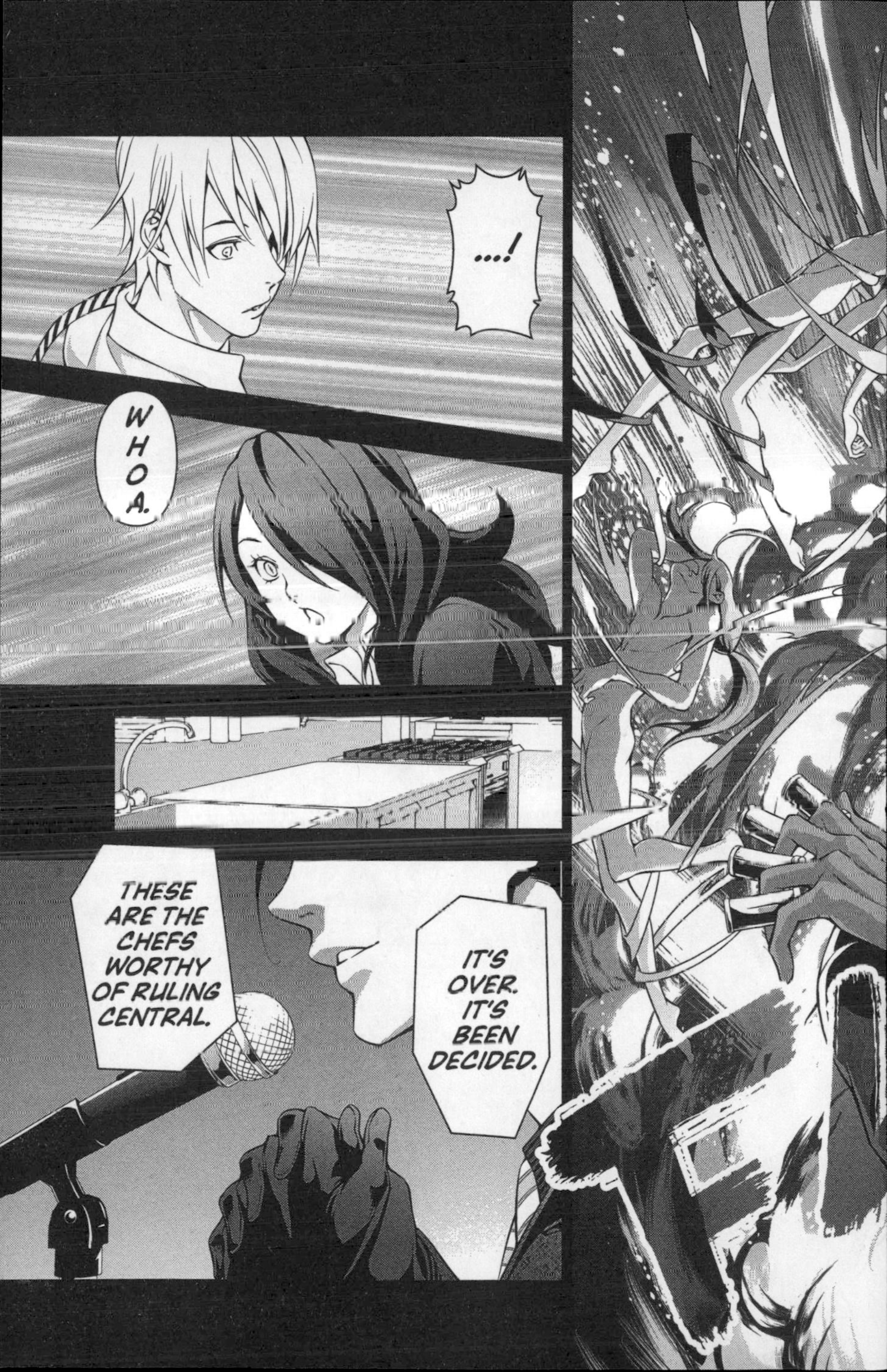

...!
WHOA.
IT'S OVER. IT'S BEEN DECIDED.
THESE ARE THE CHEFS WORTHY OF RULING CENTRAL.

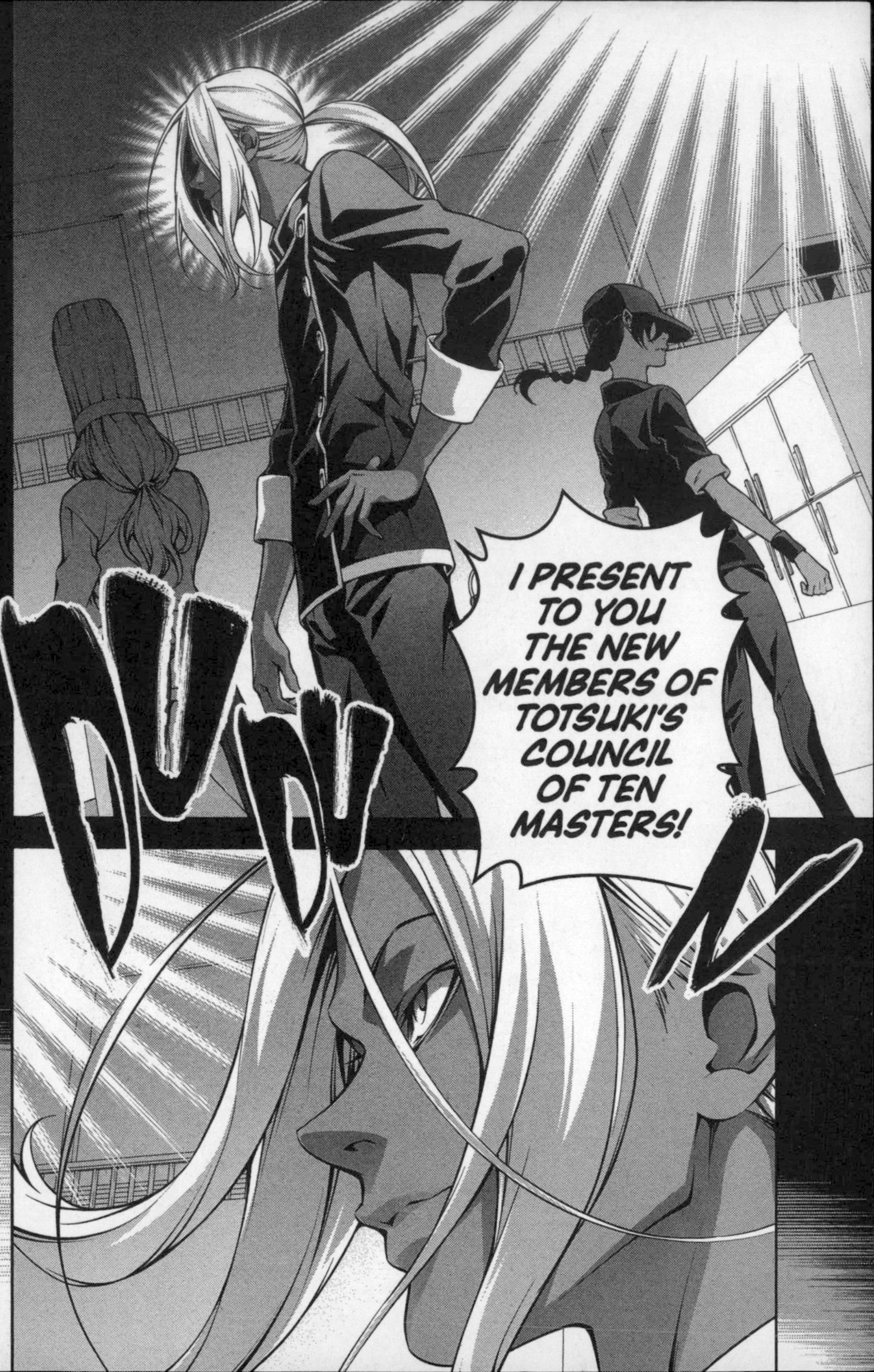
I PRESENT TO YOU THE NEW MEMBERS OF TOTSUKI'S COUNCIL OF TEN MASTERS!
DUDUN

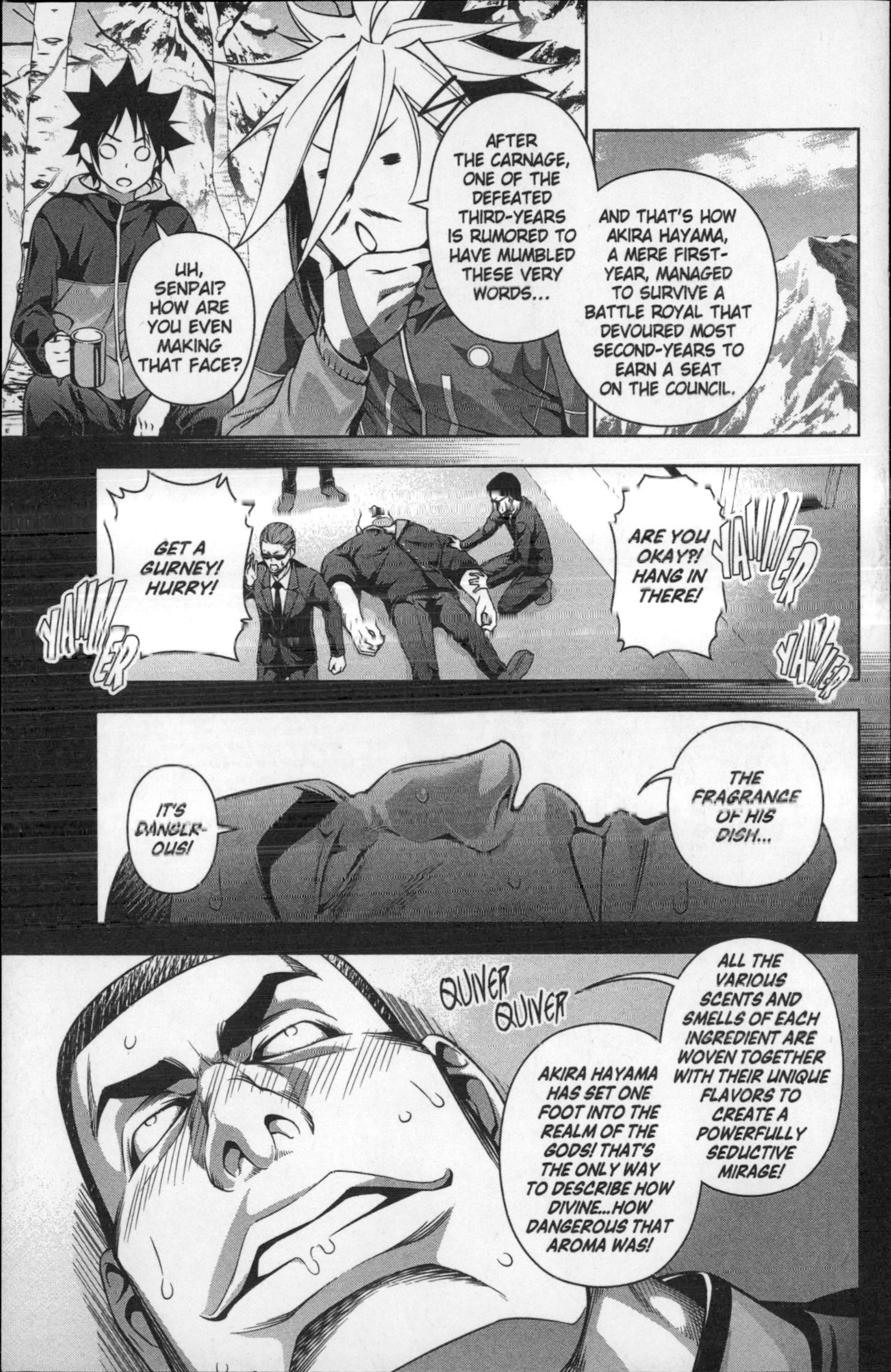
AND THAT'S HOW AKIRA HAYAMA, A MERE FIRST-YEAR, MANAGED TO SURVIVE A BATTLE ROYAL THAT DEVOURED MOST SECOND-YEARS TO EARN A SEAT ON THE COUNCIL.
AFTER THE CARNAGE, ONE OF THE DEFEATED THIRD-YEARS IS RUMORED TO HAVE MUMBLED THESE VERY WORDS...
UH, SENPAI? HOW ARE YOU EVEN MAKING THAT FACE?
YAMMER
YAMMER
ARE YOU OKAY?! HANG IN THERE!
GET A GURNEY! HURRY!
YAMMER
THE FRAGRANCE OF HIS DISH...
IT'S DANGER-OUS!
ALL THE VARIOUS SCENTS AND SMELLS OF EACH INGREDIENT ARE WOVEN TOGETHER WITH THEIR UNIQUE FLAVORS TO CREATE A POWERFULLY SEDUCTIVE MIRAGE!
QUIVER QUIVER
AKIRA HAYAMA HAS SET ONE FOOT INTO THE REALM OF THE GODS! THAT'S THE ONLY WAY TO DESCRIBE HOW DIVINE...HOW DANGEROUS THAT AROMA WAS!

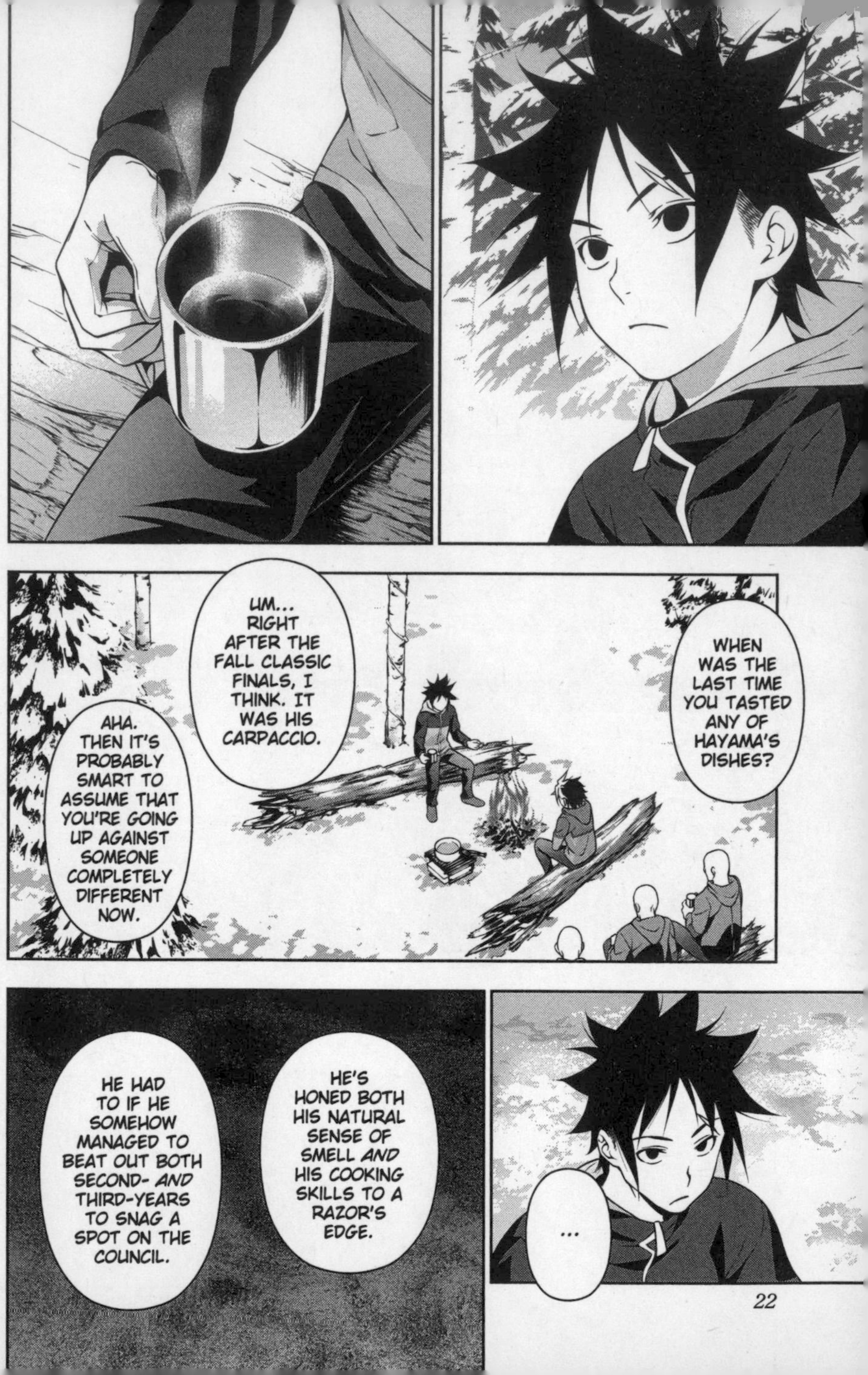
WHEN WAS THE LAST TIME YOU TASTED ANY OF HAYAMA'S DISHES?
UM... RIGHT AFTER THE FALL CLASSIC FINALS, I THINK. IT WAS HIS CARPACCIO.
AHA. THEN IT'S PROBABLY SMART TO ASSUME THAT YOU'RE GOING UP AGAINST SOMEONE COMPLETELY DIFFERENT NOW.
...
HE'S HONED BOTH HIS NATURAL SENSE OF SMELL *AND* HIS COOKING SKILLS TO A RAZOR'S EDGE.
HE HAD TO IF HE SOMEHOW MANAGED TO BEAT OUT BOTH SECOND- *AND* THIRD-YEARS TO SNAG A SPOT ON THE COUNCIL.

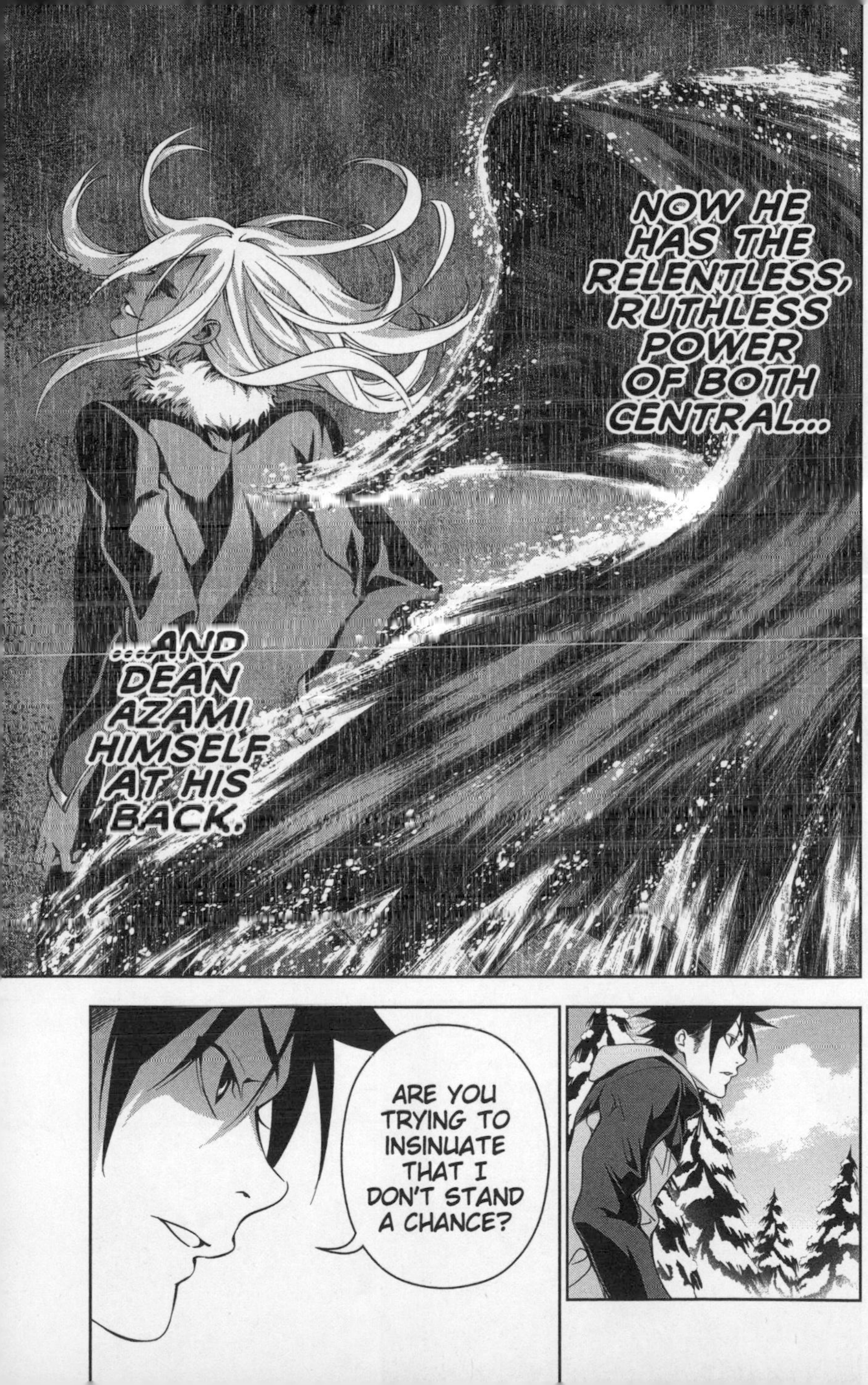
NOW HE HAS THE RELENTLESS, RUTHLESS POWER OF BOTH CENTRAL...
...AND DEAN AZAMI HIMSELF AT HIS BACK.
ARE YOU TRYING TO INSINUATE THAT I DON'T STAND A CHANCE?

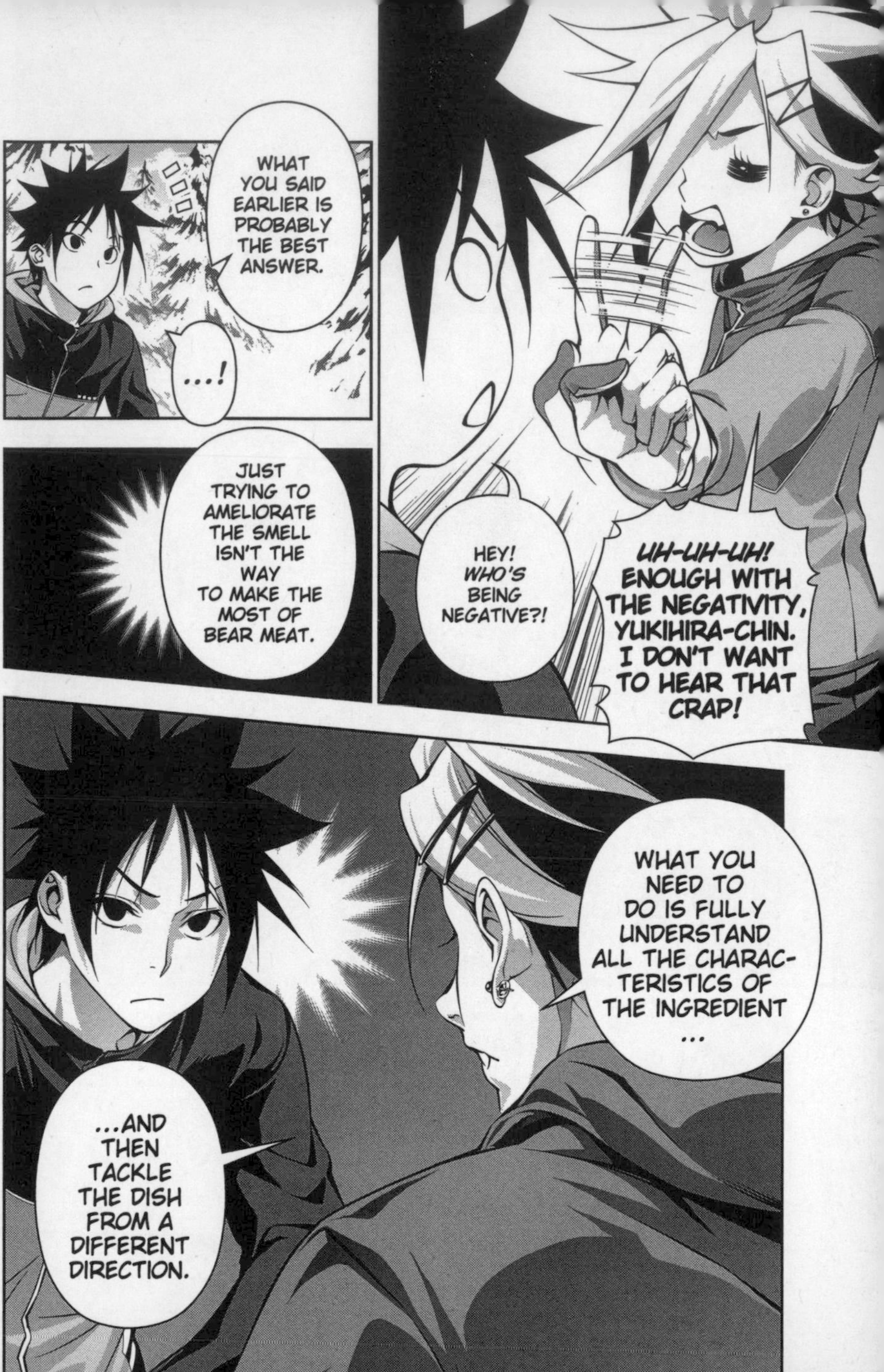
UH-UH-UH! ENOUGH WITH THE NEGATIVITY, YUKIHIRA-CHIN. I DON'T WANT TO HEAR THAT CRAP!
HEY! WHO'S BEING NEGATIVE?!
WHAT YOU SAID EARLIER IS PROBABLY THE BEST ANSWER.
...!
JUST TRYING TO AMELIORATE THE SMELL ISN'T THE WAY TO MAKE THE MOST OF BEAR MEAT.
WHAT YOU NEED TO DO IS FULLY UNDERSTAND ALL THE CHARAC-TERISTICS OF THE INGREDIENT ...
...AND THEN TACKLE THE DISH FROM A DIFFERENT DIRECTION.

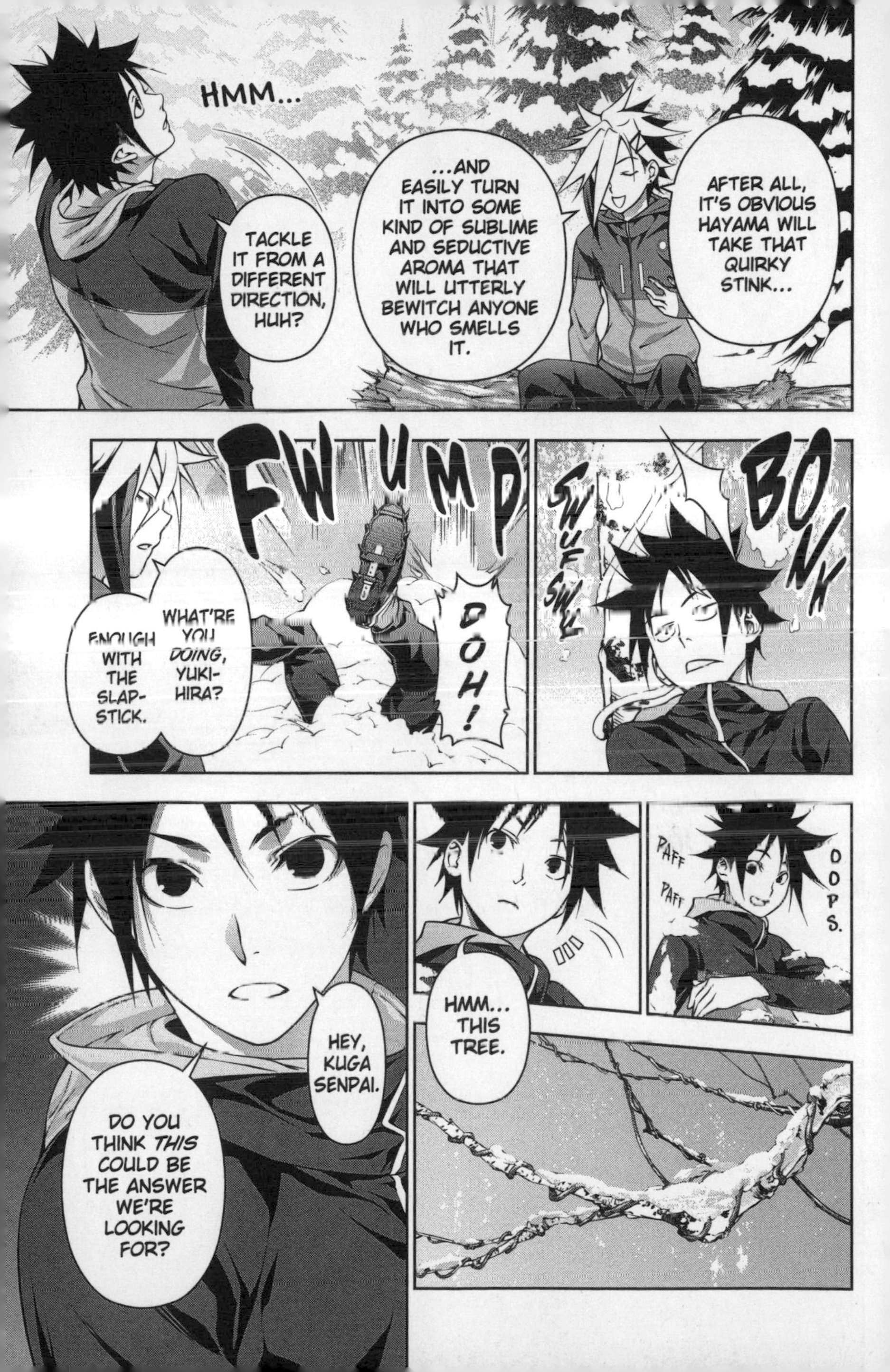
AFTER ALL, IT'S OBVIOUS HAYAMA WILL TAKE THAT QUIRKY STINK...
...AND EASILY TURN IT INTO SOME KIND OF SUBLIME AND SEDUCTIVE AROMA THAT WILL UTTERLY BEWITCH ANYONE WHO SMELLS IT.
TACKLE IT FROM A DIFFERENT DIRECTION, HUH?
HMM...
BONK
FWUMP
DOH!
WHAT'RE YOU *DOING*, YUKI-HIRA?
ENOUGH WITH THE SLAP-STICK.
PAFF
PAFF
OOPS.
HMM... THIS TREE.
HEY, KUGA SENPAI.
DO YOU THINK *THIS* COULD BE THE ANSWER WE'RE LOOKING FOR?

HOW RINDO WARMS UP AFTER A COLD DAY...

HW OOo

...

KCHAK

*SHE'S SO COLD SHE DOESN'T SPEAK AND MOVES VERY SLOWLY.

SNUGL

SNUGL

...

SHFL

SHFL

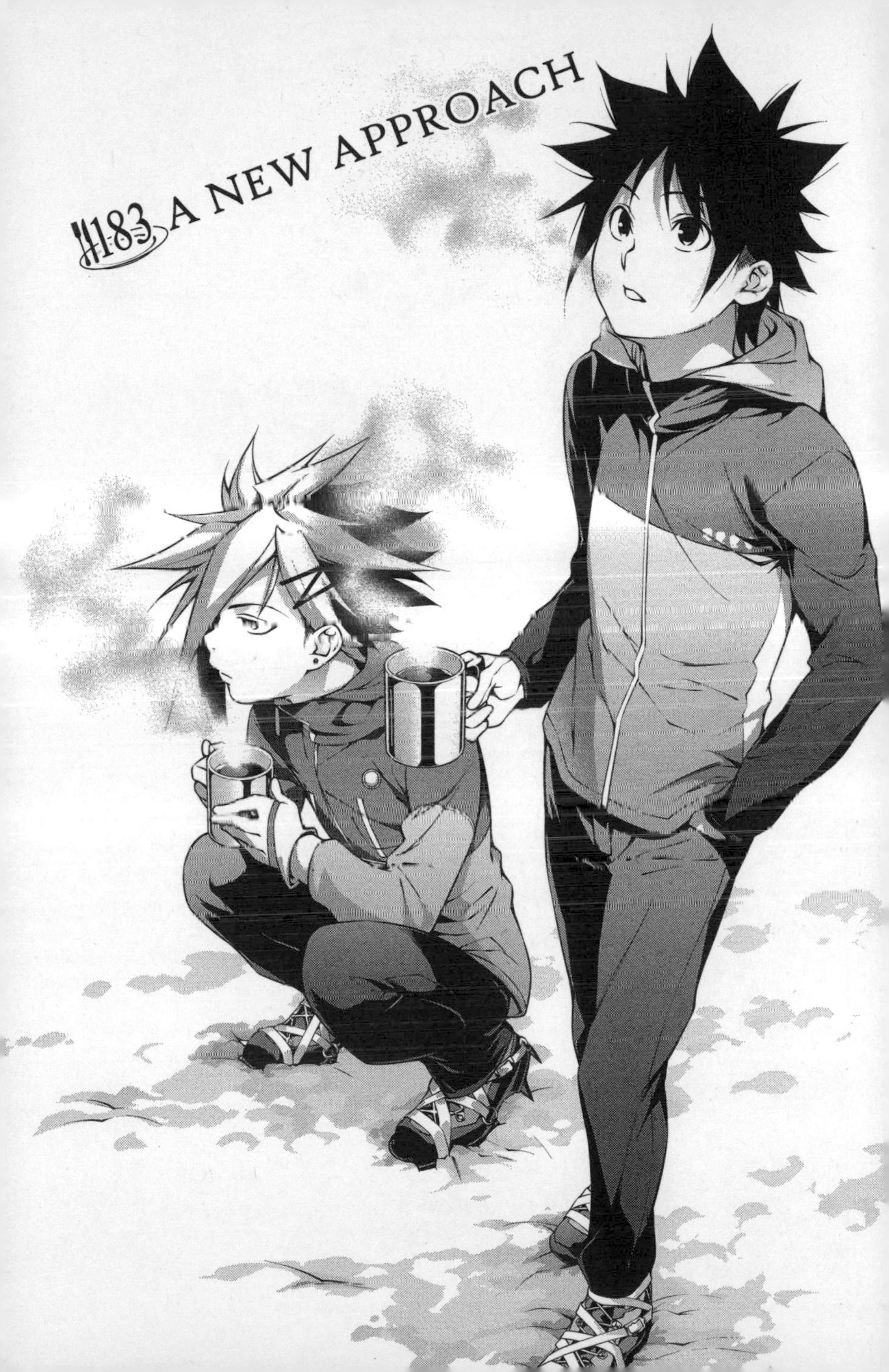
#183 A NEW APPROACH

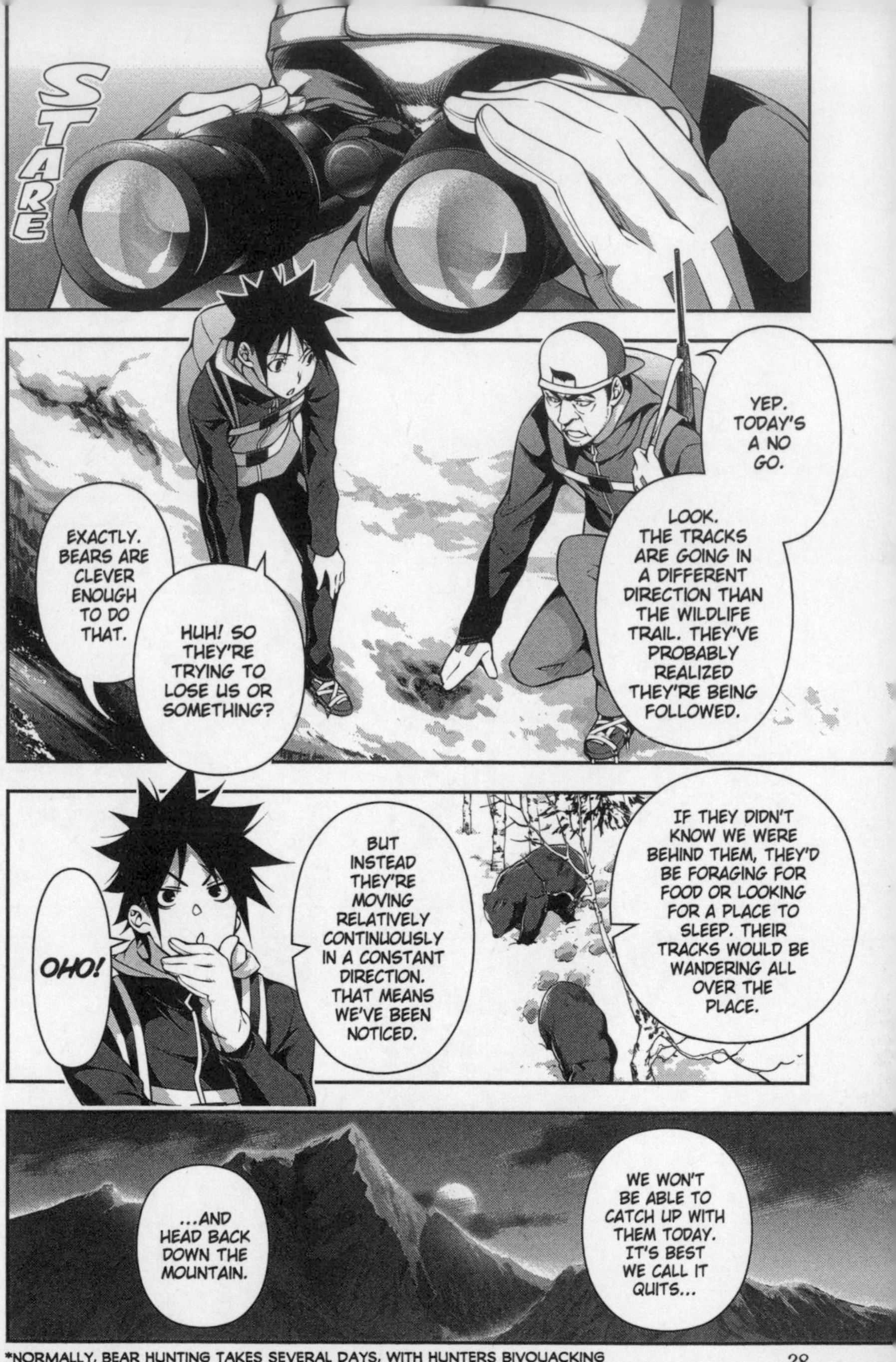
STARE
YEP. TODAY'S A NO GO.
LOOK. THE TRACKS ARE GOING IN A DIFFERENT DIRECTION THAN THE WILDLIFE TRAIL. THEY'VE PROBABLY REALIZED THEY'RE BEING FOLLOWED.
HUH! SO THEY'RE TRYING TO LOSE US OR SOMETHING?
EXACTLY. BEARS ARE CLEVER ENOUGH TO DO THAT.
IF THEY DIDN'T KNOW WE WERE BEHIND THEM, THEY'D BE FORAGING FOR FOOD OR LOOKING FOR A PLACE TO SLEEP. THEIR TRACKS WOULD BE WANDERING ALL OVER THE PLACE.
BUT INSTEAD THEY'RE MOVING RELATIVELY CONTINUOUSLY IN A CONSTANT DIRECTION. THAT MEANS WE'VE BEEN NOTICED.
OHO!
WE WON'T BE ABLE TO CATCH UP WITH THEM TODAY. IT'S BEST WE CALL IT QUITS...
...AND HEAD BACK DOWN THE MOUNTAIN.

*NORMALLY, BEAR HUNTING TAKES SEVERAL DAYS, WITH HUNTERS BIVOUACKING (SETTING UP A TEMPORARY CAMP OR SHELTER) TO KEEP FOLLOWING THEIR PREY.

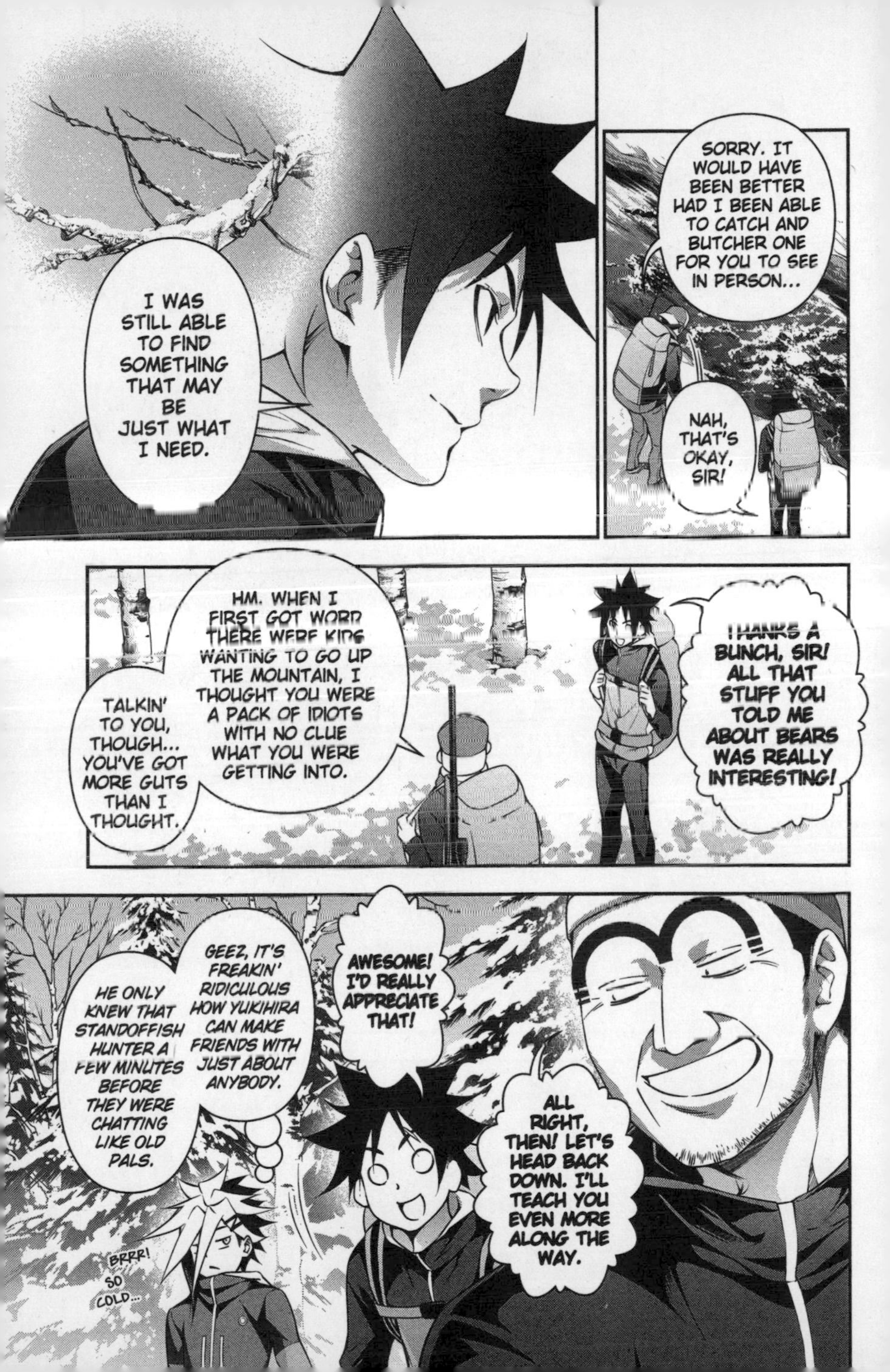
SORRY. IT WOULD HAVE BEEN BETTER HAD I BEEN ABLE TO CATCH AND BUTCHER ONE FOR YOU TO SEE IN PERSON...
NAH, THAT'S OKAY, SIR!
I WAS STILL ABLE TO FIND SOMETHING THAT MAY BE JUST WHAT I NEED.
THANKS A BUNCH, SIR! ALL THAT STUFF YOU TOLD ME ABOUT BEARS WAS REALLY INTERESTING!
HM. WHEN I FIRST GOT WORD THERE WERE KIDS WANTING TO GO UP THE MOUNTAIN, I THOUGHT YOU WERE A PACK OF IDIOTS WITH NO CLUE WHAT YOU WERE GETTING INTO.
TALKIN' TO YOU, THOUGH... YOU'VE GOT MORE GUTS THAN I THOUGHT.
ALL RIGHT, THEN! LET'S HEAD BACK DOWN. I'LL TEACH YOU EVEN MORE ALONG THE WAY.
AWESOME! I'D REALLY APPRECIATE THAT!
GEEZ, IT'S FREAKIN' RIDICULOUS HOW YUKIHIRA CAN MAKE FRIENDS WITH JUST ABOUT ANYBODY.
HE ONLY KNEW THAT STANDOFFISH HUNTER A FEW MINUTES BEFORE THEY WERE CHATTING LIKE OLD PALS.
BRRR! SO COLD...

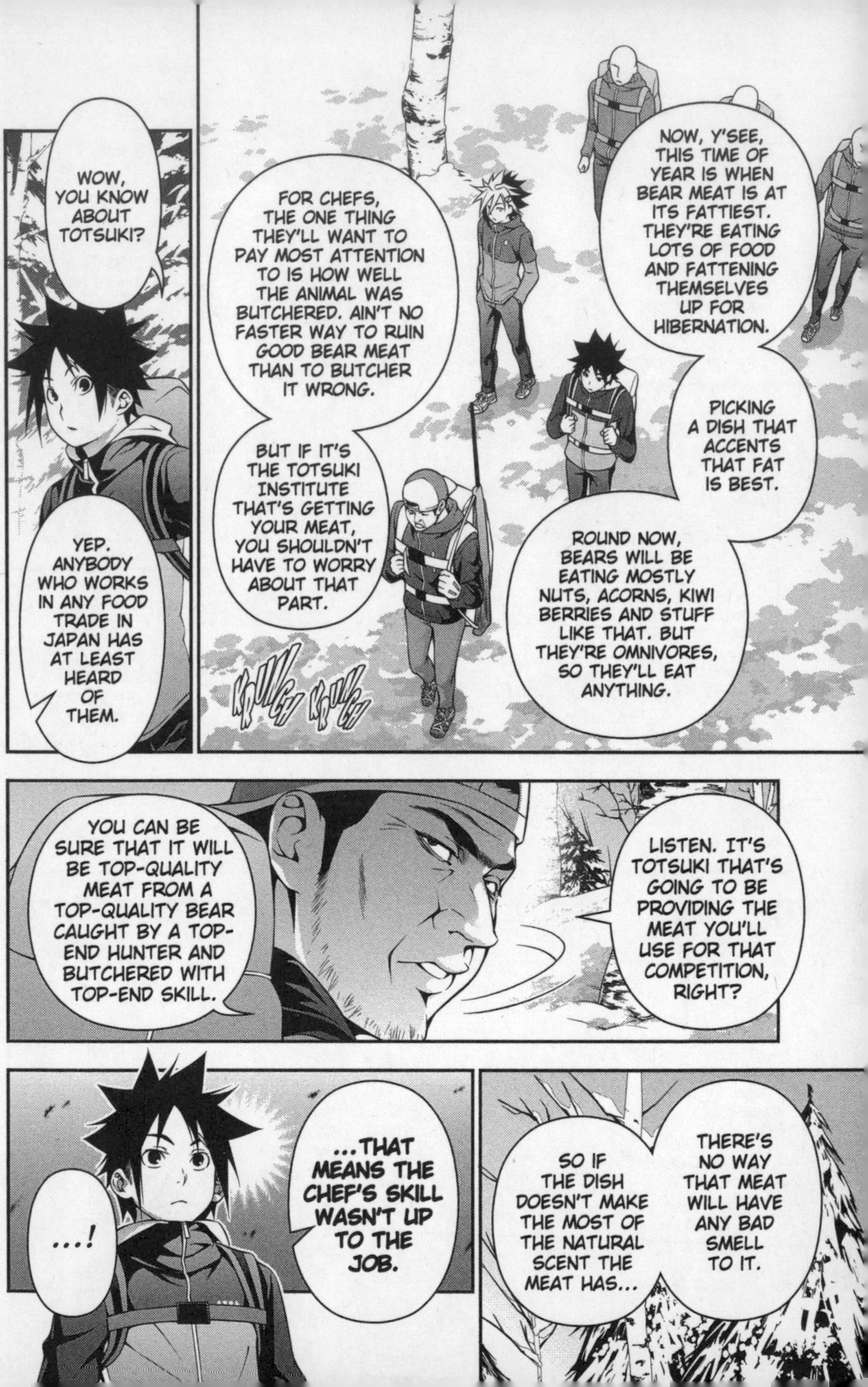
NOW, Y'SEE, THIS TIME OF YEAR IS WHEN BEAR MEAT IS AT ITS FATTIEST. THEY'RE EATING LOTS OF FOOD AND FATTENING THEMSELVES UP FOR HIBERNATION.
PICKING A DISH THAT ACCENTS THAT FAT IS BEST.
ROUND NOW, BEARS WILL BE EATING MOSTLY NUTS, ACORNS, KIWI BERRIES AND STUFF LIKE THAT. BUT THEY'RE OMNIVORES, SO THEY'LL EAT ANYTHING.
FOR CHEFS, THE ONE THING THEY'LL WANT TO PAY MOST ATTENTION TO IS HOW WELL THE ANIMAL WAS BUTCHERED. AIN'T NO FASTER WAY TO RUIN GOOD BEAR MEAT THAN TO BUTCHER IT WRONG.
BUT IF IT'S THE TOTSUKI INSTITUTE THAT'S GETTING YOUR MEAT, YOU SHOULDN'T HAVE TO WORRY ABOUT THAT PART.
KRUNCH KRUNCH
WOW, YOU KNOW ABOUT TOTSUKI?
YEP. ANYBODY WHO WORKS IN ANY FOOD TRADE IN JAPAN HAS AT LEAST HEARD OF THEM.
LISTEN. IT'S TOTSUKI THAT'S GOING TO BE PROVIDING THE MEAT YOU'LL USE FOR THAT COMPETITION, RIGHT?
YOU CAN BE SURE THAT IT WILL BE TOP-QUALITY MEAT FROM A TOP-QUALITY BEAR CAUGHT BY A TOP-END HUNTER AND BUTCHERED WITH TOP-END SKILL.
THERE'S NO WAY THAT MEAT WILL HAVE ANY BAD SMELL TO IT.
SO IF THE DISH DOESN'T MAKE THE MOST OF THE NATURAL SCENT THE MEAT HAS...
...THAT MEANS THE CHEF'S SKILL WASN'T UP TO THE JOB.
...!

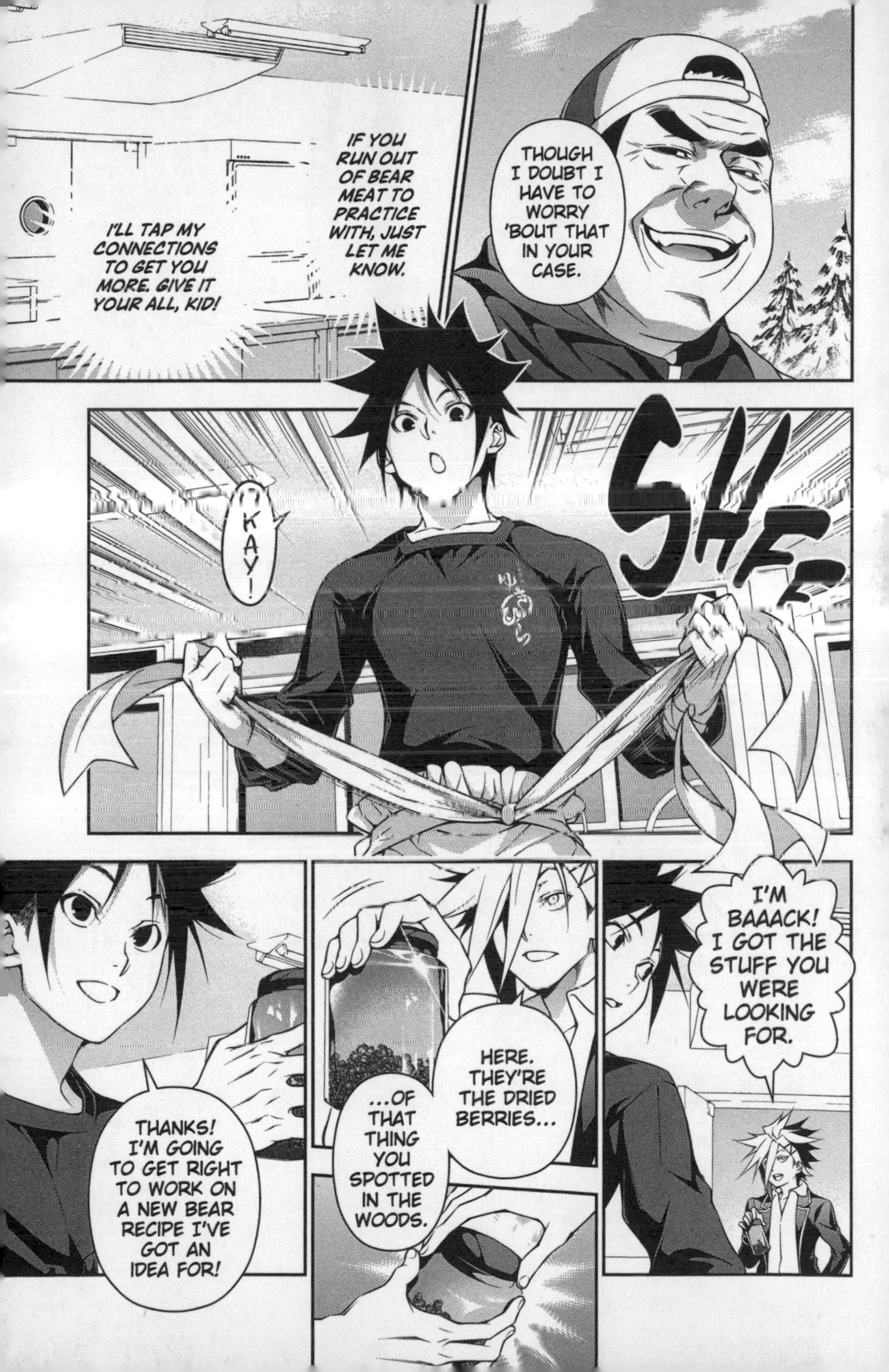
THOUGH I DOUBT I HAVE TO WORRY 'BOUT THAT IN YOUR CASE.
IF YOU RUN OUT OF BEAR MEAT TO PRACTICE WITH, JUST LET ME KNOW.
I'LL TAP MY CONNECTIONS TO GET YOU MORE. GIVE IT YOUR ALL, KID!
SHF
'KAY!
I'M BAAACK! I GOT THE STUFF YOU WERE LOOKING FOR.
HERE. THEY'RE THE DRIED BERRIES...
...OF THAT THING YOU SPOTTED IN THE WOODS.
THANKS! I'M GOING TO GET RIGHT TO WORK ON A NEW BEAR RECIPE I'VE GOT AN IDEA FOR!

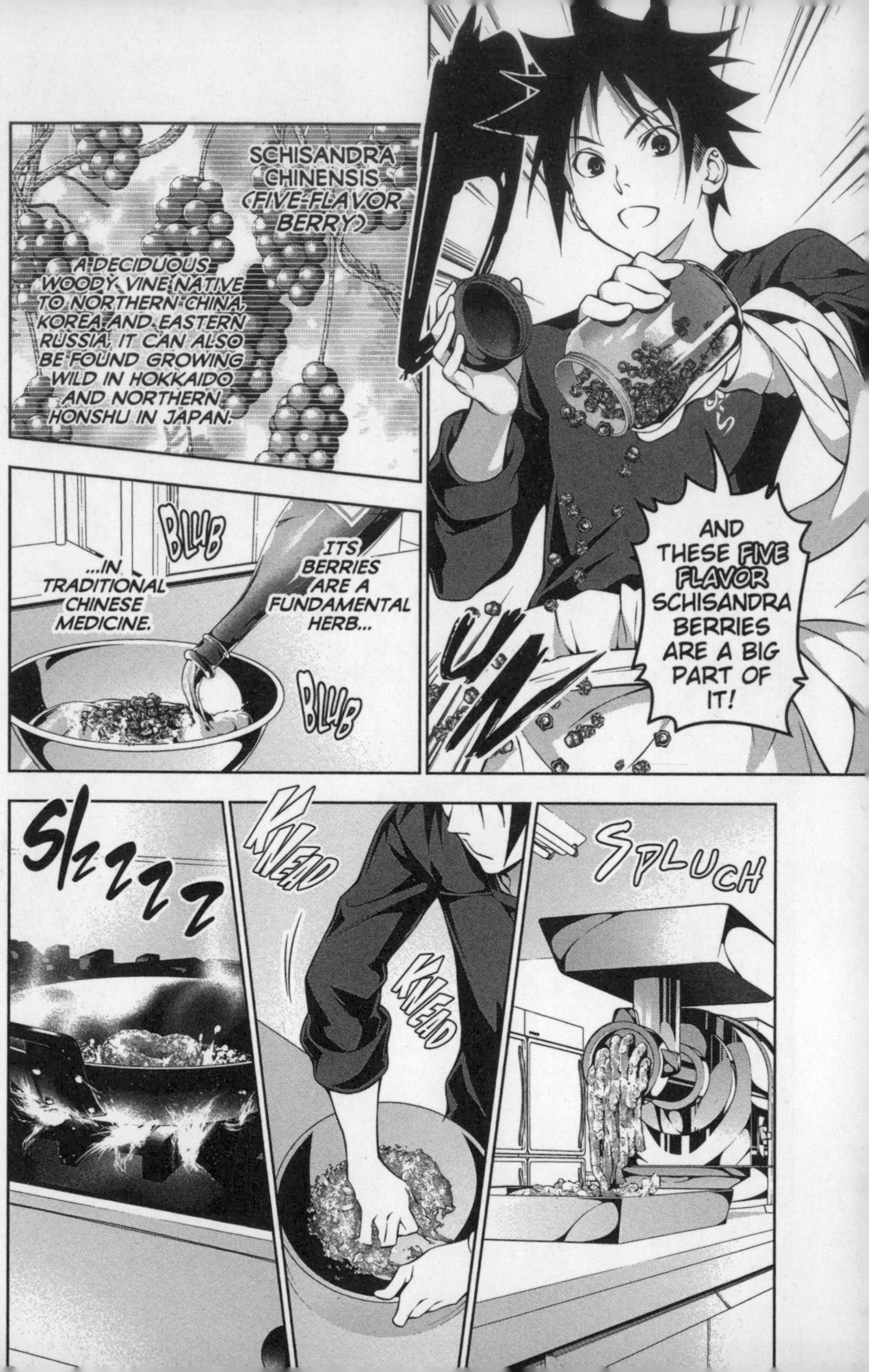
AND THESE FIVE FLAVOR SCHISANDRA BERRIES ARE A BIG PART OF IT!
SCHISANDRA CHINENSIS (FIVE-FLAVOR BERRY)
A DECIDUOUS WOODY VINE NATIVE TO NORTHERN CHINA, KOREA AND EASTERN RUSSIA, IT CAN ALSO BE FOUND GROWING WILD IN HOKKAIDO AND NORTHERN HONSHU IN JAPAN.
BLUB
ITS BERRIES ARE A FUNDAMENTAL HERB...
...IN TRADITIONAL CHINESE MEDICINE.
BLUB
SPLUCH
KNEAD
KNEAD
SIZZZZZ

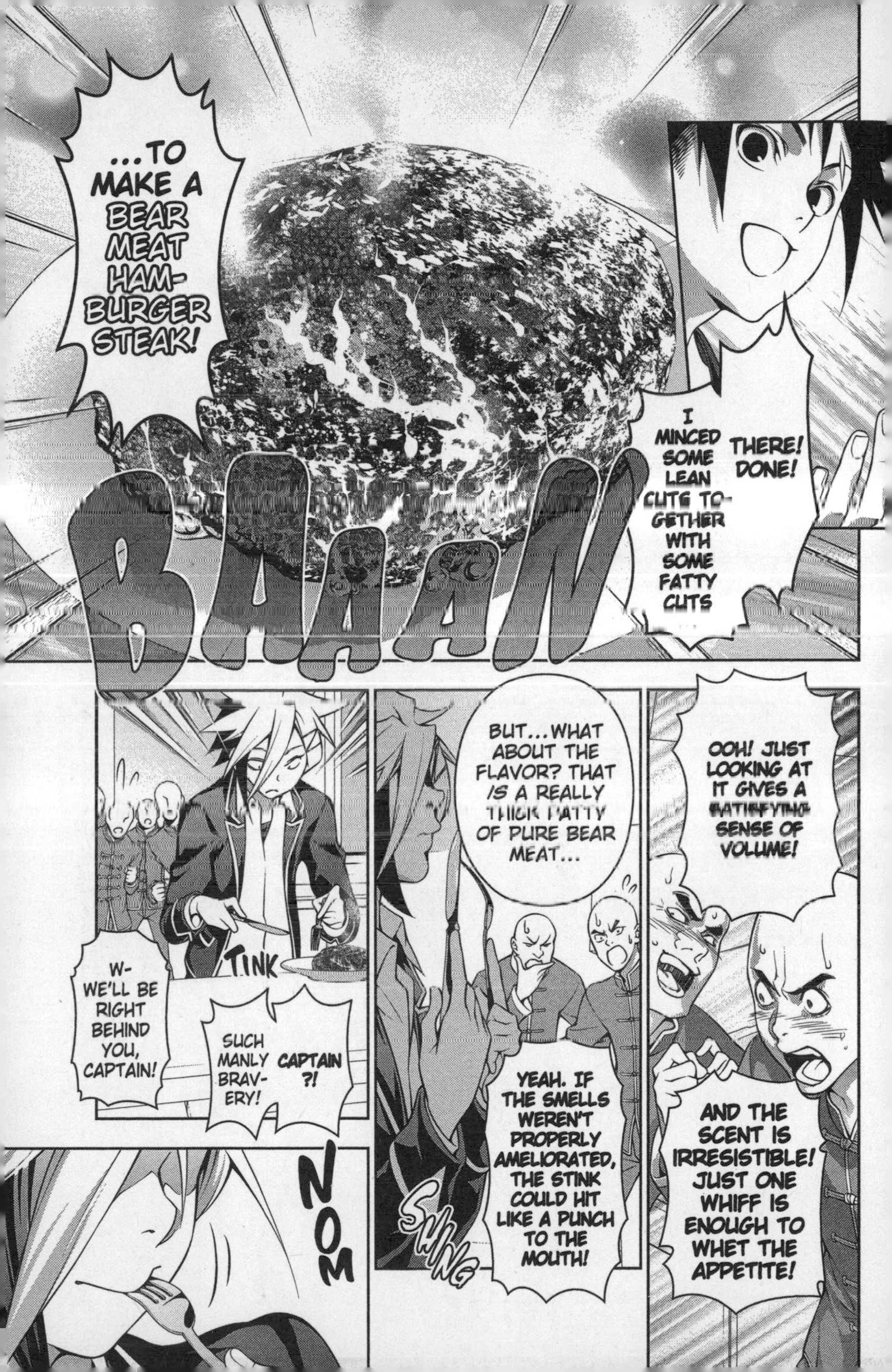
THERE! DONE!
I MINCED SOME LEAN CUTS TOGETHER WITH SOME FATTY CUTS...
...TO MAKE A BEAR MEAT HAMBURGER STEAK!
BAAAN
OOH! JUST LOOKING AT IT GIVES A SATISFYING SENSE OF VOLUME!
AND THE SCENT IS IRRESISTIBLE! JUST ONE WHIFF IS ENOUGH TO WHET THE APPETITE!
BUT...WHAT ABOUT THE FLAVOR? THAT IS A REALLY THICK PATTY OF PURE BEAR MEAT...
YEAH. IF THE SMELLS WEREN'T PROPERLY AMELIORATED, THE STINK COULD HIT LIKE A PUNCH TO THE MOUTH!
SHING
TINK
CAPTAIN?!
SUCH MANLY BRAVERY!
W-WE'LL BE RIGHT BEHIND YOU, CAPTAIN!
NOM NOM

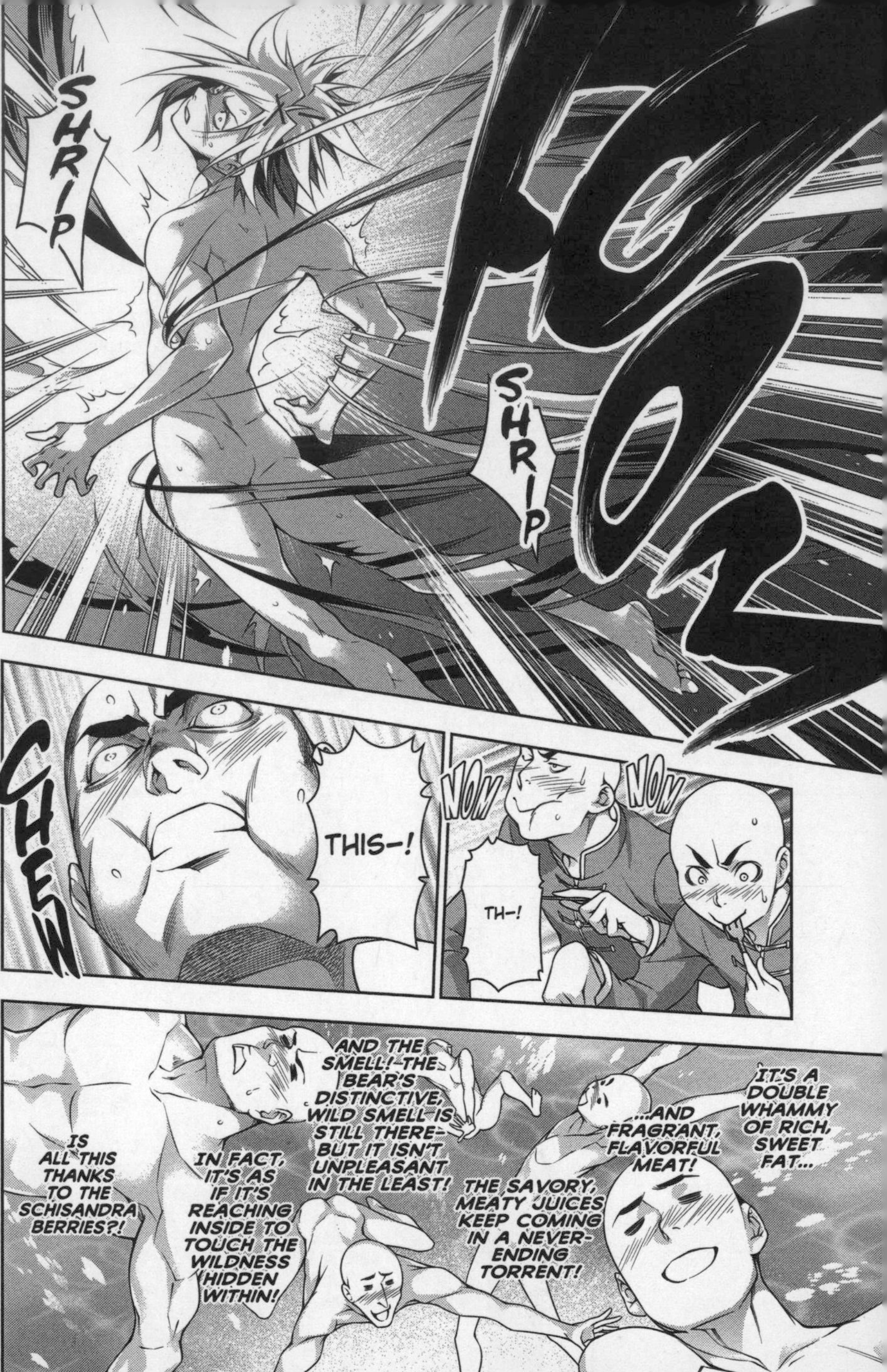
SHRIP
SHRIP
NOM
NOM
TH-!
THIS-!
CHEW
IT'S A DOUBLE WHAMMY OF RICH, SWEET FAT...
...AND FRAGRANT, FLAVORFUL MEAT!
THE SAVORY, MEATY JUICES KEEP COMING IN A NEVER-ENDING TORRENT!
AND THE SMELL! THE BEAR'S DISTINCTIVE, WILD SMELL IS STILL THERE- BUT IT ISN'T UNPLEASANT IN THE LEAST!
IN FACT, IT'S AS IF IT'S REACHING INSIDE TO TOUCH THE WILDNESS HIDDEN WITHIN!
IS ALL THIS THANKS TO THE SCHISANDRA BERRIES?!

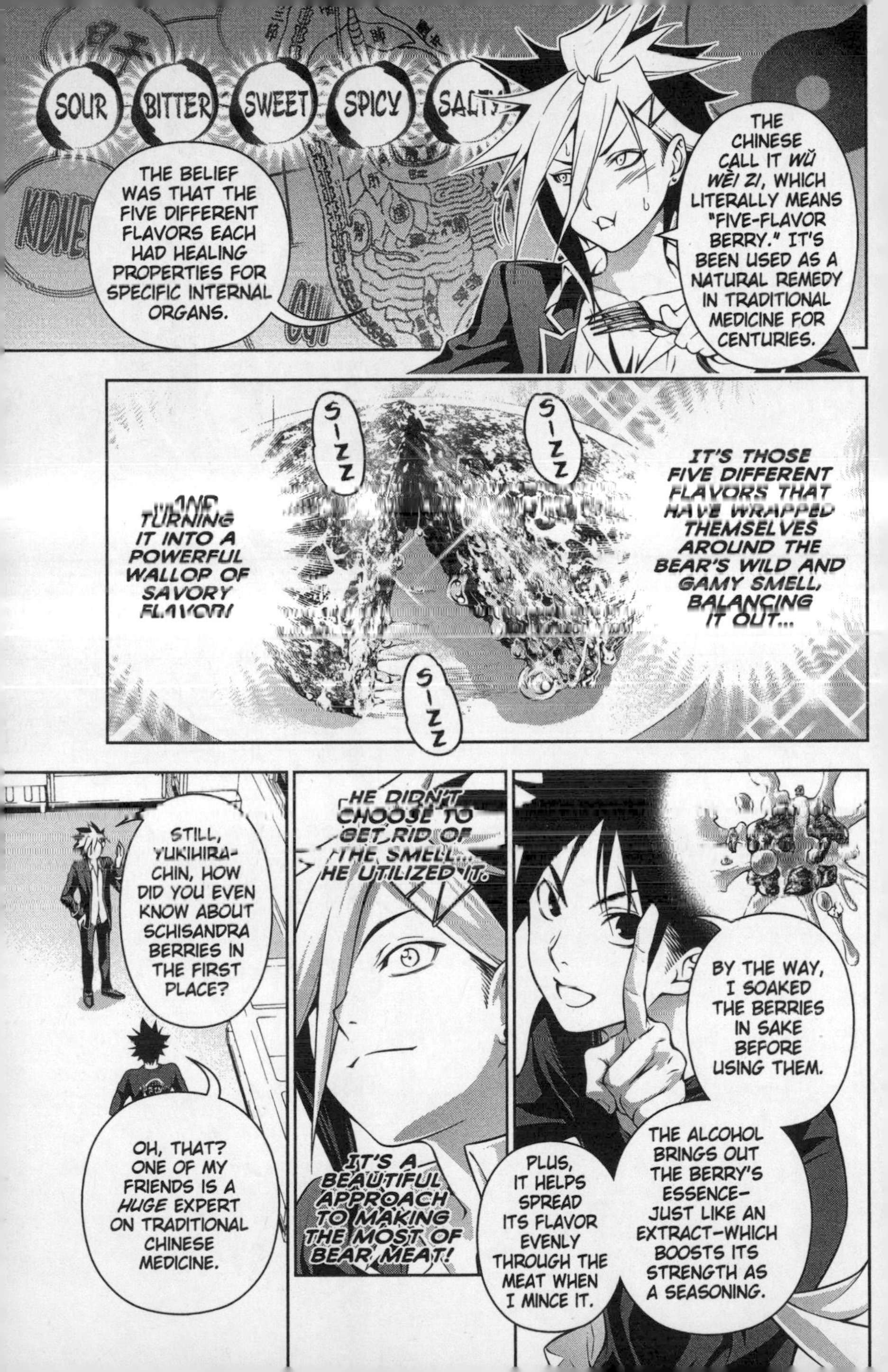
THE CHINESE CALL IT *WŬ WÈI ZI*, WHICH LITERALLY MEANS "FIVE-FLAVOR BERRY." IT'S BEEN USED AS A NATURAL REMEDY IN TRADITIONAL MEDICINE FOR CENTURIES.
SOUR
BITTER
SWEET
SPICY
THE BELIEF WAS THAT THE FIVE DIFFERENT FLAVORS EACH HAD HEALING PROPERTIES FOR SPECIFIC INTERNAL ORGANS.
IT'S THOSE FIVE DIFFERENT FLAVORS THAT HAVE WRAPPED THEMSELVES AROUND THE BEAR'S WILD AND GAMY SMELL, BALANCING IT OUT...
SIZZ
SIZZ
SIZZ
...AND TURNING IT INTO A POWERFUL WALLOP OF SAVORY FLAVOR!
BY THE WAY, I SOAKED THE BERRIES IN SAKE BEFORE USING THEM.
THE ALCOHOL BRINGS OUT THE BERRY'S ESSENCE—JUST LIKE AN EXTRACT—WHICH BOOSTS ITS STRENGTH AS A SEASONING.
PLUS, IT HELPS SPREAD ITS FLAVOR EVENLY THROUGH THE MEAT WHEN I MINCE IT.
HE DIDN'T CHOOSE TO GET RID OF THE SMELL... HE UTILIZED IT.
IT'S A BEAUTIFUL APPROACH TO MAKING THE MOST OF BEAR MEAT!
STILL, YUKIHIRA-CHIN, HOW DID YOU EVEN KNOW ABOUT SCHISANDRA BERRIES IN THE FIRST PLACE?
OH, THAT? ONE OF MY FRIENDS IS A *HUGE* EXPERT ON TRADITIONAL CHINESE MEDICINE.

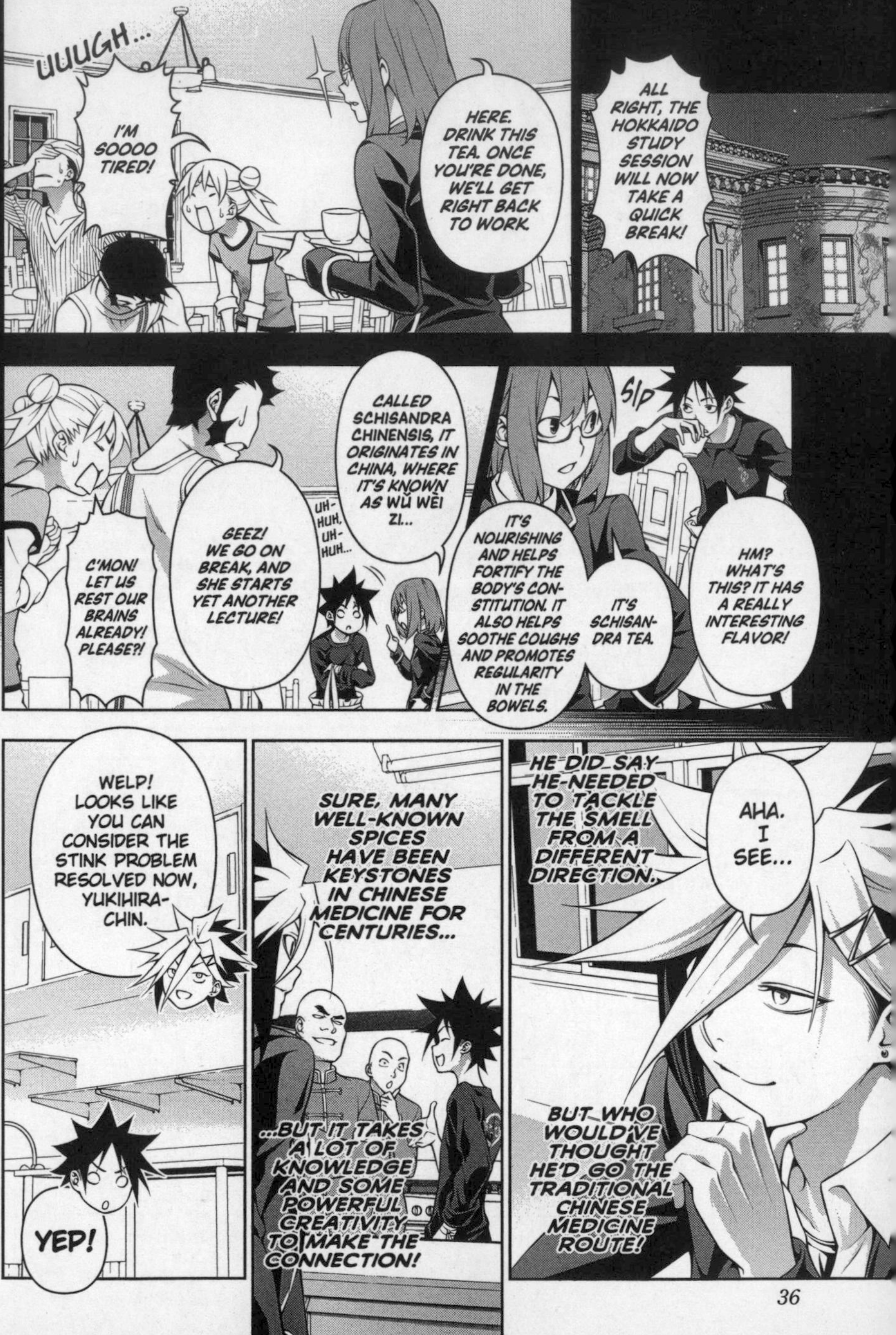
ALL RIGHT, THE HOKKAIDO STUDY SESSION WILL NOW TAKE A QUICK BREAK!
UUUGH...
I'M SOOOO TIRED!
HERE. DRINK THIS TEA. ONCE YOU'RE DONE, WE'LL GET RIGHT BACK TO WORK.
SIP
HM? WHAT'S THIS? IT HAS A REALLY INTERESTING FLAVOR!
IT'S SCHISANDRA TEA.
IT'S NOURISHING AND HELPS FORTIFY THE BODY'S CONSTITUTION. IT ALSO HELPS SOOTHE COUGHS AND PROMOTES REGULARITY IN THE BOWELS.
CALLED SCHISANDRA CHINENSIS, IT ORIGINATES IN CHINA, WHERE IT'S KNOWN AS WŬ WÈI ZI...
UH-HUH, UH-HUH...
GEEZ! WE GO ON BREAK, AND SHE STARTS YET ANOTHER LECTURE!
C'MON! LET US REST OUR BRAINS ALREADY! PLEASE?!
AHA. I SEE...
HE DID SAY HE NEEDED TO TACKLE THE SMELL FROM A DIFFERENT DIRECTION.
BUT WHO WOULD'VE THOUGHT HE'D GO THE TRADITIONAL CHINESE MEDICINE ROUTE!
SURE, MANY WELL-KNOWN SPICES HAVE BEEN KEYSTONES IN CHINESE MEDICINE FOR CENTURIES...
...BUT IT TAKES A LOT OF KNOWLEDGE AND SOME POWERFUL CREATIVITY TO MAKE THE CONNECTION!
WELP! LOOKS LIKE YOU CAN CONSIDER THE STINK PROBLEM RESOLVED NOW, YUKIHIRA-CHIN.
YEP!

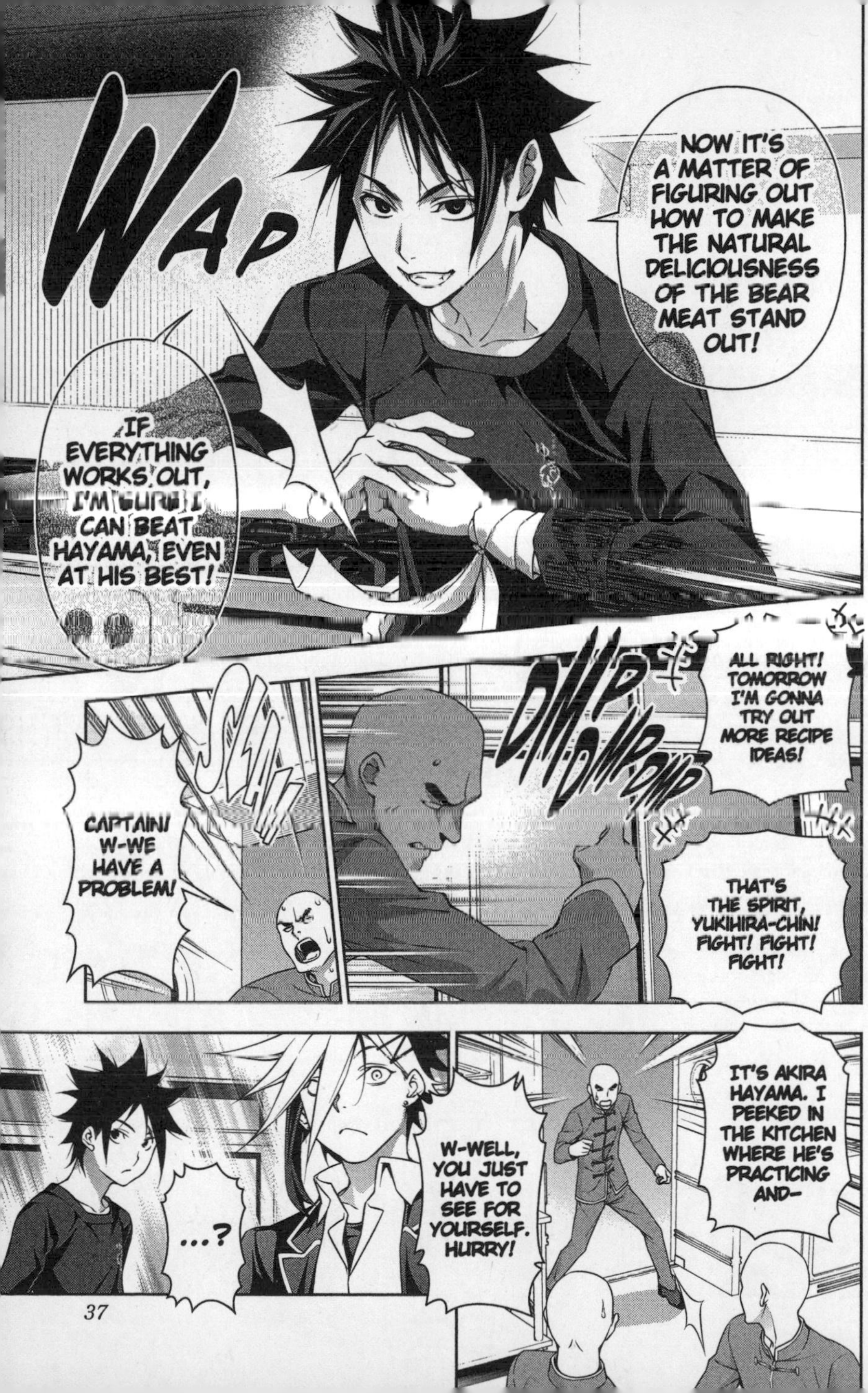
WAP
NOW IT'S A MATTER OF FIGURING OUT HOW TO MAKE THE NATURAL DELICIOUSNESS OF THE BEAR MEAT STAND OUT!
IF EVERYTHING WORKS OUT, I'M SURE I CAN BEAT HAYAMA, EVEN AT HIS BEST!
ALL RIGHT! TOMORROW I'M GONNA TRY OUT MORE RECIPE IDEAS!
DMP DMP DMP DMP
THAT'S THE SPIRIT, YUKIHIRA-CHIN! FIGHT! FIGHT! FIGHT!
SLAM
CAPTAIN! W-WE HAVE A PROBLEM!
IT'S AKIRA HAYAMA. I PEEKED IN THE KITCHEN WHERE HE'S PRACTICING AND–
W-WELL, YOU JUST HAVE TO SEE FOR YOURSELF. HURRY!
...?

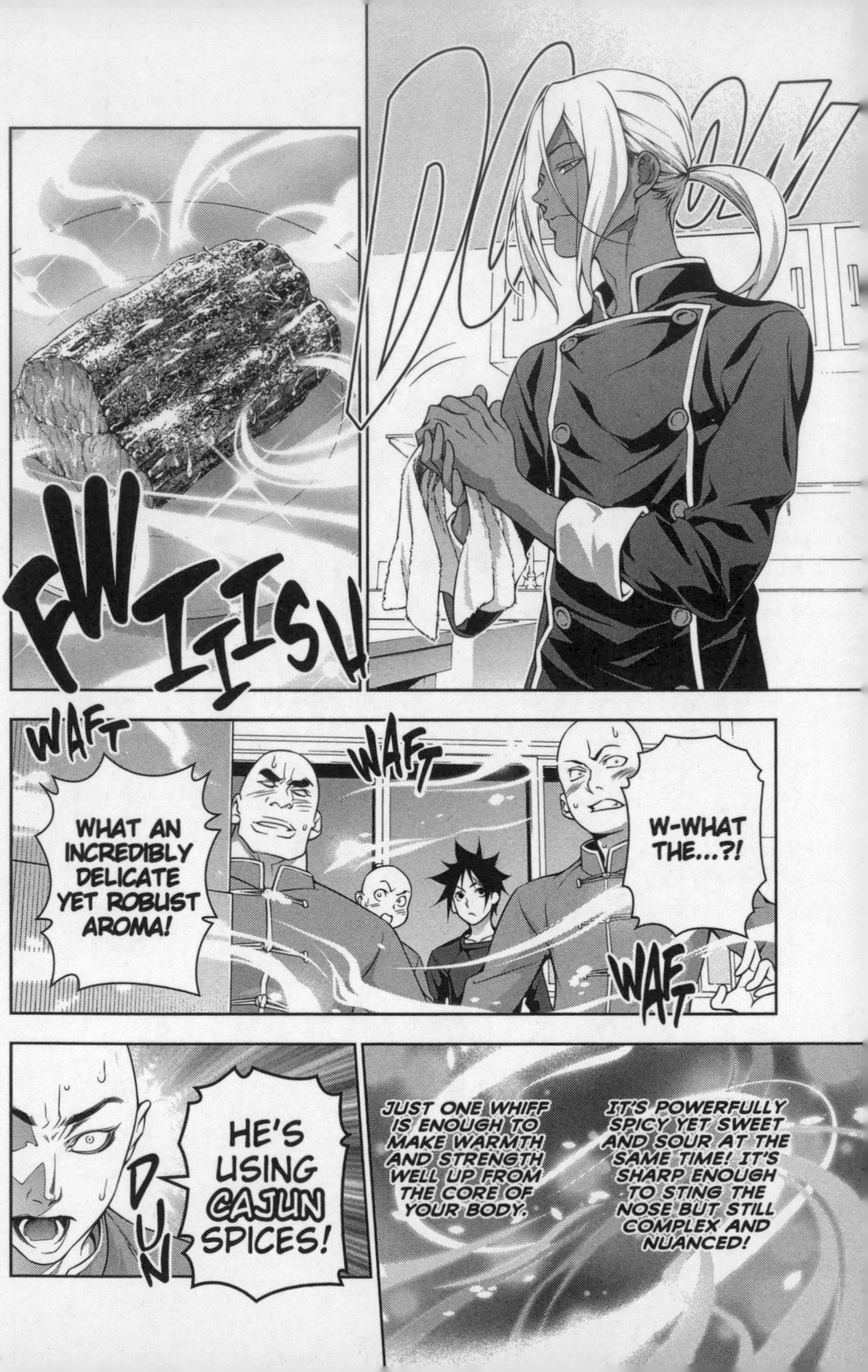
DOOOM
FWIIISH
W-WHAT THE...?!
WAFT
WAFT
WHAT AN INCREDIBLY DELICATE YET ROBUST AROMA!
WAFT
IT'S POWERFULLY SPICY YET SWEET AND SOUR AT THE SAME TIME! IT'S SHARP ENOUGH TO STING THE NOSE BUT STILL COMPLEX AND NUANCED!
JUST ONE WHIFF IS ENOUGH TO MAKE WARMTH AND STRENGTH WELL UP FROM THE CORE OF YOUR BODY.
HE'S USING CAJUN SPICES!
DUN

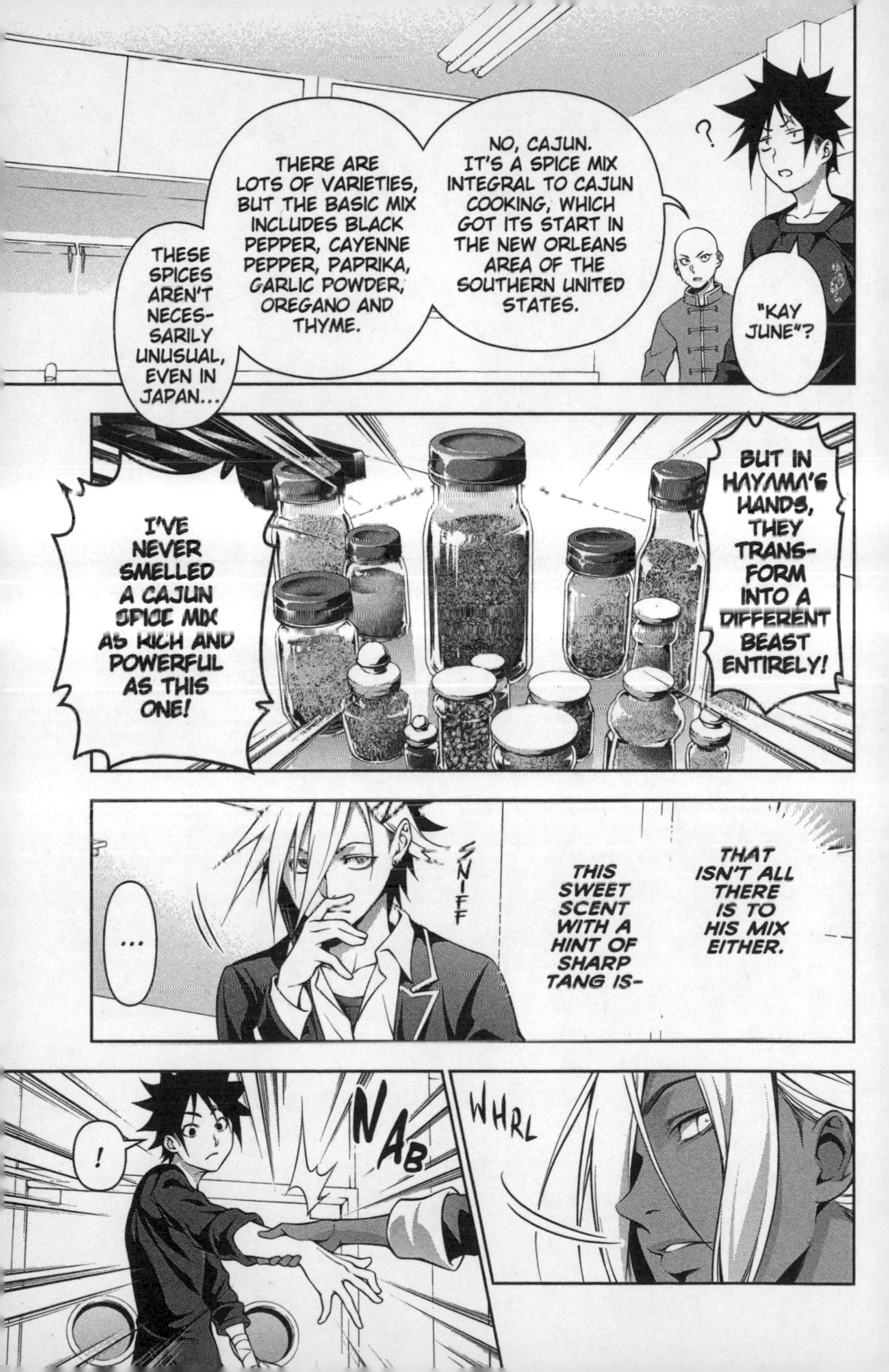
?
"KAY JUNE"?
NO, CAJUN. IT'S A SPICE MIX INTEGRAL TO CAJUN COOKING, WHICH GOT ITS START IN THE NEW ORLEANS AREA OF THE SOUTHERN UNITED STATES.
THERE ARE LOTS OF VARIETIES, BUT THE BASIC MIX INCLUDES BLACK PEPPER, CAYENNE PEPPER, PAPRIKA, GARLIC POWDER, OREGANO AND THYME.
THESE SPICES AREN'T NECES-SARILY UNUSUAL, EVEN IN JAPAN...
BUT IN HAYAMA'S HANDS, THEY TRANS-FORM INTO A DIFFERENT BEAST ENTIRELY!
I'VE NEVER SMELLED A CAJUN SPICE MIX AS RICH AND POWERFUL AS THIS ONE!
THAT ISN'T ALL THERE IS TO HIS MIX EITHER.
THIS SWEET SCENT WITH A HINT OF SHARP TANG IS-
SNIFF
...
WHRL
NAB
!

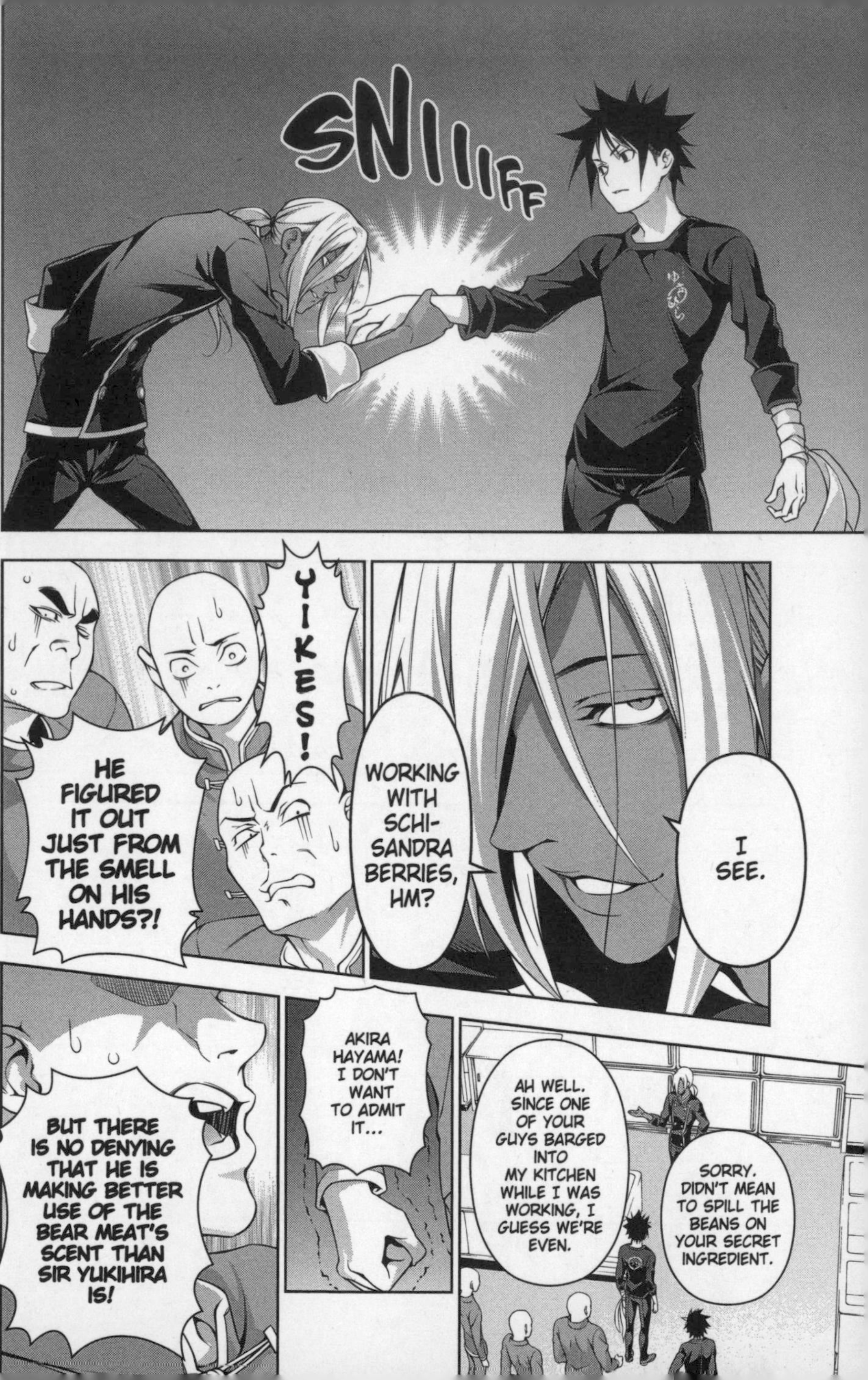
SNIIIFF
I SEE.
WORKING WITH SCHI-SANDRA BERRIES, HM?
YIKES!
HE FIGURED IT OUT JUST FROM THE SMELL ON HIS HANDS?!
SORRY. DIDN'T MEAN TO SPILL THE BEANS ON YOUR SECRET INGREDIENT.
AH WELL. SINCE ONE OF YOUR GUYS BARGED INTO MY KITCHEN WHILE I WAS WORKING, I GUESS WE'RE EVEN.
AKIRA HAYAMA! I DON'T WANT TO ADMIT IT...
BUT THERE IS NO DENYING THAT HE IS MAKING BETTER USE OF THE BEAR MEAT'S SCENT THAN SIR YUKIHIRA IS!

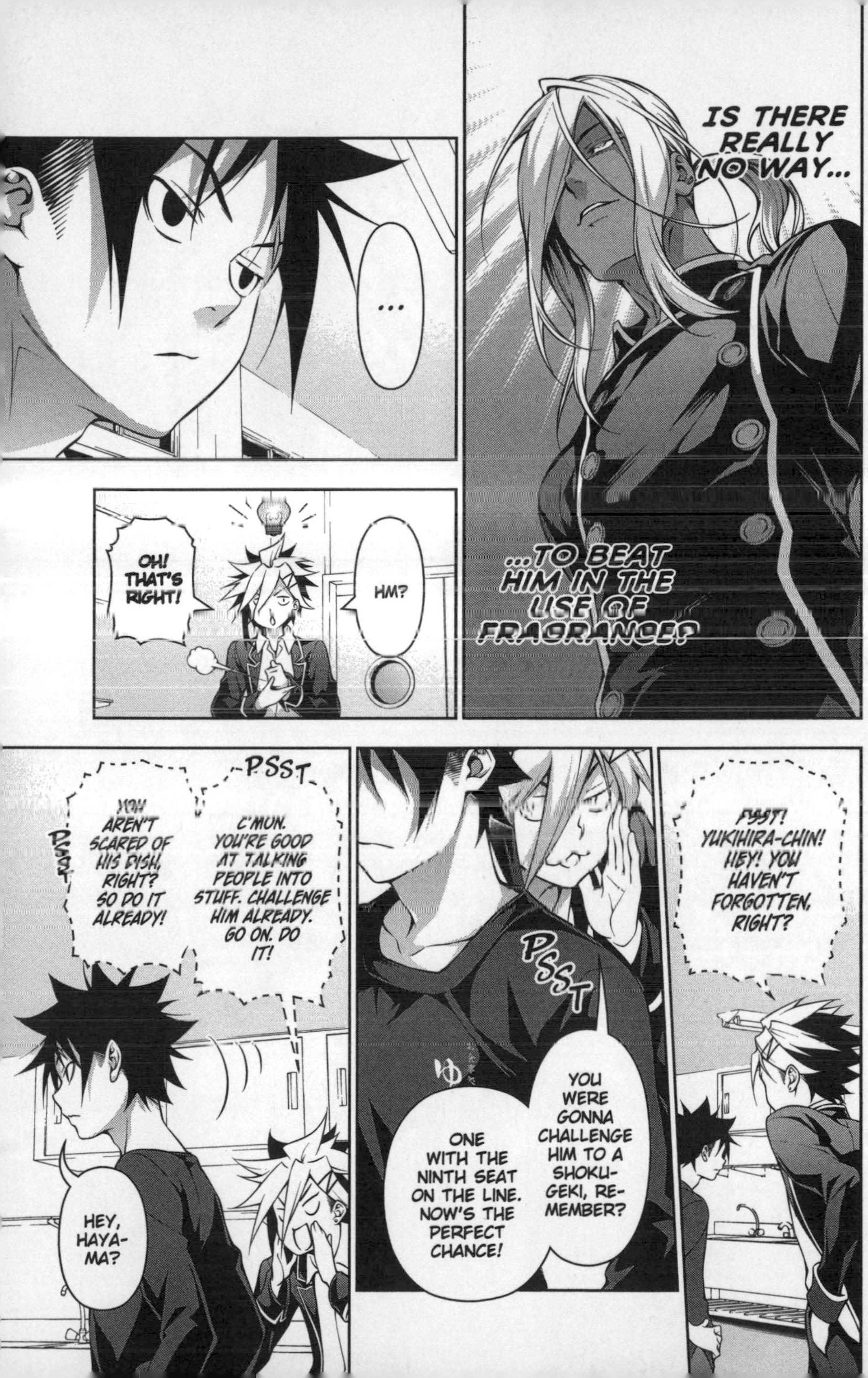
IS THERE REALLY NO WAY...
...TO BEAT HIM IN THE USE OF FRAGRANCE?
...
HM?
OH! THAT'S RIGHT!
PSST! YUKIHIRA-CHIN! HEY! YOU HAVEN'T FORGOTTEN, RIGHT?
PSST
YOU WERE GONNA CHALLENGE HIM TO A SHOKU-GEKI, RE-MEMBER?
ONE WITH THE NINTH SEAT ON THE LINE. NOW'S THE PERFECT CHANCE!
PSST
C'MON. YOU'RE GOOD AT TALKING PEOPLE INTO STUFF. CHALLENGE HIM ALREADY. GO ON. DO IT!
PSST
YOU AREN'T SCARED OF HIS DISH, RIGHT? SO DO IT ALREADY!
HEY, HAYA-MA?

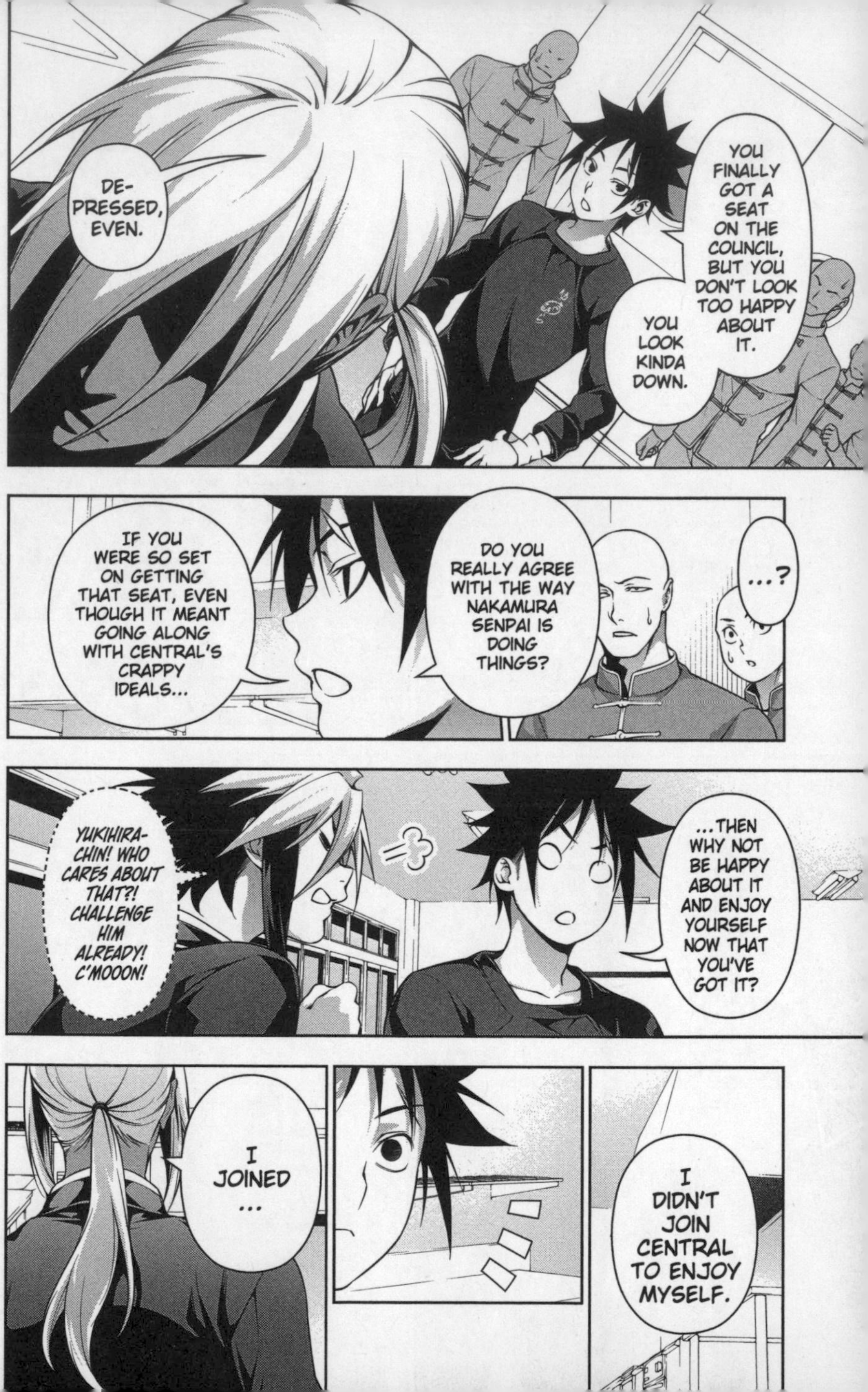
YOU FINALLY GOT A SEAT ON THE COUNCIL, BUT YOU DON'T LOOK TOO HAPPY ABOUT IT.
YOU LOOK KINDA DOWN.
DE-PRESSED, EVEN.
...?
DO YOU REALLY AGREE WITH THE WAY NAKAMURA SENPAI IS DOING THINGS?
IF YOU WERE SO SET ON GETTING THAT SEAT, EVEN THOUGH IT MEANT GOING ALONG WITH CENTRAL'S CRAPPY IDEALS...
...THEN WHY NOT BE HAPPY ABOUT IT AND ENJOY YOURSELF NOW THAT YOU'VE GOT IT?
YUKIHIRA-CHIN! WHO CARES ABOUT THAT?! CHALLENGE HIM ALREADY! C'MOOON!
I DIDN'T JOIN CENTRAL TO ENJOY MYSELF.
I JOINED ...

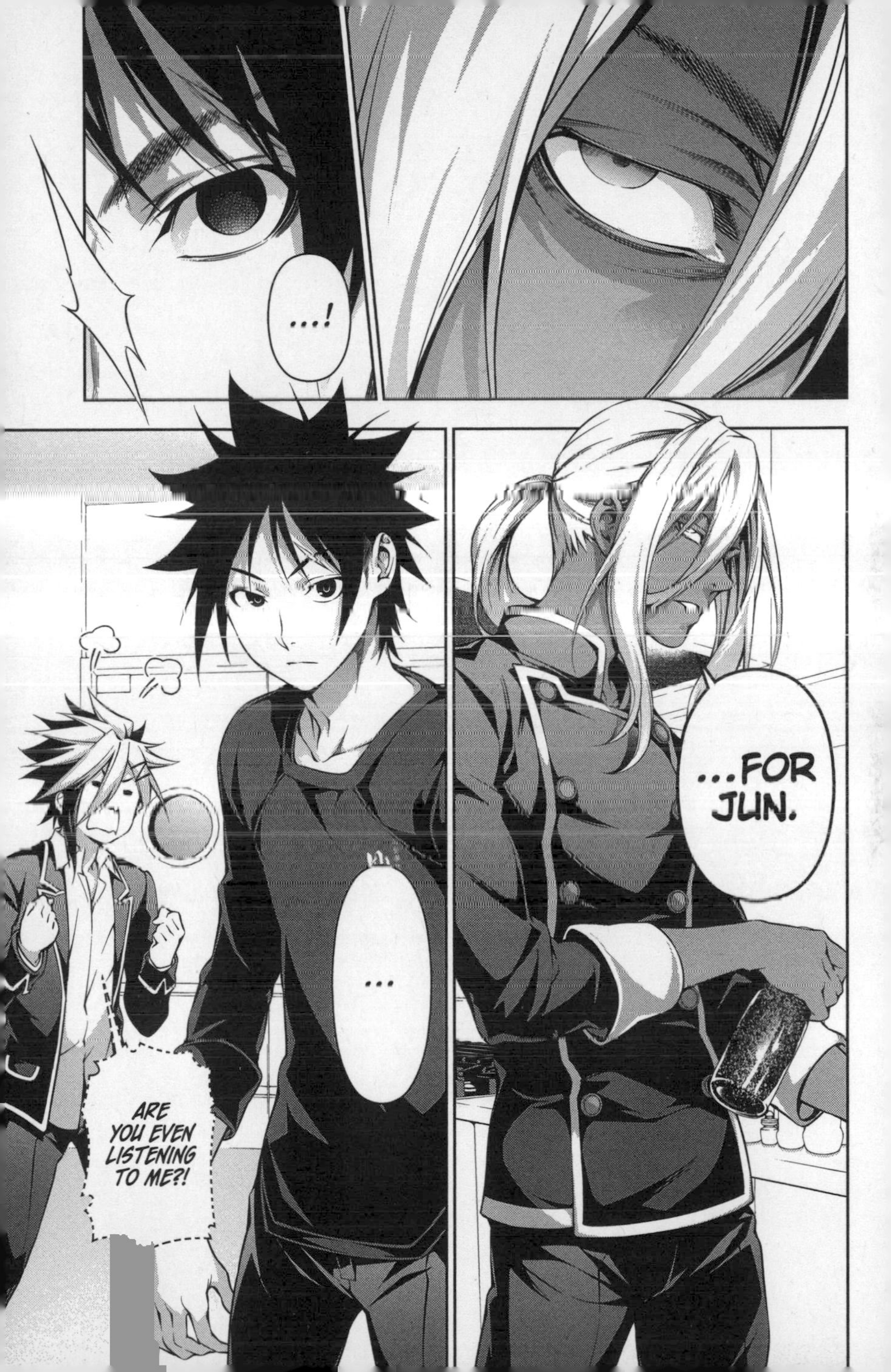
...!
...FOR JUN.
...
ARE YOU EVEN LISTENING TO ME?!

SOMA
"SNOW TREKKER"
YUKIHIRA

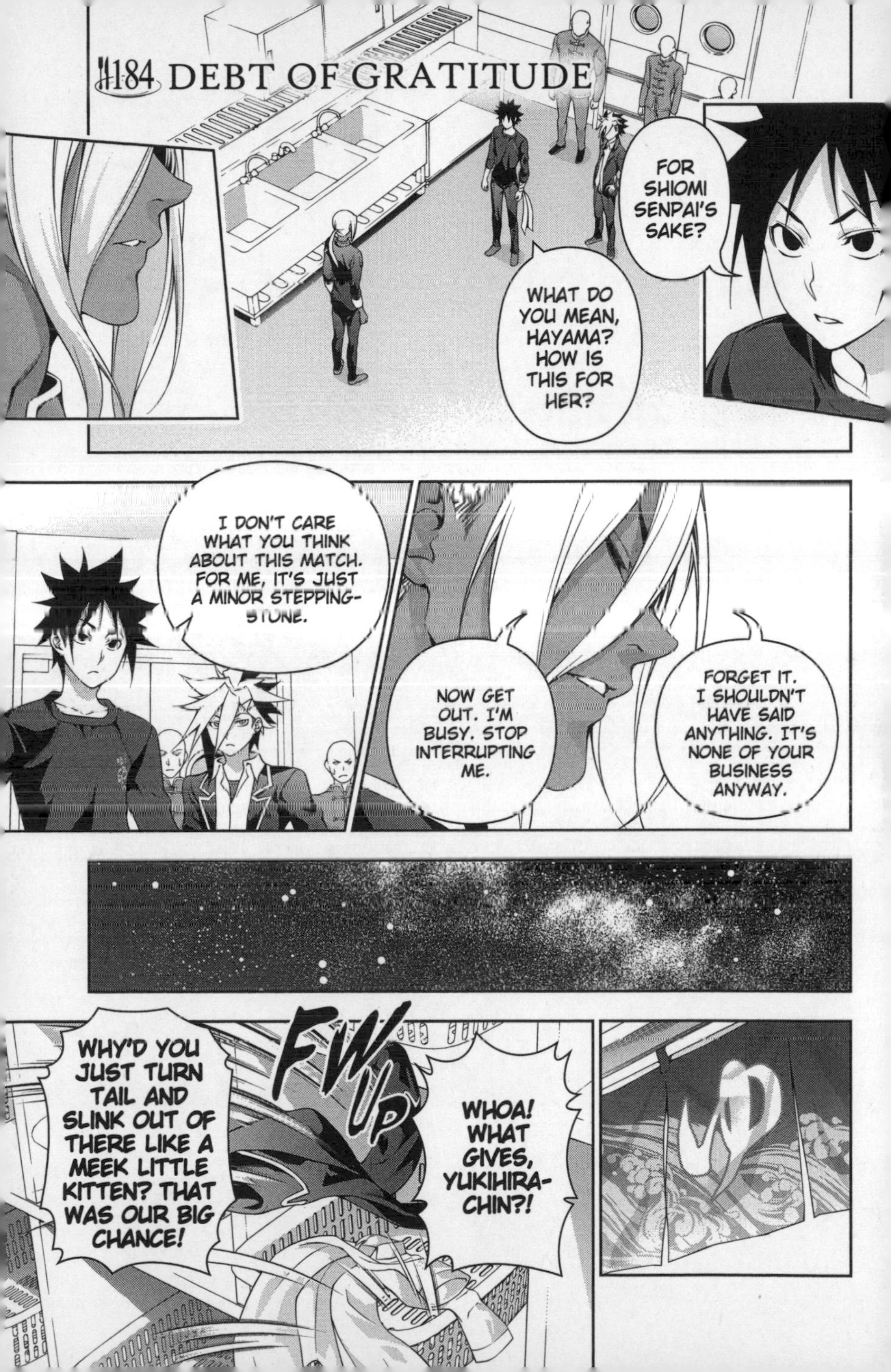
184 DEBT OF GRATITUDE
FOR SHIOMI SENPAI'S SAKE?
WHAT DO YOU MEAN, HAYAMA? HOW IS THIS FOR HER?
FORGET IT. I SHOULDN'T HAVE SAID ANYTHING. IT'S NONE OF YOUR BUSINESS ANYWAY.
NOW GET OUT. I'M BUSY. STOP INTERRUPTING ME.
I DON'T CARE WHAT YOU THINK ABOUT THIS MATCH. FOR ME, IT'S JUST A MINOR STEPPING-STONE.
FWUP
WHOA! WHAT GIVES, YUKIHIRA-CHIN?!
WHY'D YOU JUST TURN TAIL AND SLINK OUT OF THERE LIKE A MEEK LITTLE KITTEN? THAT WAS OUR BIG CHANCE!

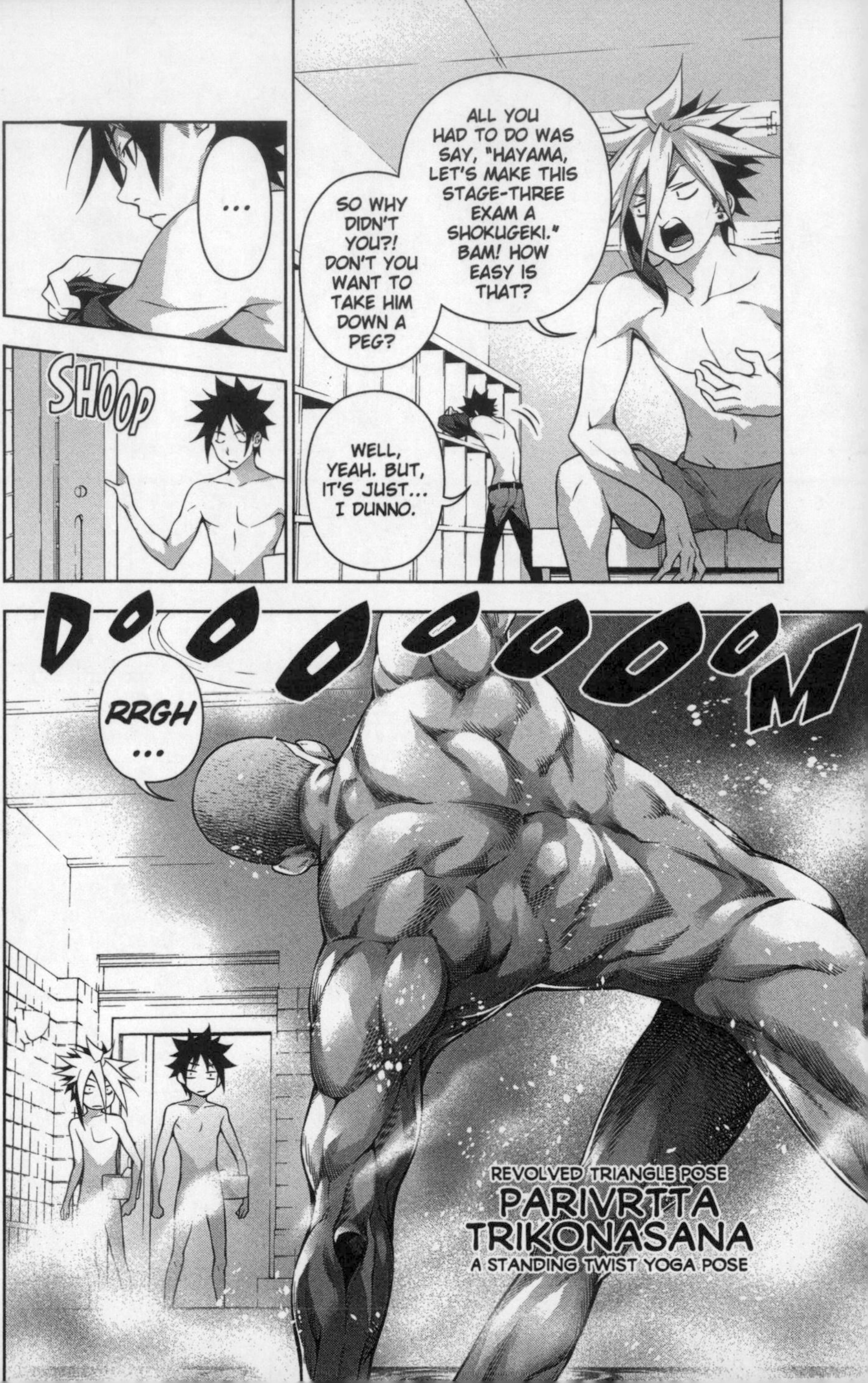
ALL YOU HAD TO DO WAS SAY, "HAYAMA, LET'S MAKE THIS STAGE-THREE EXAM A SHOKUGEKI." BAM! HOW EASY IS THAT?
SO WHY DIDN'T YOU?! DON'T YOU WANT TO TAKE HIM DOWN A PEG?
WELL, YEAH. BUT, IT'S JUST... I DUNNO.
...
SHOOP
DOOOOOOM
RRGH ...
REVOLVED TRIANGLE POSE
PARIVRTTA TRIKONASANA
A STANDING TWIST YOGA POSE

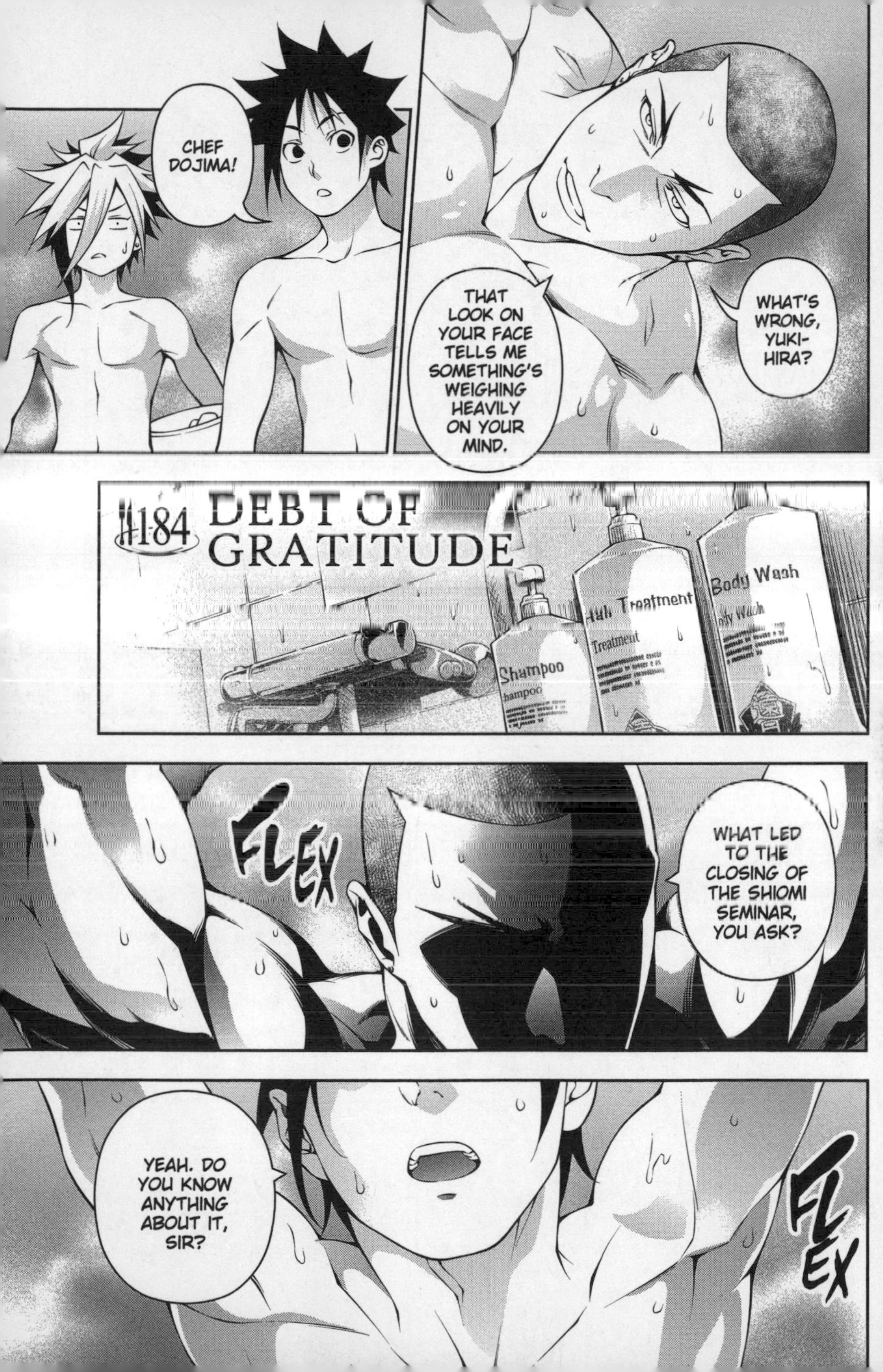
WHAT'S WRONG, YUKI-HIRA?
THAT LOOK ON YOUR FACE TELLS ME SOMETHING'S WEIGHING HEAVILY ON YOUR MIND.
CHEF DOJIMA!
#184 DEBT OF GRATITUDE
Body Wash
Hair Treatment
Treatment
Shampoo
WHAT LED TO THE CLOSING OF THE SHIOMI SEMINAR, YOU ASK?
FLEX
FLEX
YEAH. DO YOU KNOW ANYTHING ABOUT IT, SIR?

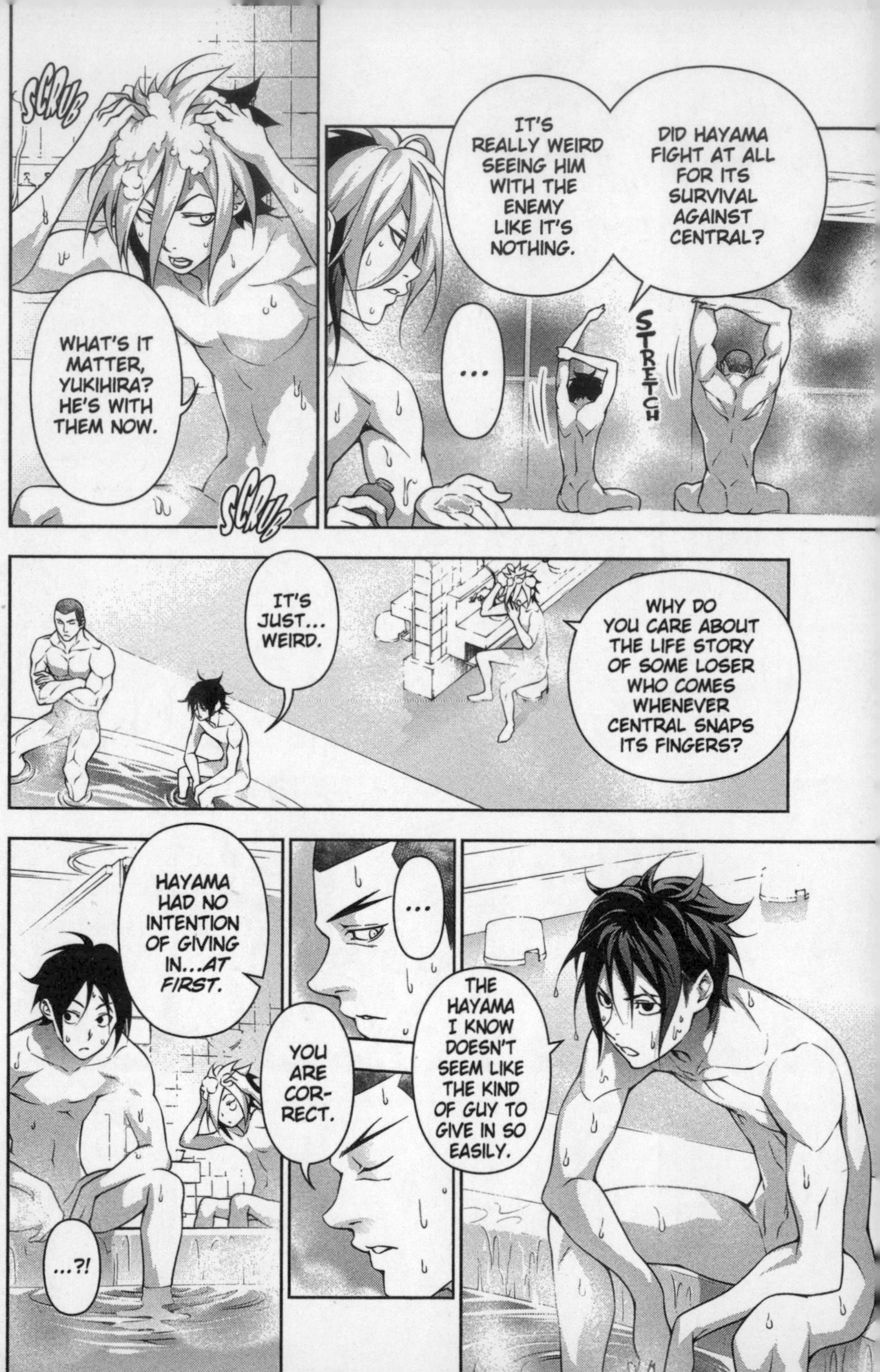
DID HAYAMA FIGHT AT ALL FOR ITS SURVIVAL AGAINST CENTRAL?
IT'S REALLY WEIRD SEEING HIM WITH THE ENEMY LIKE IT'S NOTHING.
...
STRETCH
SCRUB
WHAT'S IT MATTER, YUKIHIRA? HE'S WITH THEM NOW.
SCRUB
WHY DO YOU CARE ABOUT THE LIFE STORY OF SOME LOSER WHO COMES WHENEVER CENTRAL SNAPS ITS FINGERS?
IT'S JUST... WEIRD.
THE HAYAMA I KNOW DOESN'T SEEM LIKE THE KIND OF GUY TO GIVE IN SO EASILY.
...
YOU ARE COR-RECT.
HAYAMA HAD NO INTENTION OF GIVING IN...AT *FIRST*.
...?!

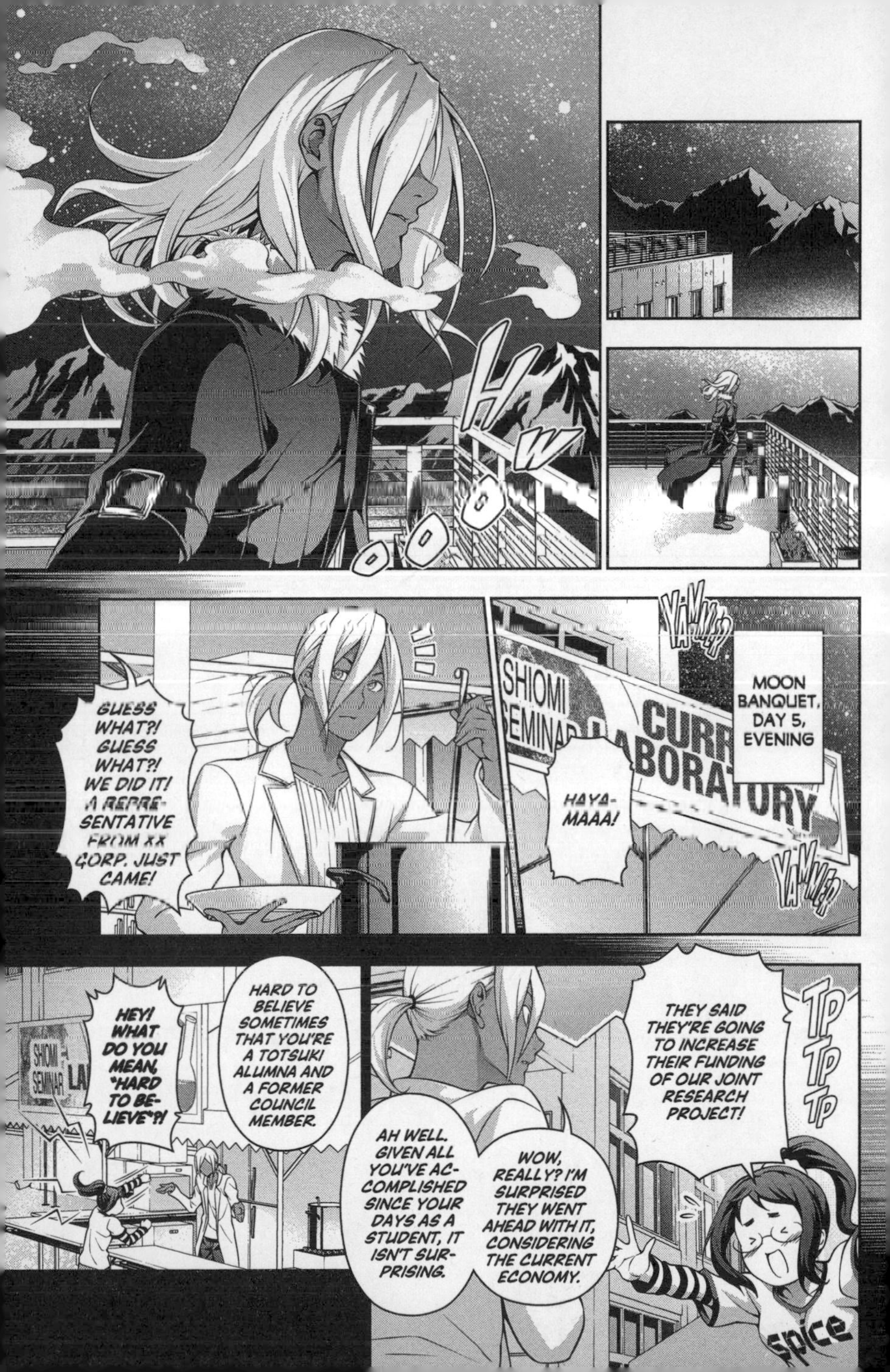
HWOOOO
YAMMER
MOON BANQUET, DAY 5, EVENING
SHIOMI SEMINAR
CURR
ABORATORY
HAYA-MAAA!
YAMMER
GUESS WHAT?! GUESS WHAT?! WE DID IT! A REPRESENTATIVE FROM XX CORP. JUST CAME!
TP TP TP
THEY SAID THEY'RE GOING TO INCREASE THEIR FUNDING OF OUR JOINT RESEARCH PROJECT!
WOW, REALLY? I'M SURPRISED THEY WENT AHEAD WITH IT, CONSIDERING THE CURRENT ECONOMY.
AH WELL. GIVEN ALL YOU'VE ACCOMPLISHED SINCE YOUR DAYS AS A STUDENT, IT ISN'T SURPRISING.
spice
HARD TO BELIEVE SOMETIMES THAT YOU'RE A TOTSUKI ALUMNA AND A FORMER COUNCIL MEMBER.
HEY! WHAT DO YOU MEAN, "HARD TO BELIEVE"?!
SHIOMI SEMINAR

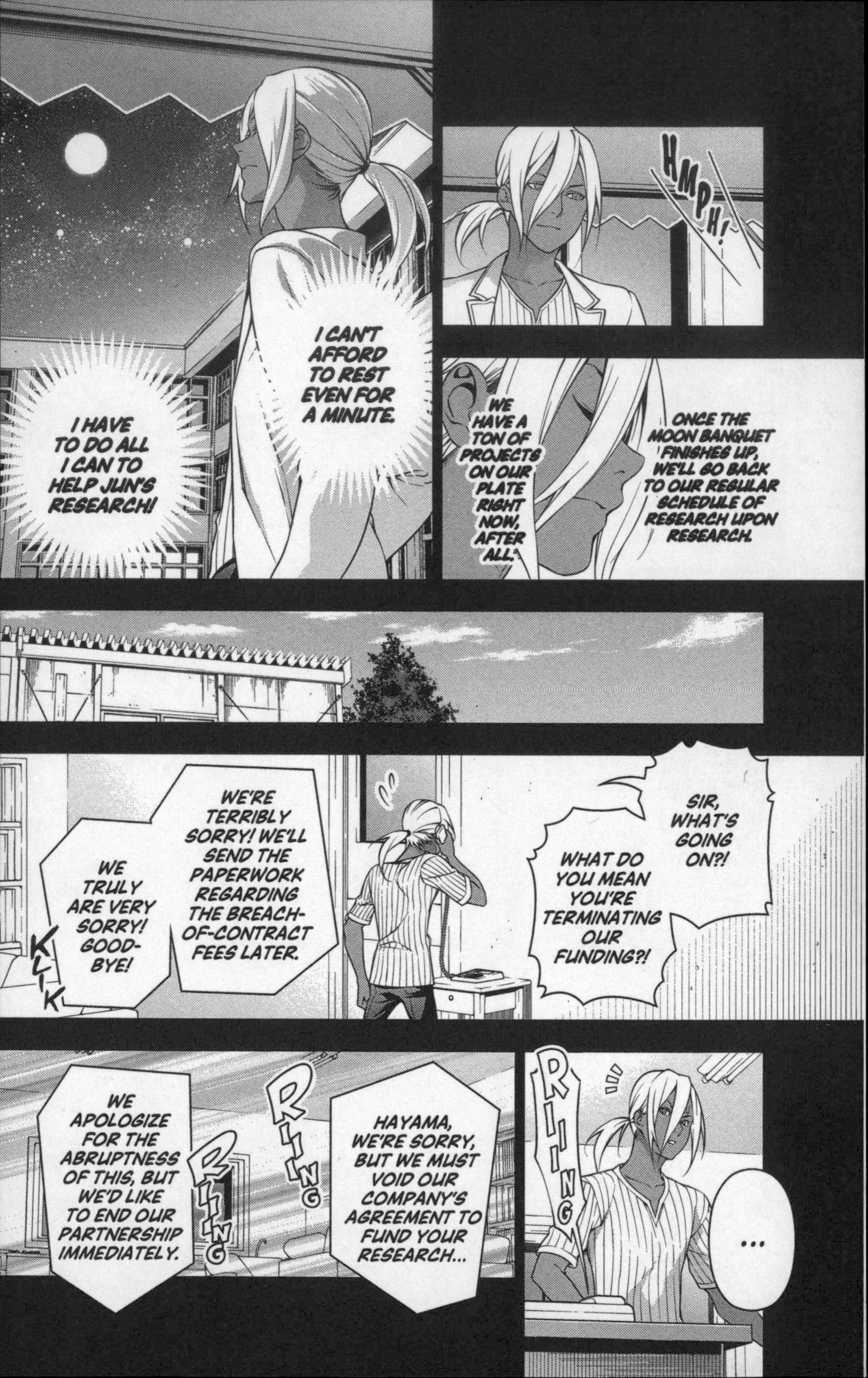
HMPH!
ONCE THE MOON BANQUET FINISHES UP, WE'LL GO BACK TO OUR REGULAR SCHEDULE OF RESEARCH UPON RESEARCH.
WE HAVE A TON OF PROJECTS ON OUR PLATE RIGHT NOW, AFTER ALL.
I CAN'T AFFORD TO REST EVEN FOR A MINUTE.
I HAVE TO DO ALL I CAN TO HELP JUN'S RESEARCH!
SIR, WHAT'S GOING ON?!
WHAT DO YOU MEAN YOU'RE TERMINATING OUR FUNDING?!
WE'RE TERRIBLY SORRY! WE'LL SEND THE PAPERWORK REGARDING THE BREACH-OF-CONTRACT FEES LATER.
WE TRULY ARE VERY SORRY! GOOD-BYE!
KLIK
RIIING
...
RIIING
HAYAMA, WE'RE SORRY, BUT WE MUST VOID OUR COMPANY'S AGREEMENT TO FUND YOUR RESEARCH...
RIIING
WE APOLOGIZE FOR THE ABRUPTNESS OF THIS, BUT WE'D LIKE TO END OUR PARTNERSHIP IMMEDIATELY.

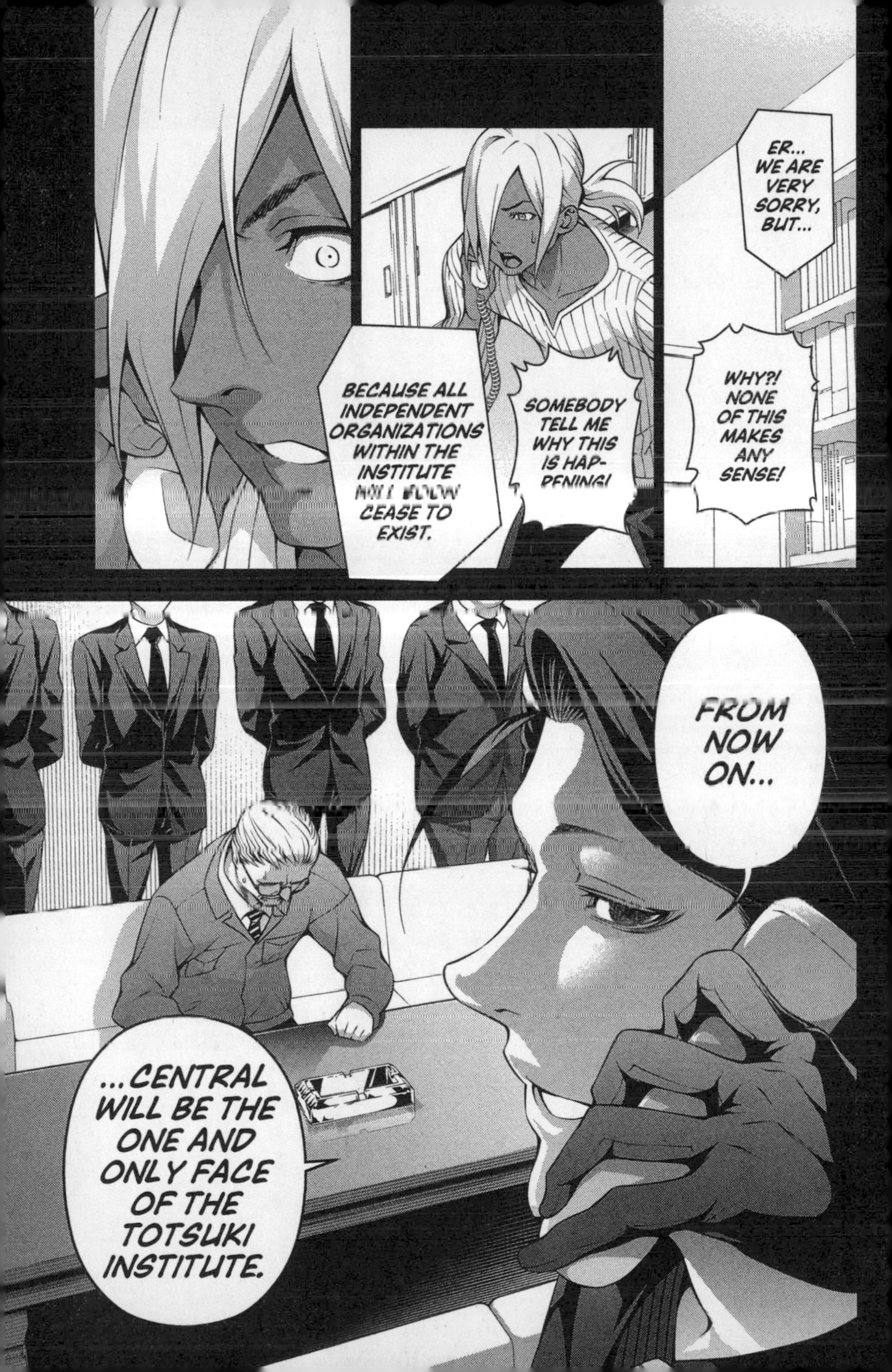
ER... WE ARE VERY SORRY, BUT...
WHY?! NONE OF THIS MAKES ANY SENSE!
SOMEBODY TELL ME WHY THIS IS HAP-PENING!
BECAUSE ALL INDEPENDENT ORGANIZATIONS WITHIN THE INSTITUTE
CEASE TO EXIST.
FROM NOW ON...
...CENTRAL WILL BE THE ONE AND ONLY FACE OF THE TOTSUKI INSTITUTE.

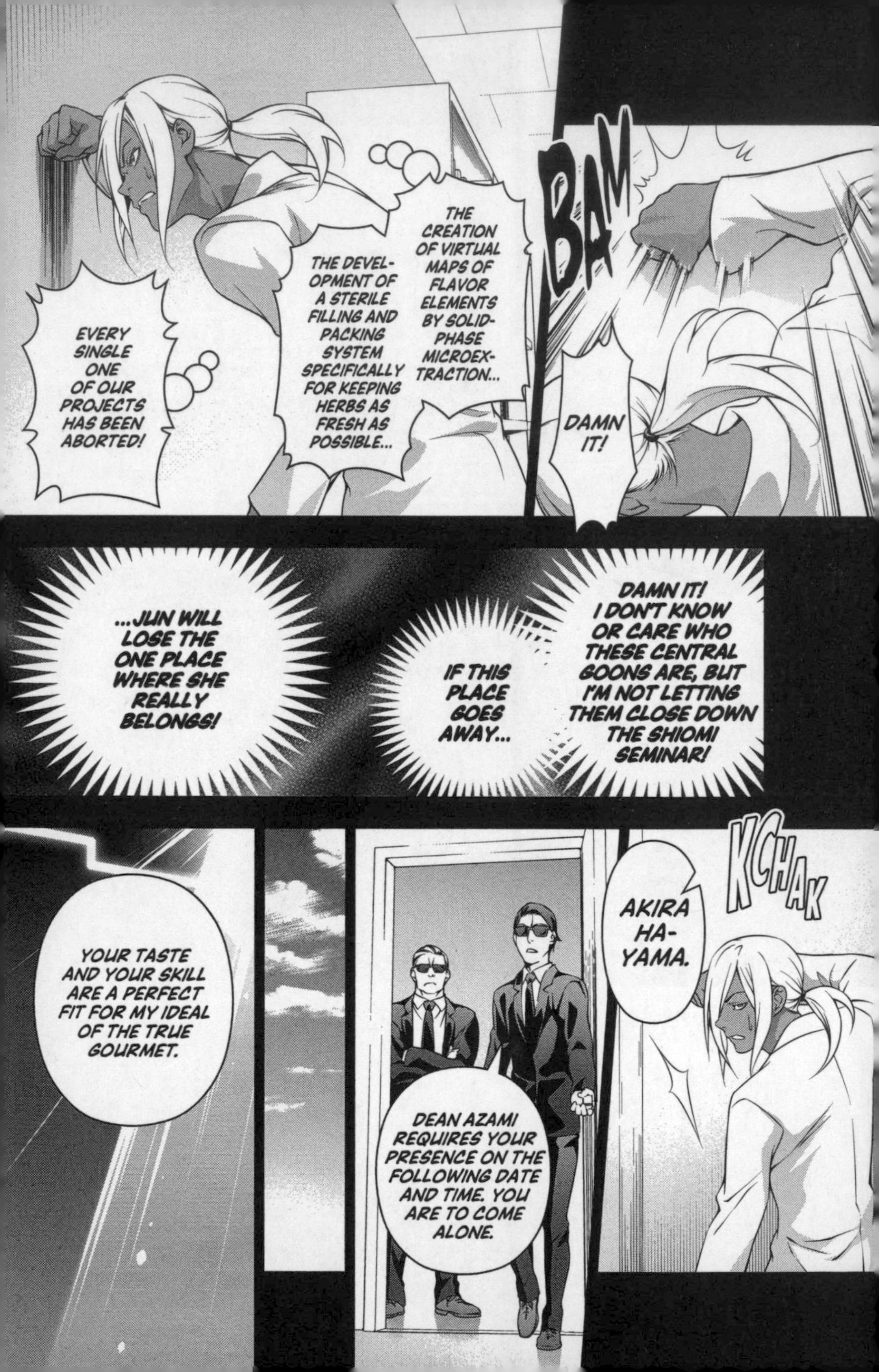
BAM
DAMN IT!
THE CREATION OF VIRTUAL MAPS OF FLAVOR ELEMENTS BY SOLID-PHASE MICROEX-TRACTION...
THE DEVEL-OPMENT OF A STERILE FILLING AND PACKING SYSTEM SPECIFICALLY FOR KEEPING HERBS AS FRESH AS POSSIBLE...
EVERY SINGLE ONE OF OUR PROJECTS HAS BEEN ABORTED!
DAMN IT! I DON'T KNOW OR CARE WHO THESE CENTRAL GOONS ARE, BUT I'M NOT LETTING THEM CLOSE DOWN THE SHIOMI SEMINAR!
IF THIS PLACE GOES AWAY...
...JUN WILL LOSE THE ONE PLACE WHERE SHE REALLY BELONGS!
KCHAK
AKIRA HA-YAMA.
DEAN AZAMI REQUIRES YOUR PRESENCE ON THE FOLLOWING DATE AND TIME. YOU ARE TO COME ALONE.
YOUR TASTE AND YOUR SKILL ARE A PERFECT FIT FOR MY IDEAL OF THE TRUE GOURMET.

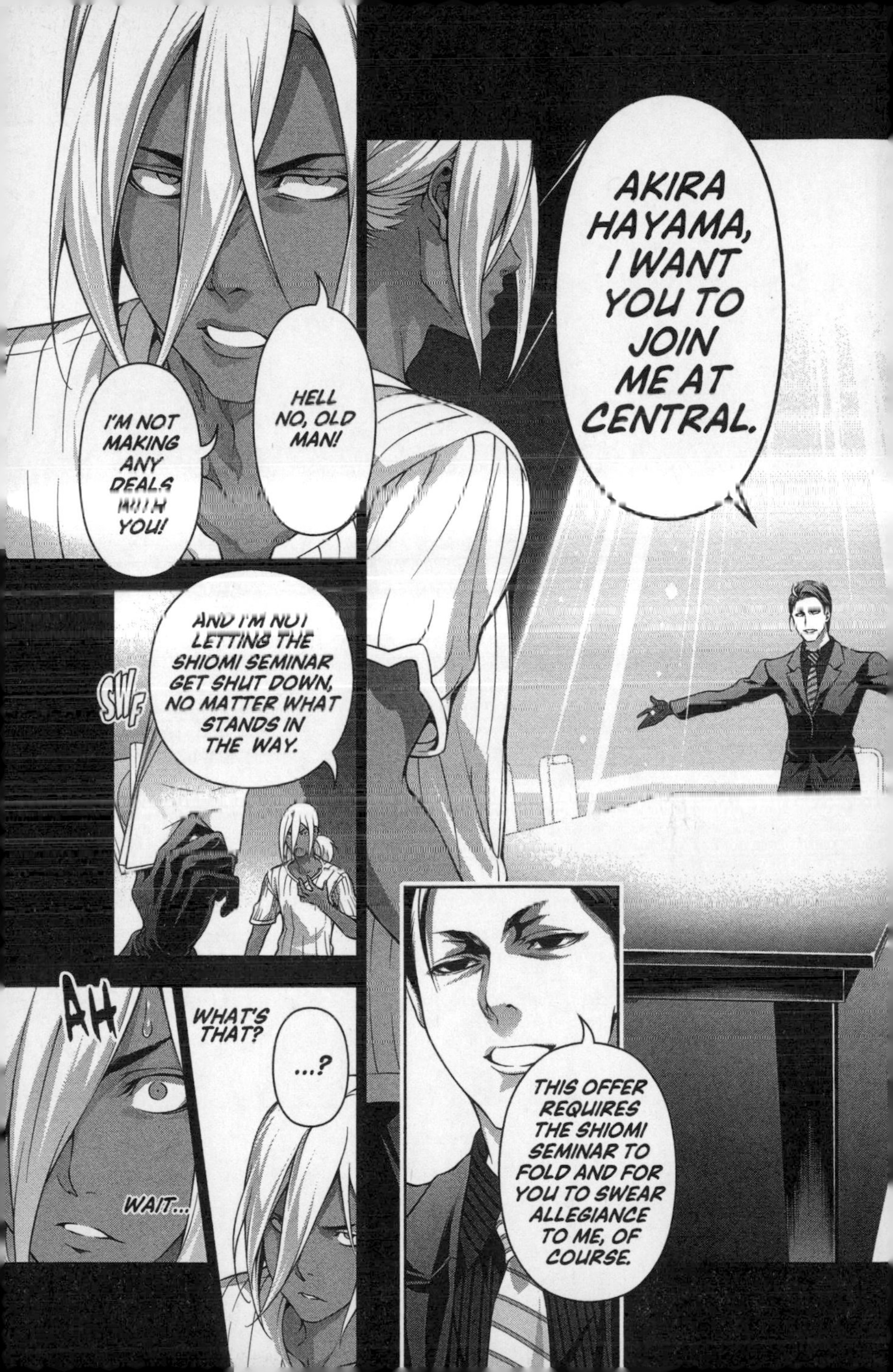
AKIRA HAYAMA, I WANT YOU TO JOIN ME AT CENTRAL.
HELL NO, OLD MAN!
I'M NOT MAKING ANY DEALS WITH YOU!
AND I'M NOT LETTING THE SHIOMI SEMINAR GET SHUT DOWN, NO MATTER WHAT STANDS IN THE WAY.
SWF
THIS OFFER REQUIRES THE SHIOMI SEMINAR TO FOLD AND FOR YOU TO SWEAR ALLEGIANCE TO ME, OF COURSE.
...?
AH
WHAT'S THAT?
WAIT...

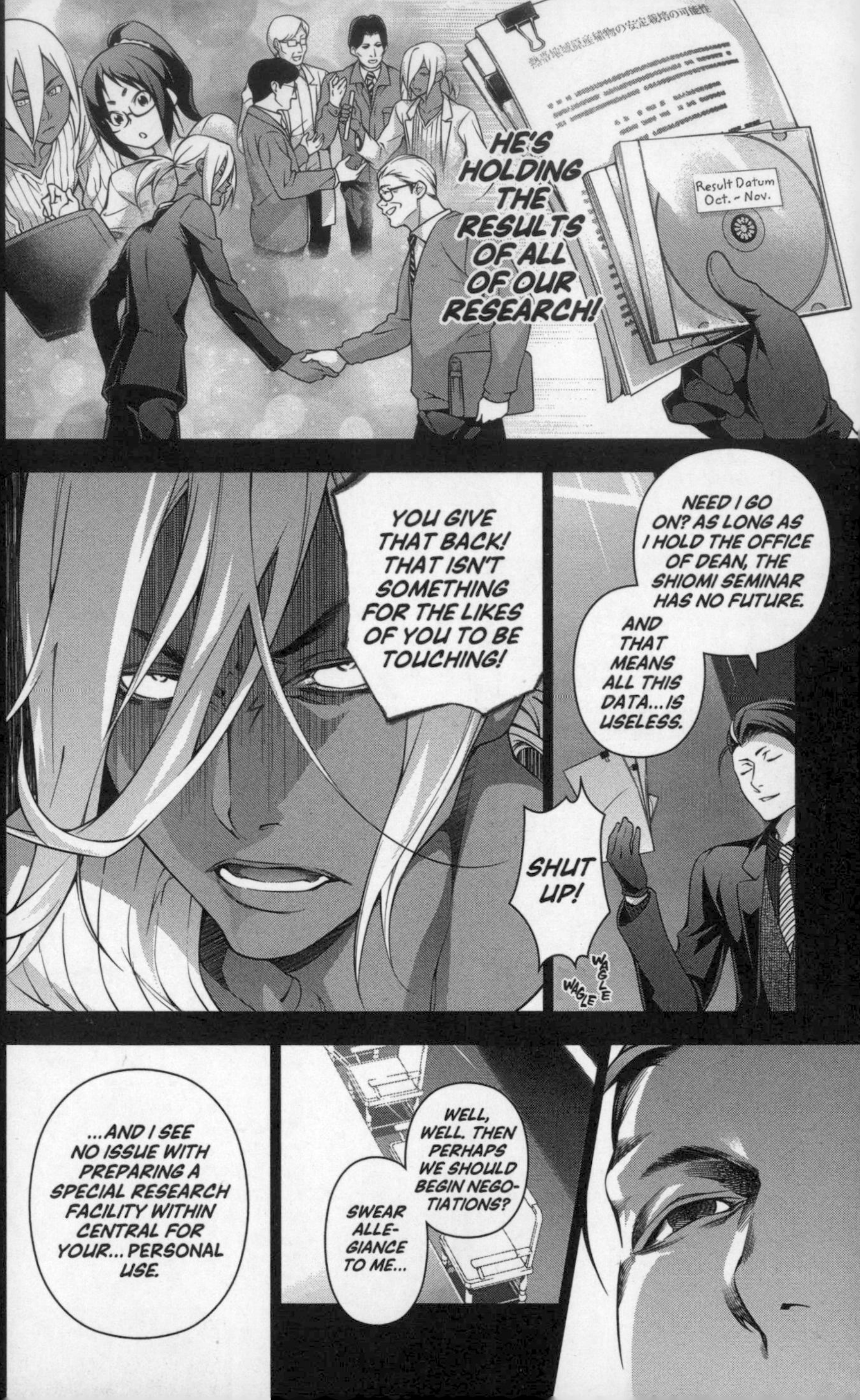
HE'S HOLDING THE RESULTS OF ALL OF OUR RESEARCH!
Result Datum Oct. ~ Nov.
NEED I GO ON? AS LONG AS I HOLD THE OFFICE OF DEAN, THE SHIOMI SEMINAR HAS NO FUTURE.
AND THAT MEANS ALL THIS DATA... IS USELESS.
SHUT UP!
WAGLE WAGLE
YOU GIVE THAT BACK! THAT ISN'T SOMETHING FOR THE LIKES OF YOU TO BE TOUCHING!
WELL, WELL. THEN PERHAPS WE SHOULD BEGIN NEGO-TIATIONS?
SWEAR ALLE-GIANCE TO ME...
...AND I SEE NO ISSUE WITH PREPARING A SPECIAL RESEARCH FACILITY WITHIN CENTRAL FOR YOUR... PERSONAL USE.

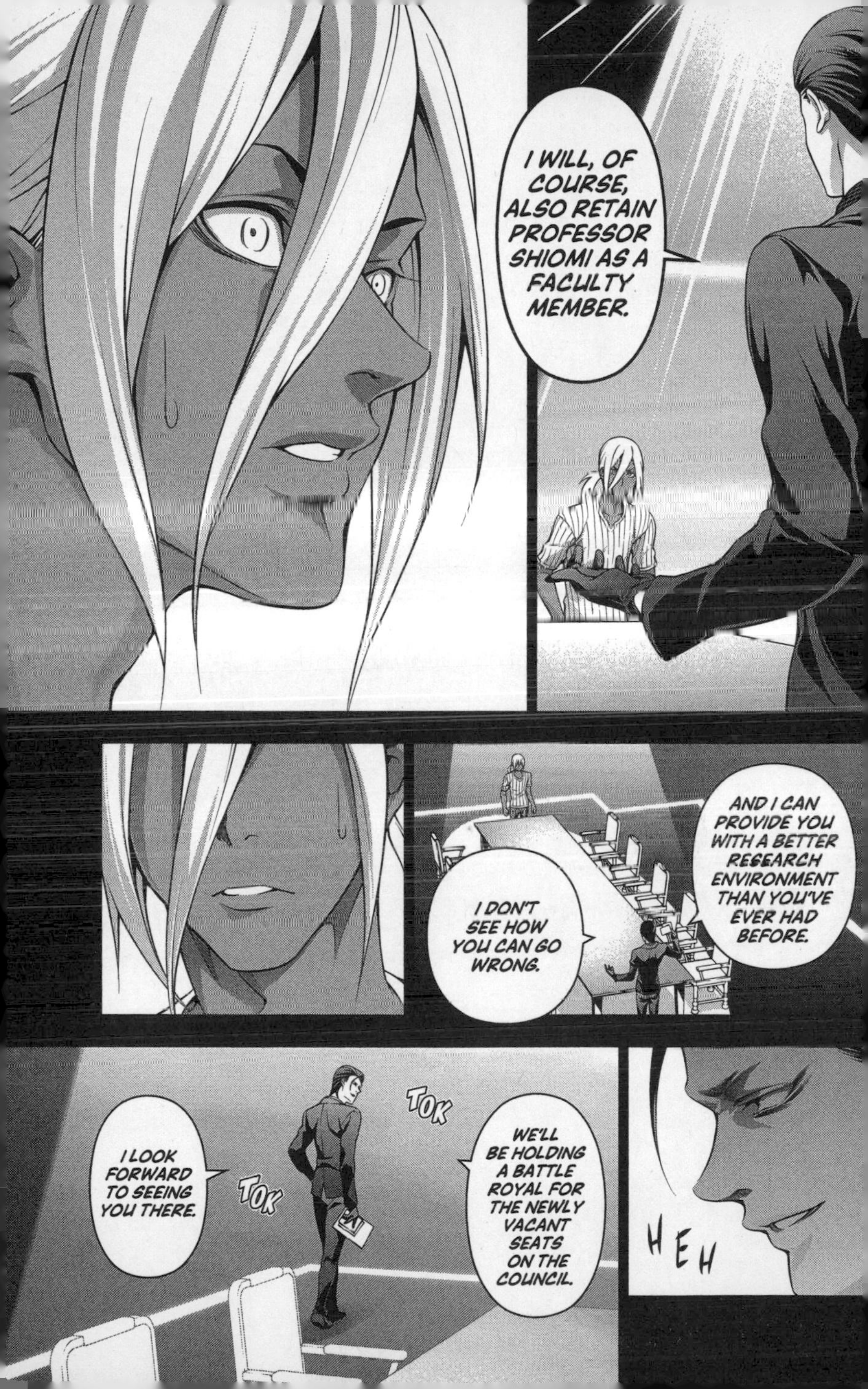
I WILL, OF COURSE, ALSO RETAIN PROFESSOR SHIOMI AS A FACULTY MEMBER.
AND I CAN PROVIDE YOU WITH A BETTER RESEARCH ENVIRONMENT THAN YOU'VE EVER HAD BEFORE.
I DON'T SEE HOW YOU CAN GO WRONG.
HEH
TOK
WE'LL BE HOLDING A BATTLE ROYAL FOR THE NEWLY VACANT SEATS ON THE COUNCIL.
TOK
I LOOK FORWARD TO SEEING YOU THERE.

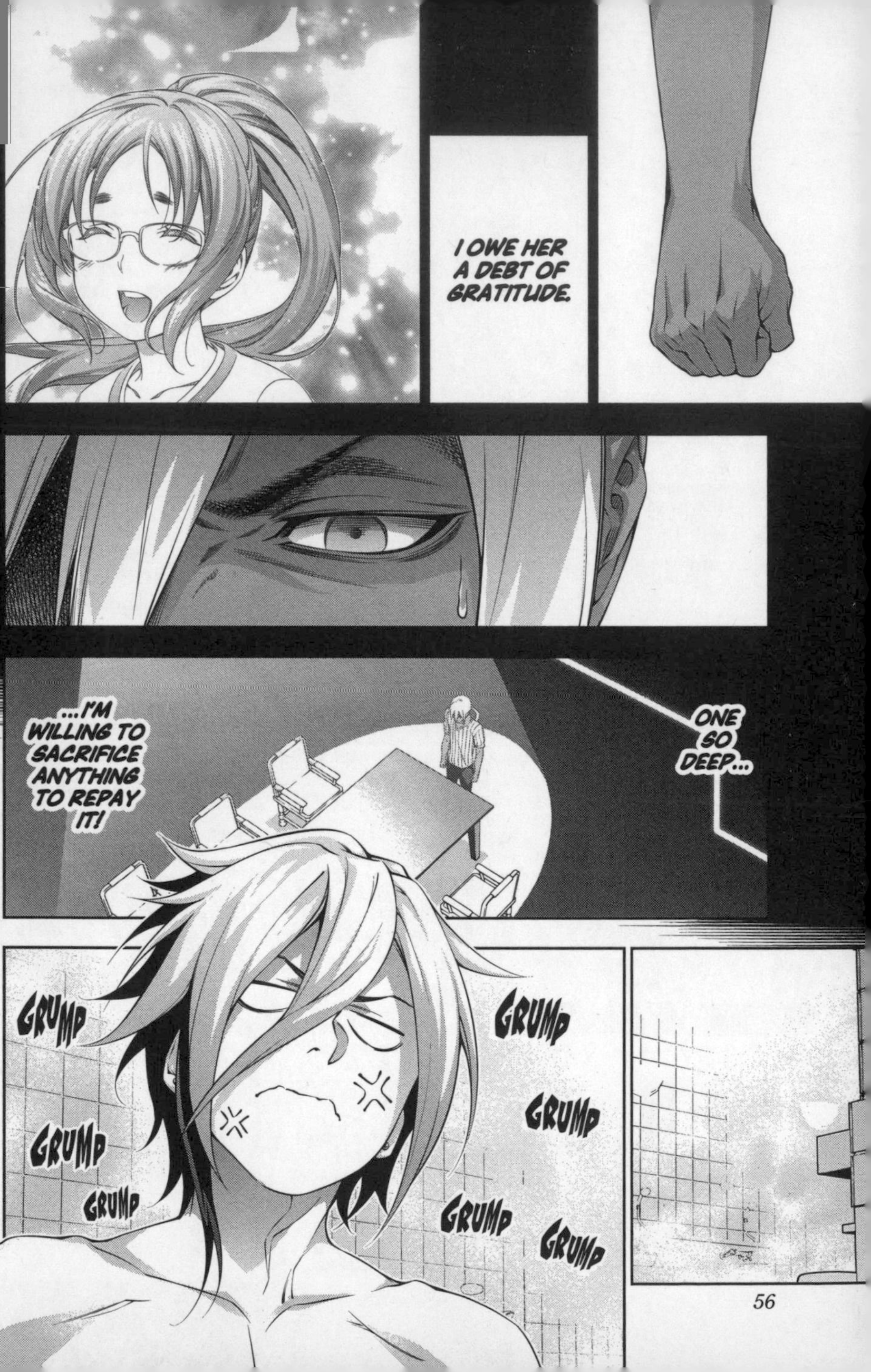
I OWE HER A DEBT OF GRATITUDE.
ONE SO DEEP...
...I'M WILLING TO SACRIFICE ANYTHING TO REPAY IT!
GRUMP
GRUMP
GRUMP
GRUMP
GRUMP
GRUMP
GRUMP

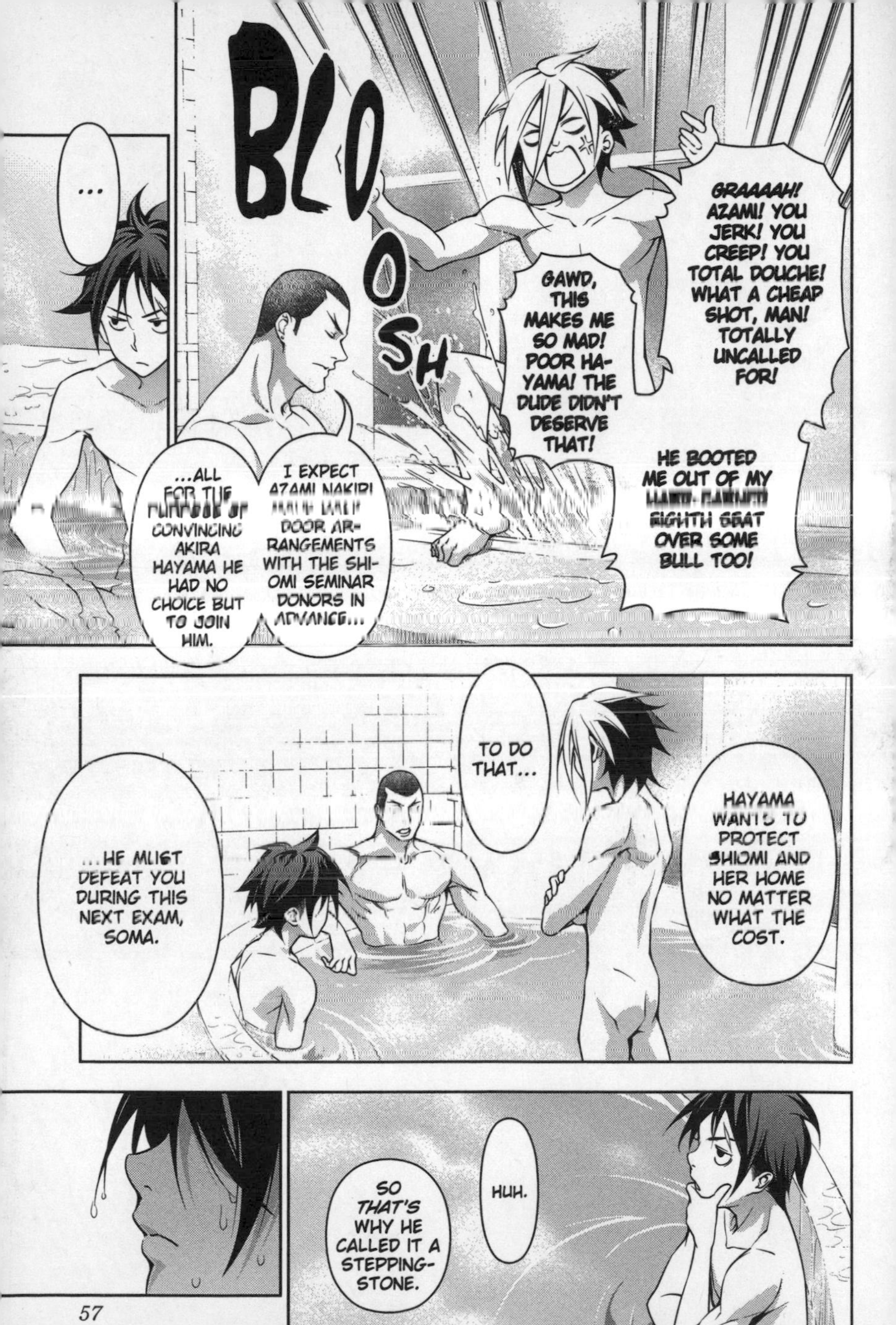
GRAAAAH! AZAMI! YOU JERK! YOU CREEP! YOU TOTAL DOUCHE! WHAT A CHEAP SHOT, MAN! TOTALLY UNCALLED FOR!
GAWD, THIS MAKES ME SO MAD! POOR HAYAMA! THE DUDE DIDN'T DESERVE THAT!
HE BOOTED ME OUT OF MY HARD-EARNED EIGHTH SEAT OVER SOME BULL TOO!
BLOOSH
I EXPECT AZAMI NAKIRI MADE BACK-DOOR ARRANGEMENTS WITH THE SHIOMI SEMINAR DONORS IN ADVANCE...
...ALL FOR THE PURPOSE OF CONVINCING AKIRA HAYAMA HE HAD NO CHOICE BUT TO JOIN HIM.
...
HAYAMA WANTS TO PROTECT SHIOMI AND HER HOME NO MATTER WHAT THE COST.
TO DO THAT...
...HE MUST DEFEAT YOU DURING THIS NEXT EXAM, SOMA.
HUH.
SO THAT'S WHY HE CALLED IT A STEPPING-STONE.

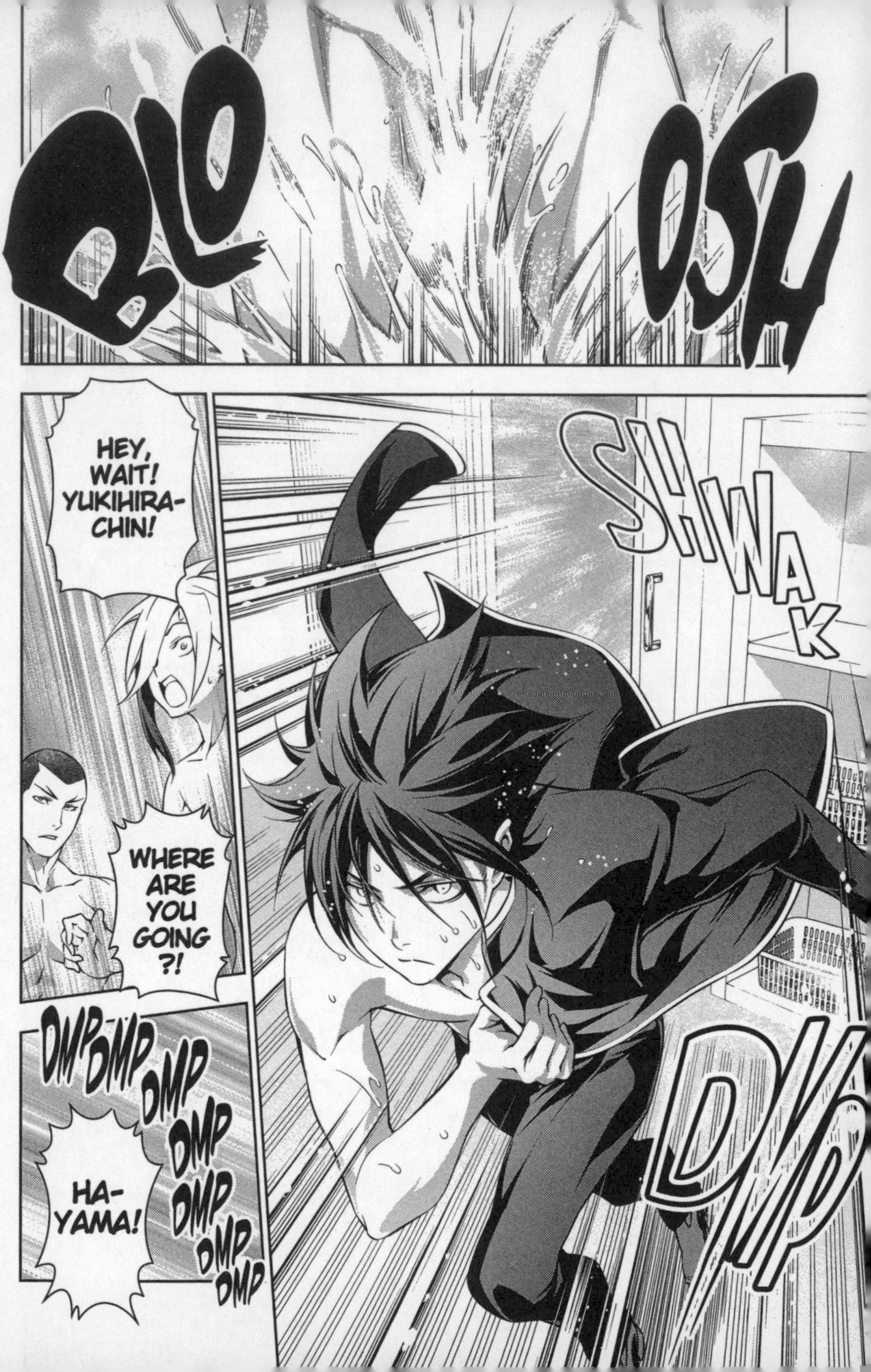
BLOOSH
SHWAK
HEY, WAIT! YUKIHIRA-CHIN!
WHERE ARE YOU GOING?!
DMP DMP DMP DMP DMP DMP DMP DMP
HA-YAMA!

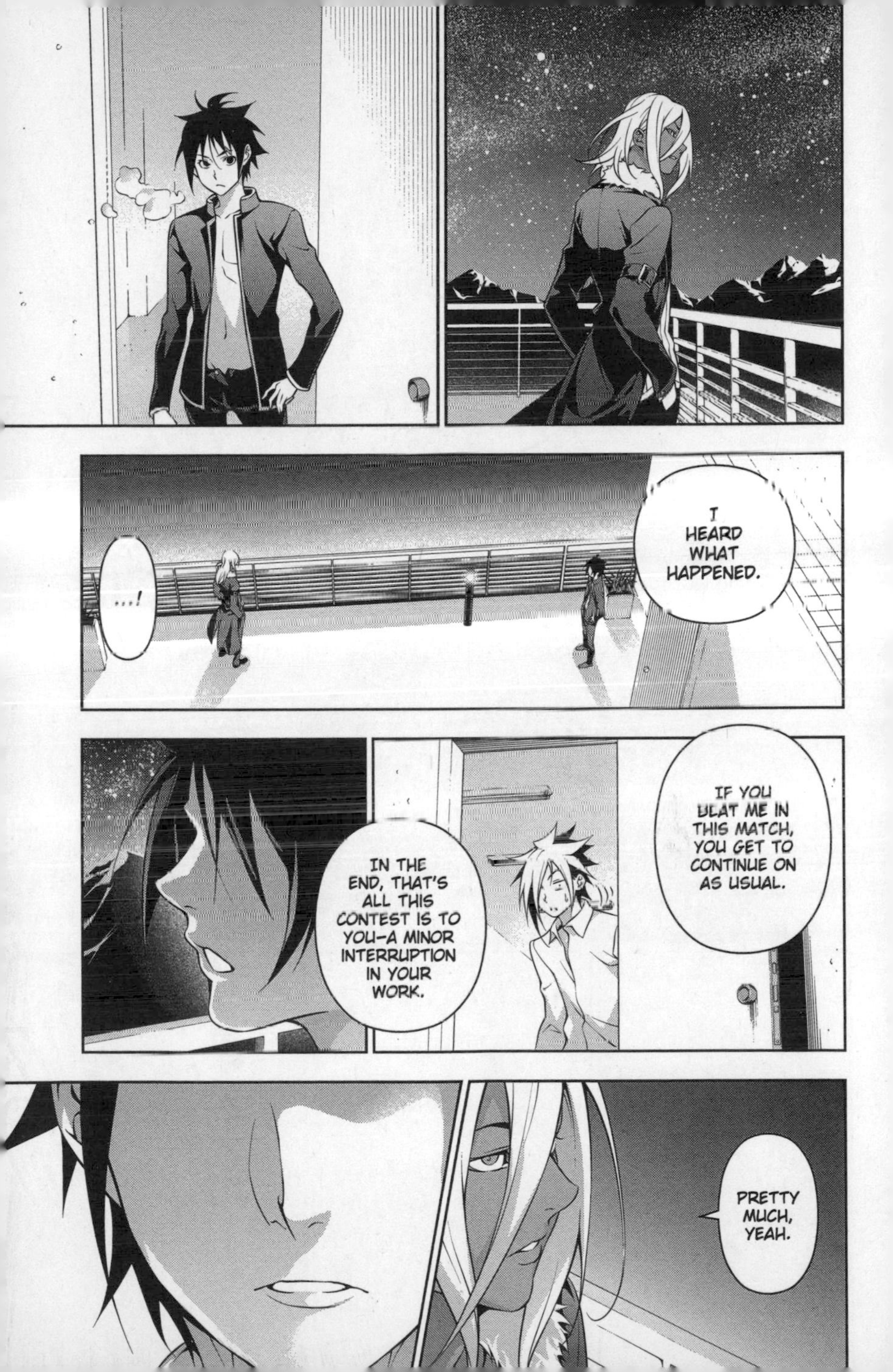
I HEARD WHAT HAPPENED.
...!
IF YOU BEAT ME IN THIS MATCH, YOU GET TO CONTINUE ON AS USUAL.
IN THE END, THAT'S ALL THIS CONTEST IS TO YOU—A MINOR INTERRUPTION IN YOUR WORK.
PRETTY MUCH, YEAH.

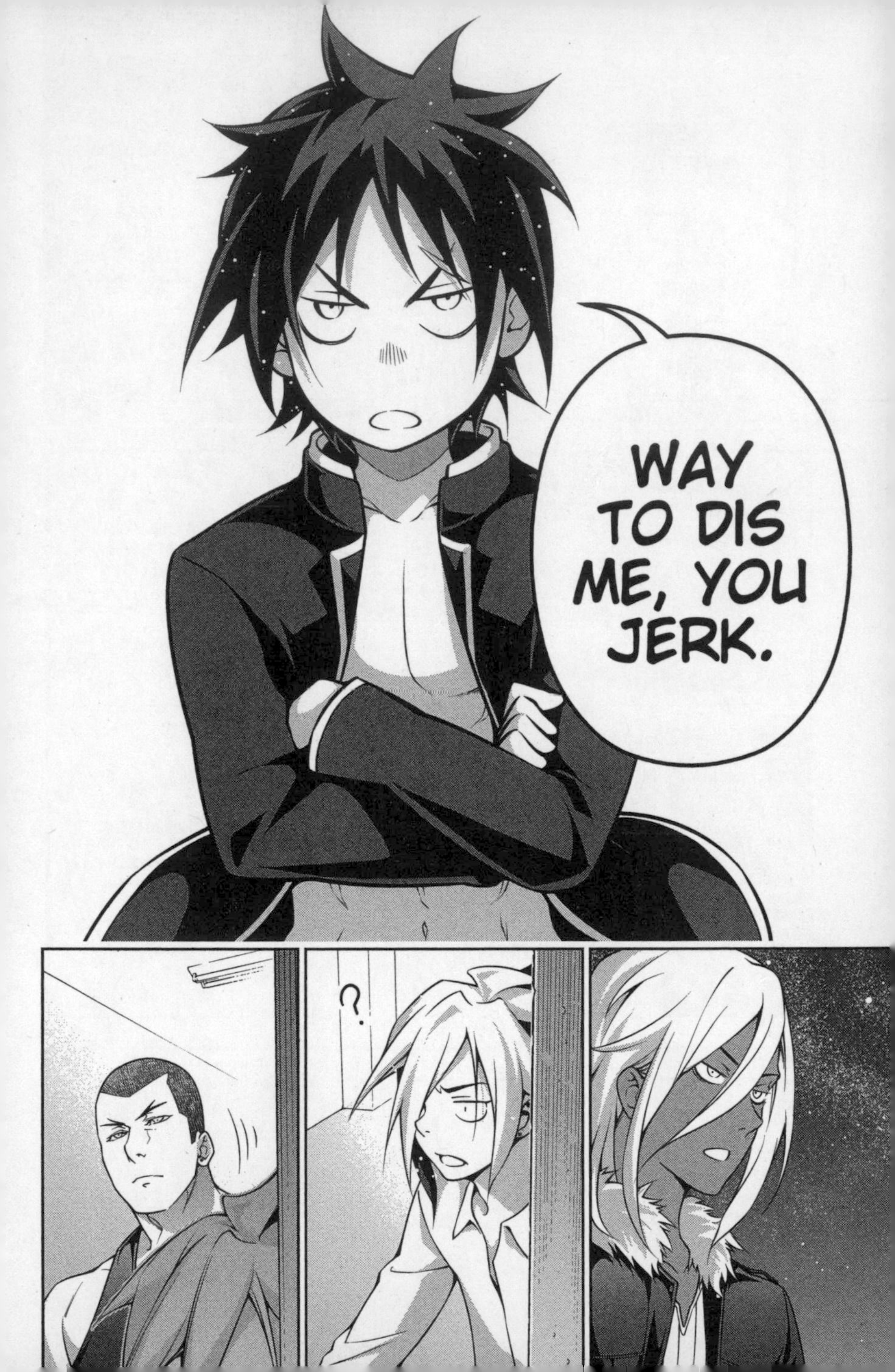
WAY TO DIS ME, YOU JERK.
?

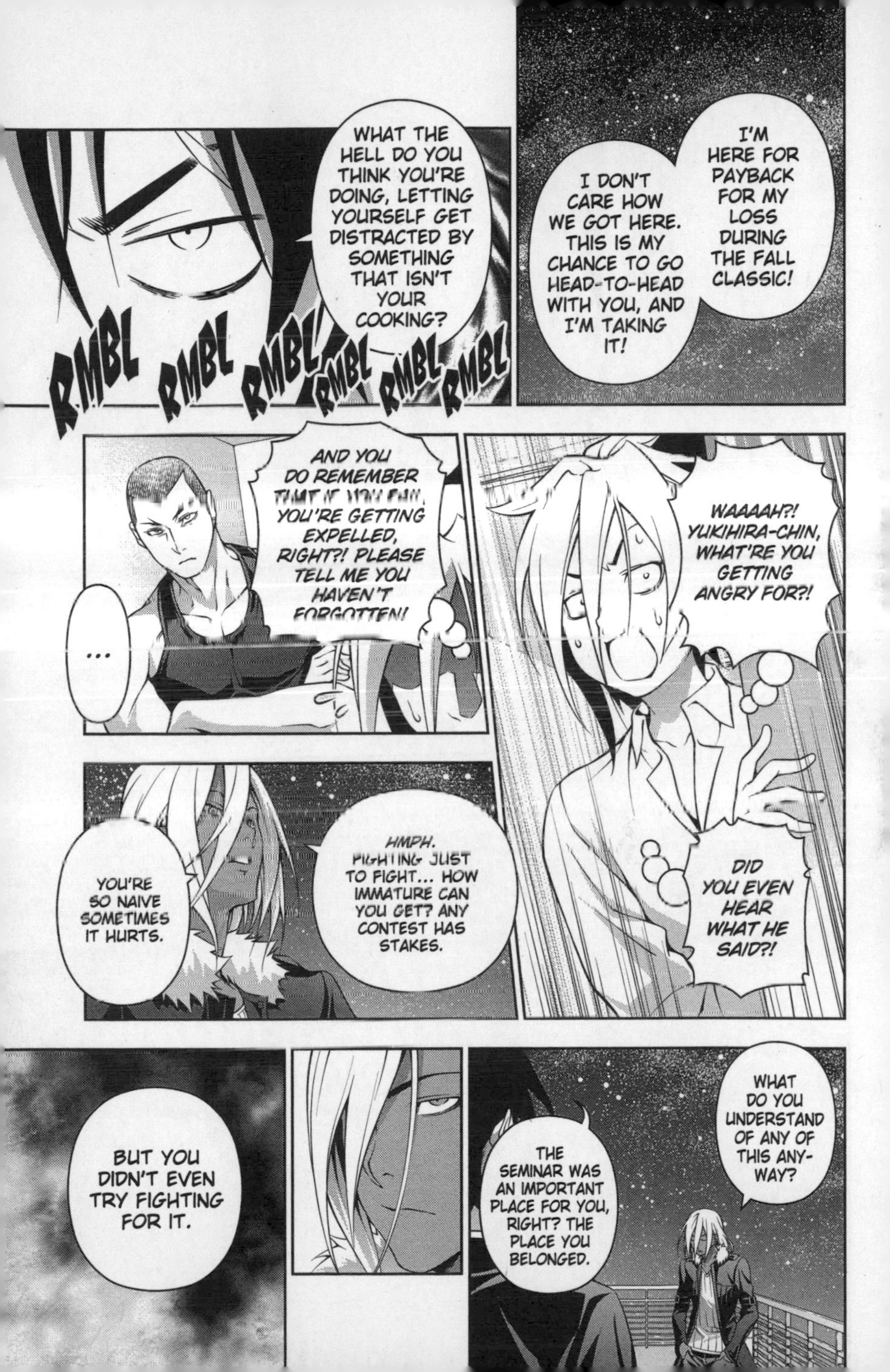
I'M HERE FOR PAYBACK FOR MY LOSS DURING THE FALL CLASSIC!
I DON'T CARE HOW WE GOT HERE. THIS IS MY CHANCE TO GO HEAD-TO-HEAD WITH YOU, AND I'M TAKING IT!
WHAT THE HELL DO YOU THINK YOU'RE DOING, LETTING YOURSELF GET DISTRACTED BY SOMETHING THAT ISN'T YOUR COOKING?
RMBL RMBL RMBL RMBL RMBL RMBL
WAAAAH?! YUKIHIRA-CHIN, WHAT'RE YOU GETTING ANGRY FOR?!
DID YOU EVEN HEAR WHAT HE SAID?!
AND YOU DO REMEMBER THAT IF YOU FAIL, YOU'RE GETTING EXPELLED, RIGHT?! PLEASE TELL ME YOU HAVEN'T FORGOTTEN!
...
HMPH. FIGHTING JUST TO FIGHT... HOW IMMATURE CAN YOU GET? ANY CONTEST HAS STAKES.
YOU'RE SO NAIVE SOMETIMES IT HURTS.
WHAT DO YOU UNDERSTAND OF ANY OF THIS ANY-WAY?
THE SEMINAR WAS AN IMPORTANT PLACE FOR YOU, RIGHT? THE PLACE YOU BELONGED.
BUT YOU DIDN'T EVEN TRY FIGHTING FOR IT.

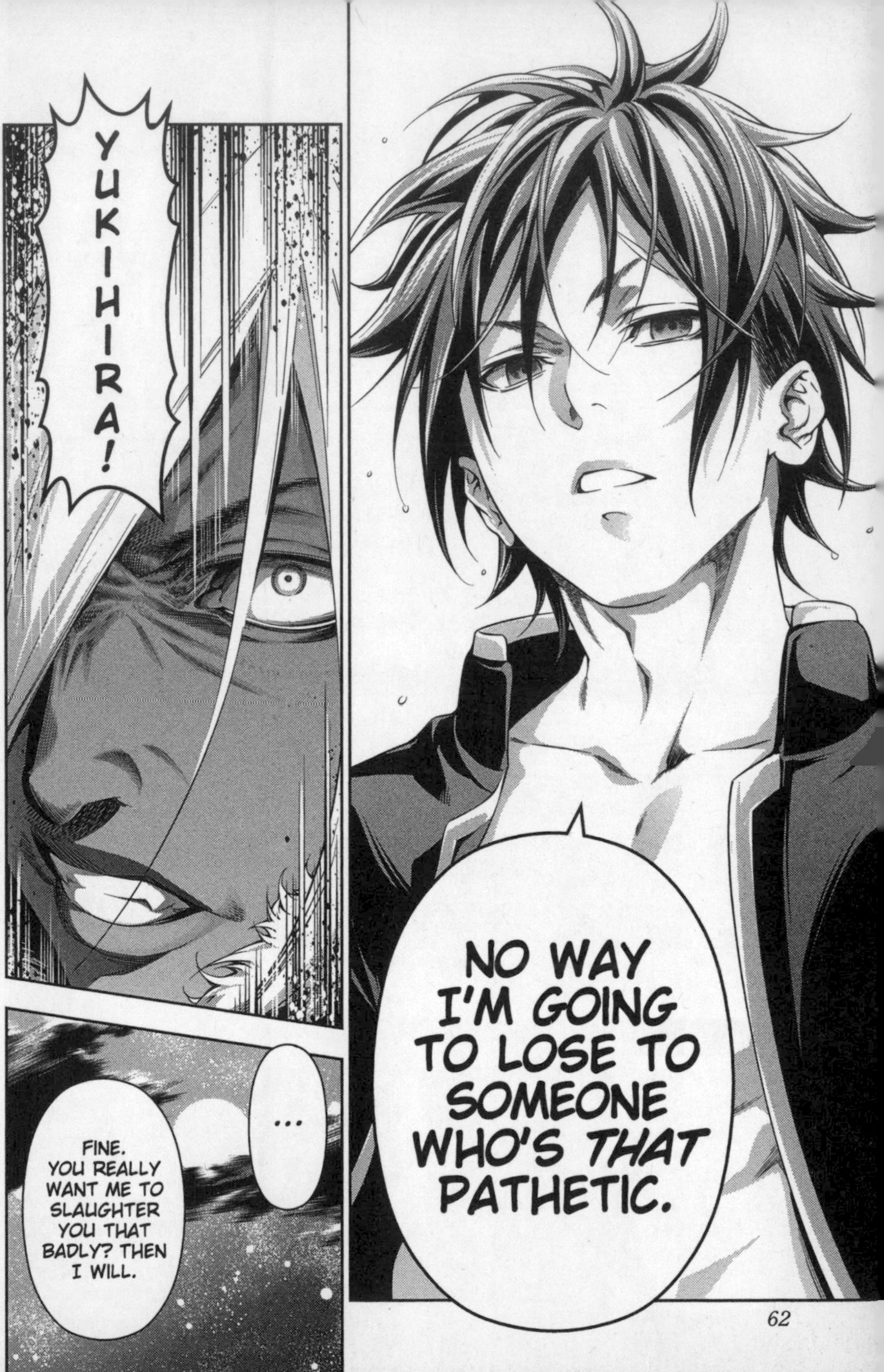
NO WAY I'M GOING TO LOSE TO SOMEONE WHO'S *THAT* PATHETIC.
YUKIHIRA!
...
FINE. YOU REALLY WANT ME TO SLAUGHTER YOU THAT BADLY? THEN I WILL.

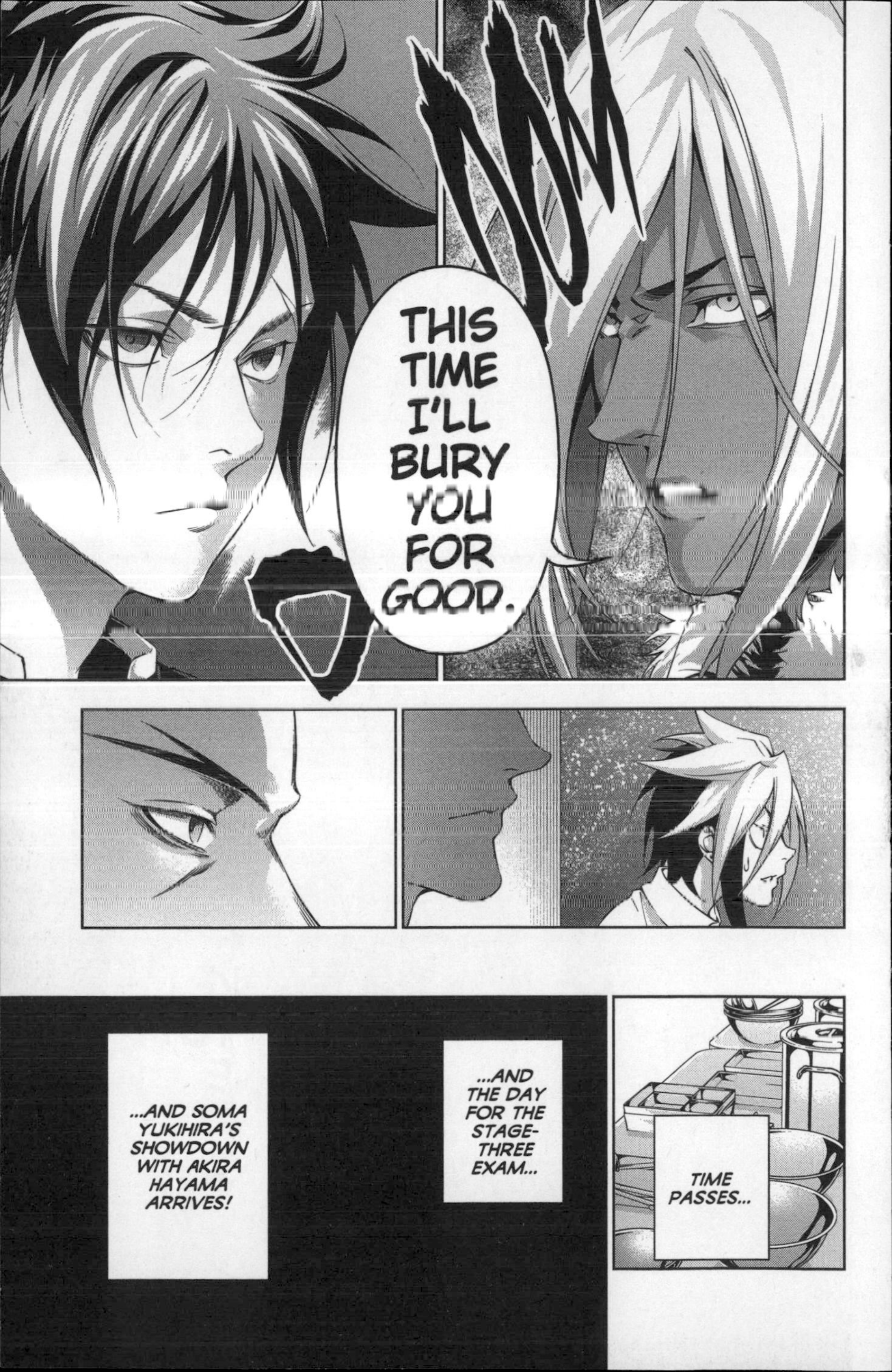
THIS TIME I'LL BURY YOU FOR GOOD.
TIME PASSES...
...AND THE DAY FOR THE STAGE-THREE EXAM...
...AND SOMA YUKIHIRA'S SHOWDOWN WITH AKIRA HAYAMA ARRIVES!

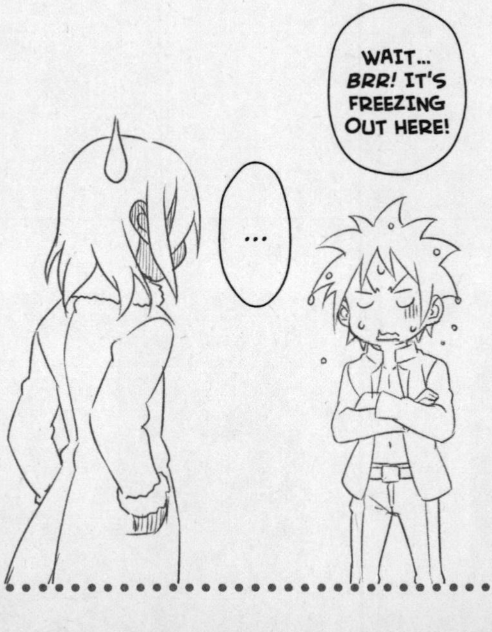
WAIT... *BRR!* IT'S FREEZING OUT HERE!
...

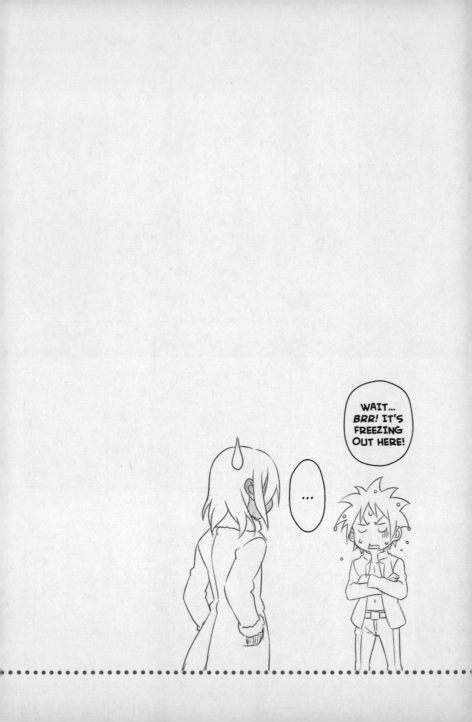

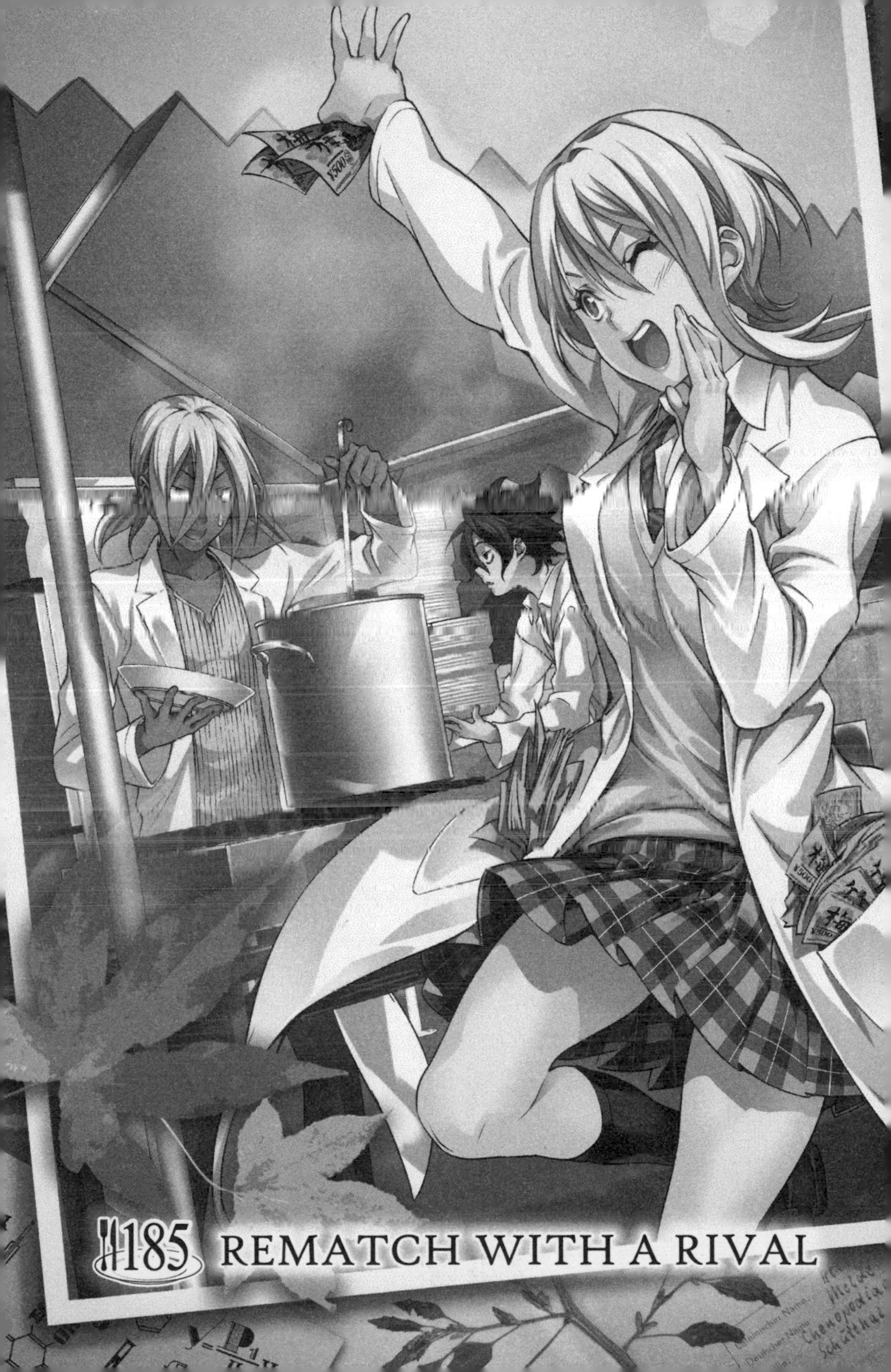

#185 REMATCH WITH A RIVAL

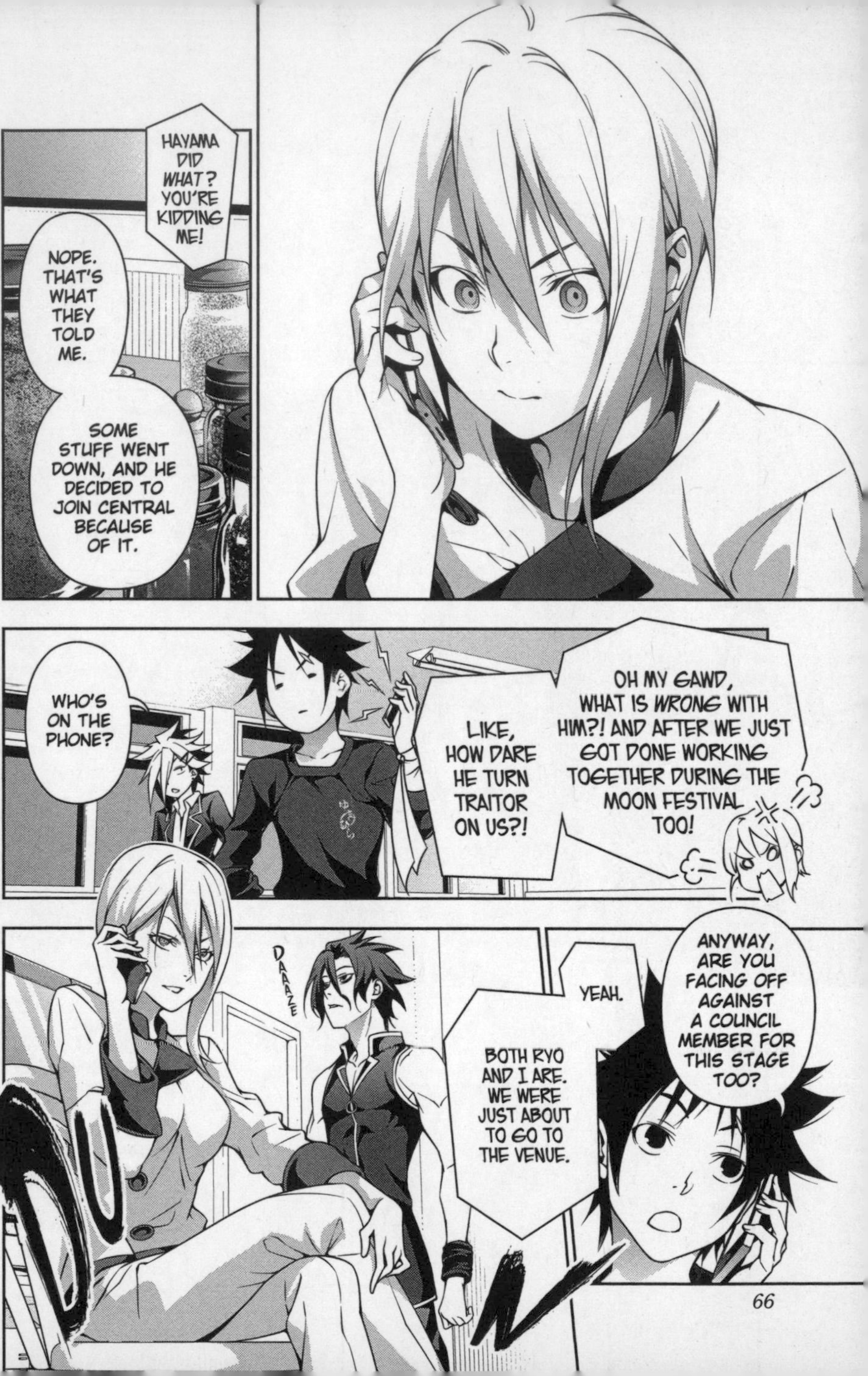
HAYAMA DID WHAT? YOU'RE KIDDING ME!
NOPE. THAT'S WHAT THEY TOLD ME.
SOME STUFF WENT DOWN, AND HE DECIDED TO JOIN CENTRAL BECAUSE OF IT.
OH MY GAWD, WHAT IS *WRONG* WITH HIM?! AND AFTER WE JUST GOT DONE WORKING TOGETHER DURING THE MOON FESTIVAL TOO!
LIKE, HOW DARE HE TURN TRAITOR ON US?!
WHO'S ON THE PHONE?
ANYWAY, ARE YOU FACING OFF AGAINST A COUNCIL MEMBER FOR THIS STAGE TOO?
YEAH.
BOTH RYO AND I ARE. WE WERE JUST ABOUT TO GO TO THE VENUE.
DAAAZE

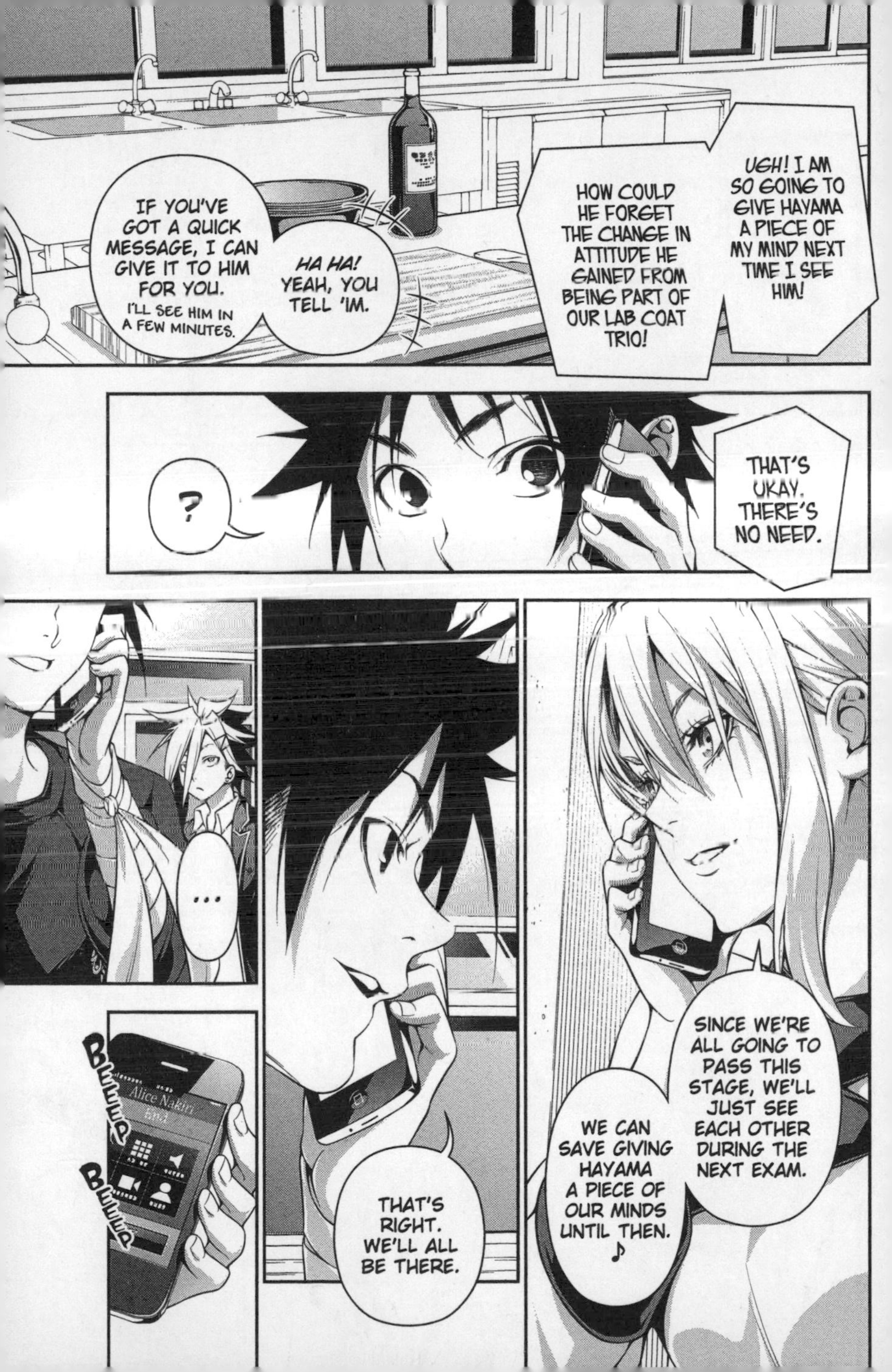
UGH! I AM SO GOING TO GIVE HAYAMA A PIECE OF MY MIND NEXT TIME I SEE HIM!
HOW COULD HE FORGET THE CHANGE IN ATTITUDE HE GAINED FROM BEING PART OF OUR LAB COAT TRIO!
HA HA! YEAH, YOU TELL 'IM.
IF YOU'VE GOT A QUICK MESSAGE, I CAN GIVE IT TO HIM FOR YOU.
I'LL SEE HIM IN A FEW MINUTES.
THAT'S OKAY. THERE'S NO NEED.
?
SINCE WE'RE ALL GOING TO PASS THIS STAGE, WE'LL JUST SEE EACH OTHER DURING THE NEXT EXAM.
WE CAN SAVE GIVING HAYAMA A PIECE OF OUR MINDS UNTIL THEN. ♪
THAT'S RIGHT. WE'LL ALL BE THERE.
...
Alice Nakiri
End
BEEEP
BEEEP

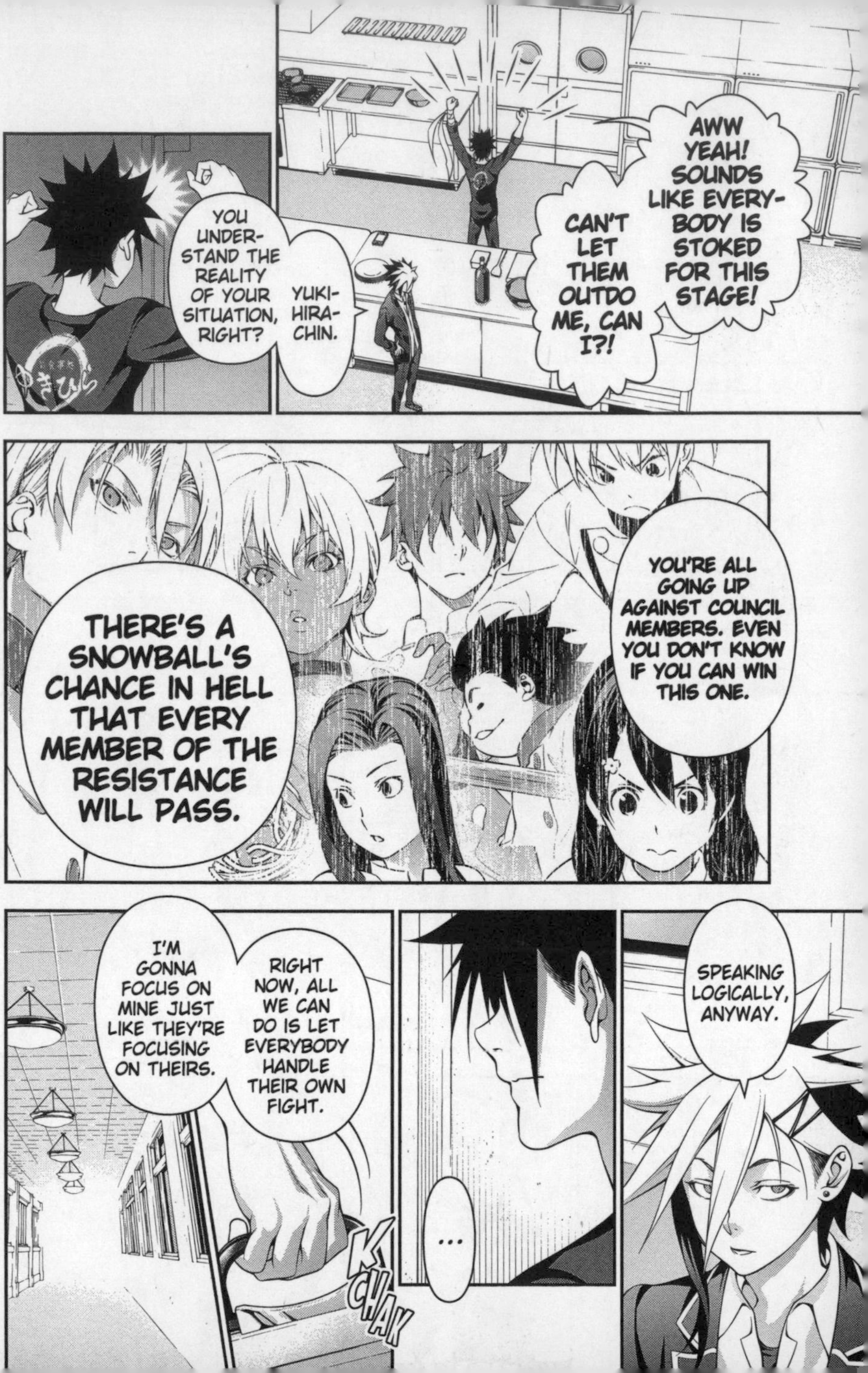
AWW YEAH! SOUNDS LIKE EVERY-BODY IS STOKED FOR THIS STAGE!
CAN'T LET THEM OUTDO ME, CAN I?!
YUKI-HIRA-CHIN.
YOU UNDER-STAND THE REALITY OF YOUR SITUATION, RIGHT?
YOU'RE ALL GOING UP AGAINST COUNCIL MEMBERS. EVEN YOU DON'T KNOW IF YOU CAN WIN THIS ONE.
THERE'S A SNOWBALL'S CHANCE IN HELL THAT EVERY MEMBER OF THE RESISTANCE WILL PASS.
SPEAKING LOGICALLY, ANYWAY.
...
RIGHT NOW, ALL WE CAN DO IS LET EVERYBODY HANDLE THEIR OWN FIGHT.
I'M GONNA FOCUS ON MINE JUST LIKE THEY'RE FOCUSING ON THEIRS.
KCHAK

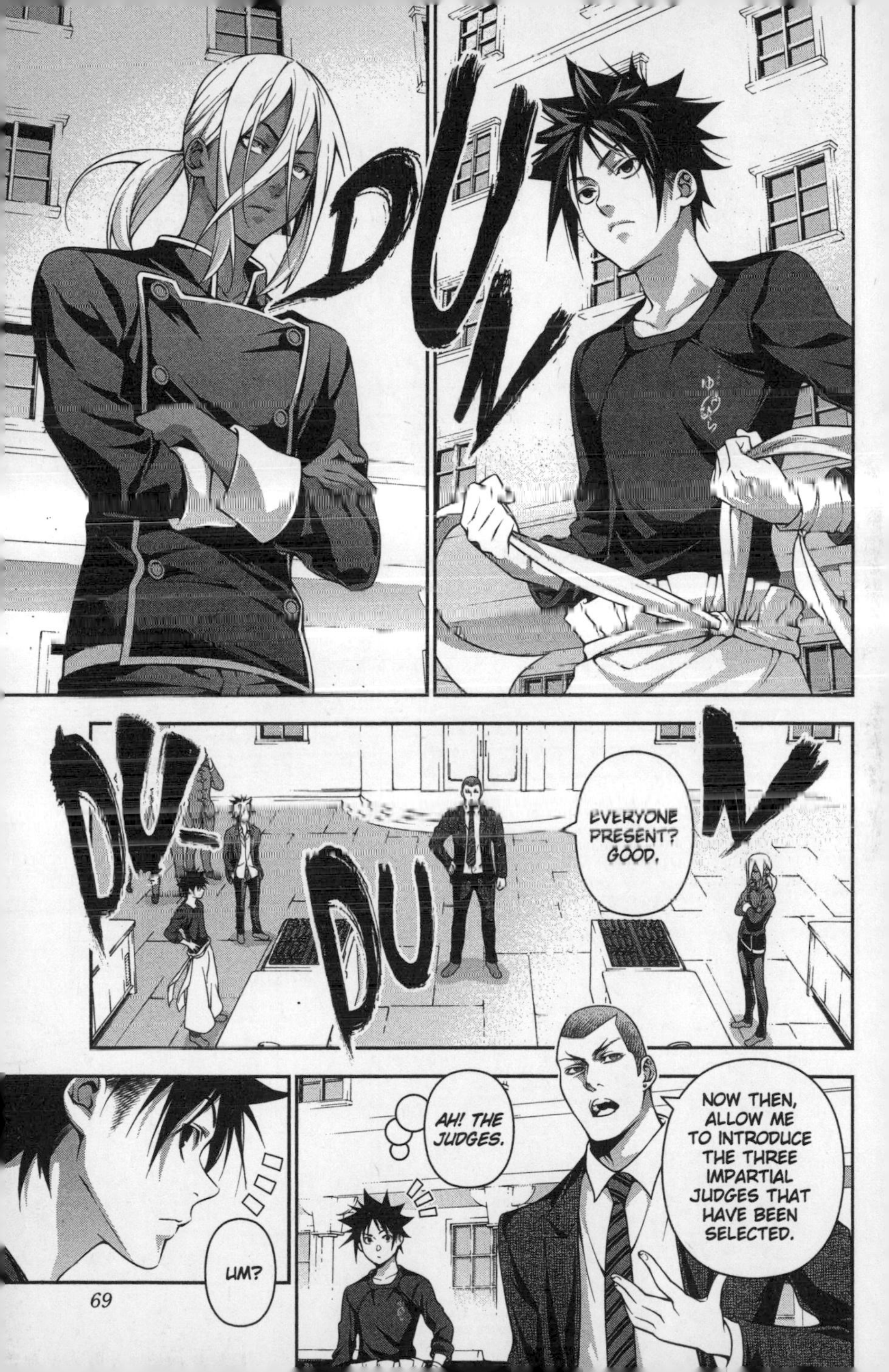
DUN
DU- DUN
EVERYONE PRESENT? GOOD.
NOW THEN, ALLOW ME TO INTRODUCE THE THREE IMPARTIAL JUDGES THAT HAVE BEEN SELECTED.
AH! THE JUDGES.
UM?

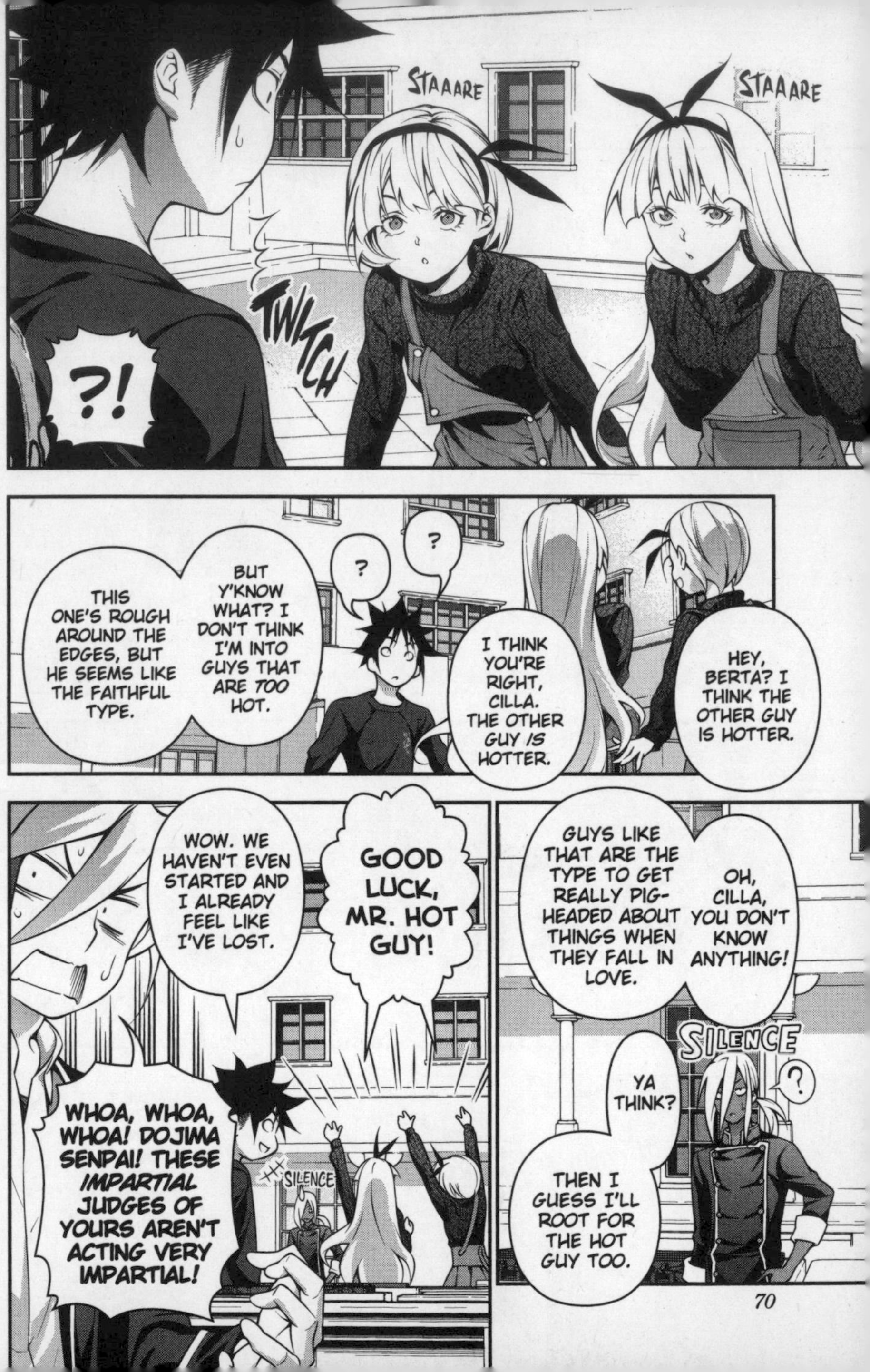
STAAARE
STAAARE
TWITCH
?!
HEY, BERTA? I THINK THE OTHER GUY IS HOTTER.
I THINK YOU'RE RIGHT, CILLA. THE OTHER GUY *IS* HOTTER.
?
?
BUT Y'KNOW WHAT? I DON'T THINK I'M INTO GUYS THAT ARE *TOO* HOT.
THIS ONE'S ROUGH AROUND THE EDGES, BUT HE SEEMS LIKE THE FAITHFUL TYPE.
OH, CILLA, YOU DON'T KNOW ANYTHING!
GUYS LIKE THAT ARE THE TYPE TO GET REALLY PIG-HEADED ABOUT THINGS WHEN THEY FALL IN LOVE.
SILENCE
?
YA THINK?
THEN I GUESS I'LL ROOT FOR THE HOT GUY TOO.
GOOD LUCK, MR. HOT GUY!
WOW. WE HAVEN'T EVEN STARTED AND I ALREADY FEEL LIKE I'VE LOST.
SILENCE
WHOA, WHOA, WHOA! DOJIMA SENPAI! THESE *IMPARTIAL* JUDGES OF YOURS AREN'T ACTING VERY IMPARTIAL!

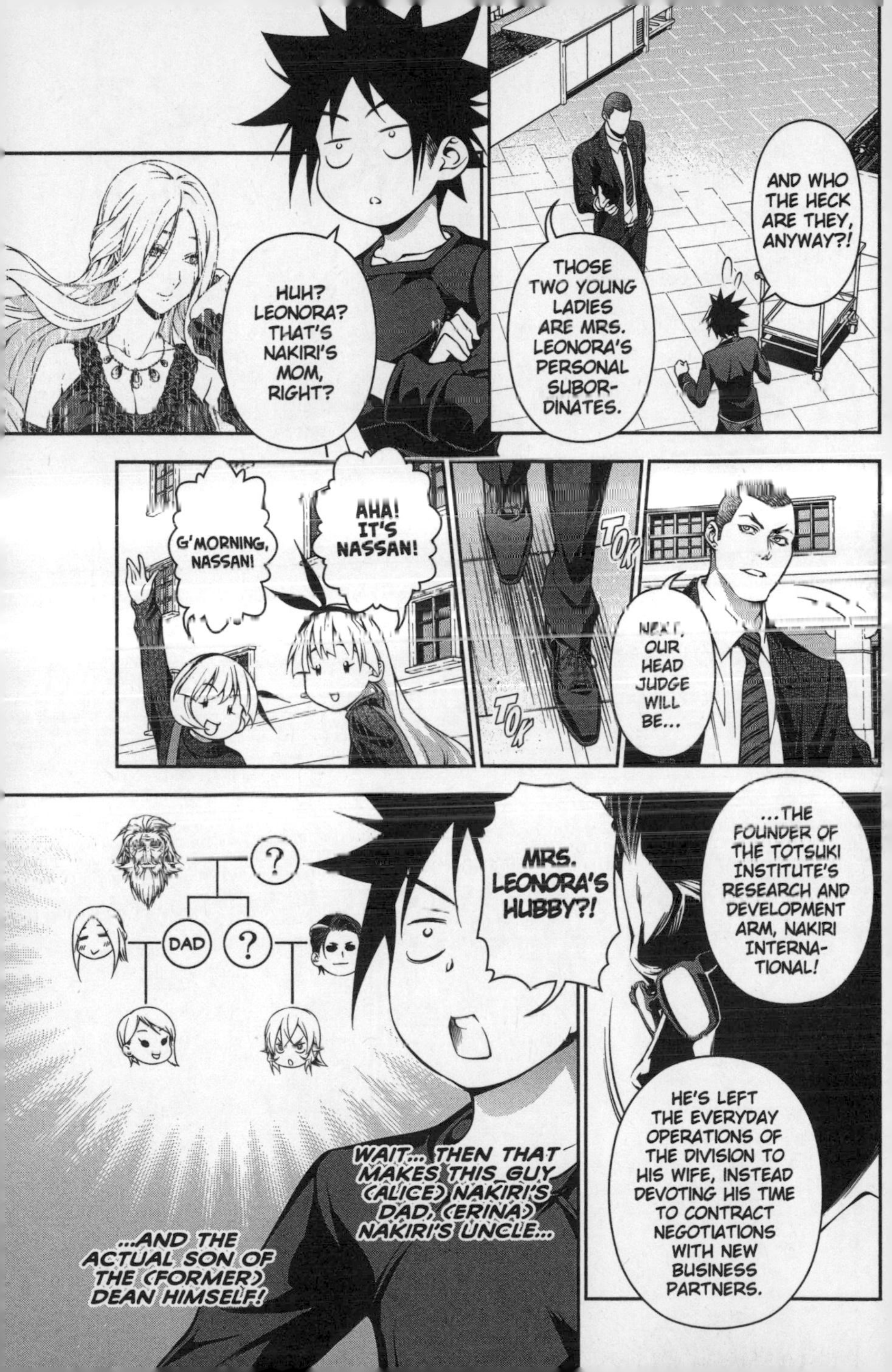
AND WHO THE HECK ARE THEY, ANYWAY?!
THOSE TWO YOUNG LADIES ARE MRS. LEONORA'S PERSONAL SUBOR-DINATES.
HUH? LEONORA? THAT'S NAKIRI'S MOM, RIGHT?
NEXT, OUR HEAD JUDGE WILL BE...
TOK
TOK
AHA! IT'S NASSAN!
G'MORNING, NASSAN!
...THE FOUNDER OF THE TOTSUKI INSTITUTE'S RESEARCH AND DEVELOPMENT ARM, NAKIRI INTERNA-TIONAL!
HE'S LEFT THE EVERYDAY OPERATIONS OF THE DIVISION TO HIS WIFE, INSTEAD DEVOTING HIS TIME TO CONTRACT NEGOTIATIONS WITH NEW BUSINESS PARTNERS.
MRS. LEONORA'S HUBBY?!
WAIT... THEN THAT MAKES THIS GUY (ALICE) NAKIRI'S DAD, (ERINA) NAKIRI'S UNCLE...
...AND THE ACTUAL SON OF THE (FORMER) DEAN HIMSELF!
?
?
DAD

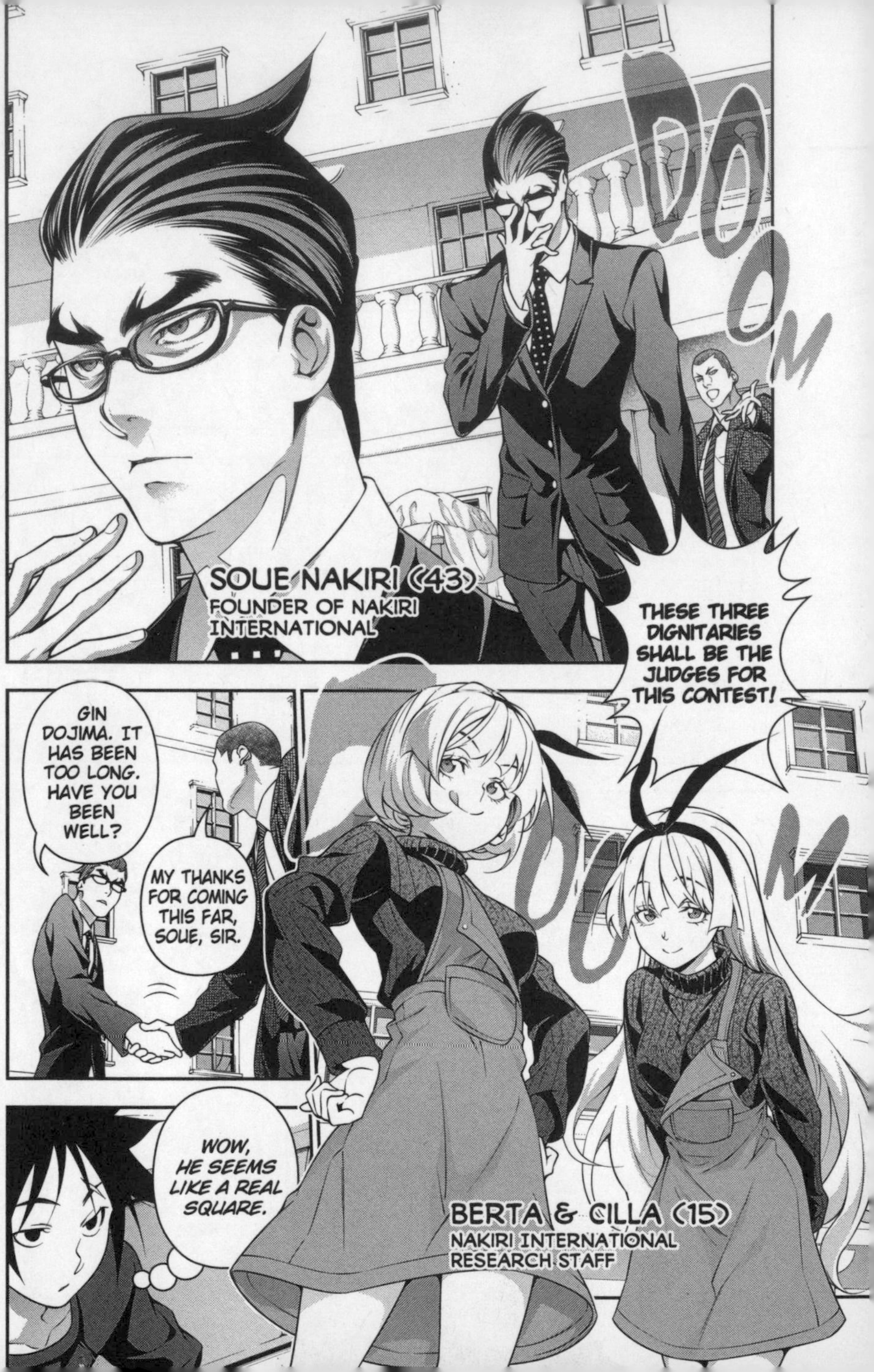
DOOOM
SOUE NAKIRI (43)
FOUNDER OF NAKIRI INTERNATIONAL
THESE THREE DIGNITARIES SHALL BE THE JUDGES FOR THIS CONTEST!
OOOM
BERTA & CILLA (15)
NAKIRI INTERNATIONAL RESEARCH STAFF
GIN DOJIMA. IT HAS BEEN TOO LONG. HAVE YOU BEEN WELL?
MY THANKS FOR COMING THIS FAR, SOUE, SIR.
WOW, HE SEEMS LIKE A REAL SQUARE.

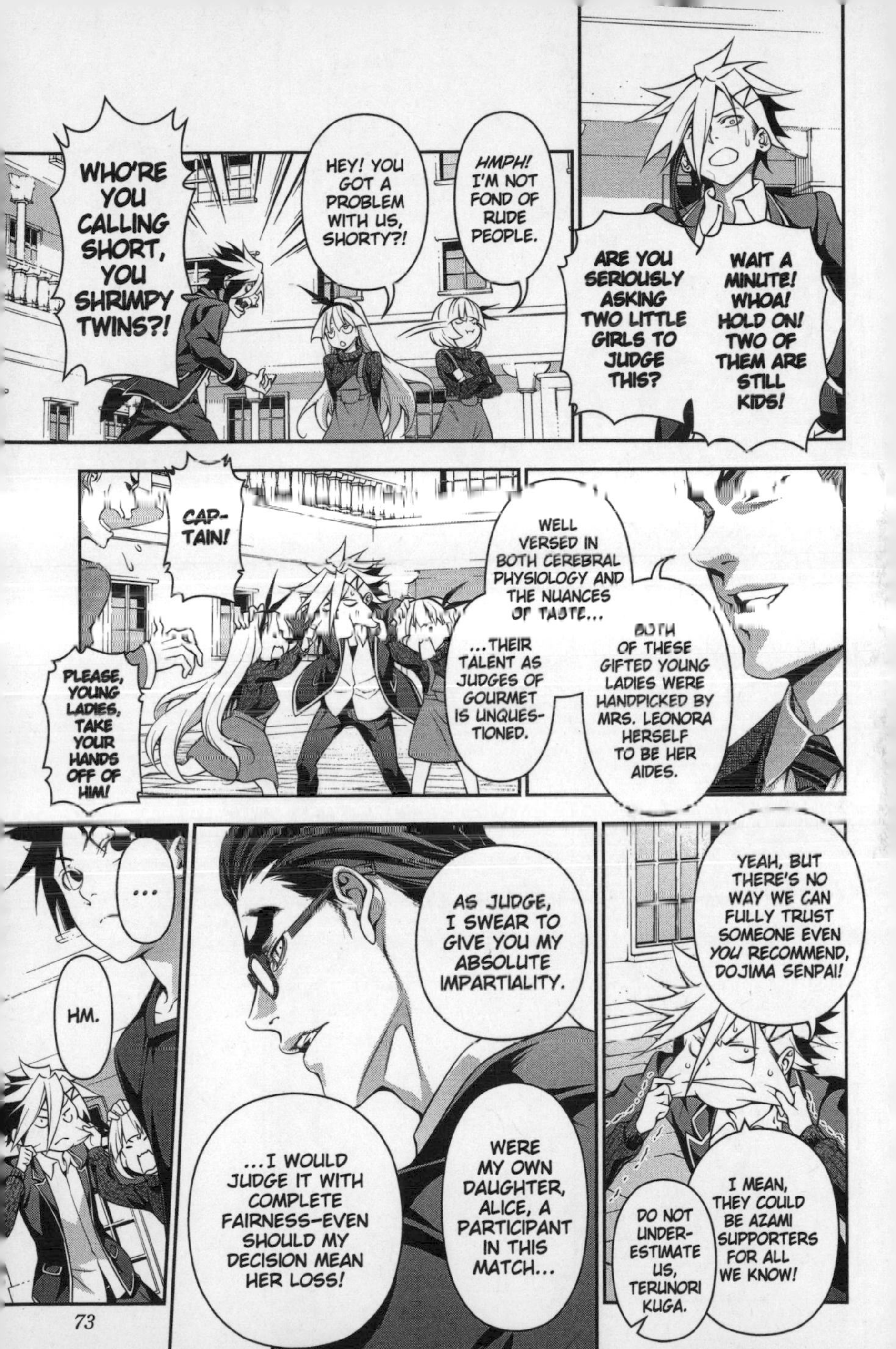
WAIT A MINUTE! WHOA! HOLD ON! TWO OF THEM ARE STILL KIDS!
ARE YOU SERIOUSLY ASKING TWO LITTLE GIRLS TO JUDGE THIS?
HMPH! I'M NOT FOND OF RUDE PEOPLE.
HEY! YOU GOT A PROBLEM WITH US, SHORTY?!
WHO'RE YOU CALLING SHORT, YOU SHRIMPY TWINS?!
BOTH OF THESE GIFTED YOUNG LADIES WERE HANDPICKED BY MRS. LEONORA HERSELF TO BE HER AIDES.
WELL VERSED IN BOTH CEREBRAL PHYSIOLOGY AND THE NUANCES OF TASTE...
...THEIR TALENT AS JUDGES OF GOURMET IS UNQUES-TIONED.
CAP-TAIN!
PLEASE, YOUNG LADIES, TAKE YOUR HANDS OFF OF HIM!
YEAH, BUT THERE'S NO WAY WE CAN FULLY TRUST SOMEONE EVEN YOU RECOMMEND, DOJIMA SENPAI!
I MEAN, THEY COULD BE AZAMI SUPPORTERS FOR ALL WE KNOW!
DO NOT UNDER-ESTIMATE US, TERUNORI KUGA.
AS JUDGE, I SWEAR TO GIVE YOU MY ABSOLUTE IMPARTIALITY.
WERE MY OWN DAUGHTER, ALICE, A PARTICIPANT IN THIS MATCH...
...I WOULD JUDGE IT WITH COMPLETE FAIRNESS—EVEN SHOULD MY DECISION MEAN HER LOSS!
...
HM.

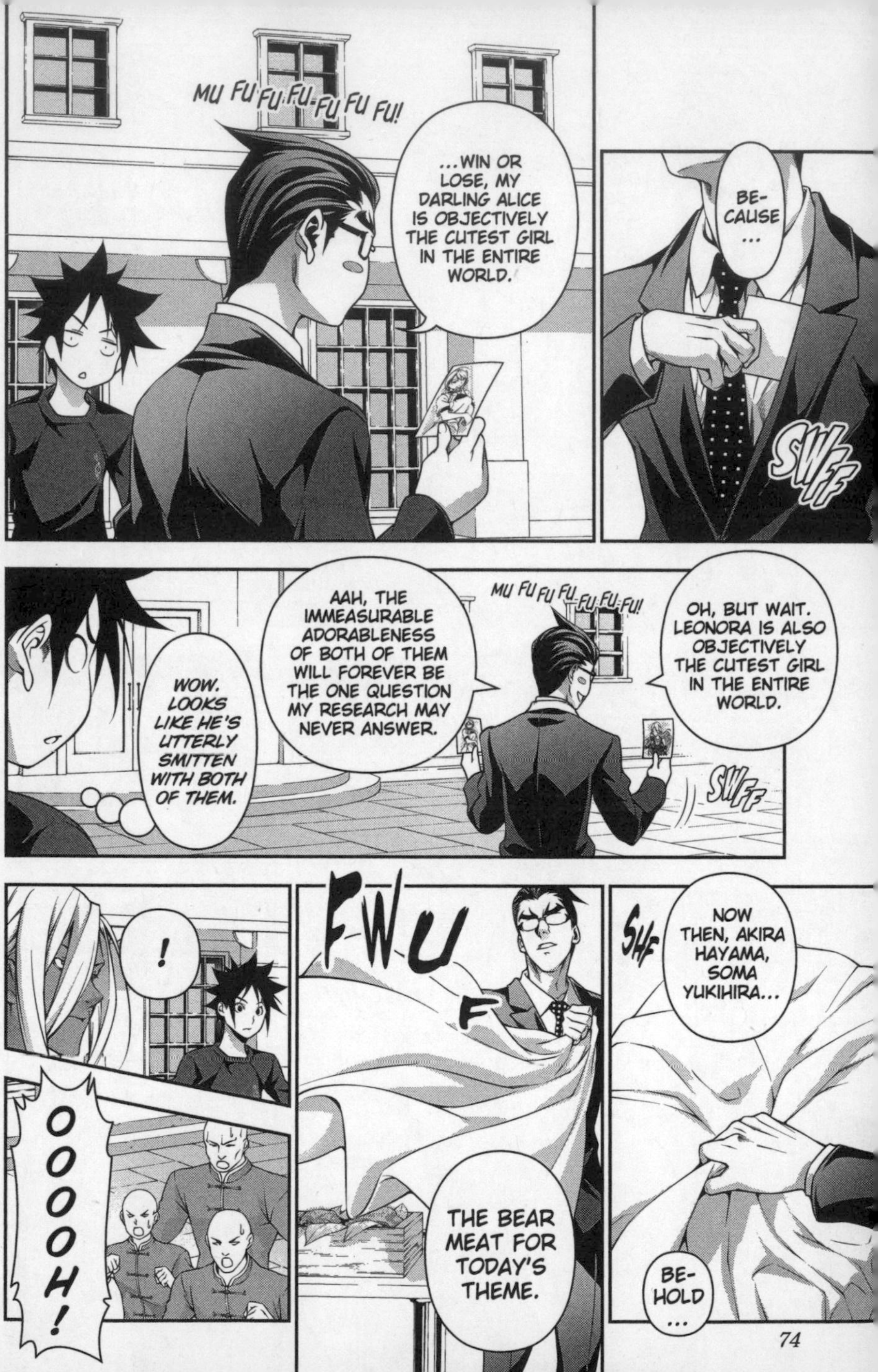
BE-CAUSE...
SWFF
MU FU FU FU FU FU FU!
...WIN OR LOSE, MY DARLING ALICE IS OBJECTIVELY THE CUTEST GIRL IN THE ENTIRE WORLD.
OH, BUT WAIT. LEONORA IS ALSO OBJECTIVELY THE CUTEST GIRL IN THE ENTIRE WORLD.
SWFF
MU FU FU FU FU FU FU!
AAH, THE IMMEASURABLE ADORABLENESS OF BOTH OF THEM WILL FOREVER BE THE ONE QUESTION MY RESEARCH MAY NEVER ANSWER.
WOW. LOOKS LIKE HE'S UTTERLY SMITTEN WITH BOTH OF THEM.
SHF
NOW THEN, AKIRA HAYAMA, SOMA YUKIHIRA...
BE-HOLD...
FWUF
THE BEAR MEAT FOR TODAY'S THEME.
!
OOOOOH!

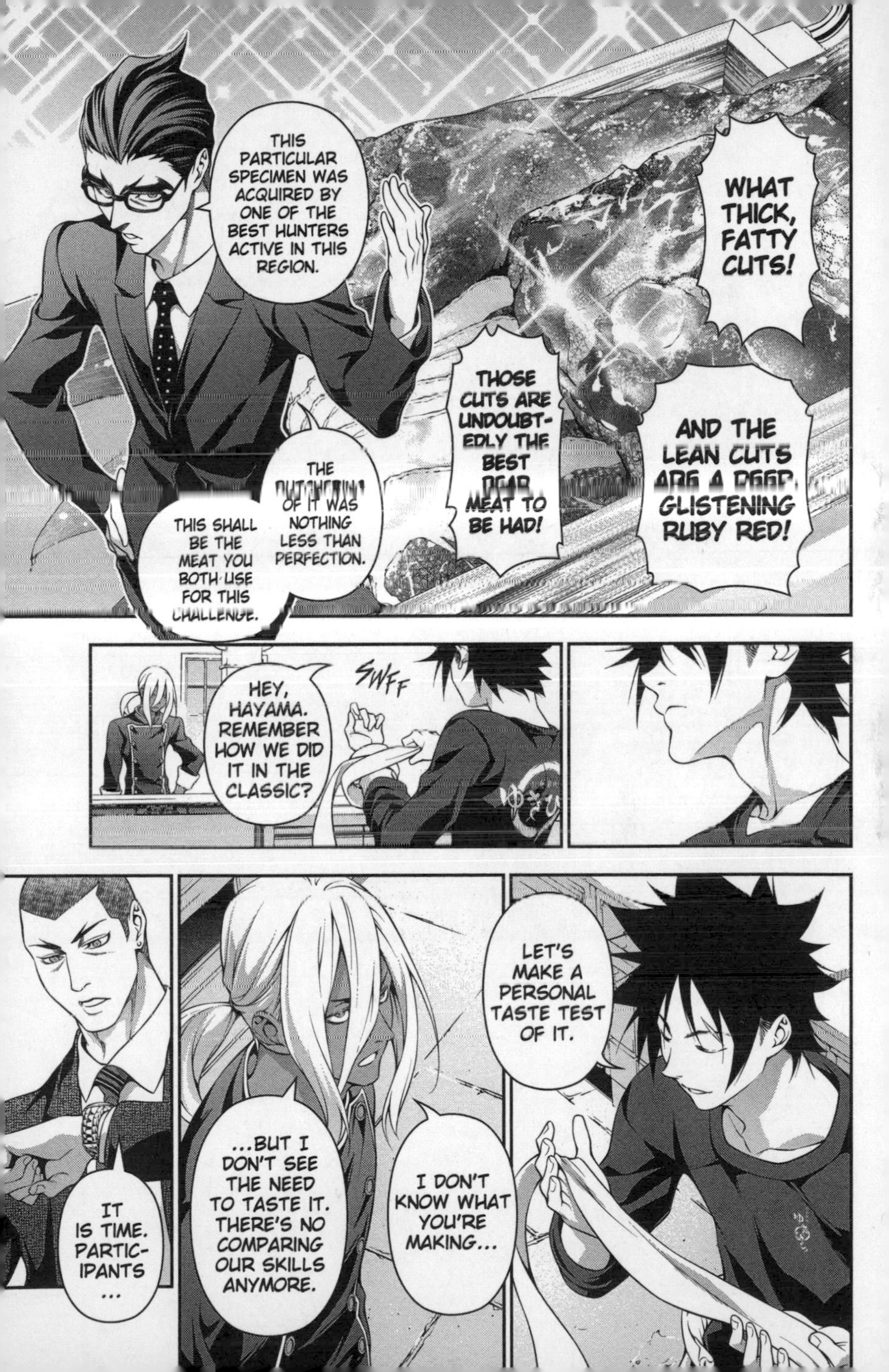
WHAT THICK, FATTY CUTS!
AND THE LEAN CUTS ARE A DEEP, GLISTENING RUBY RED!
THOSE CUTS ARE UNDOUBTEDLY THE BEST BEAR MEAT TO BE HAD!
THIS PARTICULAR SPECIMEN WAS ACQUIRED BY ONE OF THE BEST HUNTERS ACTIVE IN THIS REGION.
THE BUTCHERING OF IT WAS NOTHING LESS THAN PERFECTION.
THIS SHALL BE THE MEAT YOU BOTH USE FOR THIS CHALLENGE.
SWFF
HEY, HAYAMA. REMEMBER HOW WE DID IT IN THE CLASSIC?
LET'S MAKE A PERSONAL TASTE TEST OF IT.
I DON'T KNOW WHAT YOU'RE MAKING...
...BUT I DON'T SEE THE NEED TO TASTE IT. THERE'S NO COMPARING OUR SKILLS ANYMORE.
IT IS TIME. PARTICIPANTS ...

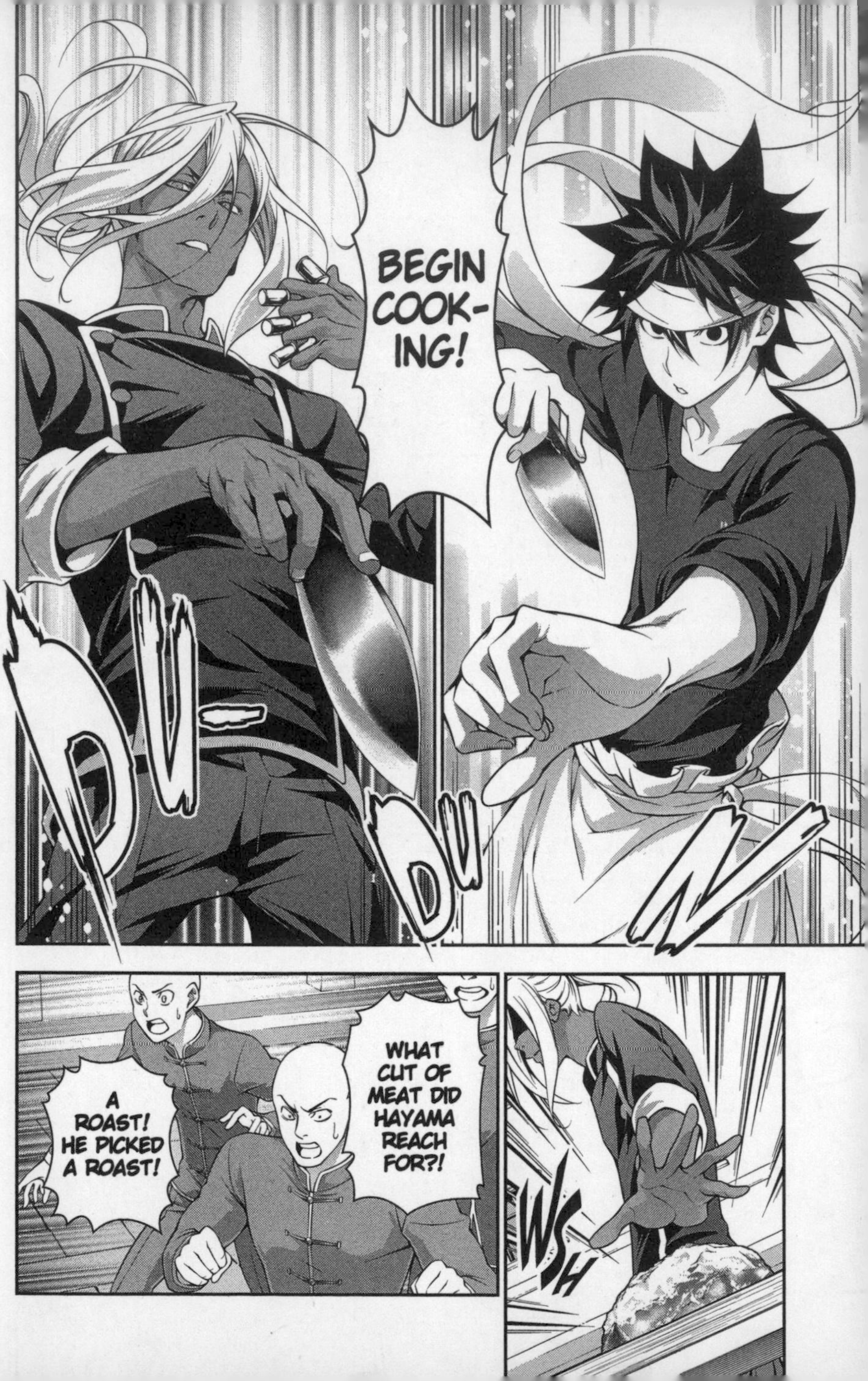
BEGIN COOKING!
DU DU DUN
WSH
WHAT CUT OF MEAT DID HAYAMA REACH FOR?!
A ROAST! HE PICKED A ROAST!

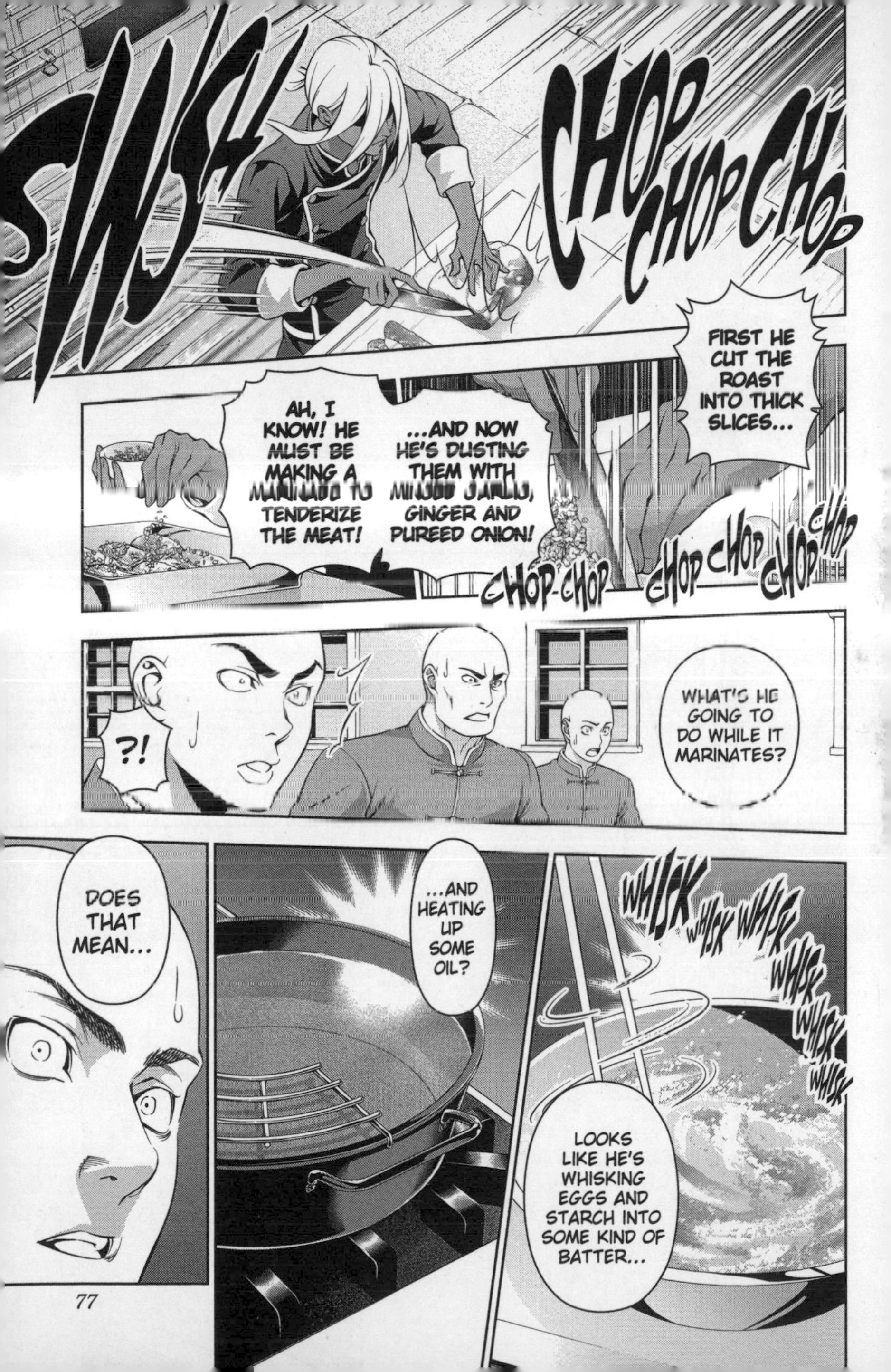
CHOP CHOP CHOP CHOP
SWISH
FIRST HE CUT THE ROAST INTO THICK SLICES...
...AND NOW HE'S DUSTING THEM WITH MINCED GARLIC, GINGER AND PUREED ONION!
CHOP CHOP CHOP CHOP
AH, I KNOW! HE MUST BE MAKING A MARINADE TO TENDERIZE THE MEAT!
CHOP-CHOP
WHAT'S HE GOING TO DO WHILE IT MARINATES?
?!
WHISK WHISK WHISK WHISK WHISK WHISK
LOOKS LIKE HE'S WHISKING EGGS AND STARCH INTO SOME KIND OF BATTER...
...AND HEATING UP SOME OIL?
DOES THAT MEAN...

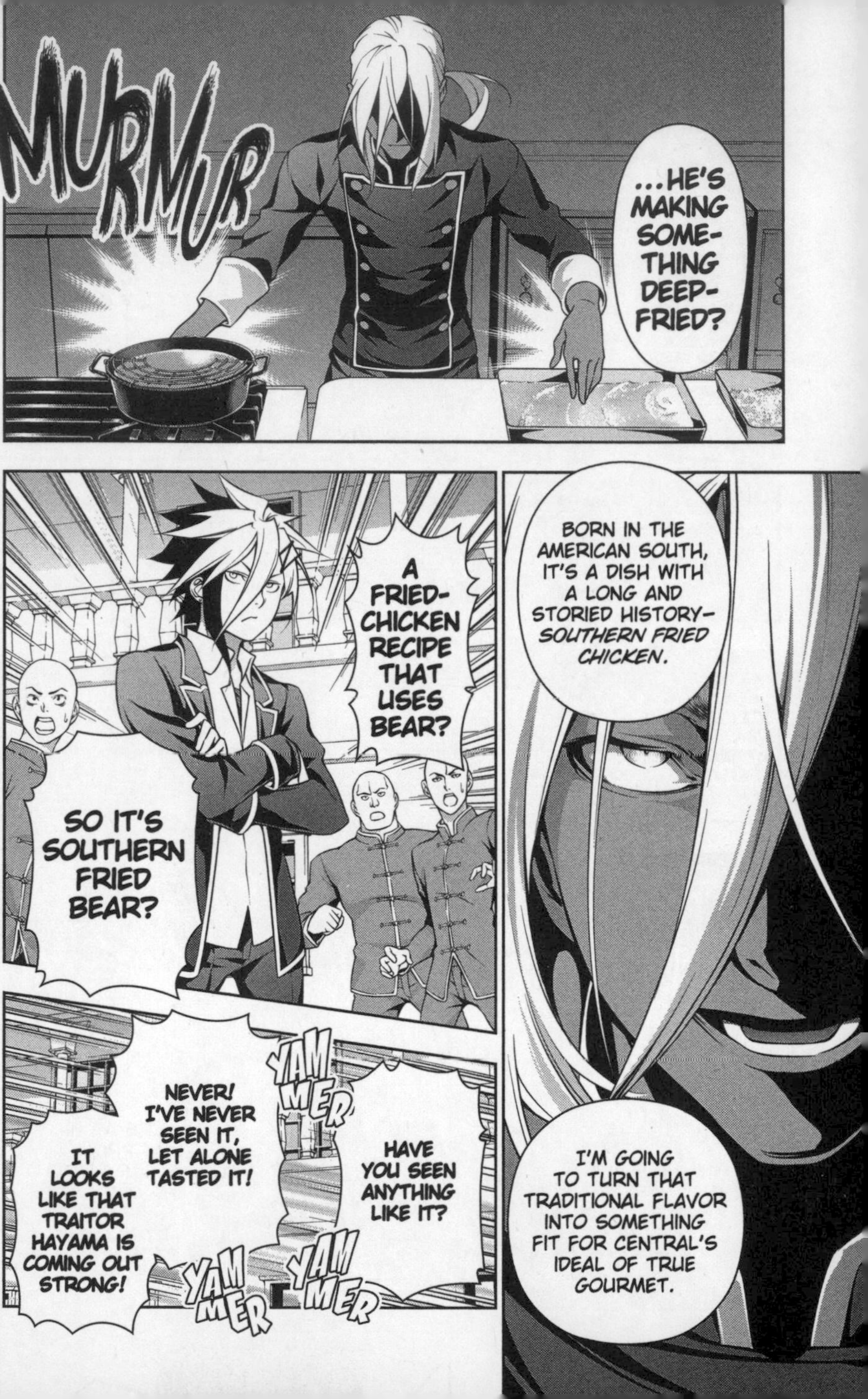
...HE'S MAKING SOME-THING DEEP-FRIED?
MURMUR
BORN IN THE AMERICAN SOUTH, IT'S A DISH WITH A LONG AND STORIED HISTORY- *SOUTHERN FRIED CHICKEN.*
I'M GOING TO TURN THAT TRADITIONAL FLAVOR INTO SOMETHING FIT FOR CENTRAL'S IDEAL OF TRUE GOURMET.
A FRIED-CHICKEN RECIPE THAT USES BEAR?
SO IT'S SOUTHERN FRIED BEAR?
YAMMER
HAVE YOU SEEN ANYTHING LIKE IT?
NEVER! I'VE NEVER SEEN IT, LET ALONE TASTED IT!
IT LOOKS LIKE THAT TRAITOR HAYAMA IS COMING OUT STRONG!
YAMMER
YAMMER

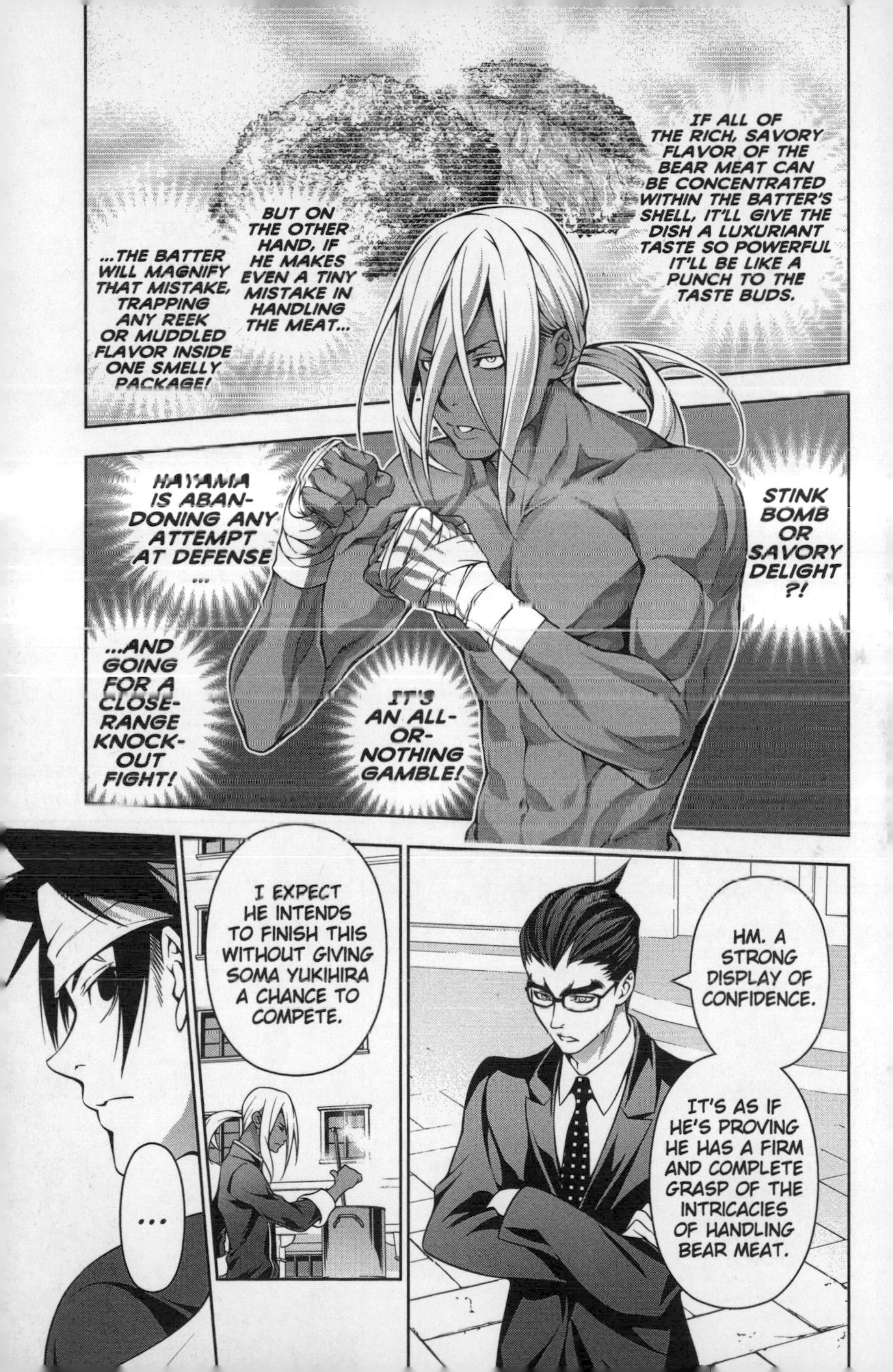
IF ALL OF THE RICH, SAVORY FLAVOR OF THE BEAR MEAT CAN BE CONCENTRATED WITHIN THE BATTER'S SHELL, IT'LL GIVE THE DISH A LUXURIANT TASTE SO POWERFUL IT'LL BE LIKE A PUNCH TO THE TASTE BUDS.
BUT ON THE OTHER HAND, IF HE MAKES EVEN A TINY MISTAKE IN HANDLING THE MEAT...
...THE BATTER WILL MAGNIFY THAT MISTAKE, TRAPPING ANY REEK OR MUDDLED FLAVOR INSIDE ONE SMELLY PACKAGE!
STINK BOMB OR SAVORY DELIGHT?!
HAYAMA IS ABANDONING ANY ATTEMPT AT DEFENSE...
...AND GOING FOR A CLOSE-RANGE KNOCKOUT FIGHT!
IT'S AN ALL-OR-NOTHING GAMBLE!
HM. A STRONG DISPLAY OF CONFIDENCE.
IT'S AS IF HE'S PROVING HE HAS A FIRM AND COMPLETE GRASP OF THE INTRICACIES OF HANDLING BEAR MEAT.
I EXPECT HE INTENDS TO FINISH THIS WITHOUT GIVING SOMA YUKIHIRA A CHANCE TO COMPETE.
...

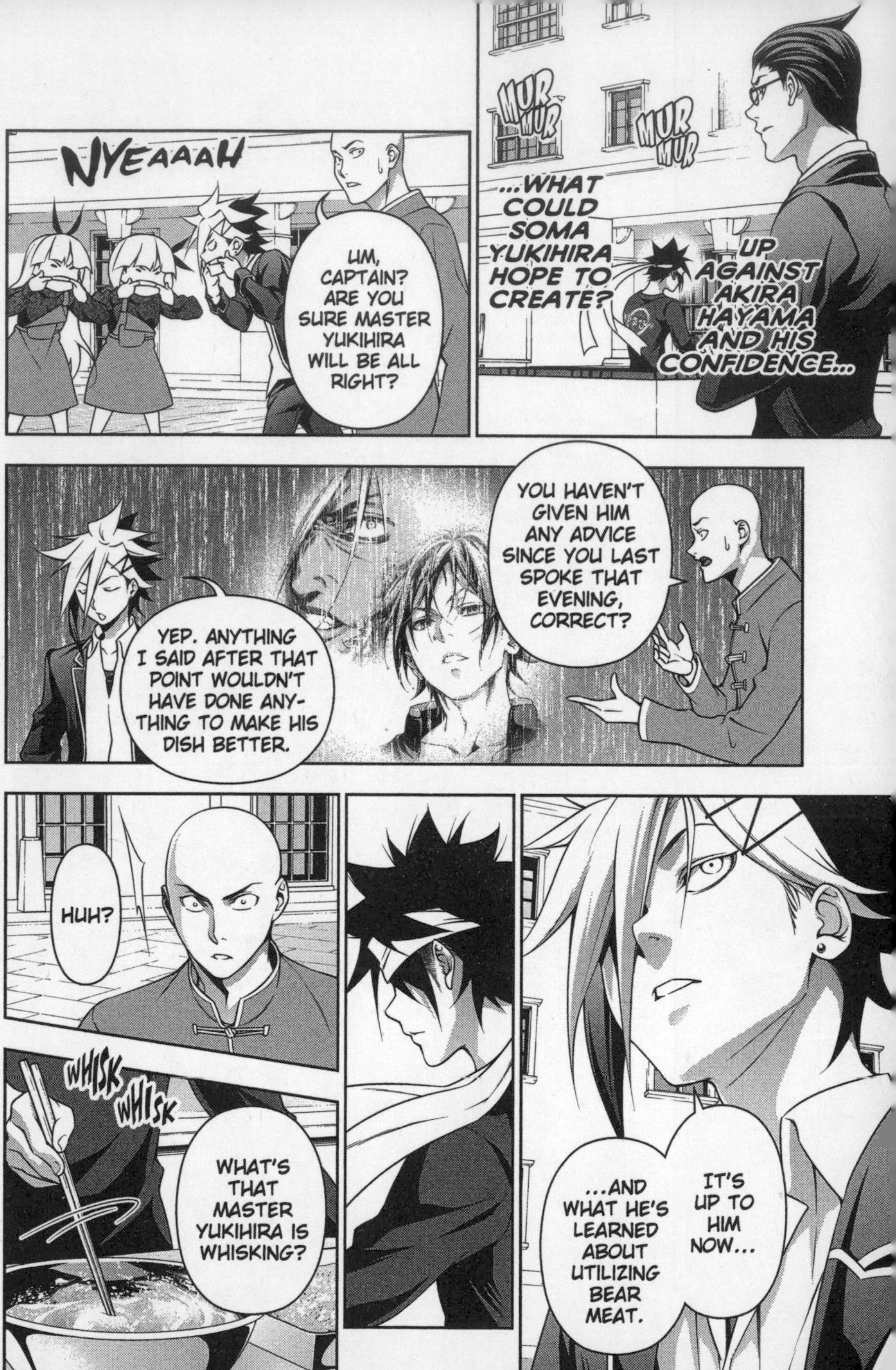

MUR MUR
MUR MUR
...WHAT COULD SOMA YUKIHIRA HOPE TO CREATE?
UP AGAINST AKIRA HAYAMA AND HIS CONFIDENCE...
NYEAAAH
UM, CAPTAIN? ARE YOU SURE MASTER YUKIHIRA WILL BE ALL RIGHT?
YOU HAVEN'T GIVEN HIM ANY ADVICE SINCE YOU LAST SPOKE THAT EVENING, CORRECT?
YEP. ANYTHING I SAID AFTER THAT POINT WOULDN'T HAVE DONE ANY-THING TO MAKE HIS DISH BETTER.
IT'S UP TO HIM NOW...
...AND WHAT HE'S LEARNED ABOUT UTILIZING BEAR MEAT.
HUH?
WHISK WHISK
WHAT'S THAT MASTER YUKIHIRA IS WHISKING?

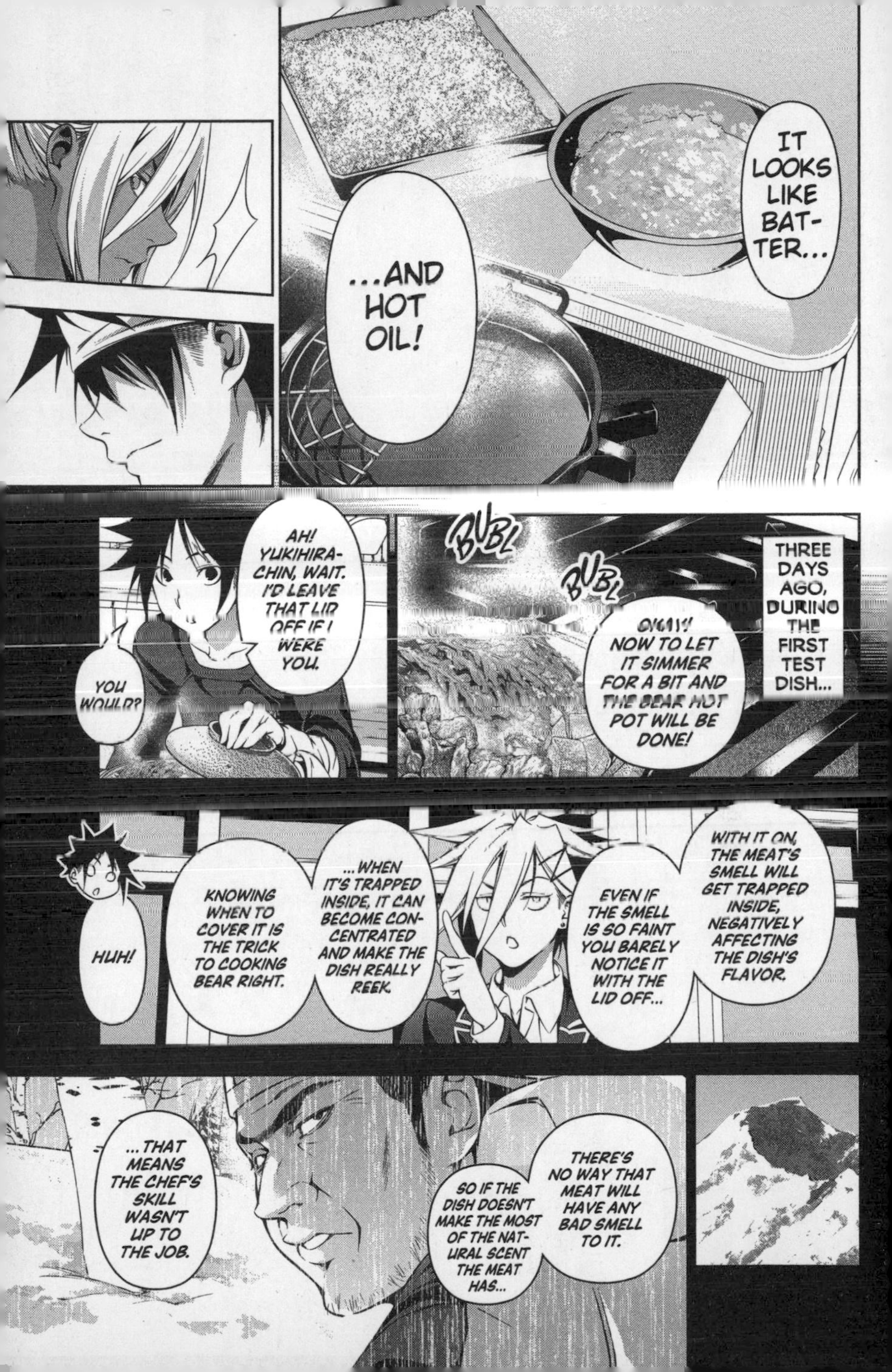
IT LOOKS LIKE BAT-TER...
...AND HOT OIL!
THREE DAYS AGO, DURING THE FIRST TEST DISH...
BUBL
BUBL
OKAY! NOW TO LET IT SIMMER FOR A BIT AND THE BEAR HOT POT WILL BE DONE!
AH! YUKIHIRA-CHIN, WAIT. I'D LEAVE THAT LID OFF IF I WERE YOU.
YOU WOULD?
WITH IT ON, THE MEAT'S SMELL WILL GET TRAPPED INSIDE, NEGATIVELY AFFECTING THE DISH'S FLAVOR.
EVEN IF THE SMELL IS SO FAINT YOU BARELY NOTICE IT WITH THE LID OFF...
...WHEN IT'S TRAPPED INSIDE, IT CAN BECOME CON-CENTRATED AND MAKE THE DISH REALLY REEK.
KNOWING WHEN TO COVER IT IS THE TRICK TO COOKING BEAR RIGHT.
HUH!
THERE'S NO WAY THAT MEAT WILL HAVE ANY BAD SMELL TO IT.
SO IF THE DISH DOESN'T MAKE THE MOST OF THE NAT-URAL SCENT THE MEAT HAS...
...THAT MEANS THE CHEF'S SKILL WASN'T UP TO THE JOB.

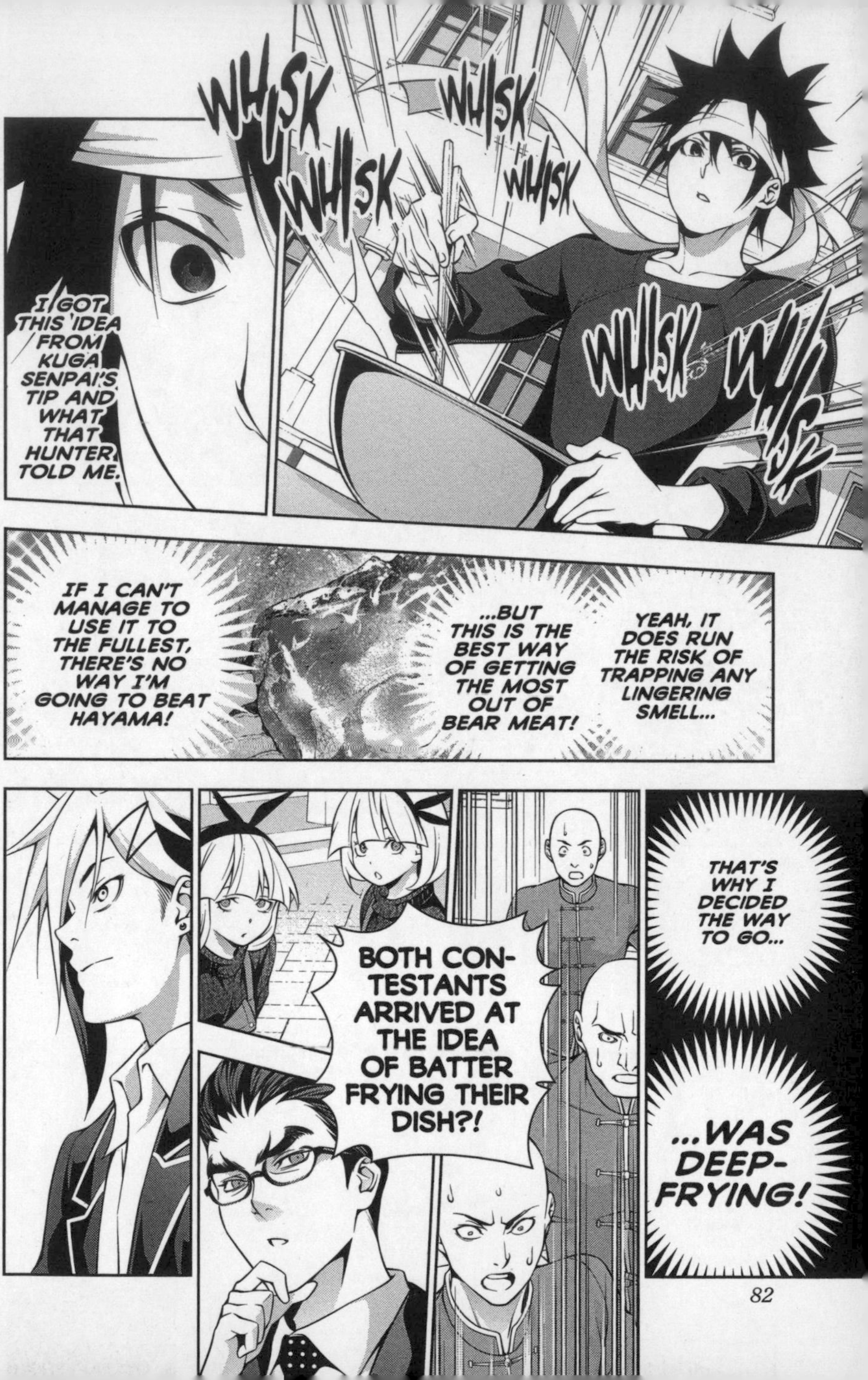
WHISK
WHISK
WHISK
WHISK
WHISK
WHISK
I GOT THIS IDEA FROM KUGA SENPAI'S TIP AND WHAT THAT HUNTER TOLD ME.
YEAH, IT DOES RUN THE RISK OF TRAPPING ANY LINGERING SMELL...
...BUT THIS IS THE BEST WAY OF GETTING THE MOST OUT OF BEAR MEAT!
IF I CAN'T MANAGE TO USE IT TO THE FULLEST, THERE'S NO WAY I'M GOING TO BEAT HAYAMA!
THAT'S WHY I DECIDED THE WAY TO GO...
...WAS DEEP-FRYING!
BOTH CON-TESTANTS ARRIVED AT THE IDEA OF BATTER FRYING THEIR DISH?!

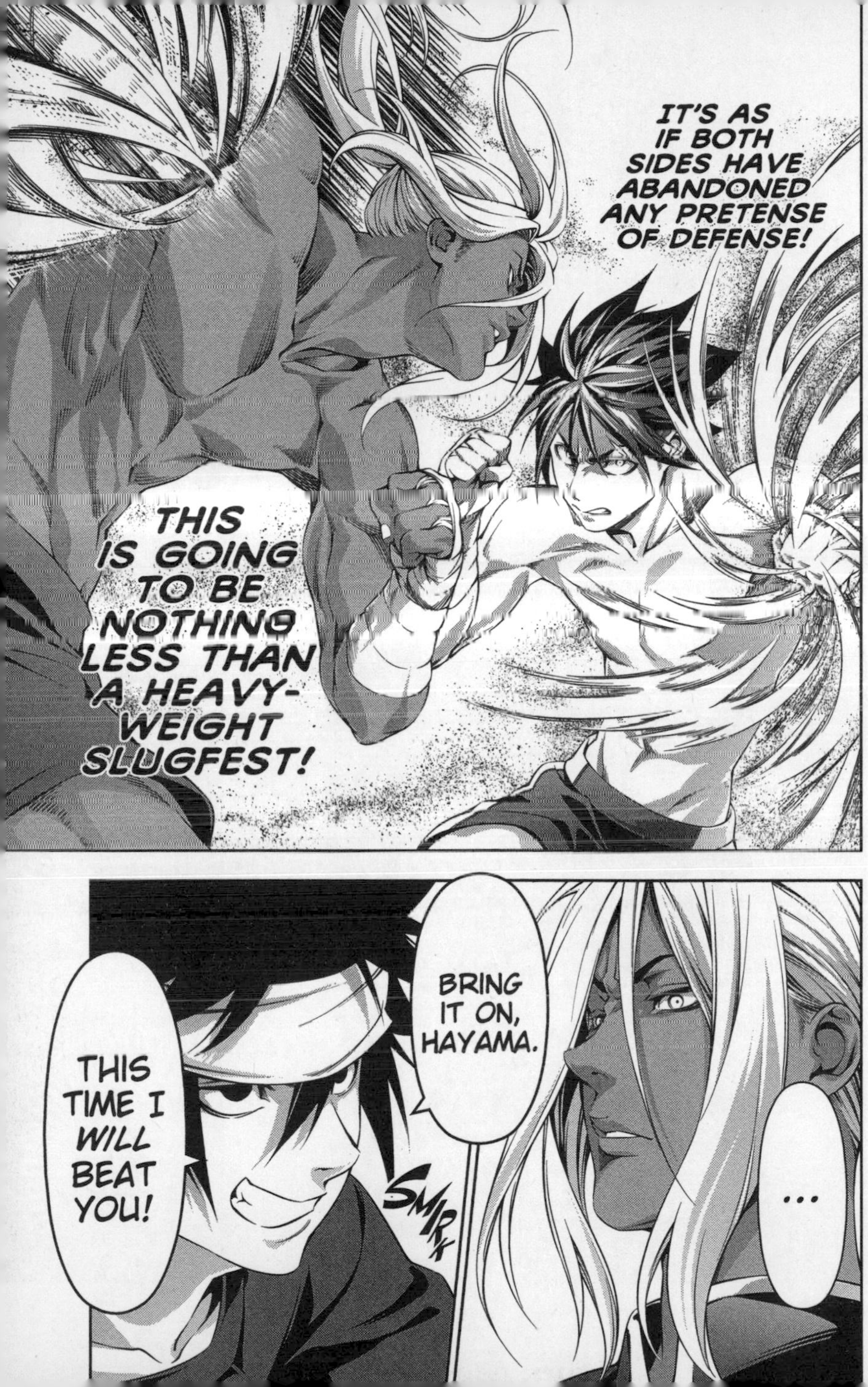
IT'S AS IF BOTH SIDES HAVE ABANDONED ANY PRETENSE OF DEFENSE!
THIS IS GOING TO BE NOTHING LESS THAN A HEAVY-WEIGHT SLUGFEST!
...
BRING IT ON, HAYAMA.
SMRK
THIS TIME I *WILL* BEAT YOU!

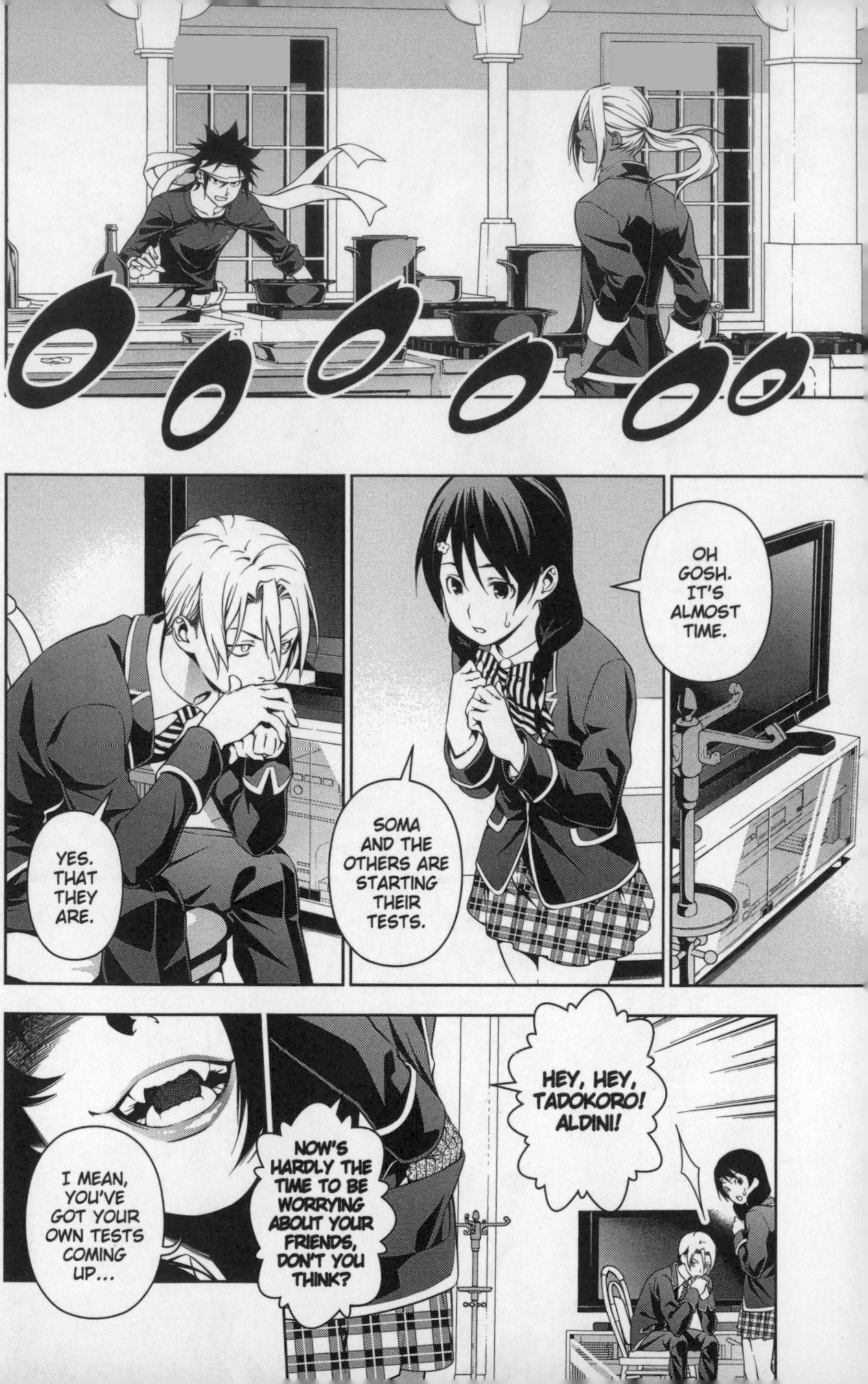
OH GOSH. IT'S ALMOST TIME.
SOMA AND THE OTHERS ARE STARTING THEIR TESTS.
YES. THAT THEY ARE.
HEY, HEY, TADOKORO! ALDINI!
NOW'S HARDLY THE TIME TO BE WORRYING ABOUT YOUR FRIENDS, DON'T YOU THINK?
I MEAN, YOU'VE GOT YOUR OWN TESTS COMING UP...

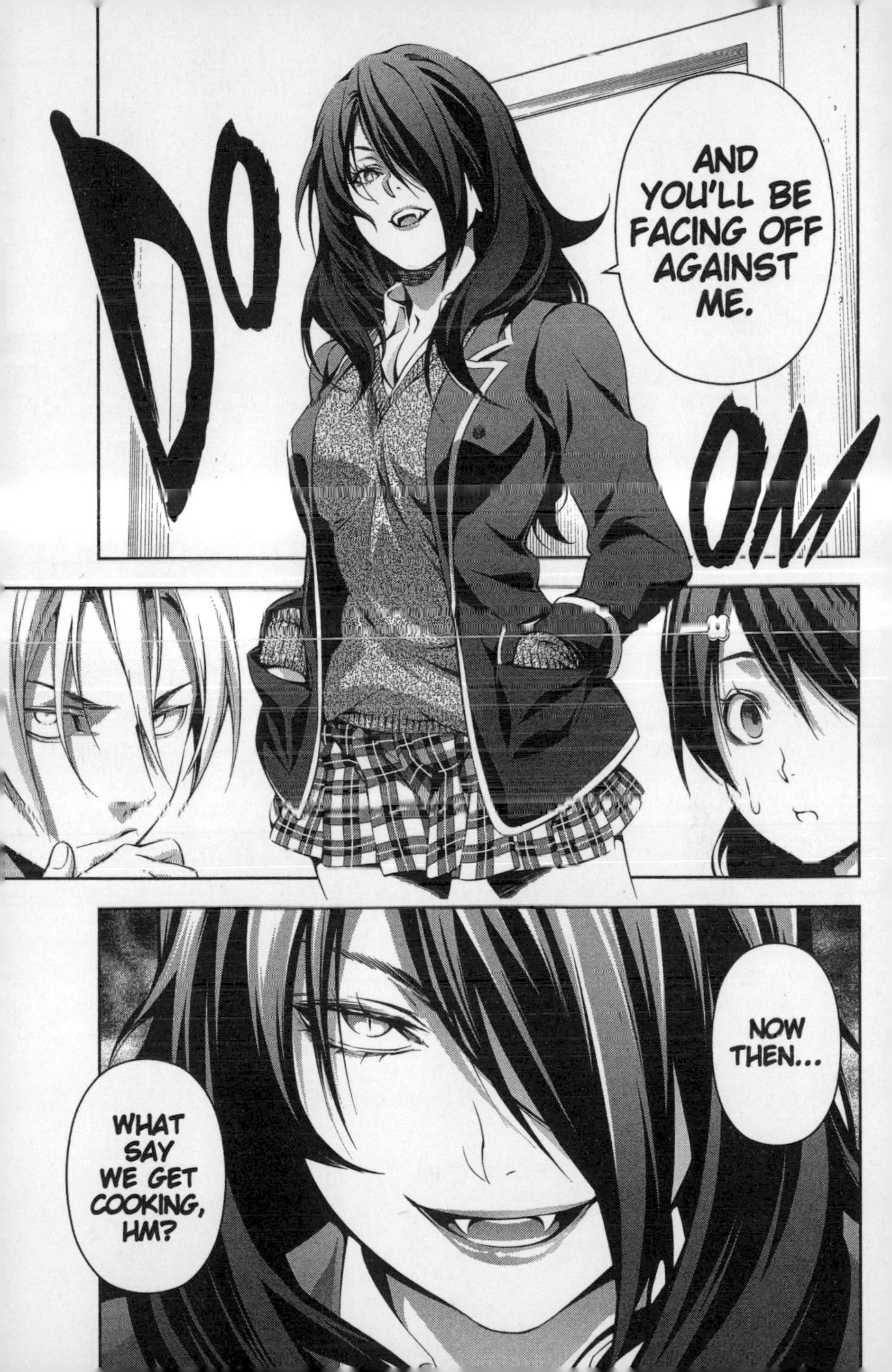
AND YOU'LL BE FACING OFF AGAINST ME.
DO OM
NOW THEN...
WHAT SAY WE GET COOKING, HM?

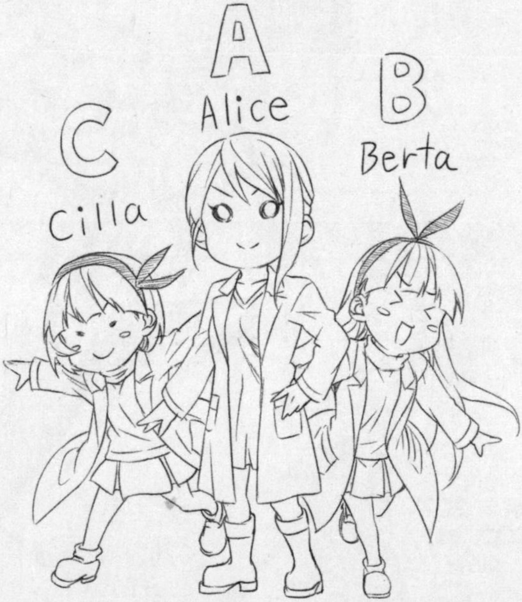
C
Cilla
A
Alice
B
Berta

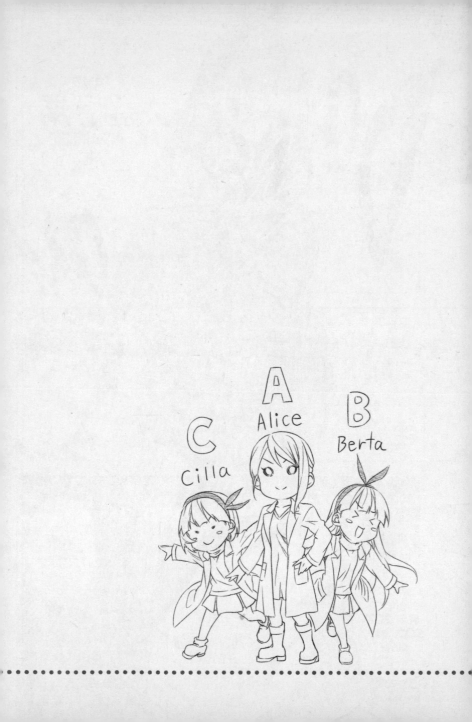

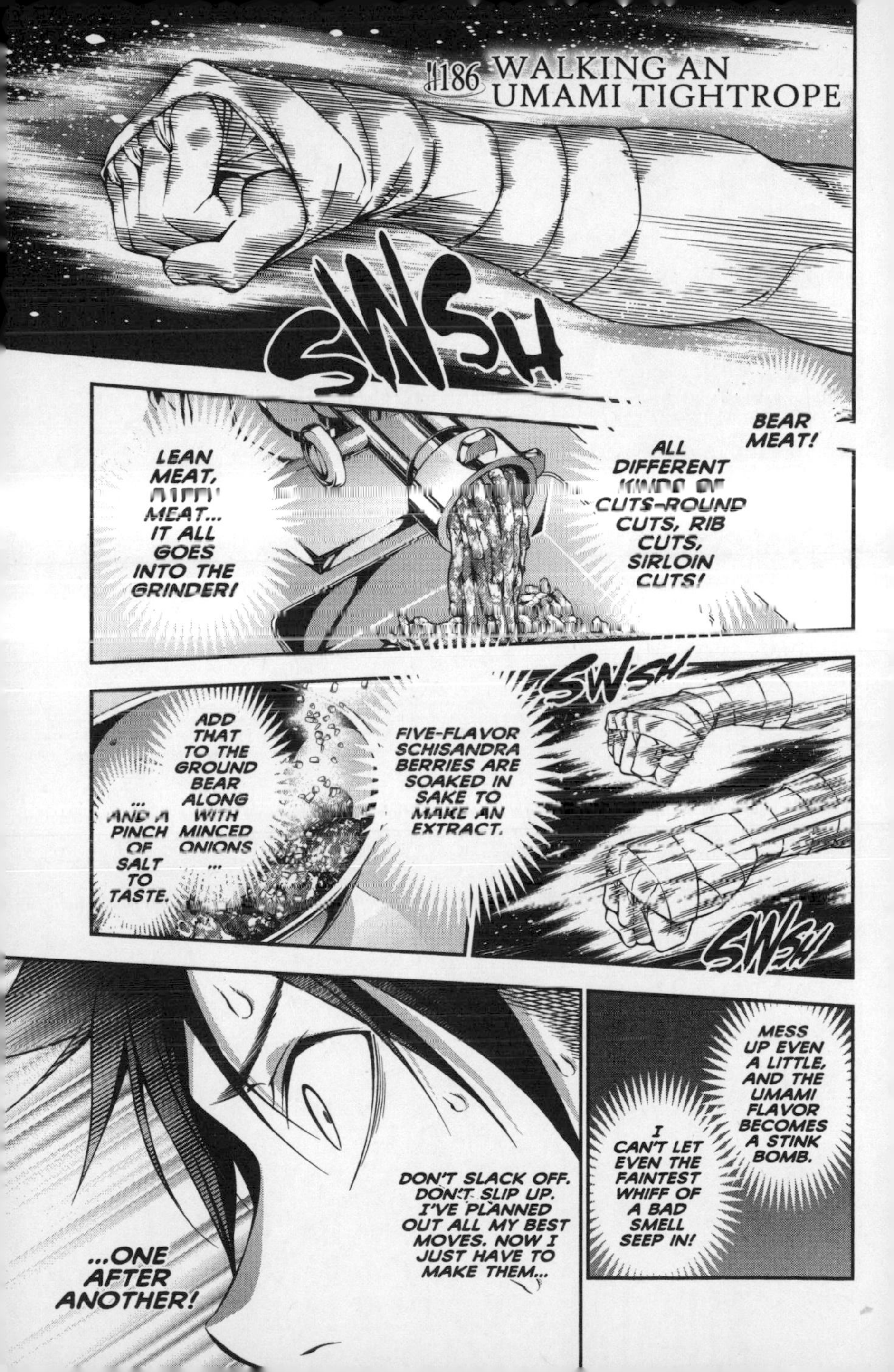
#186 WALKING AN UMAMI TIGHTROPE
SWSH
BEAR MEAT!
ALL DIFFERENT KINDS OF CUTS—ROUND CUTS, RIB CUTS, SIRLOIN CUTS!
LEAN MEAT, FATTY MEAT... IT ALL GOES INTO THE GRINDER!
SWSH
FIVE-FLAVOR SCHISANDRA BERRIES ARE SOAKED IN SAKE TO MAKE AN EXTRACT.
ADD THAT TO THE GROUND BEAR ALONG WITH MINCED ONIONS...
...AND A PINCH OF SALT TO TASTE.
SWSH
MESS UP EVEN A LITTLE, AND THE UMAMI FLAVOR BECOMES A STINK BOMB.
I CAN'T LET EVEN THE FAINTEST WHIFF OF A BAD SMELL SEEP IN!
DON'T SLACK OFF. DON'T SLIP UP. I'VE PLANNED OUT ALL MY BEST MOVES. NOW I JUST HAVE TO MAKE THEM...
...ONE AFTER ANOTHER!

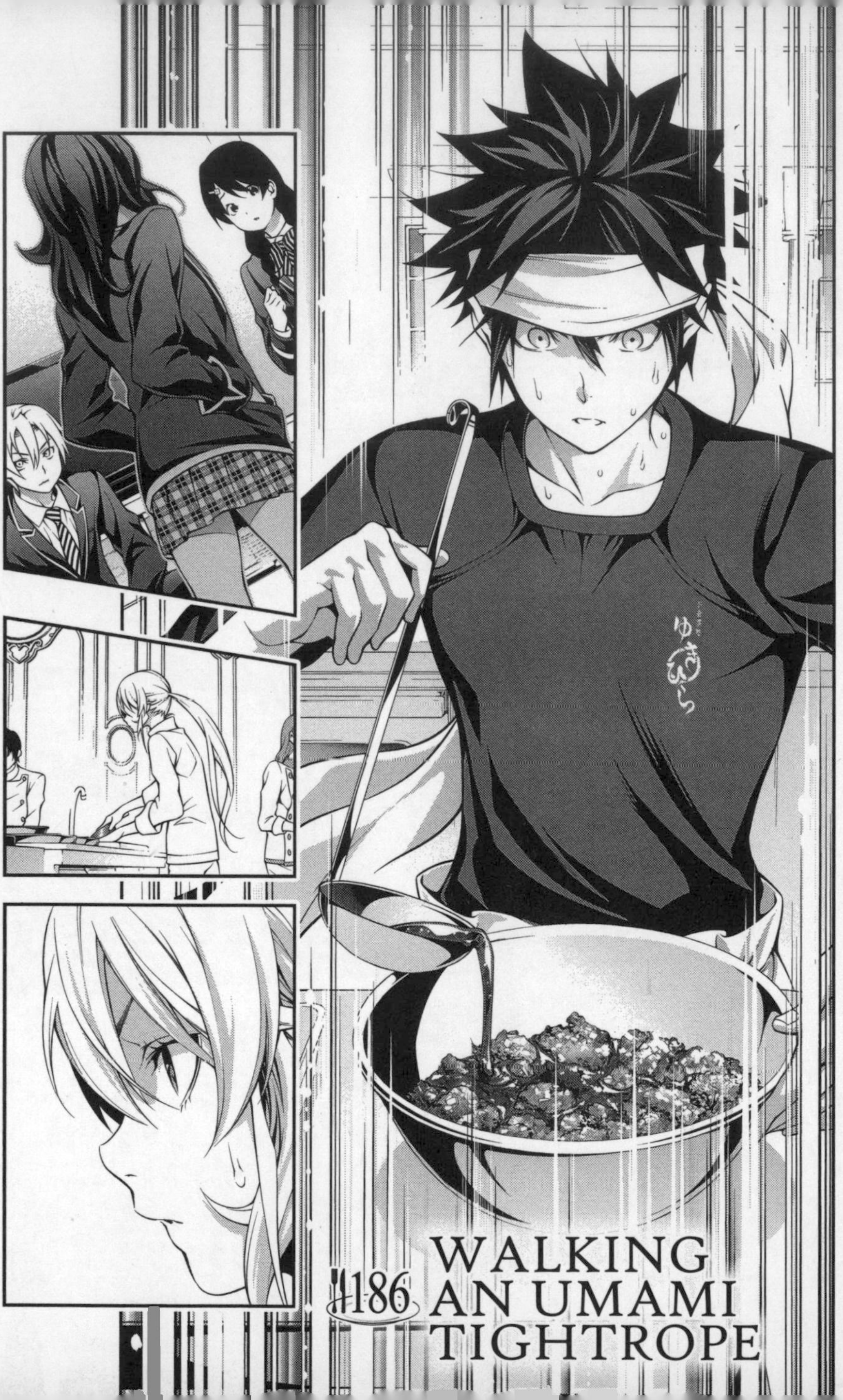
ゆきひら
186
WALKING
AN UMAMI
TIGHTROPE

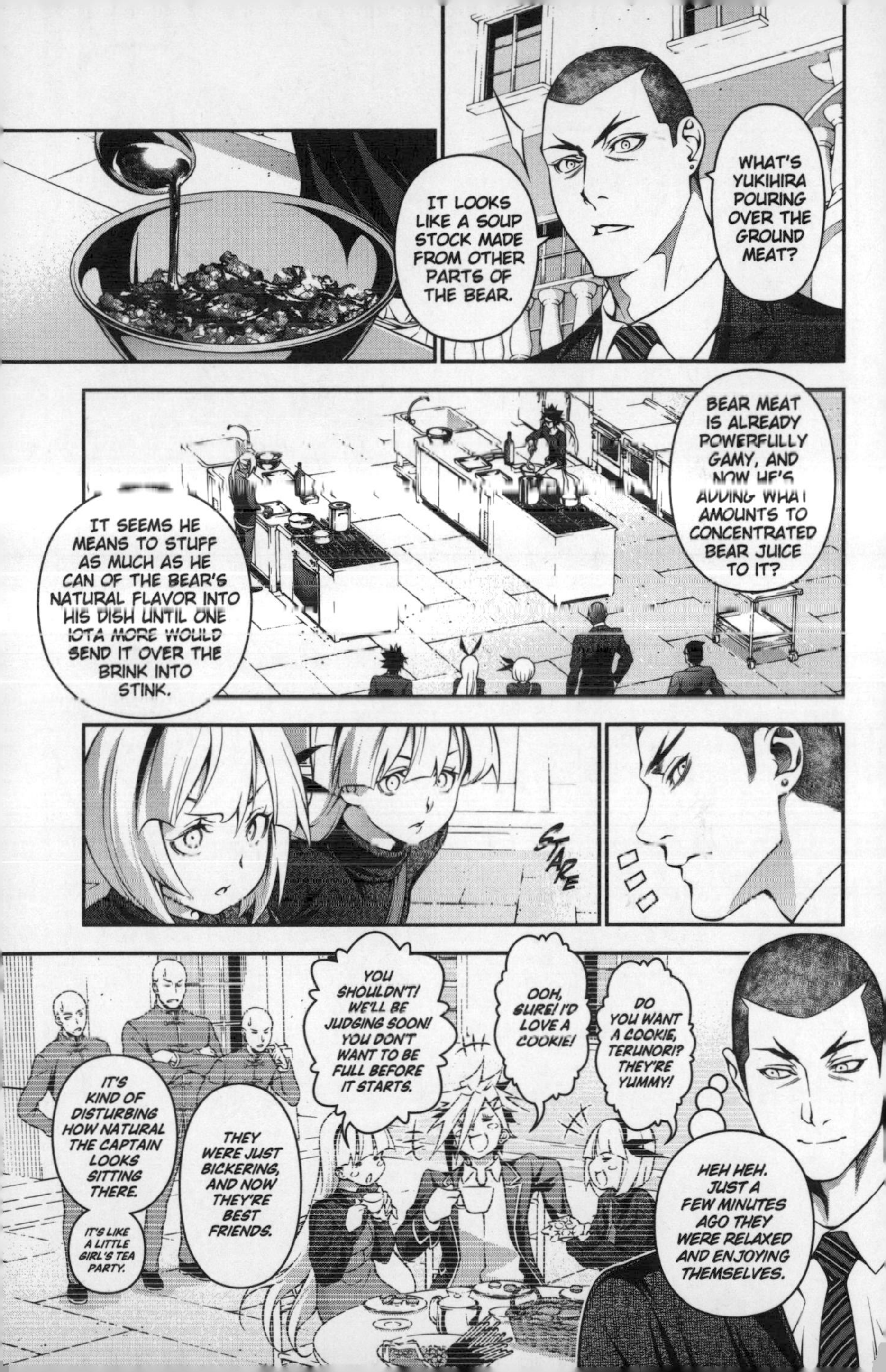
WHAT'S YUKIHIRA POURING OVER THE GROUND MEAT?
IT LOOKS LIKE A SOUP STOCK MADE FROM OTHER PARTS OF THE BEAR.
BEAR MEAT IS ALREADY POWERFULLY GAMY, AND NOW HE'S ADDING WHAT AMOUNTS TO CONCENTRATED BEAR JUICE TO IT?
IT SEEMS HE MEANS TO STUFF AS MUCH AS HE CAN OF THE BEAR'S NATURAL FLAVOR INTO HIS DISH UNTIL ONE IOTA MORE WOULD SEND IT OVER THE BRINK INTO STINK.
STARE
HEH HEH. JUST A FEW MINUTES AGO THEY WERE RELAXED AND ENJOYING THEMSELVES.
DO YOU WANT A COOKIE, TERUNORI? THEY'RE YUMMY!
OOH, SURE! I'D LOVE A COOKIE!
YOU SHOULDN'T! WE'LL BE JUDGING SOON! YOU DON'T WANT TO BE FULL BEFORE IT STARTS.
THEY WERE JUST BICKERING, AND NOW THEY'RE BEST FRIENDS.
IT'S KIND OF DISTURBING HOW NATURAL THE CAPTAIN LOOKS SITTING THERE.
IT'S LIKE A LITTLE GIRL'S TEA PARTY.

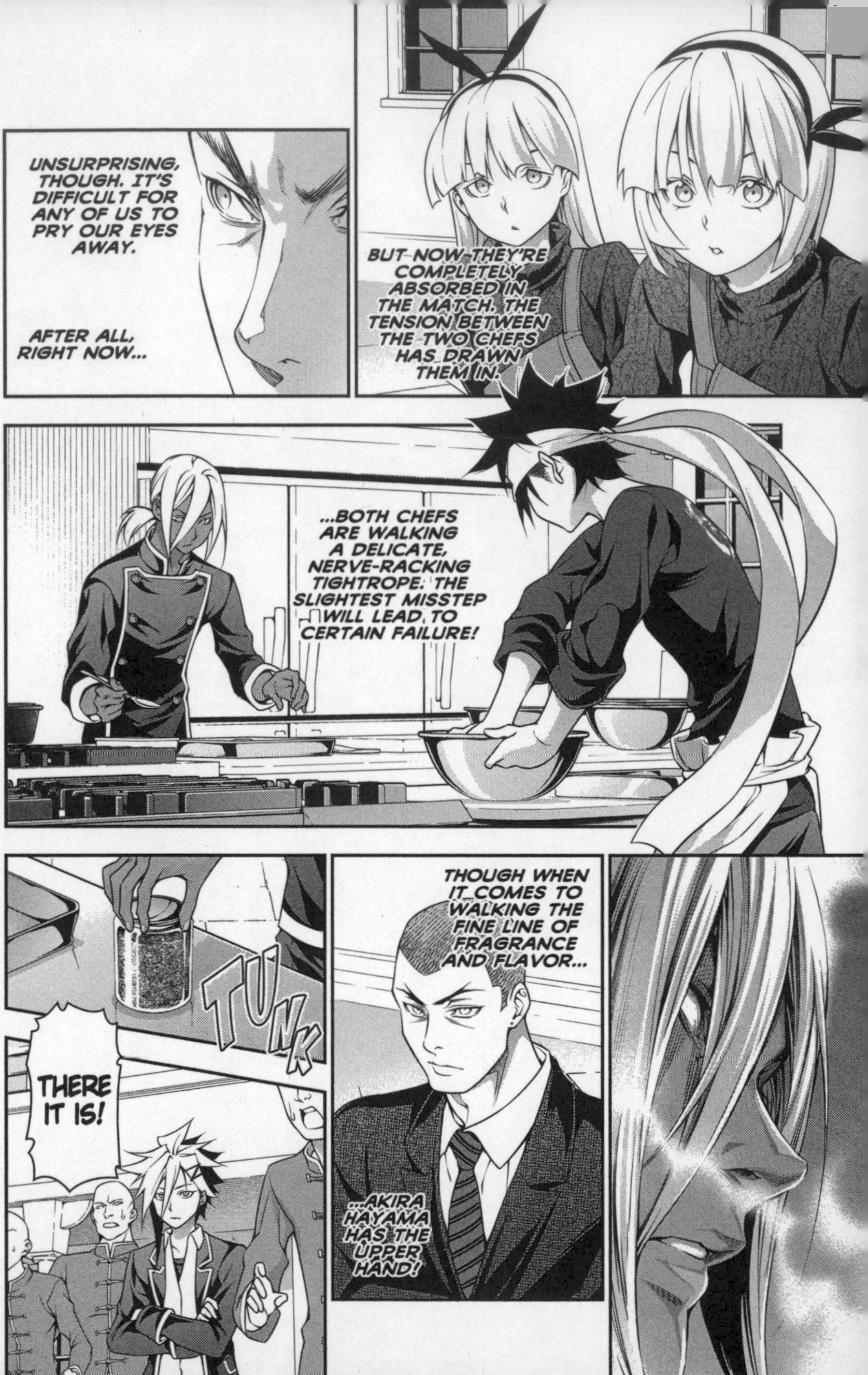
BUT NOW THEY'RE COMPLETELY ABSORBED IN THE MATCH. THE TENSION BETWEEN THE TWO CHEFS HAS DRAWN THEM IN.
UNSURPRISING, THOUGH. IT'S DIFFICULT FOR ANY OF US TO PRY OUR EYES AWAY.
AFTER ALL, RIGHT NOW...
...BOTH CHEFS ARE WALKING A DELICATE, NERVE-RACKING TIGHTROPE. THE SLIGHTEST MISSTEP WILL LEAD TO CERTAIN FAILURE!
THOUGH WHEN IT COMES TO WALKING THE FINE LINE OF FRAGRANCE AND FLAVOR...
...AKIRA HAYAMA HAS THE UPPER HAND!
TUNK
THERE IT IS!

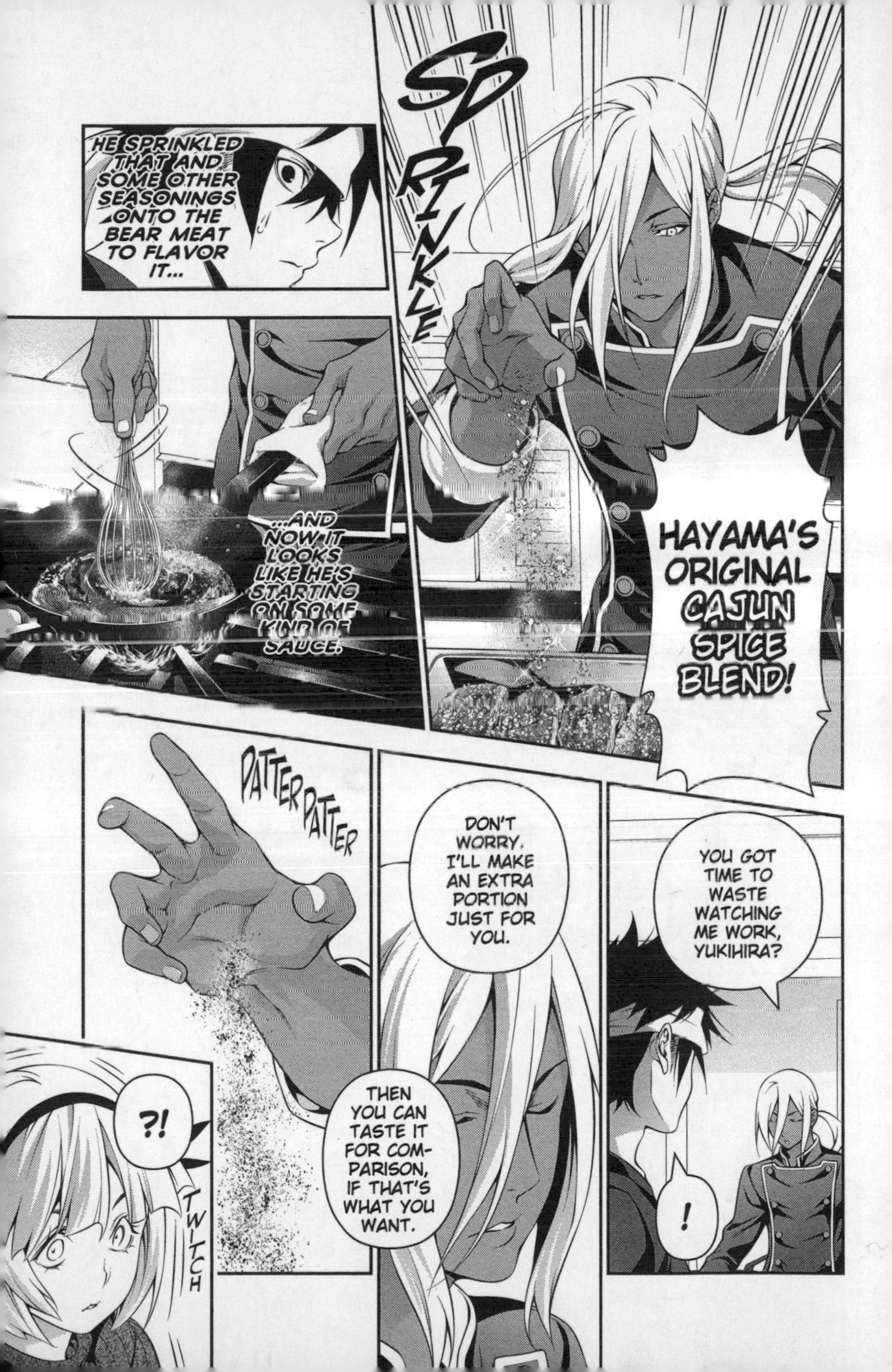
SPRINKLE
HAYAMA'S ORIGINAL CAJUN SPICE BLEND!
HE SPRINKLED THAT AND SOME OTHER SEASONINGS ONTO THE BEAR MEAT TO FLAVOR IT...
...AND NOW IT LOOKS LIKE HE'S STARTING ON SOME KIND OF SAUCE.
YOU GOT TIME TO WASTE WATCHING ME WORK, YUKIHIRA?
!
DON'T WORRY. I'LL MAKE AN EXTRA PORTION JUST FOR YOU.
THEN YOU CAN TASTE IT FOR COM-PARISON, IF THAT'S WHAT YOU WANT.
PATTER PATTER
?!
TWITCH

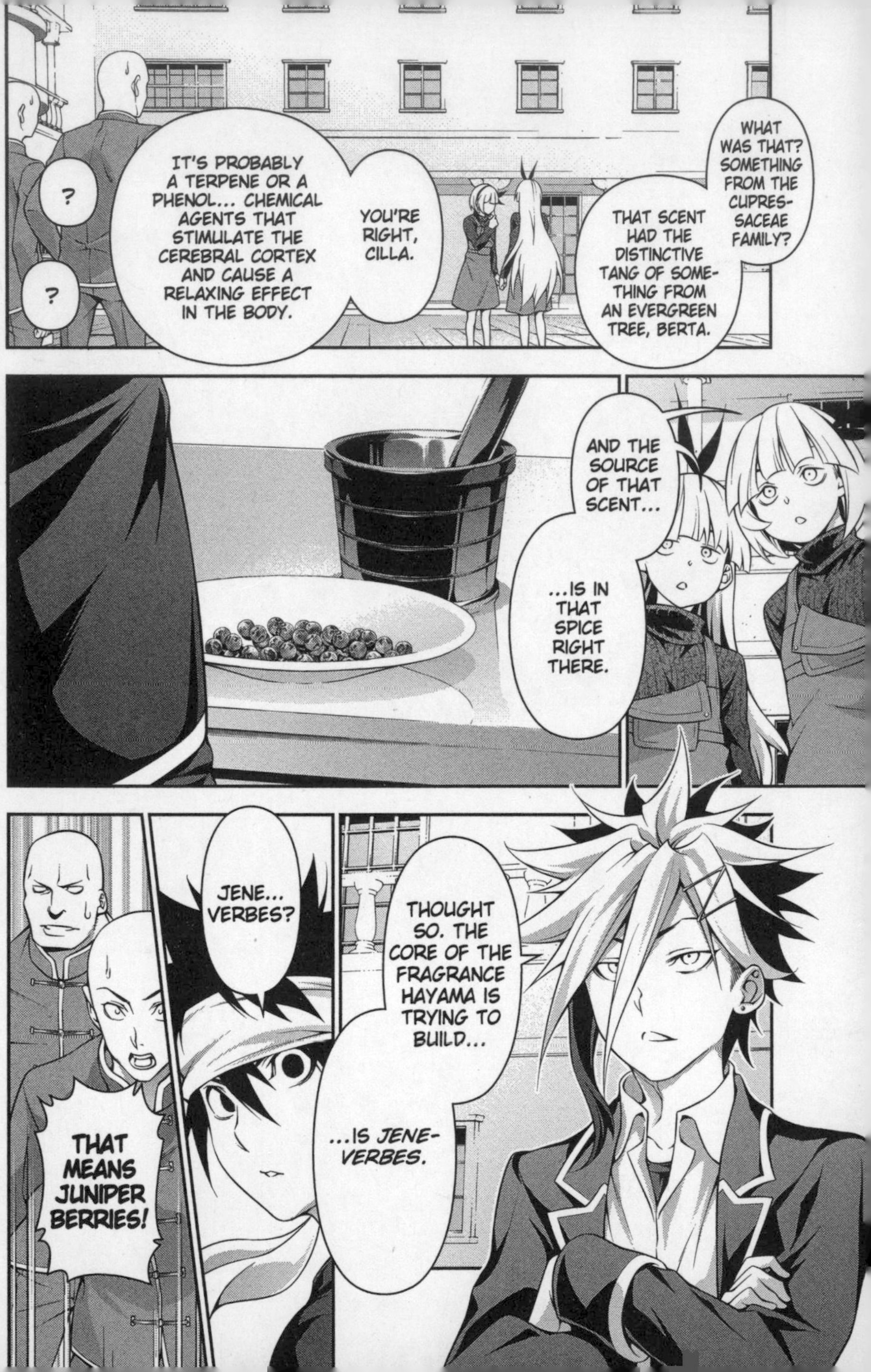

WHAT WAS THAT? SOMETHING FROM THE CUPRES-SACEAE FAMILY?
THAT SCENT HAD THE DISTINCTIVE TANG OF SOME-THING FROM AN EVERGREEN TREE, BERTA.
YOU'RE RIGHT, CILLA.
IT'S PROBABLY A TERPENE OR A PHENOL... CHEMICAL AGENTS THAT STIMULATE THE CEREBRAL CORTEX AND CAUSE A RELAXING EFFECT IN THE BODY.
?
?
AND THE SOURCE OF THAT SCENT...
...IS IN THAT SPICE RIGHT THERE.
THOUGHT SO. THE CORE OF THE FRAGRANCE HAYAMA IS TRYING TO BUILD...
...IS JENE-VERBES.
JENE... VERBES?
THAT MEANS JUNIPER BERRIES!

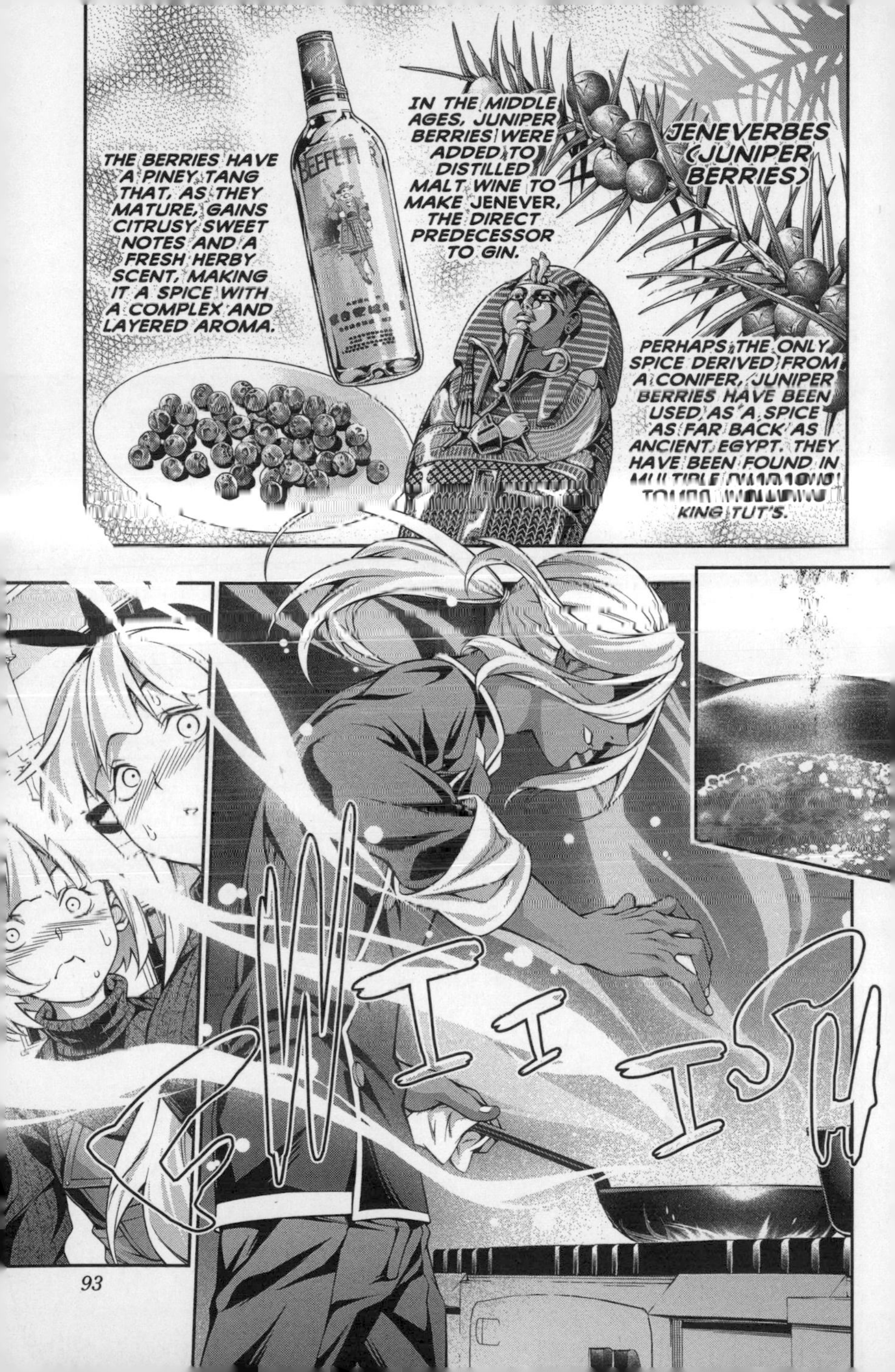
JENEVERBES (JUNIPER BERRIES)
IN THE MIDDLE AGES, JUNIPER BERRIES WERE ADDED TO DISTILLED MALT WINE TO MAKE JENEVER, THE DIRECT PREDECESSOR TO GIN.
THE BERRIES HAVE A PINEY TANG THAT, AS THEY MATURE, GAINS CITRUSY SWEET NOTES AND A FRESH HERBY SCENT, MAKING IT A SPICE WITH A COMPLEX AND LAYERED AROMA.
BEEFEATER
PERHAPS THE ONLY SPICE DERIVED FROM A CONIFER, JUNIPER BERRIES HAVE BEEN USED AS A SPICE AS FAR BACK AS ANCIENT EGYPT. THEY HAVE BEEN FOUND IN
KING TUT'S.
SWIIISH

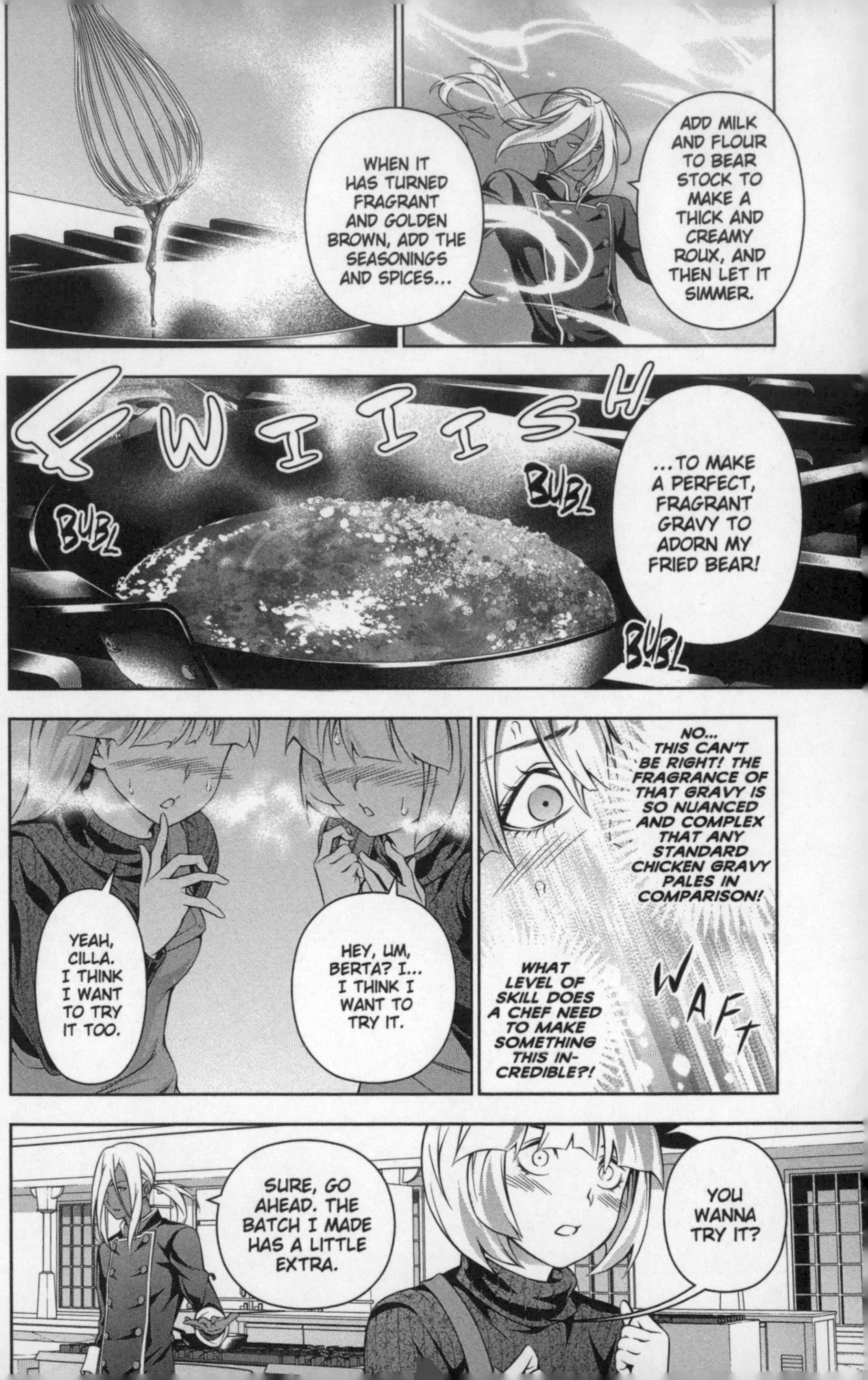
ADD MILK AND FLOUR TO BEAR STOCK TO MAKE A THICK AND CREAMY ROUX, AND THEN LET IT SIMMER.
WHEN IT HAS TURNED FRAGRANT AND GOLDEN BROWN, ADD THE SEASONINGS AND SPICES...
FWIIISH
...TO MAKE A PERFECT, FRAGRANT GRAVY TO ADORN MY FRIED BEAR!
BUBL
BUBL
BUBL
NO... THIS CAN'T BE RIGHT! THE FRAGRANCE OF THAT GRAVY IS SO NUANCED AND COMPLEX THAT ANY STANDARD CHICKEN GRAVY PALES IN COMPARISON!
WAFT
WHAT LEVEL OF SKILL DOES A CHEF NEED TO MAKE SOMETHING THIS IN-CREDIBLE?!
HEY, UM, BERTA? I... I THINK I WANT TO TRY IT.
YEAH, CILLA. I THINK I WANT TO TRY IT TOO.
YOU WANNA TRY IT?
SURE, GO AHEAD. THE BATCH I MADE HAS A LITTLE EXTRA.

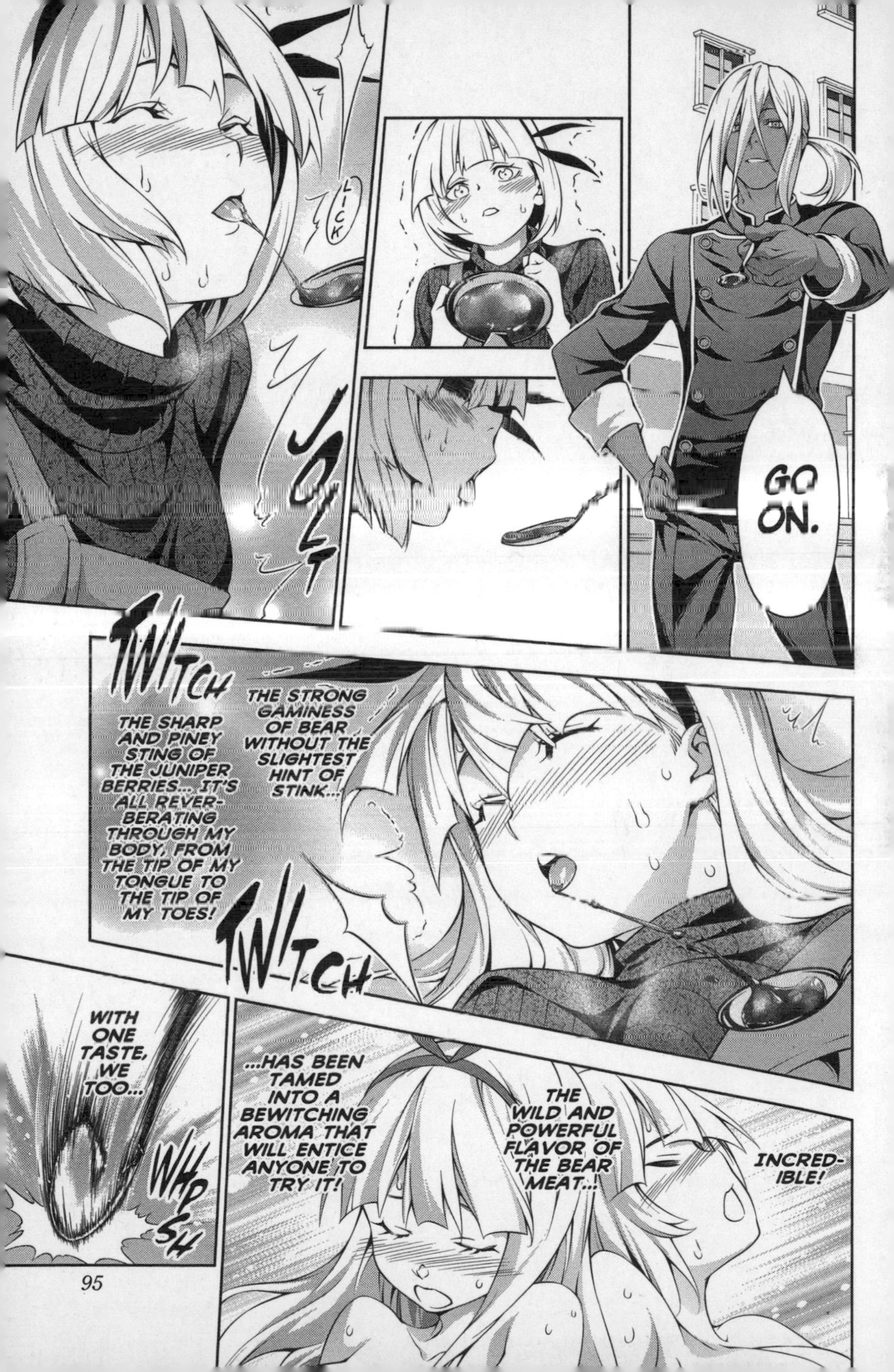
GO ON.
JOLT
LICK
THE STRONG GAMINESS OF BEAR WITHOUT THE SLIGHTEST HINT OF STINK...
TWITCH
THE SHARP AND PINEY STING OF THE JUNIPER BERRIES... IT'S ALL REVER-BERATING THROUGH MY BODY, FROM THE TIP OF MY TONGUE TO THE TIP OF MY TOES!
TWITCH
INCRED-IBLE!
THE WILD AND POWERFUL FLAVOR OF THE BEAR MEAT...!
...HAS BEEN TAMED INTO A BEWITCHING AROMA THAT WILL ENTICE ANYONE TO TRY IT!
WITH ONE TASTE, WE TOO...
WHPSH

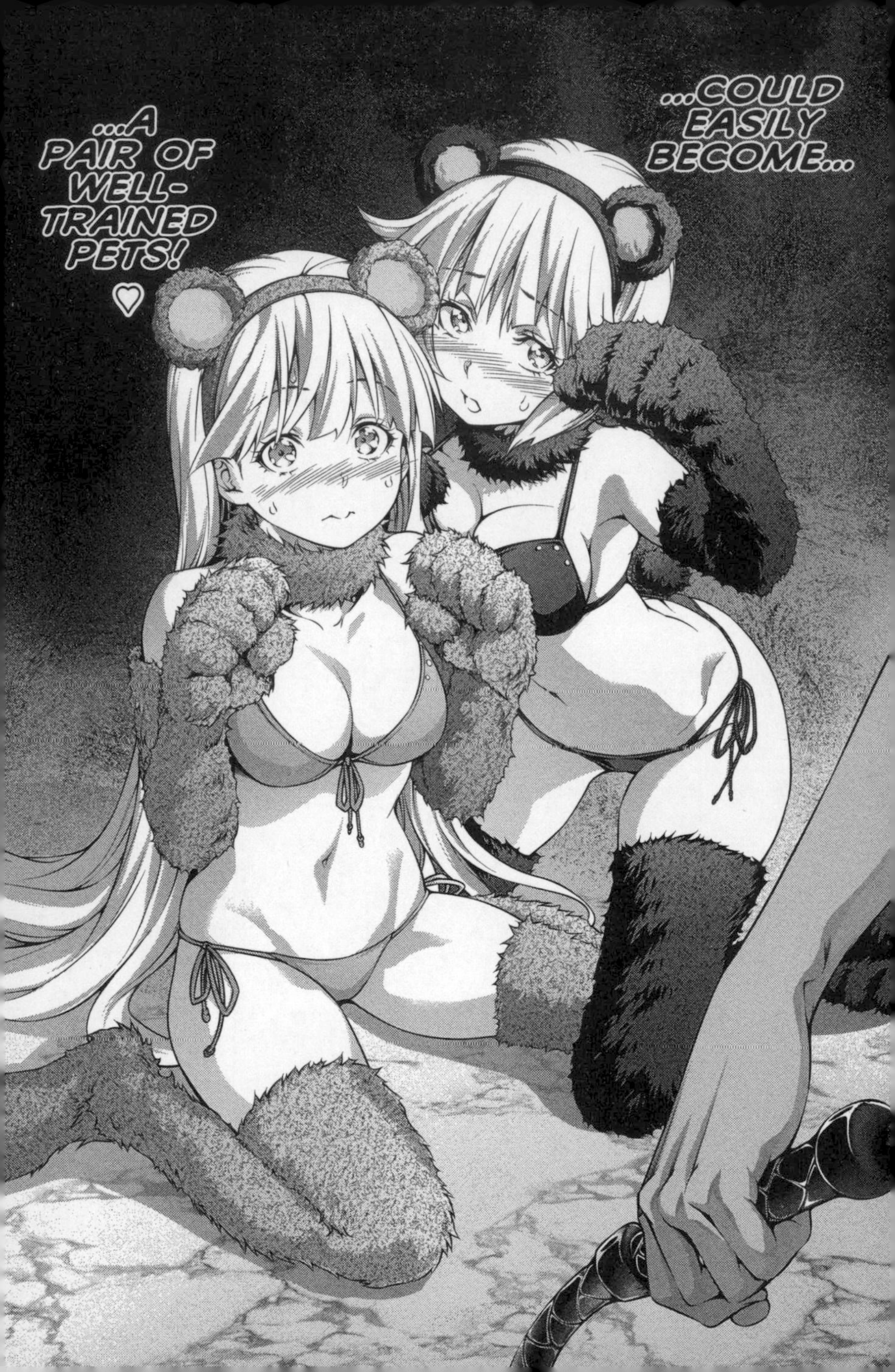
...COULD EASILY BECOME...
...A PAIR OF WELL-TRAINED PETS! ♥

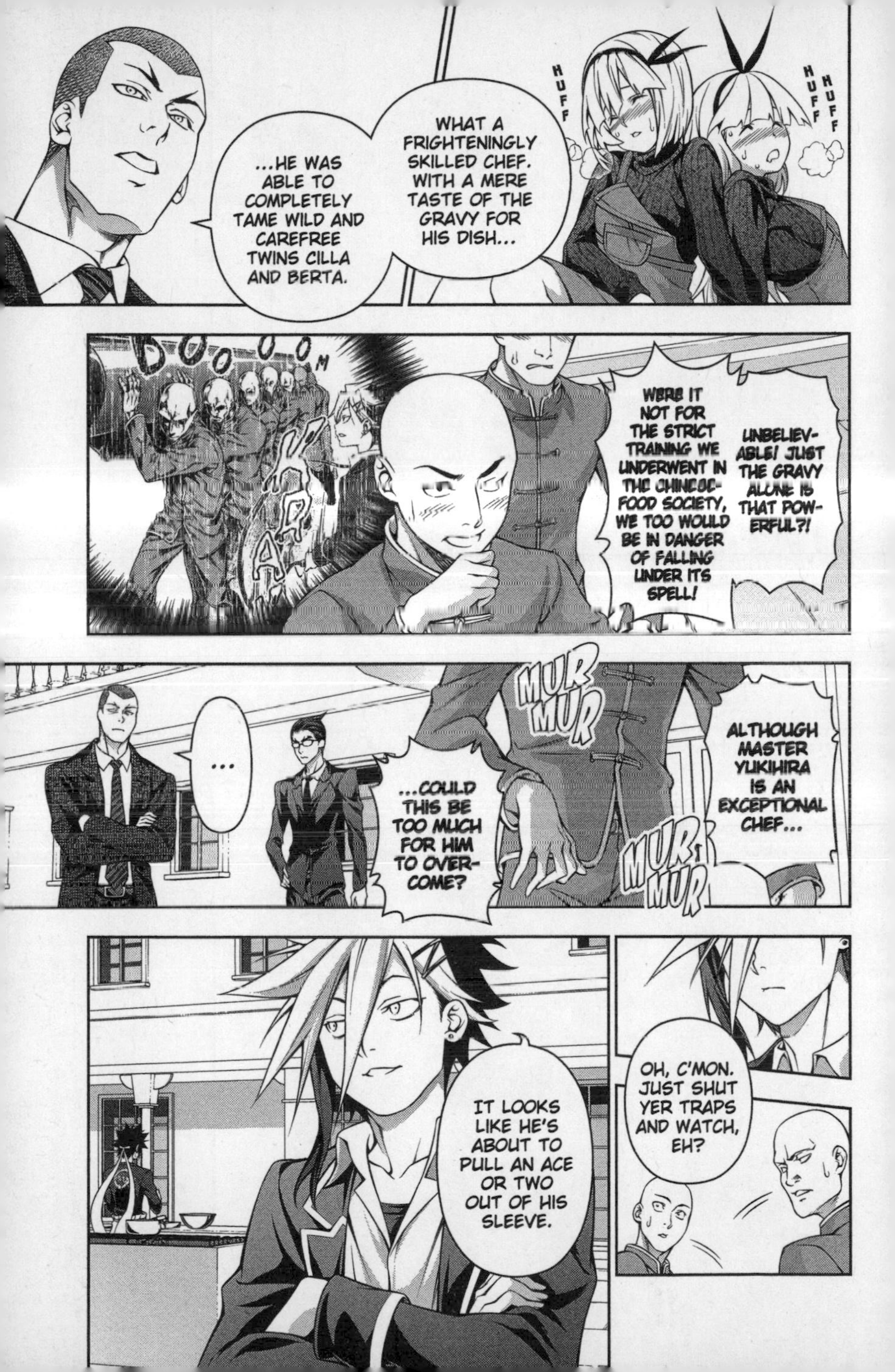
HUFF
HUFF HUFF
WHAT A FRIGHTENINGLY SKILLED CHEF. WITH A MERE TASTE OF THE GRAVY FOR HIS DISH...
...HE WAS ABLE TO COMPLETELY TAME WILD AND CAREFREE TWINS CILLA AND BERTA.
UNBELIEV-ABLE! JUST THE GRAVY ALONE IS THAT POW-ERFUL?!
WERE IT NOT FOR THE STRICT TRAINING WE UNDERWENT IN THE CHINESE-FOOD SOCIETY, WE TOO WOULD BE IN DANGER OF FALLING UNDER ITS SPELL!
BOOOOOM
ALTHOUGH MASTER YUKIHIRA IS AN EXCEPTIONAL CHEF...
MUR MUR
MUR MUR
...COULD THIS BE TOO MUCH FOR HIM TO OVER-COME?
...
OH, C'MON. JUST SHUT YER TRAPS AND WATCH, EH?
IT LOOKS LIKE HE'S ABOUT TO PULL AN ACE OR TWO OUT OF HIS SLEEVE.

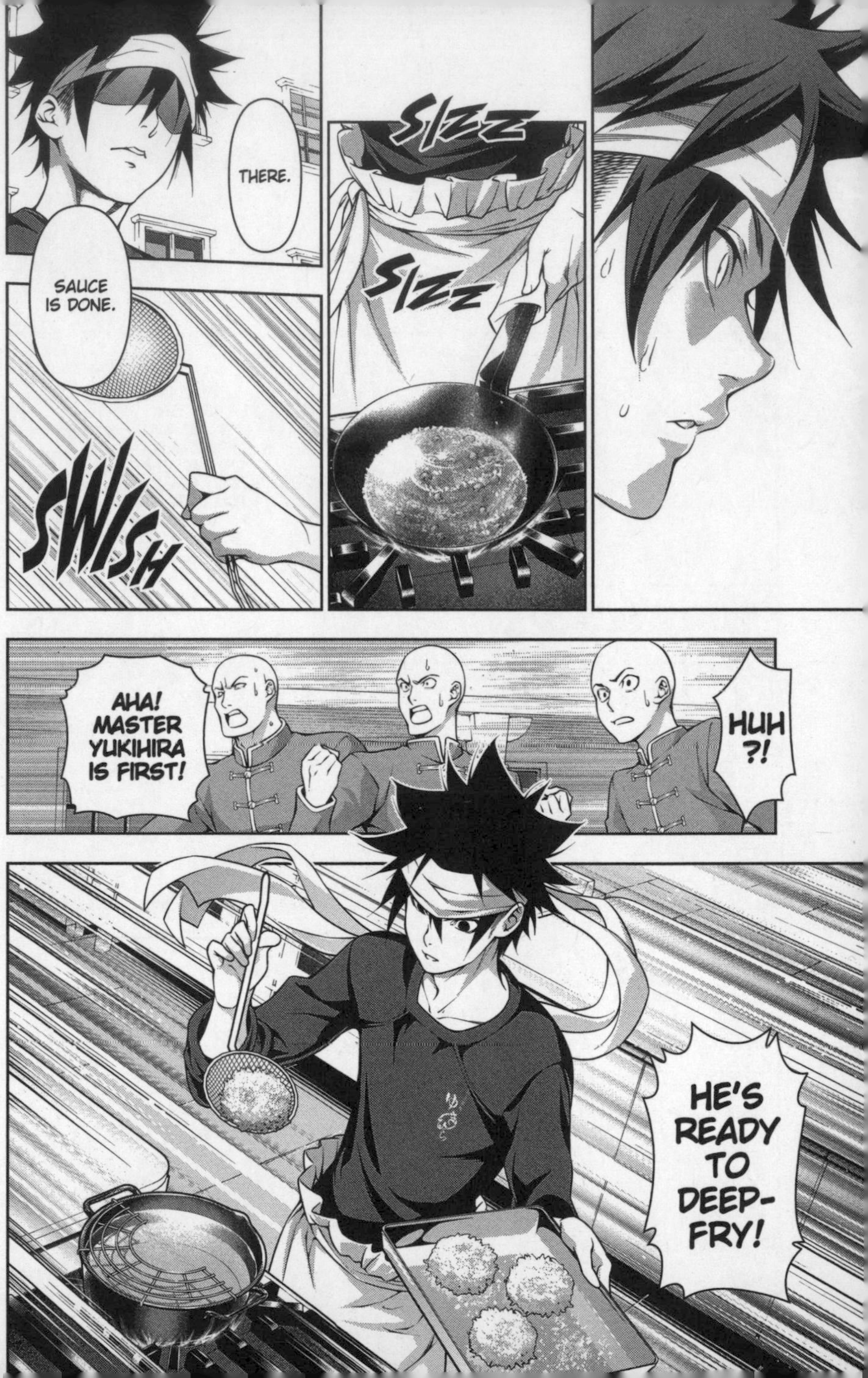
SIZZ
SIZZ
THERE.
SAUCE IS DONE.
SWISH
HUH?!
AHA! MASTER YUKIHIRA IS FIRST!
HE'S READY TO DEEP-FRY!

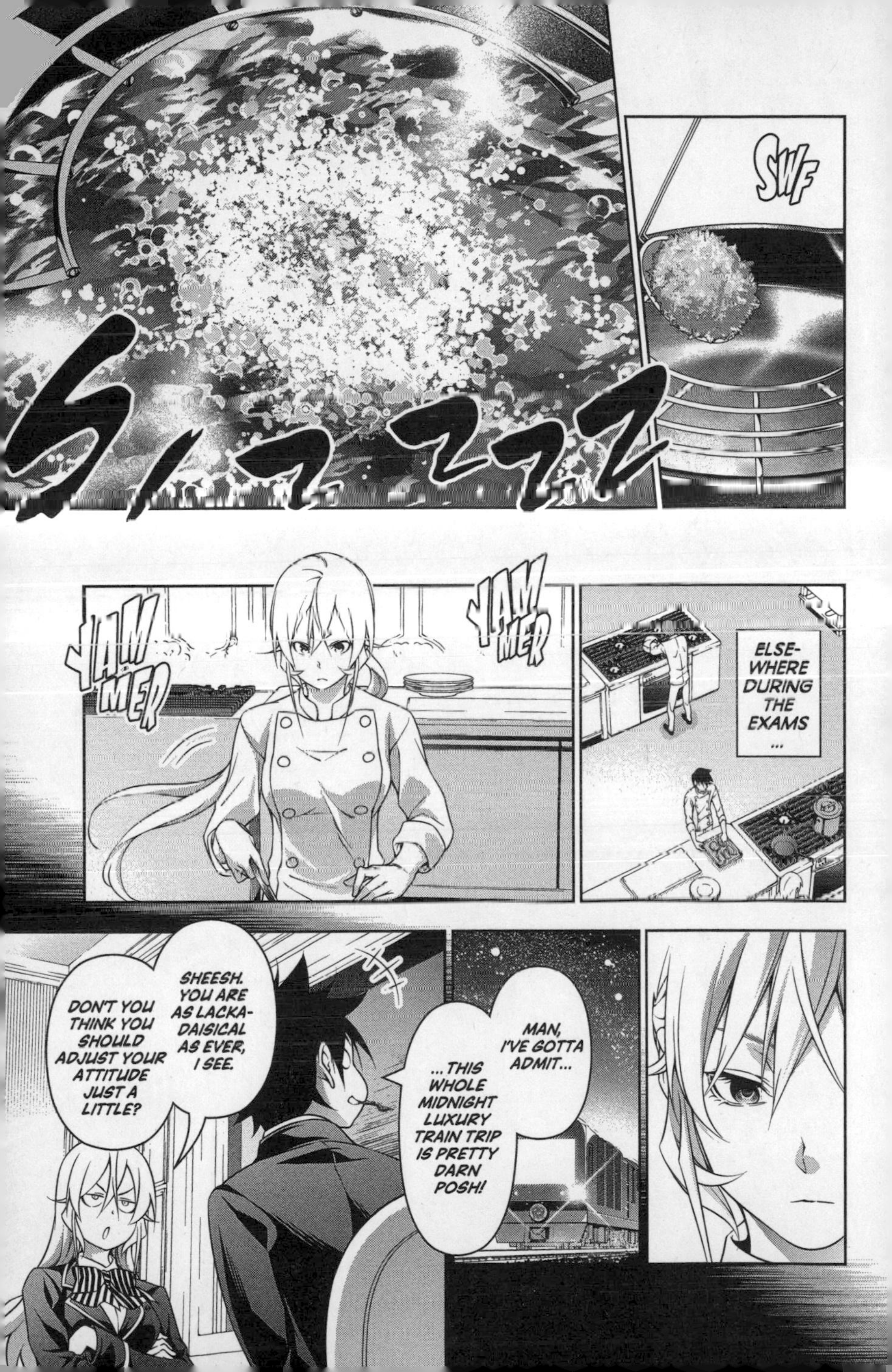
SWF
ELSE-WHERE DURING THE EXAMS ...
HAMMER
HAMMER
MAN, I'VE GOTTA ADMIT...
...THIS WHOLE MIDNIGHT LUXURY TRAIN TRIP IS PRETTY DARN POSH!
SHEESH. YOU ARE AS LACKADAISICAL AS EVER, I SEE.
DON'T YOU THINK YOU SHOULD ADJUST YOUR ATTITUDE JUST A LITTLE?

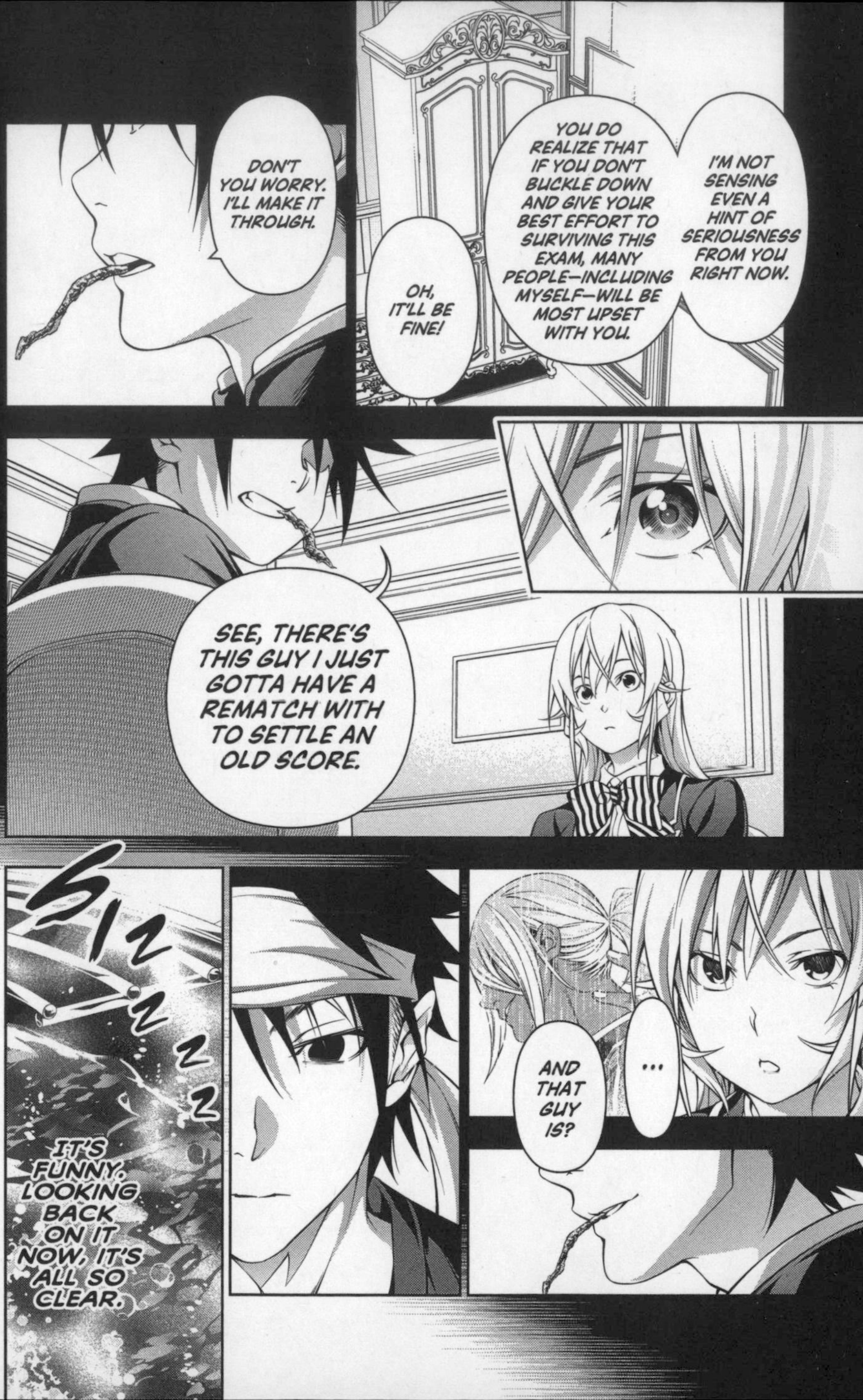

I'M NOT SENSING EVEN A HINT OF SERIOUSNESS FROM YOU RIGHT NOW.
YOU DO REALIZE THAT IF YOU DON'T BUCKLE DOWN AND GIVE YOUR BEST EFFORT TO SURVIVING THIS EXAM, MANY PEOPLE—INCLUDING MYSELF—WILL BE MOST UPSET WITH YOU.
OH, IT'LL BE FINE!
DON'T YOU WORRY. I'LL MAKE IT THROUGH.
SEE, THERE'S THIS GUY I JUST GOTTA HAVE A REMATCH WITH TO SETTLE AN OLD SCORE.
...
AND THAT GUY IS?
SIZZZZZ
IT'S FUNNY. LOOKING BACK ON IT NOW, IT'S ALL SO CLEAR.

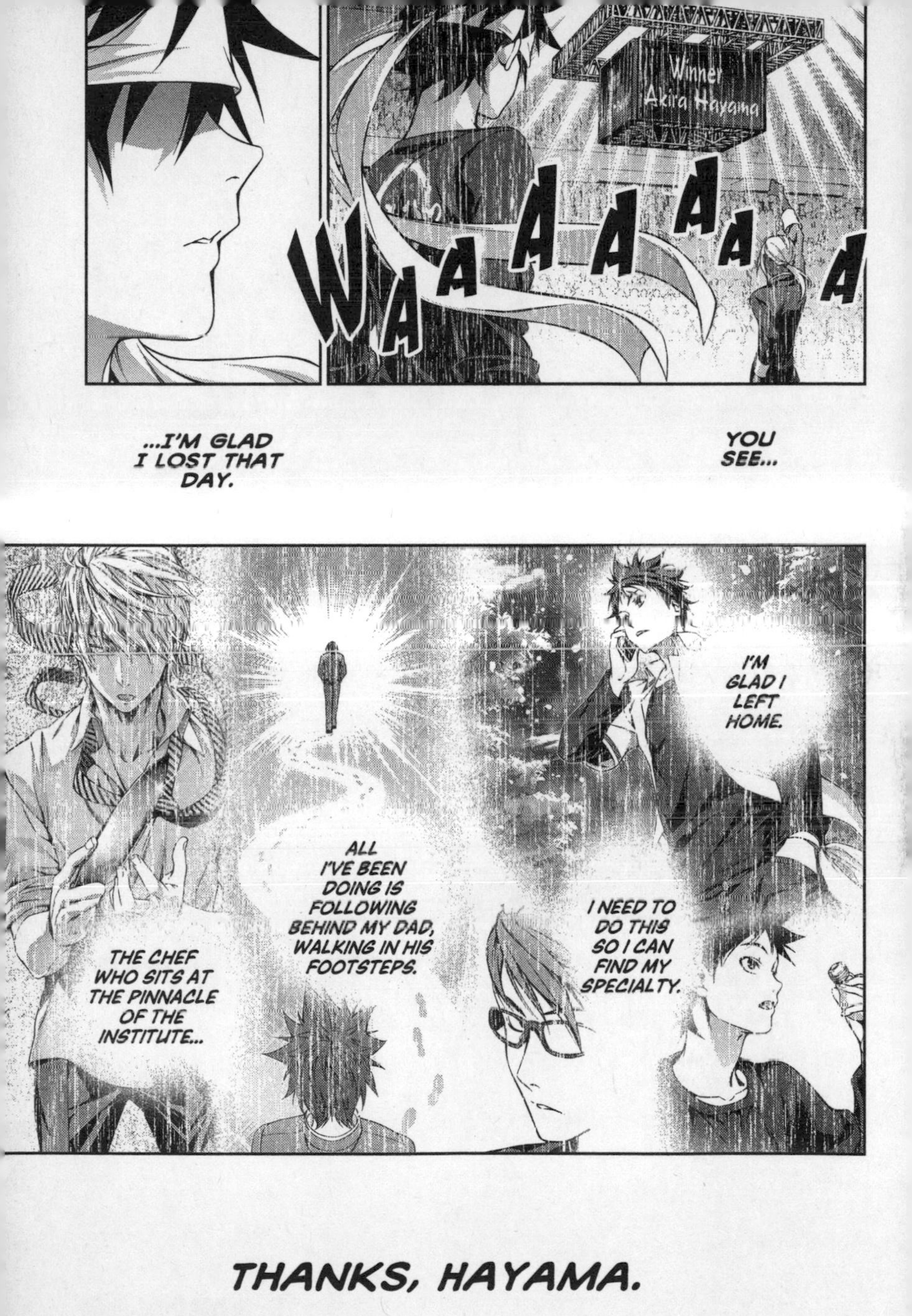
Winner Akira Hayama
WAAAAAAAAA
YOU SEE...
...I'M GLAD I LOST THAT DAY.
I'M GLAD I LEFT HOME.
I NEED TO DO THIS SO I CAN FIND MY SPECIALTY.
ALL I'VE BEEN DOING IS FOLLOWING BEHIND MY DAD, WALKING IN HIS FOOTSTEPS.
THE CHEF WHO SITS AT THE PINNACLE OF THE INSTITUTE...
THANKS, HAYAMA.

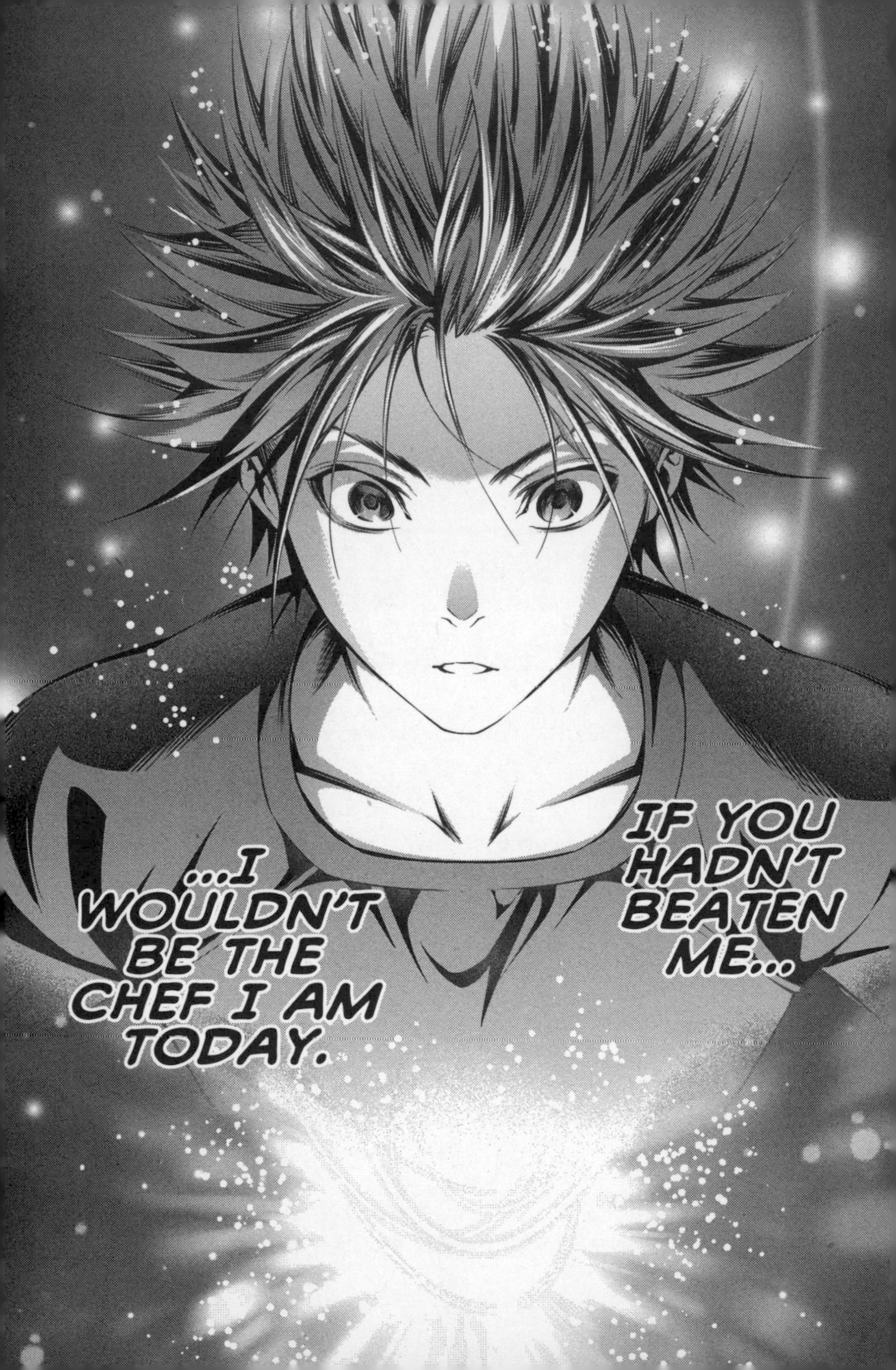
IF YOU HADN'T BEATEN ME...
...I WOULDN'T BE THE CHEF I AM TODAY.

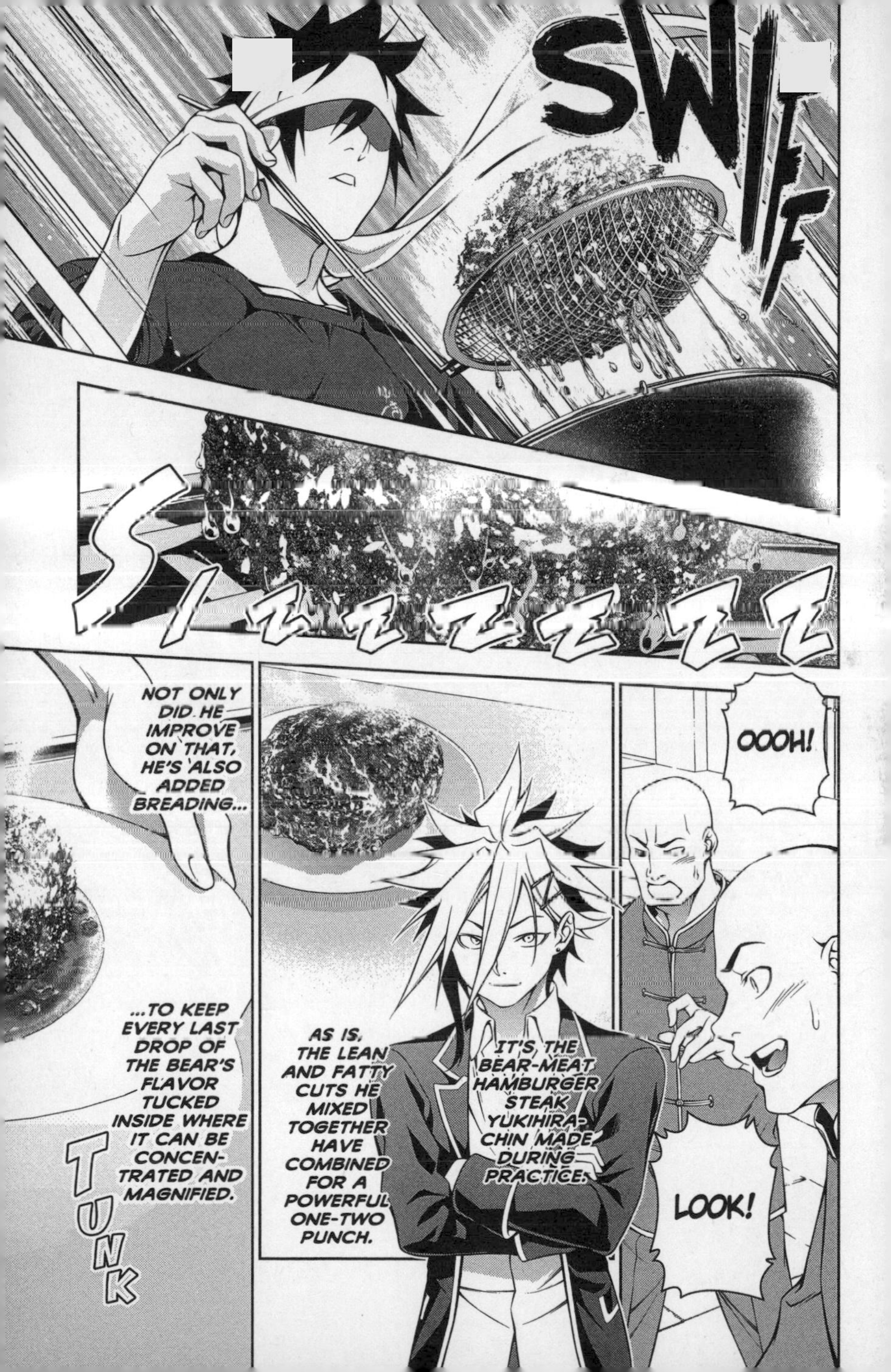
SWIFF
SIZZZZZZZ
OOOH!
LOOK!
IT'S THE BEAR-MEAT HAMBURGER STEAK YUKIHIRA-CHIN MADE DURING PRACTICE.
AS IS, THE LEAN AND FATTY CUTS HE MIXED TOGETHER HAVE COMBINED FOR A POWERFUL ONE-TWO PUNCH.
NOT ONLY DID HE IMPROVE ON THAT, HE'S ALSO ADDED BREADING...
...TO KEEP EVERY LAST DROP OF THE BEAR'S FLAVOR TUCKED INSIDE WHERE IT CAN BE CONCENTRATED AND MAGNIFIED.
TUNK

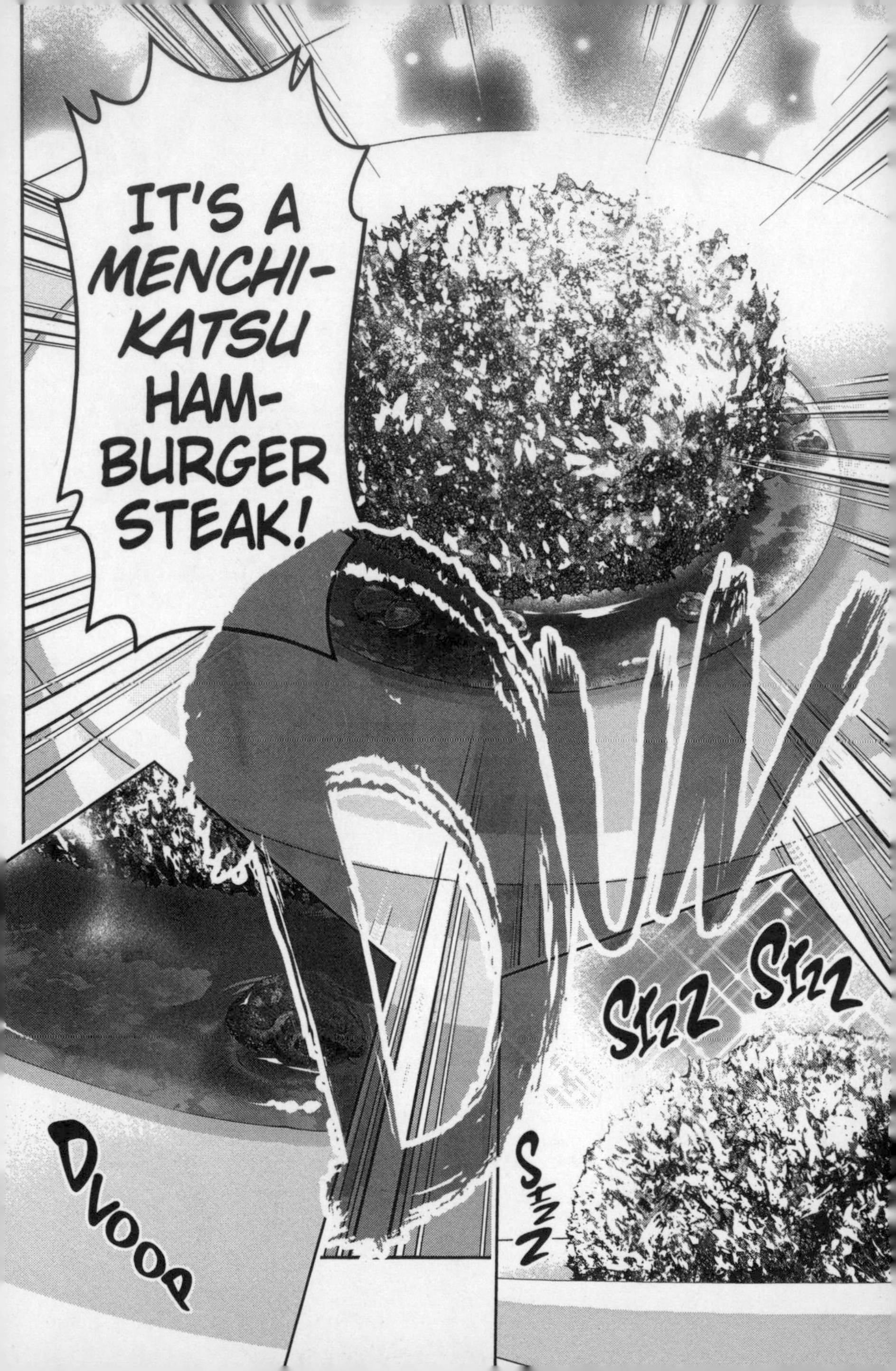
IT'S A MENCHI-KATSU HAM-BURGER STEAK!
SIZZ SIZZ
SIZZ
DVOOP

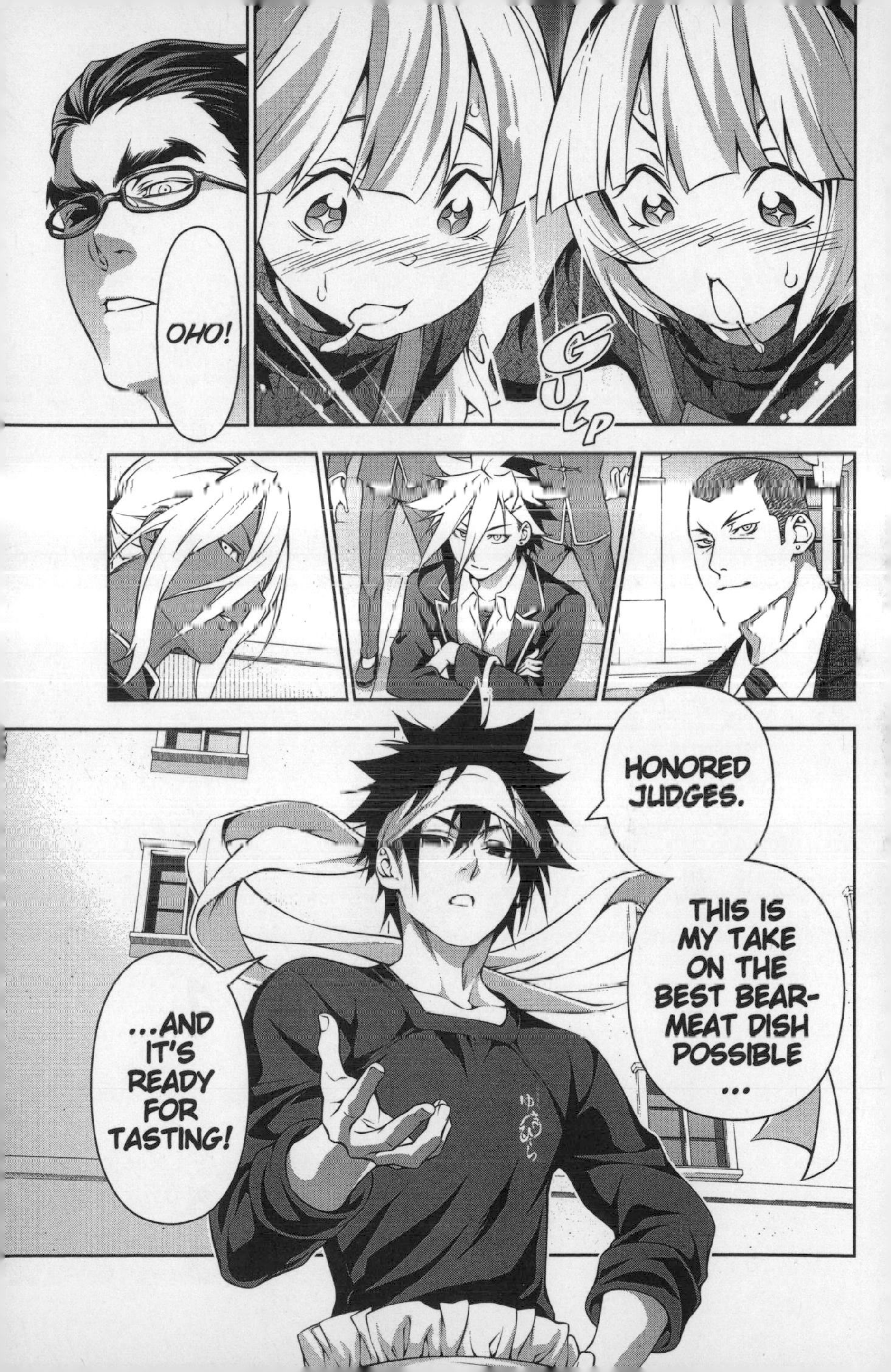
GULP
OHO!
HONORED JUDGES.
THIS IS MY TAKE ON THE BEST BEAR-MEAT DISH POSSIBLE ...
...AND IT'S READY FOR TASTING!

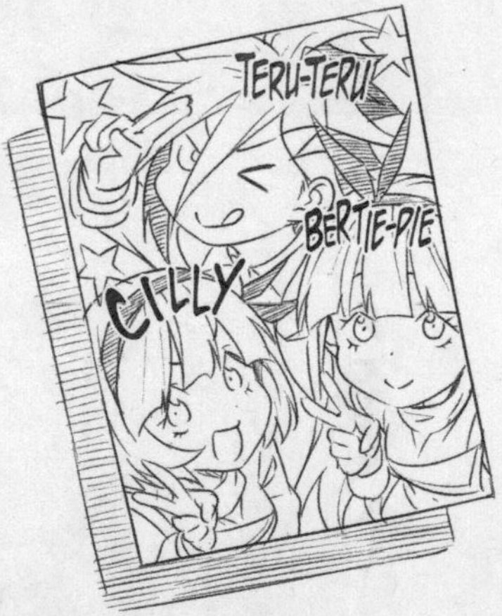
TERU-TERU
BERTIE-PIE
CILLY

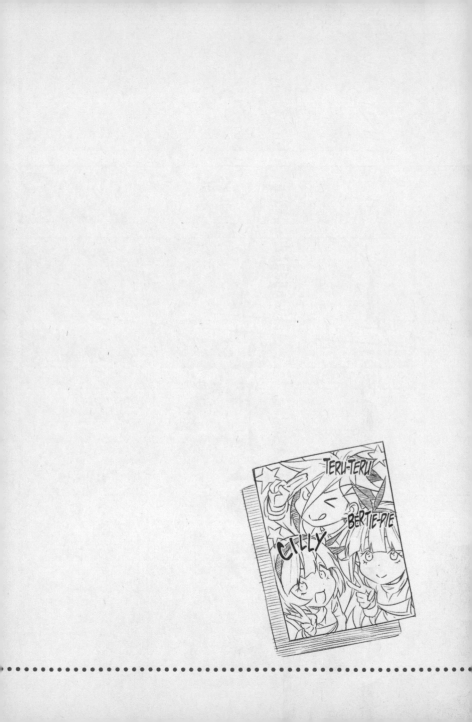

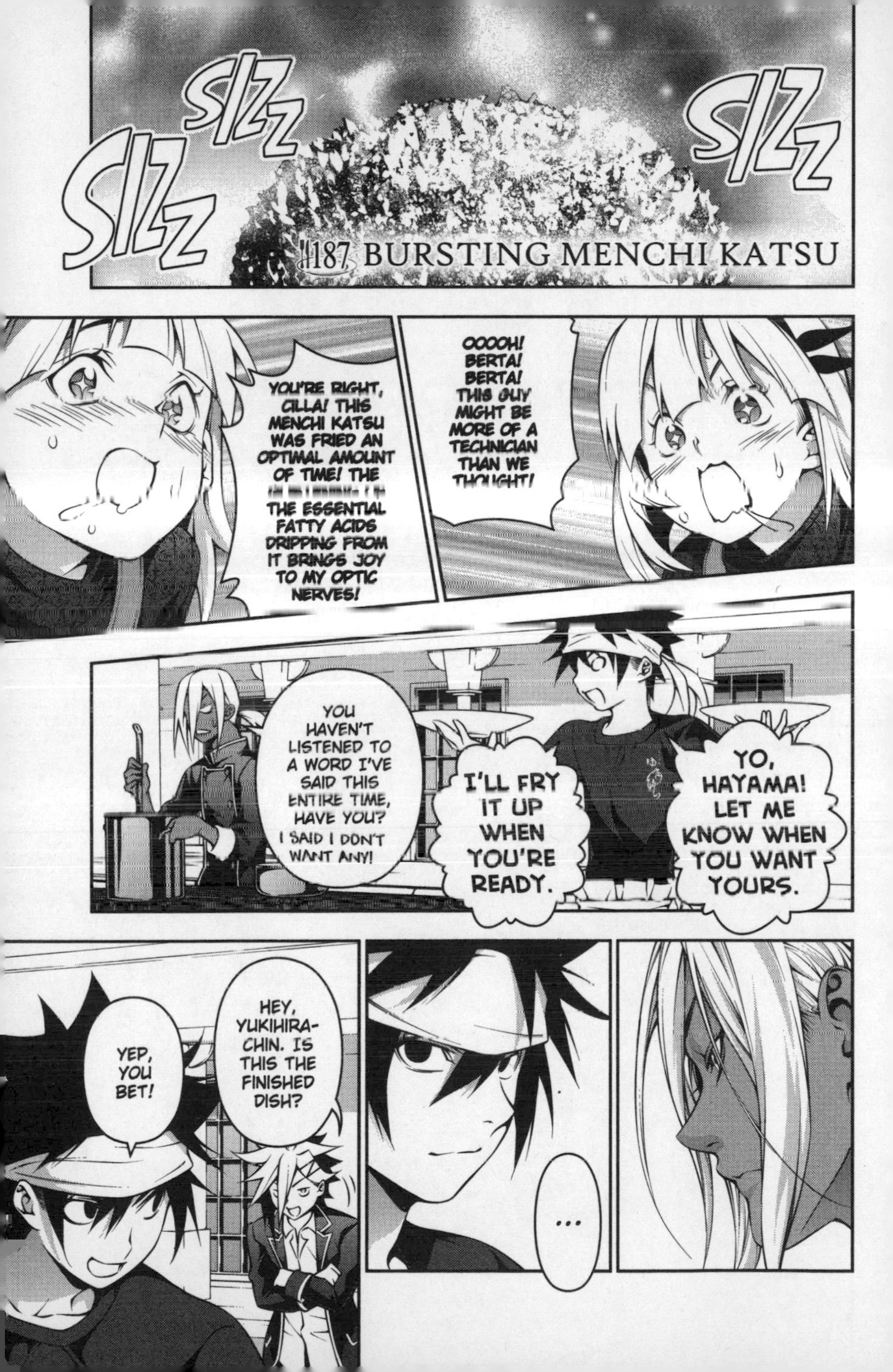
SIZZ
SIZZ
SIZZ
#187 BURSTING MENCHI KATSU
OOOOH! BERTA! BERTA! THIS GUY MIGHT BE MORE OF A TECHNICIAN THAN WE THOUGHT!
YOU'RE RIGHT, CILLA! THIS MENCHI KATSU WAS FRIED AN OPTIMAL AMOUNT OF TIME! THE THE ESSENTIAL FATTY ACIDS DRIPPING FROM IT BRINGS JOY TO MY OPTIC NERVES!
YO, HAYAMA! LET ME KNOW WHEN YOU WANT YOURS.
I'LL FRY IT UP WHEN YOU'RE READY.
YOU HAVEN'T LISTENED TO A WORD I'VE SAID THIS ENTIRE TIME, HAVE YOU?
I SAID I DON'T WANT ANY!
...
HEY, YUKIHIRA-CHIN. IS THIS THE FINISHED DISH?
YEP, YOU BET!

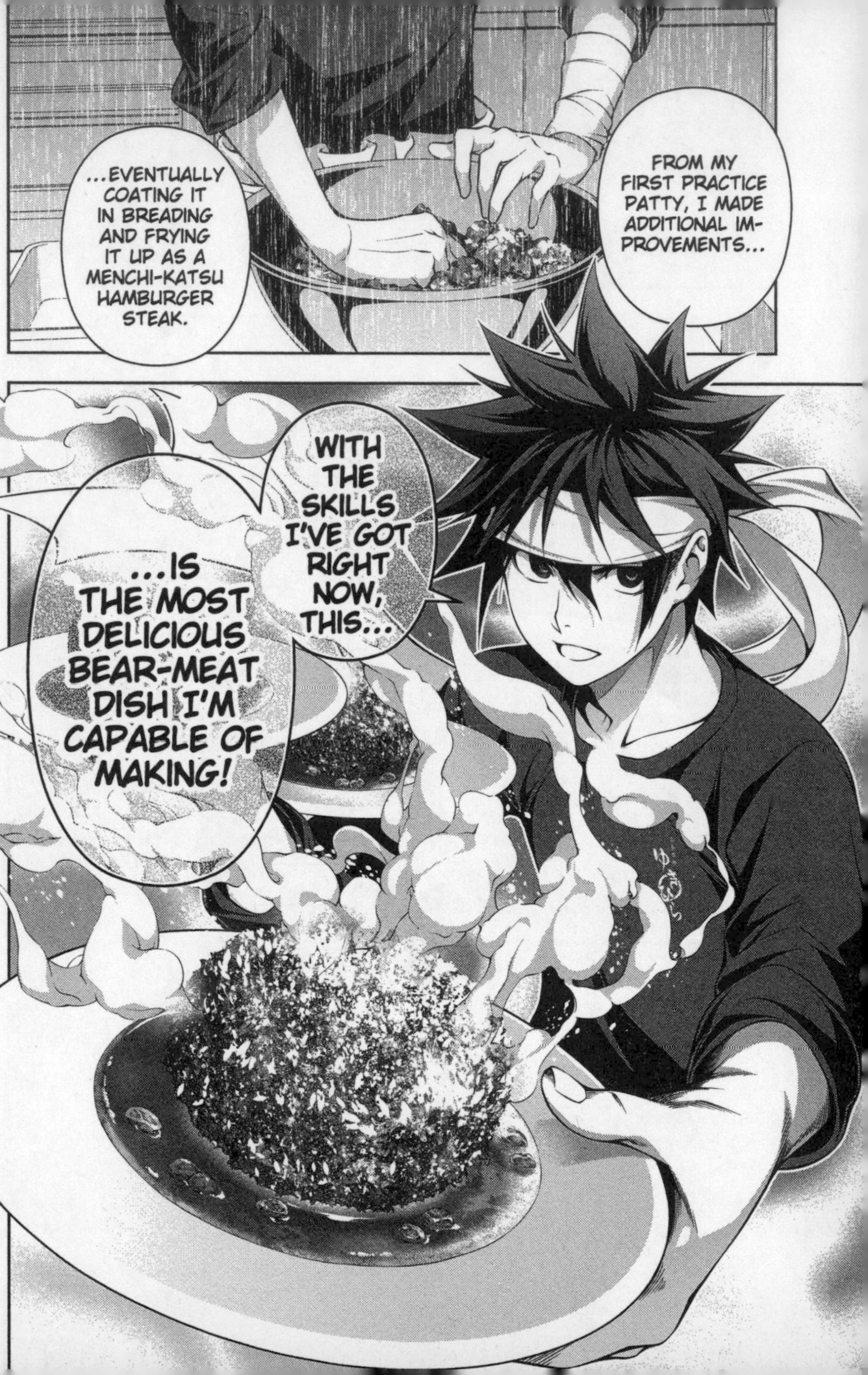
FROM MY FIRST PRACTICE PATTY, I MADE ADDITIONAL IM-PROVEMENTS...
...EVENTUALLY COATING IT IN BREADING AND FRYING IT UP AS A MENCHI-KATSU HAMBURGER STEAK.
WITH THE SKILLS I'VE GOT RIGHT NOW, THIS...
...IS THE MOST DELICIOUS BEAR-MEAT DISH I'M CAPABLE OF MAKING!

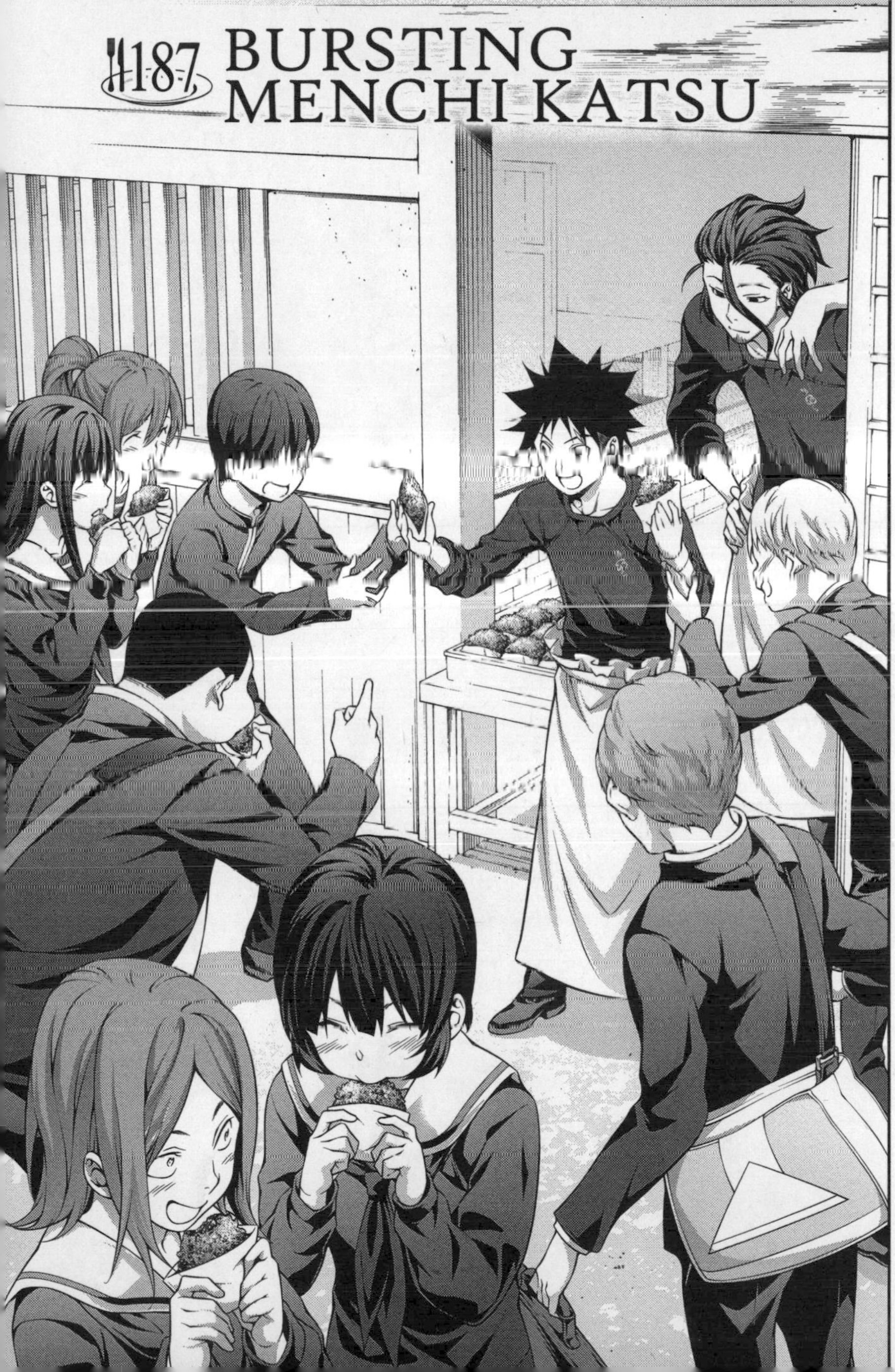
187
BURSTING
MENCHI KATSU

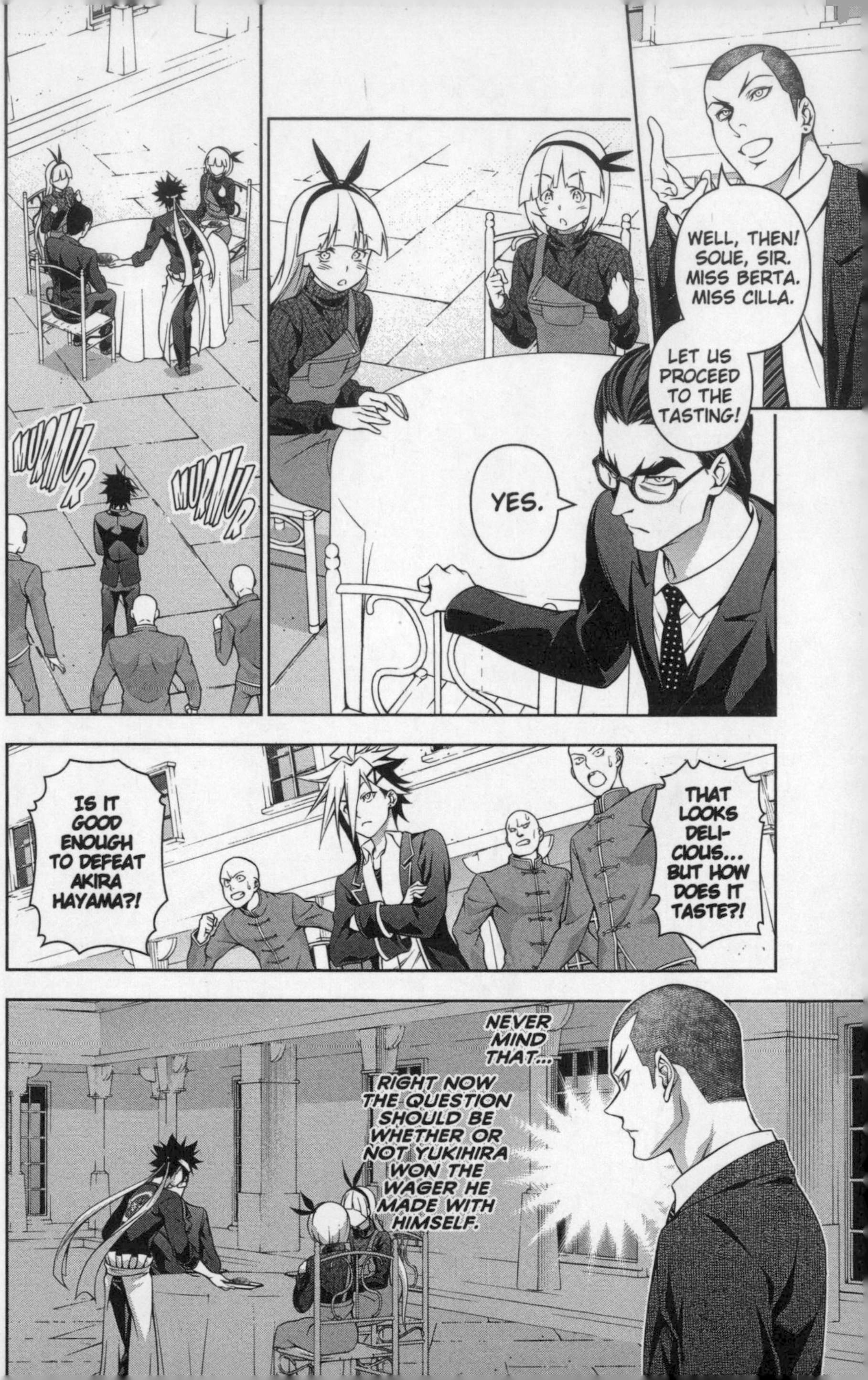
WELL, THEN! SOUE, SIR. MISS BERTA. MISS CILLA.
LET US PROCEED TO THE TASTING!
YES.
MURMUR
MURMUR
THAT LOOKS DELI-CIOUS... BUT HOW DOES IT TASTE?!
IS IT GOOD ENOUGH TO DEFEAT AKIRA HAYAMA?!
NEVER MIND THAT...
RIGHT NOW THE QUESTION SHOULD BE WHETHER OR NOT YUKIHIRA WON THE WAGER HE MADE WITH HIMSELF.

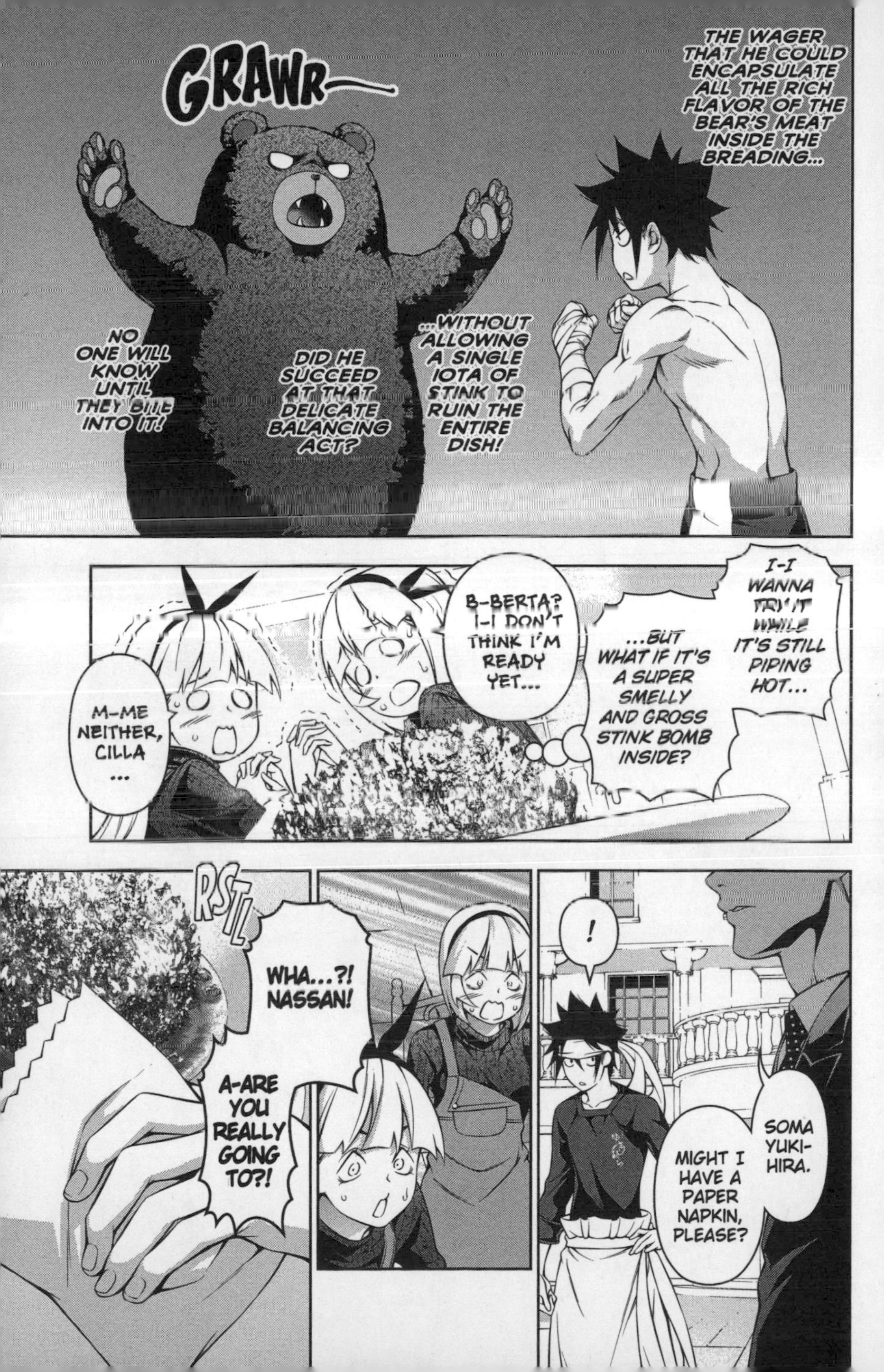
THE WAGER THAT HE COULD ENCAPSULATE ALL THE RICH FLAVOR OF THE BEAR'S MEAT INSIDE THE BREADING...
GRAWR
...WITHOUT ALLOWING A SINGLE IOTA OF STINK TO RUIN THE ENTIRE DISH!
DID HE SUCCEED AT THAT DELICATE BALANCING ACT?
NO ONE WILL KNOW UNTIL THEY BITE INTO IT!
I-I WANNA TRY IT WHILE IT'S STILL PIPING HOT...
...BUT WHAT IF IT'S A SUPER SMELLY AND GROSS STINK BOMB INSIDE?
B-BERTA? I-I DON'T THINK I'M READY YET...
M-ME NEITHER, CILLA...
!
SOMA YUKIHIRA.
MIGHT I HAVE A PAPER NAPKIN, PLEASE?
WHA...?! NASSAN!
A-ARE YOU REALLY GOING TO?!
RSTL

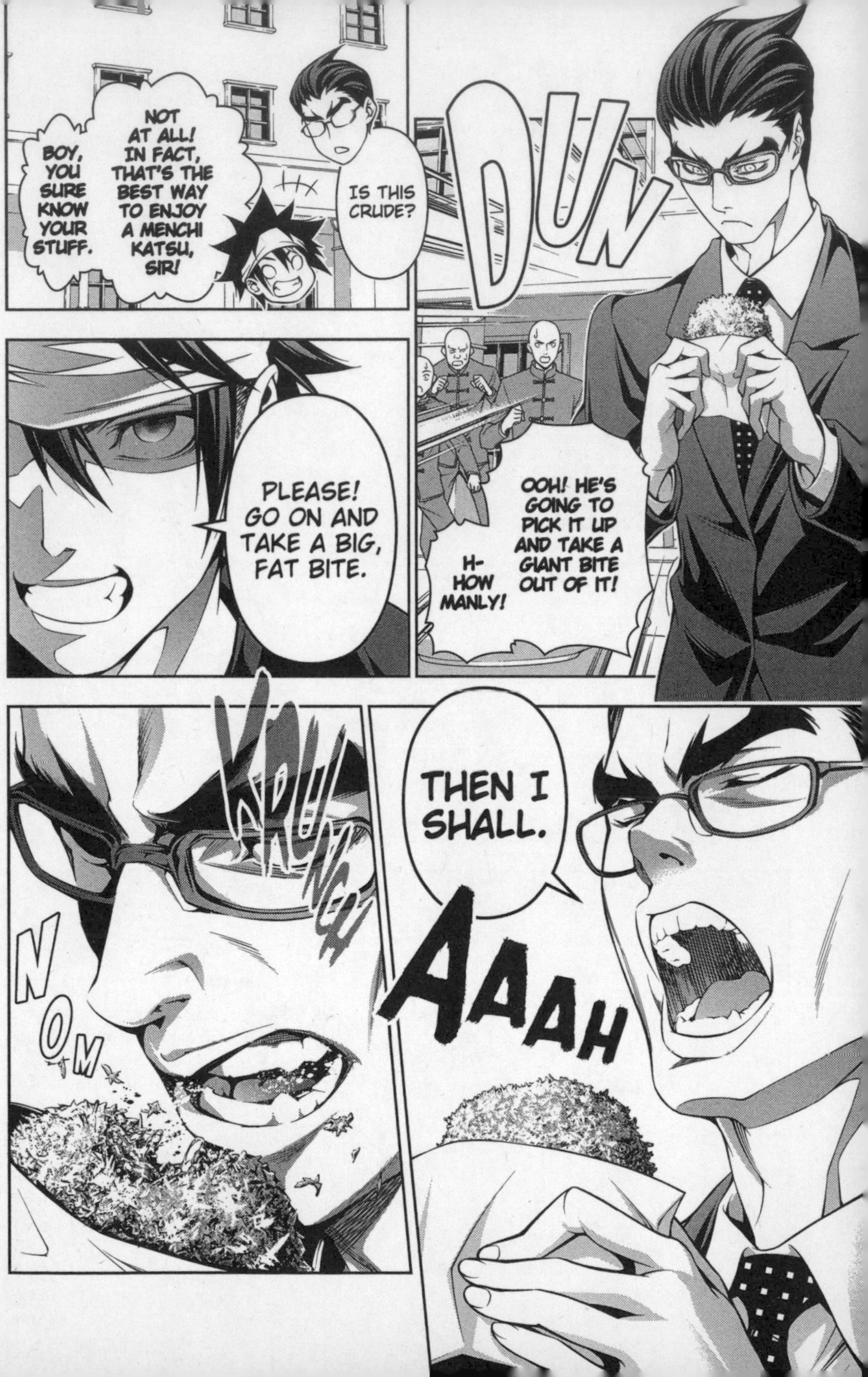
DUN
OOH! HE'S GOING TO PICK IT UP AND TAKE A GIANT BITE OUT OF IT!
H-HOW MANLY!
IS THIS CRUDE?
NOT AT ALL! IN FACT, THAT'S THE BEST WAY TO ENJOY A MENCHI KATSU, SIR!
BOY, YOU SURE KNOW YOUR STUFF.
PLEASE! GO ON AND TAKE A BIG, FAT BITE.
THEN I SHALL.
AAAH
NOM

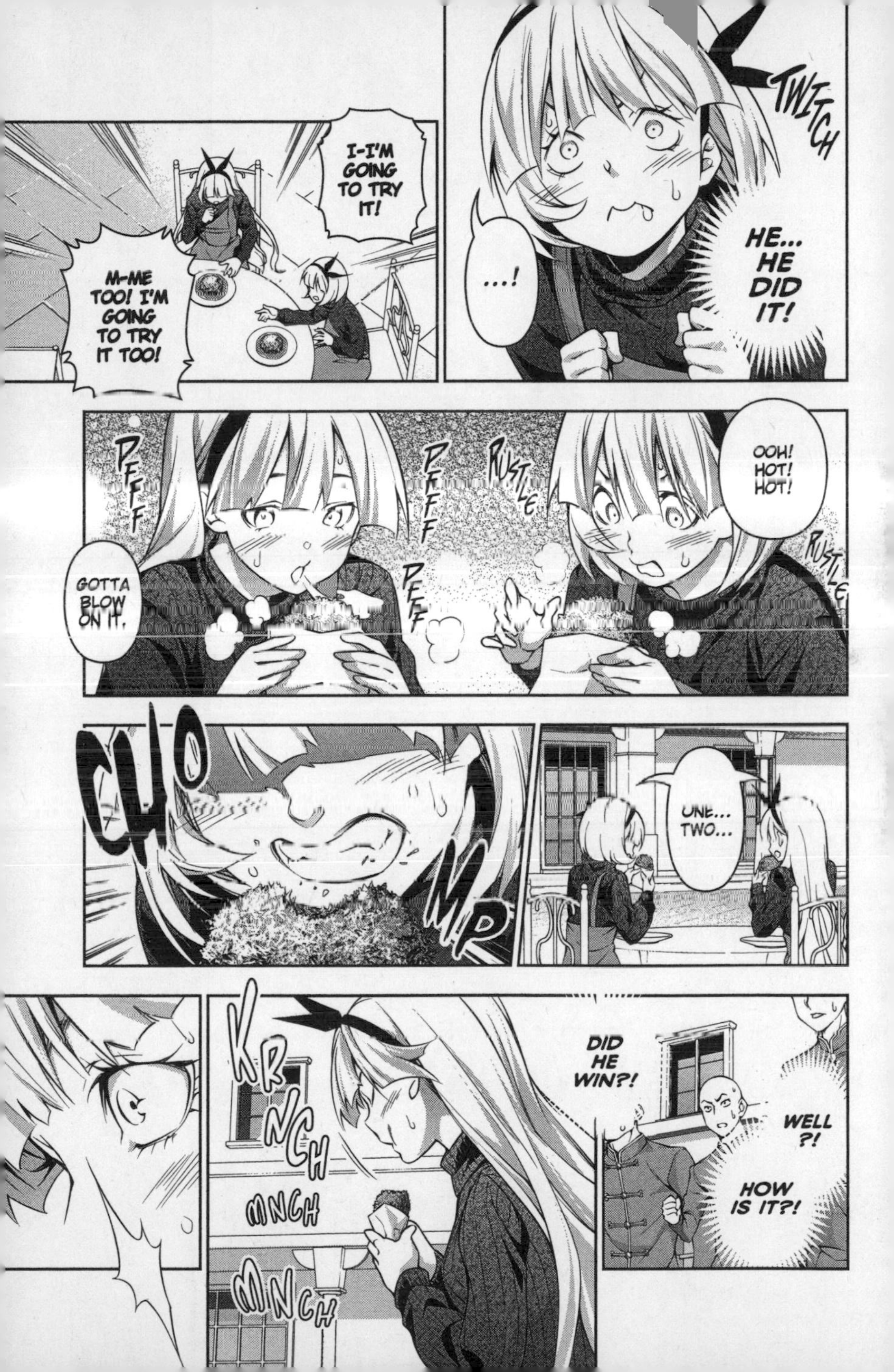
TWITCH
...!
HE... HE DID IT!
I-I'M GOING TO TRY IT!
M-ME TOO! I'M GOING TO TRY IT TOO!
OOH! HOT! HOT!
RUSTLE
RUSTLE
PFFF
PFFF
PFFF
PFFF
GOTTA BLOW ON IT.
ONE... TWO...
CHOMP
DID HE WIN?!
WELL?!
HOW IS IT?!
KRNCH
MNCH
MNCH

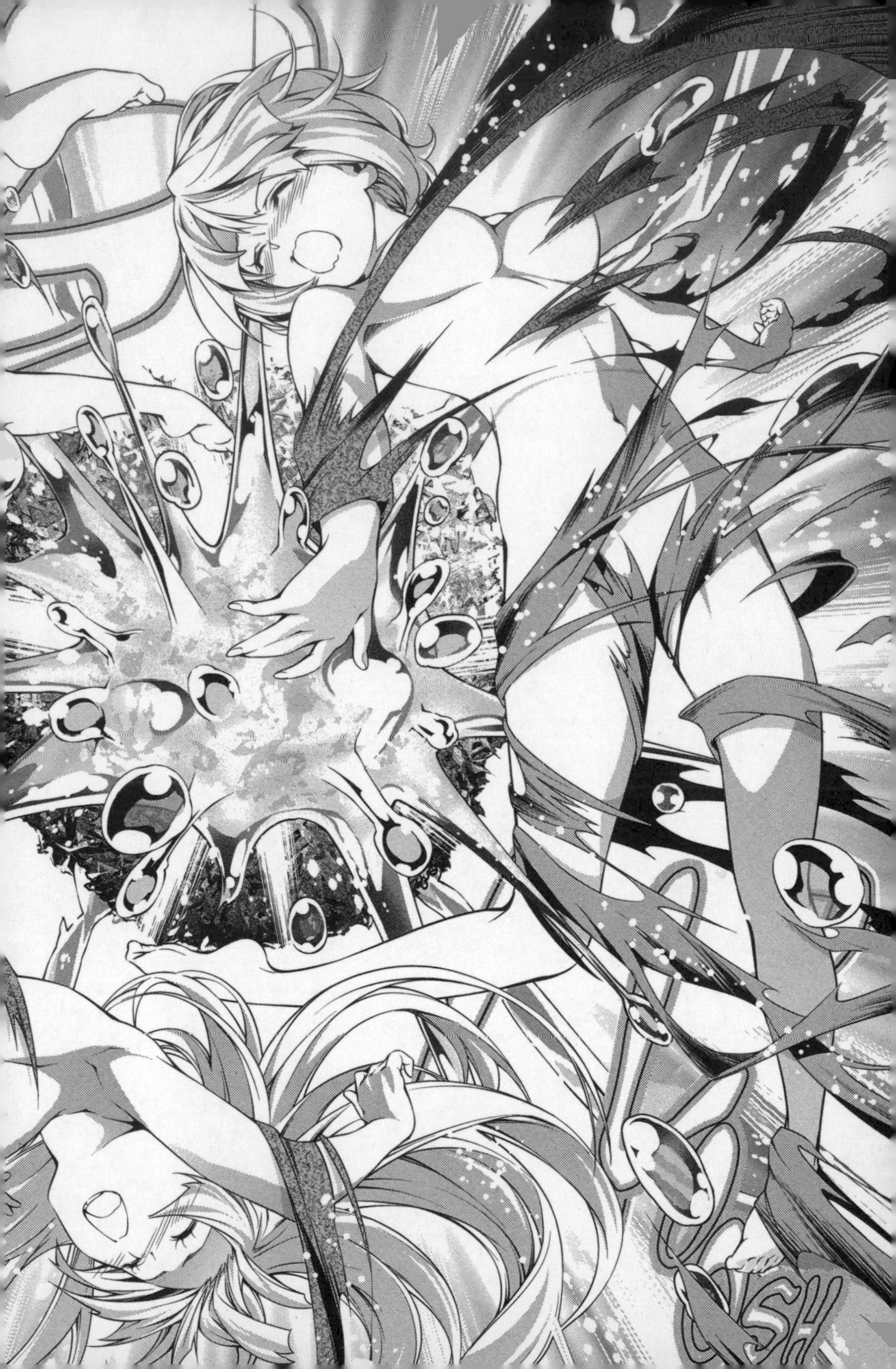
SH

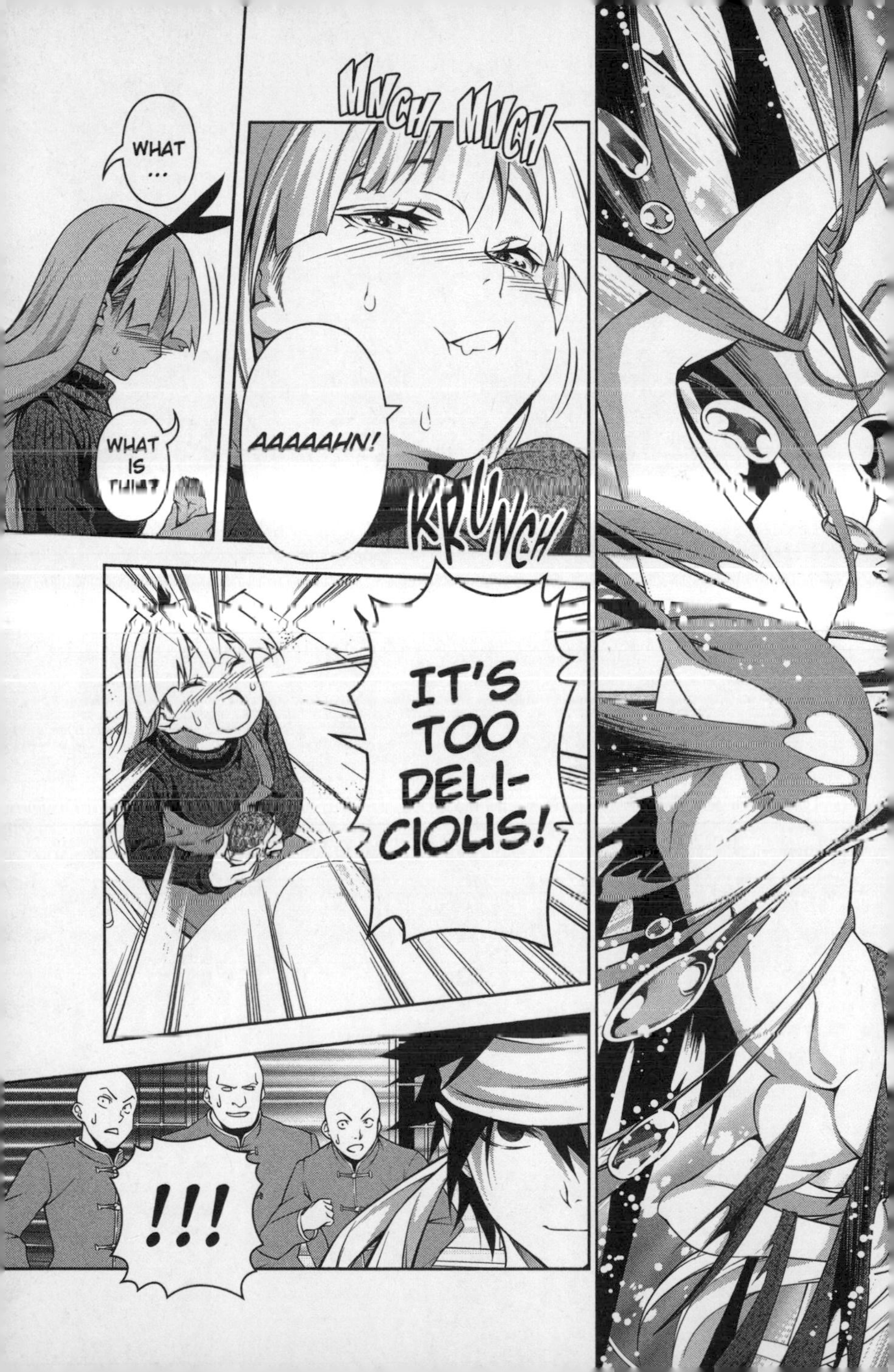
MNCH, MNCH
AAAAAHN!
KRUNCH
WHAT ...
WHAT IS THIS?
IT'S TOO DELI-CIOUS!
!!!

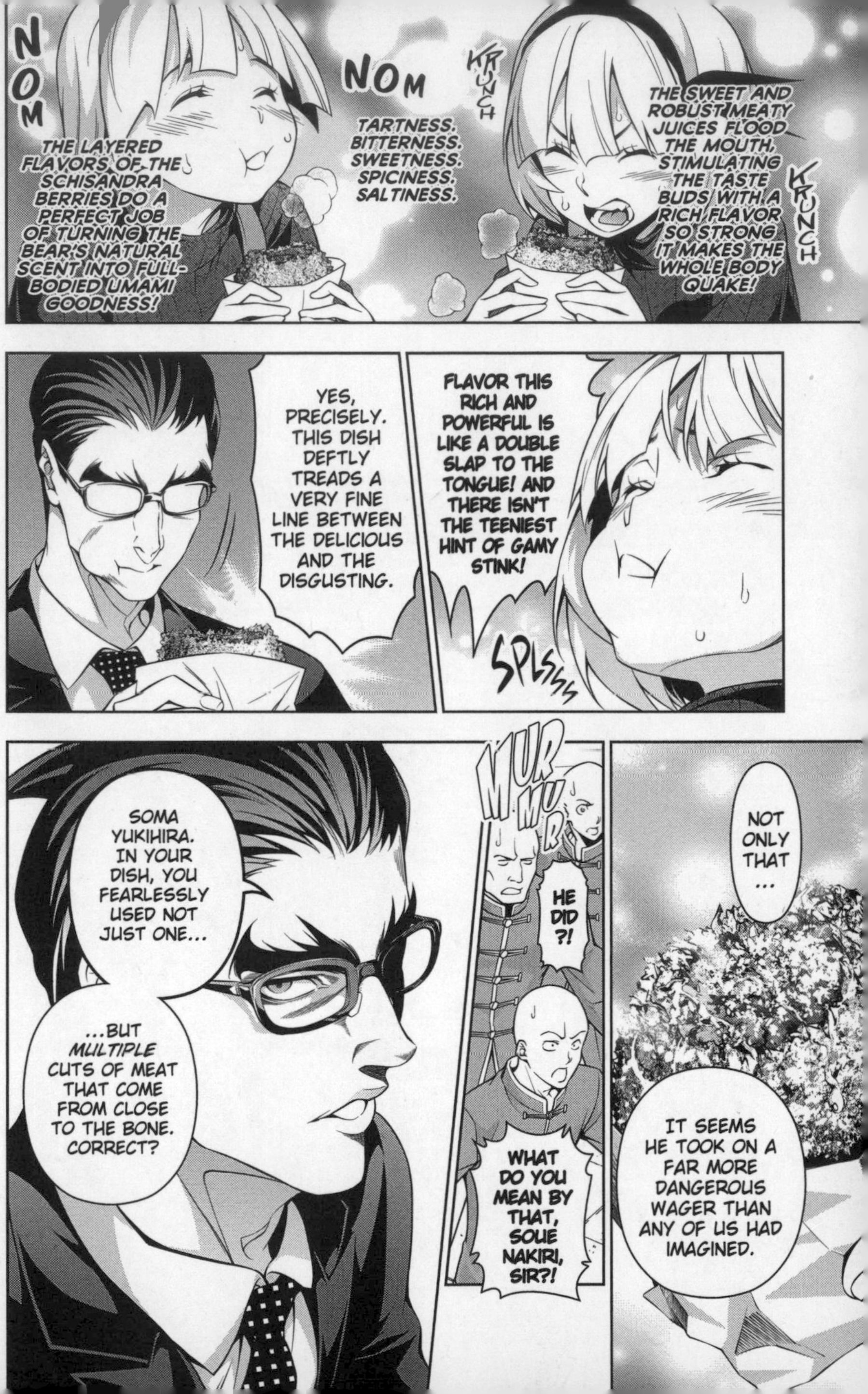
KRUNCH
THE SWEET AND ROBUST MEATY JUICES FLOOD THE MOUTH, STIMULATING THE TASTE BUDS WITH A RICH FLAVOR SO STRONG IT MAKES THE WHOLE BODY QUAKE!
KRUNCH
NOM
TARTNESS. BITTERNESS. SWEETNESS. SPICINESS. SALTINESS.
NOM
NOM
THE LAYERED FLAVORS OF THE SCHISANDRA BERRIES DO A PERFECT JOB OF TURNING THE BEAR'S NATURAL SCENT INTO FULL-BODIED UMAMI GOODNESS!
FLAVOR THIS RICH AND POWERFUL IS LIKE A DOUBLE SLAP TO THE TONGUE! AND THERE ISN'T THE TEENIEST HINT OF GAMY STINK!
SPLSSSS
YES, PRECISELY. THIS DISH DEFTLY TREADS A VERY FINE LINE BETWEEN THE DELICIOUS AND THE DISGUSTING.
NOT ONLY THAT...
IT SEEMS HE TOOK ON A FAR MORE DANGEROUS WAGER THAN ANY OF US HAD IMAGINED.
MUR MUR MUR
HE DID?!
WHAT DO YOU MEAN BY THAT, SOUE NAKIRI, SIR?!
SOMA YUKIHIRA. IN YOUR DISH, YOU FEARLESSLY USED NOT JUST ONE...
...BUT *MULTIPLE* CUTS OF MEAT THAT COME FROM CLOSE TO THE BONE. CORRECT?

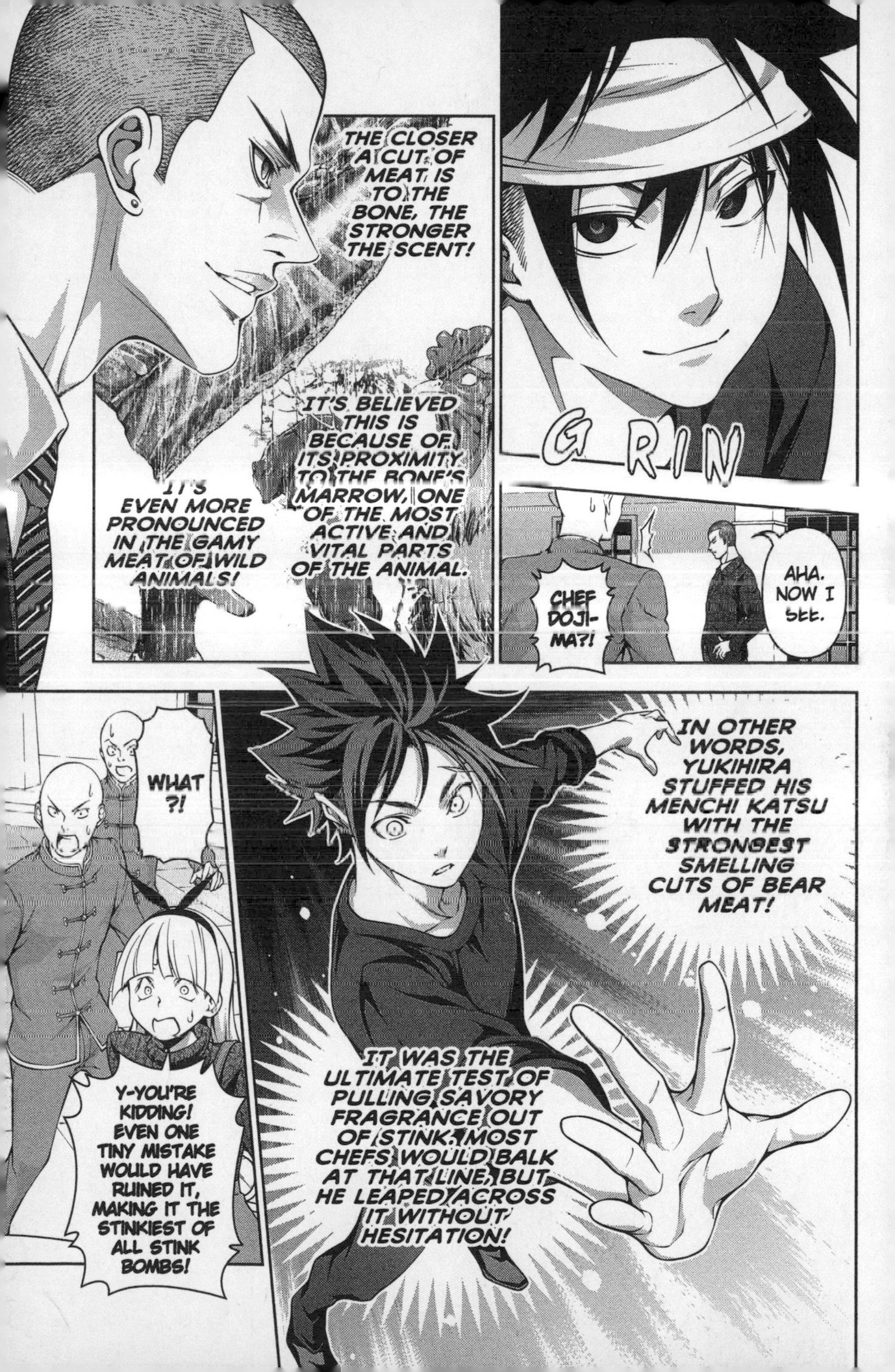
GRIN
AHA. NOW I SEE.
CHEF DOJIMA?!
THE CLOSER A CUT OF MEAT IS TO THE BONE, THE STRONGER THE SCENT!
IT'S BELIEVED THIS IS BECAUSE OF ITS PROXIMITY TO THE BONE'S MARROW, ONE OF THE MOST ACTIVE AND VITAL PARTS OF THE ANIMAL.
IT'S EVEN MORE PRONOUNCED IN THE GAMY MEAT OF WILD ANIMALS!
IN OTHER WORDS, YUKIHIRA STUFFED HIS MENCHI KATSU WITH THE STRONGEST SMELLING CUTS OF BEAR MEAT!
IT WAS THE ULTIMATE TEST OF PULLING SAVORY FRAGRANCE OUT OF STINK. MOST CHEFS WOULD BALK AT THAT LINE, BUT HE LEAPED ACROSS IT WITHOUT HESITATION!
WHAT ?!
Y-YOU'RE KIDDING! EVEN ONE TINY MISTAKE WOULD HAVE RUINED IT, MAKING IT THE STINKIEST OF ALL STINK BOMBS!

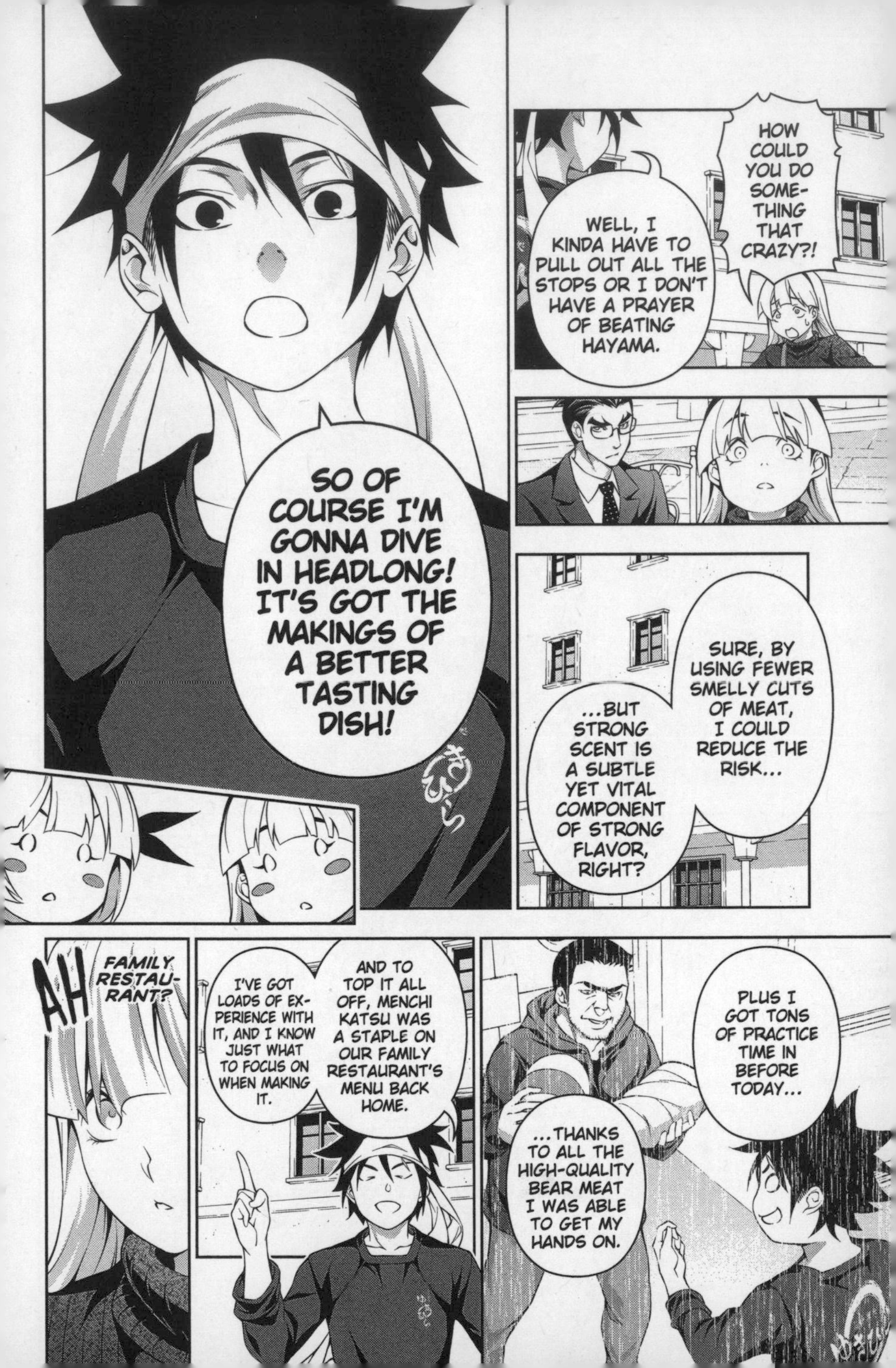
HOW COULD YOU DO SOME-THING THAT CRAZY?!
WELL, I KINDA HAVE TO PULL OUT ALL THE STOPS OR I DON'T HAVE A PRAYER OF BEATING HAYAMA.
SURE, BY USING FEWER SMELLY CUTS OF MEAT, I COULD REDUCE THE RISK...
...BUT STRONG SCENT IS A SUBTLE YET VITAL COMPONENT OF STRONG FLAVOR, RIGHT?
SO OF COURSE I'M GONNA DIVE IN HEADLONG! IT'S GOT THE MAKINGS OF A BETTER TASTING DISH!
PLUS I GOT TONS OF PRACTICE TIME IN BEFORE TODAY...
...THANKS TO ALL THE HIGH-QUALITY BEAR MEAT I WAS ABLE TO GET MY HANDS ON.
AND TO TOP IT ALL OFF, MENCHI KATSU WAS A STAPLE ON OUR FAMILY RESTAURANT'S MENU BACK HOME.
I'VE GOT LOADS OF EX-PERIENCE WITH IT, AND I KNOW JUST WHAT TO FOCUS ON WHEN MAKING IT.
FAMILY RESTAU-RANT?
AH

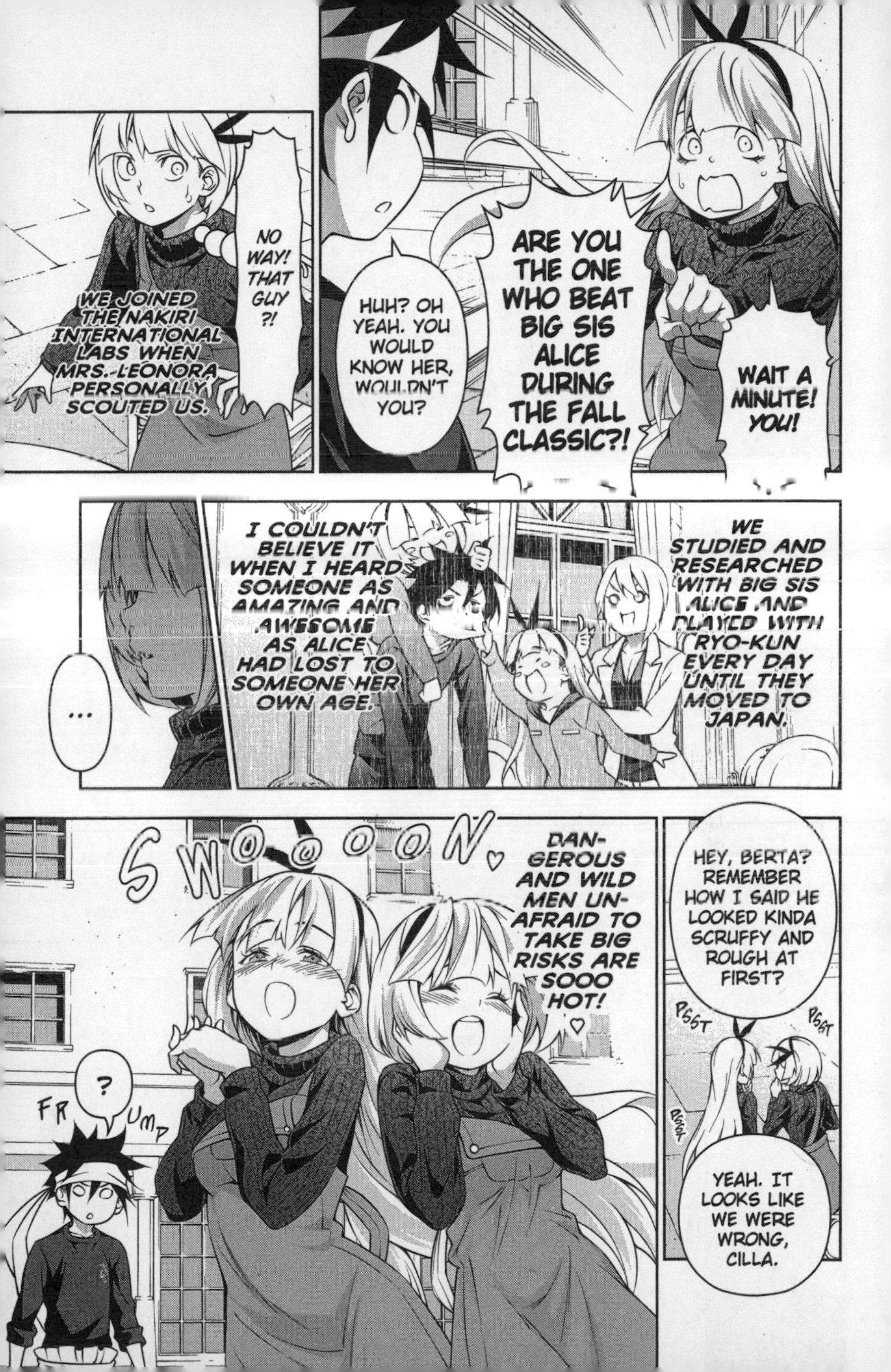
WAIT A MINUTE! YOU!
ARE YOU THE ONE WHO BEAT BIG SIS ALICE DURING THE FALL CLASSIC?!
HUH? OH YEAH. YOU WOULD KNOW HER, WOULDN'T YOU?
NO WAY! THAT GUY?!
WE JOINED THE NAKIRI INTERNATIONAL LABS WHEN MRS. LEONORA PERSONALLY SCOUTED US.
WE STUDIED AND RESEARCHED WITH BIG SIS ALICE AND PLAYED WITH RYO-KUN EVERY DAY UNTIL THEY MOVED TO JAPAN.
I COULDN'T BELIEVE IT WHEN I HEARD SOMEONE AS AMAZING AND AWESOME AS ALICE HAD LOST TO SOMEONE HER OWN AGE.
...
HEY, BERTA? REMEMBER HOW I SAID HE LOOKED KINDA SCRUFFY AND ROUGH AT FIRST?
PSST
PSST
PSST
YEAH. IT LOOKS LIKE WE WERE WRONG, CILLA.
SWOOOOON
DAN-GEROUS AND WILD MEN UN-AFRAID TO TAKE BIG RISKS ARE SOOO HOT!
?
FRUMP

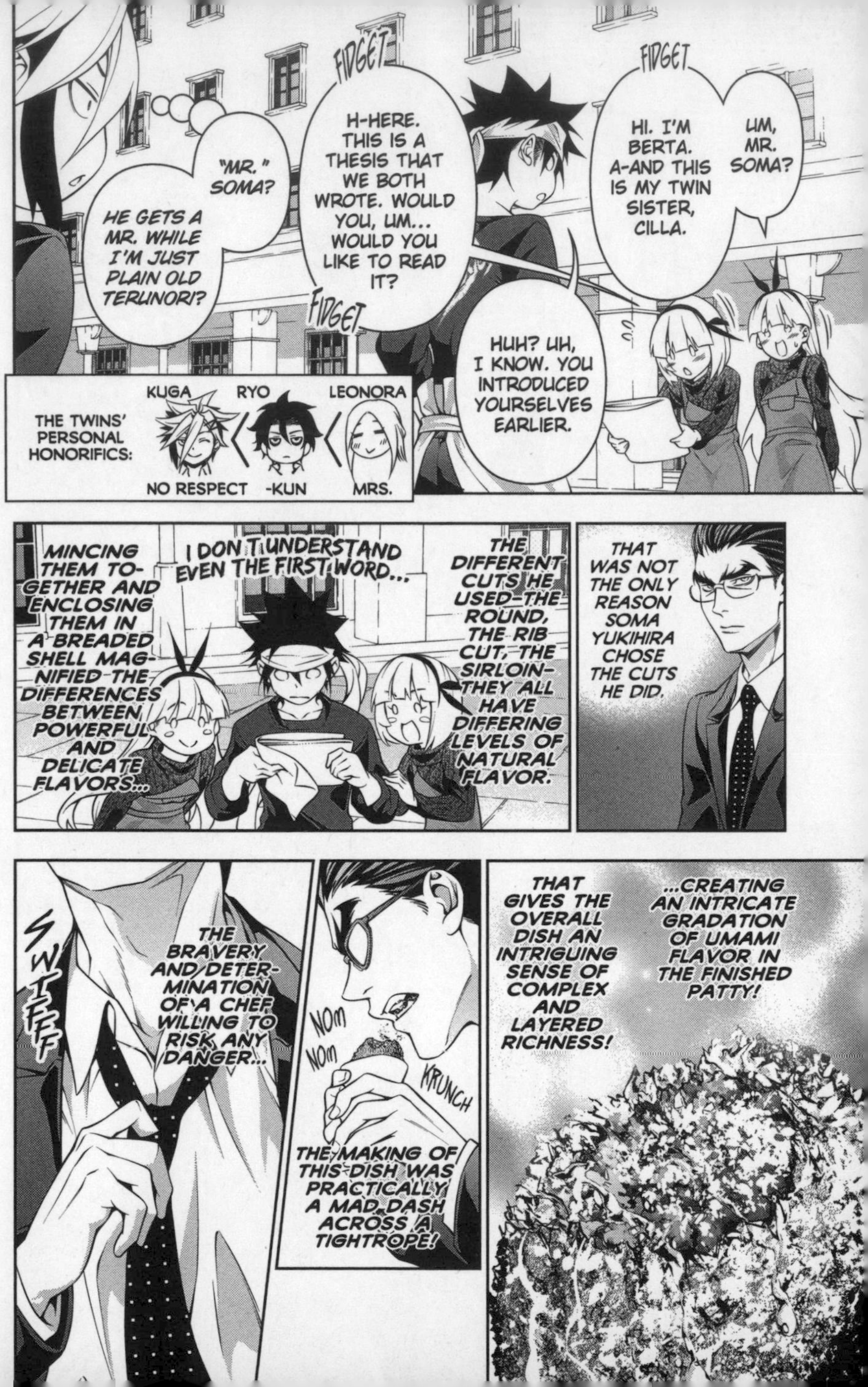
FIDGET
UM, MR. SOMA?
HI. I'M BERTA. A-AND THIS IS MY TWIN SISTER, CILLA.
FIDGET
H-HERE. THIS IS A THESIS THAT WE BOTH WROTE. WOULD YOU, UM... WOULD YOU LIKE TO READ IT?
FIDGET
HUH? UH, I KNOW. YOU INTRODUCED YOURSELVES EARLIER.
"MR." SOMA?
HE GETS A MR. WHILE I'M JUST PLAIN OLD TERUNORI?
THE TWINS' PERSONAL HONORIFICS:
KUGA
RYO
LEONORA
NO RESPECT
-KUN
MRS.
THAT WAS NOT THE ONLY REASON SOMA YUKIHIRA CHOSE THE CUTS HE DID.
THE DIFFERENT CUTS HE USED—THE ROUND, THE RIB CUT, THE SIRLOIN—THEY ALL HAVE DIFFERING LEVELS OF NATURAL FLAVOR.
I DONT UNDERSTAND EVEN THE FIRST WORD...
MINCING THEM TOGETHER AND ENCLOSING THEM IN A BREADED SHELL MAGNIFIED THE DIFFERENCES BETWEEN POWERFUL AND DELICATE FLAVORS...
...CREATING AN INTRICATE GRADATION OF UMAMI FLAVOR IN THE FINISHED PATTY!
THAT GIVES THE OVERALL DISH AN INTRIGUING SENSE OF COMPLEX AND LAYERED RICHNESS!
NOM NOM
KRUNCH
THE MAKING OF THIS DISH WAS PRACTICALLY A MAD DASH ACROSS A TIGHTROPE!
THE BRAVERY AND DETERMINATION OF A CHEF WILLING TO RISK ANY DANGER...
SWIFFF

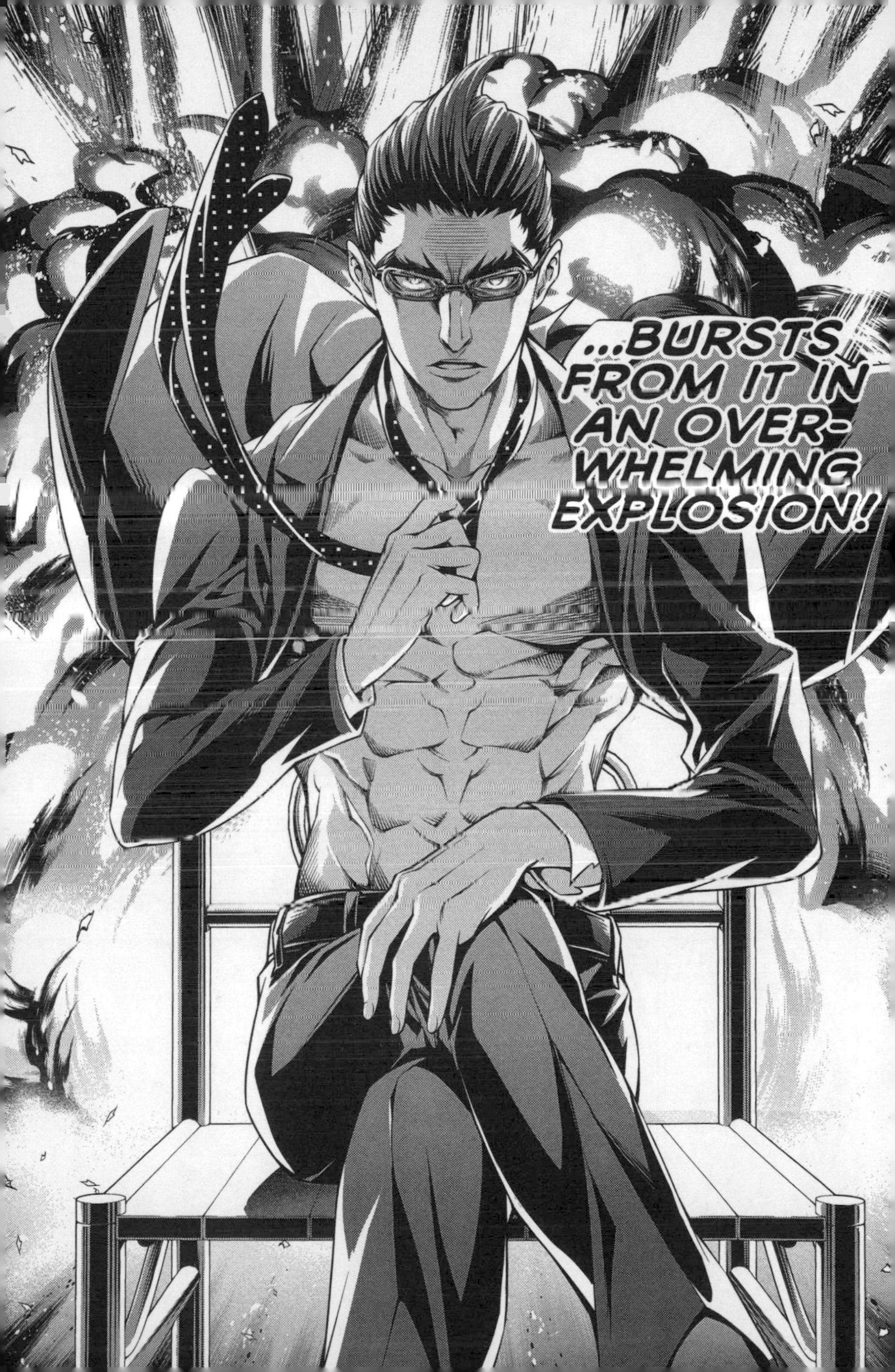
...BURSTS FROM IT IN AN OVER-WHELMING EXPLOSION!

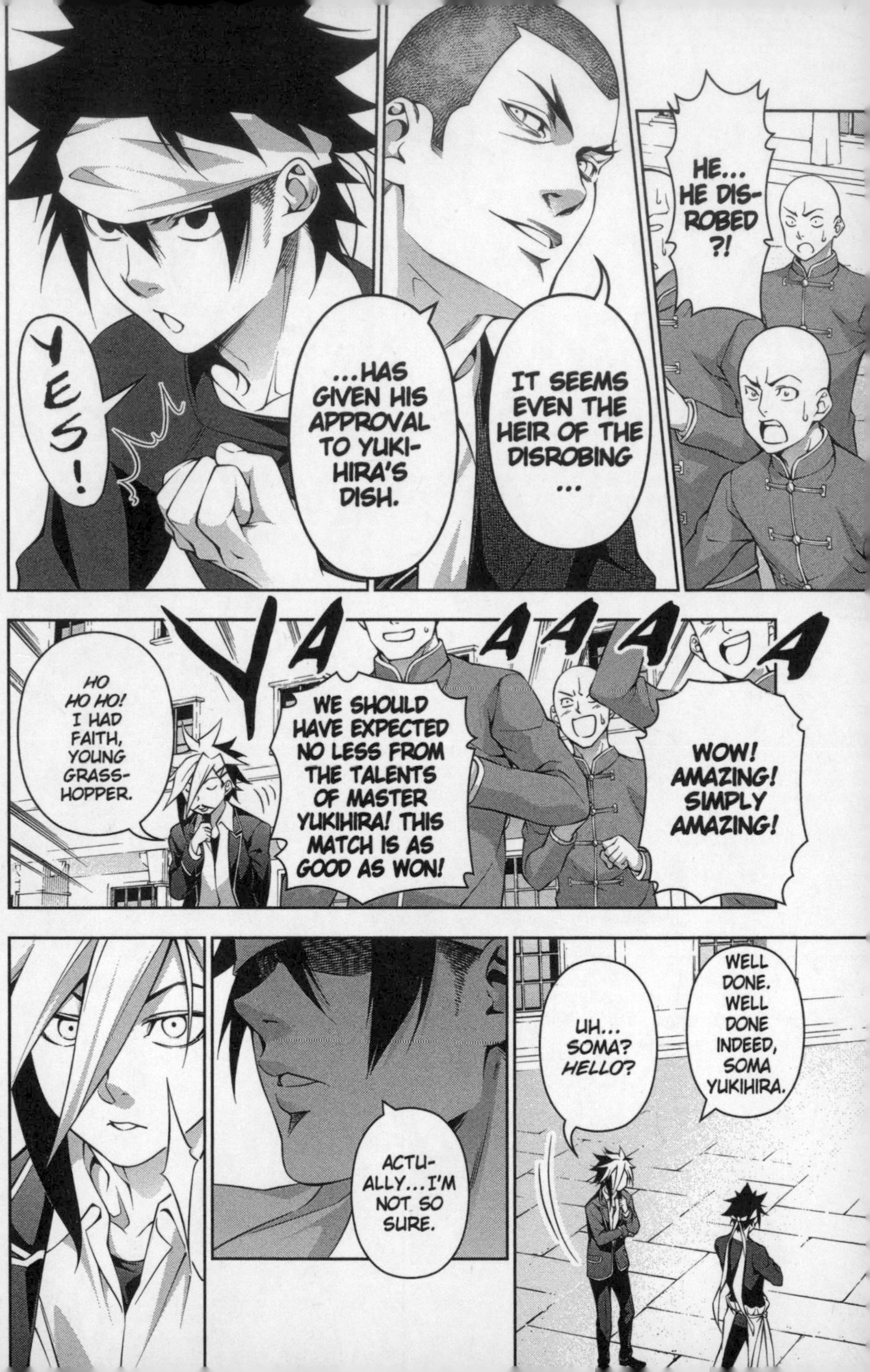
HE... HE DIS-ROBED ?!
IT SEEMS EVEN THE HEIR OF THE DISROBING ...
...HAS GIVEN HIS APPROVAL TO YUKI-HIRA'S DISH.
YES!
YAAAAAA
WOW! AMAZING! SIMPLY AMAZING!
WE SHOULD HAVE EXPECTED NO LESS FROM THE TALENTS OF MASTER YUKIHIRA! THIS MATCH IS AS GOOD AS WON!
HO HO HO! I HAD FAITH, YOUNG GRASS-HOPPER.
WELL DONE. WELL DONE INDEED, SOMA YUKIHIRA.
UH... SOMA? HELLO?
ACTU-ALLY...I'M NOT SO SURE.

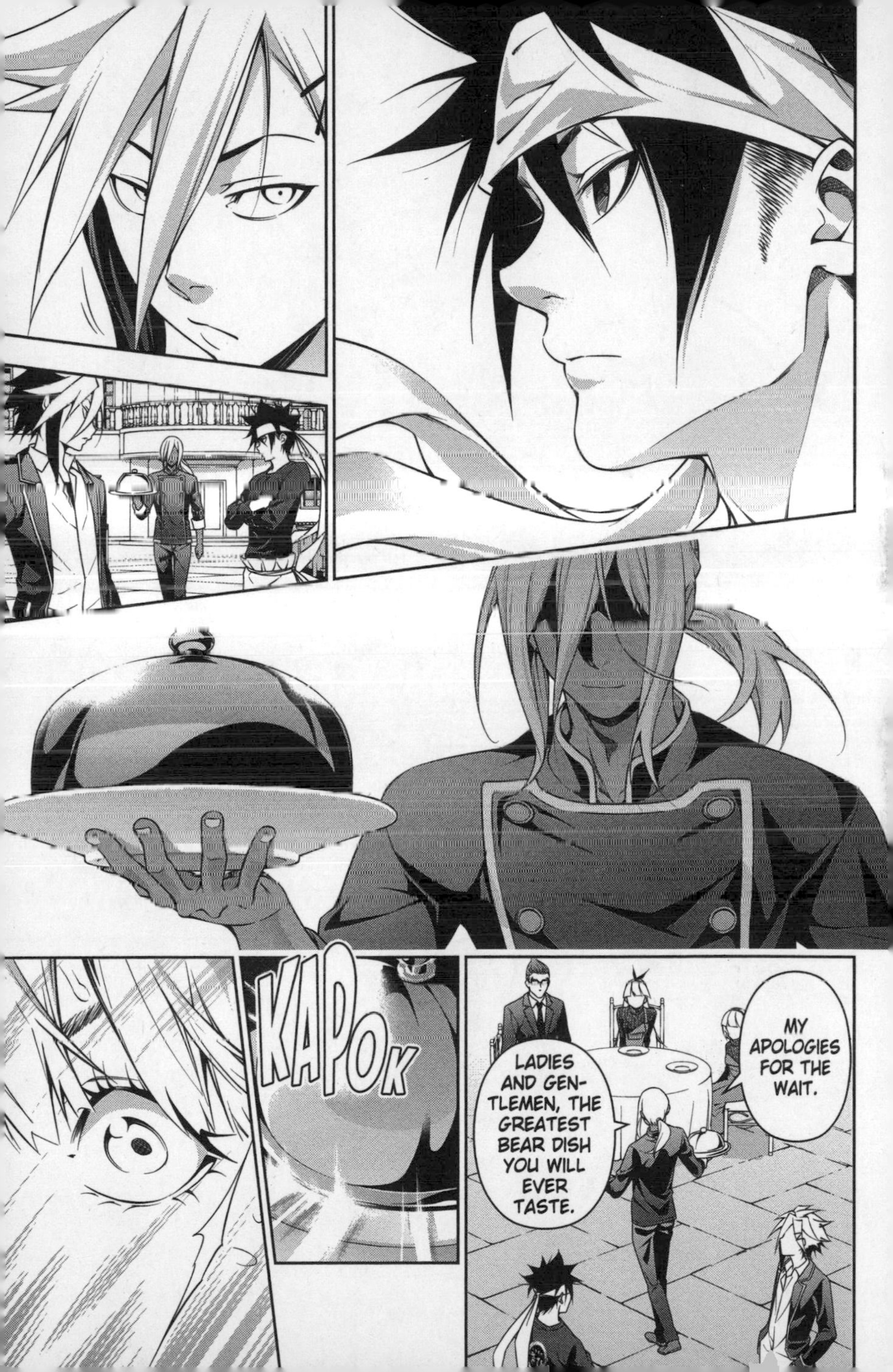
MY APOLOGIES FOR THE WAIT.
LADIES AND GEN-TLEMEN, THE GREATEST BEAR DISH YOU WILL EVER TASTE.
KAPOK

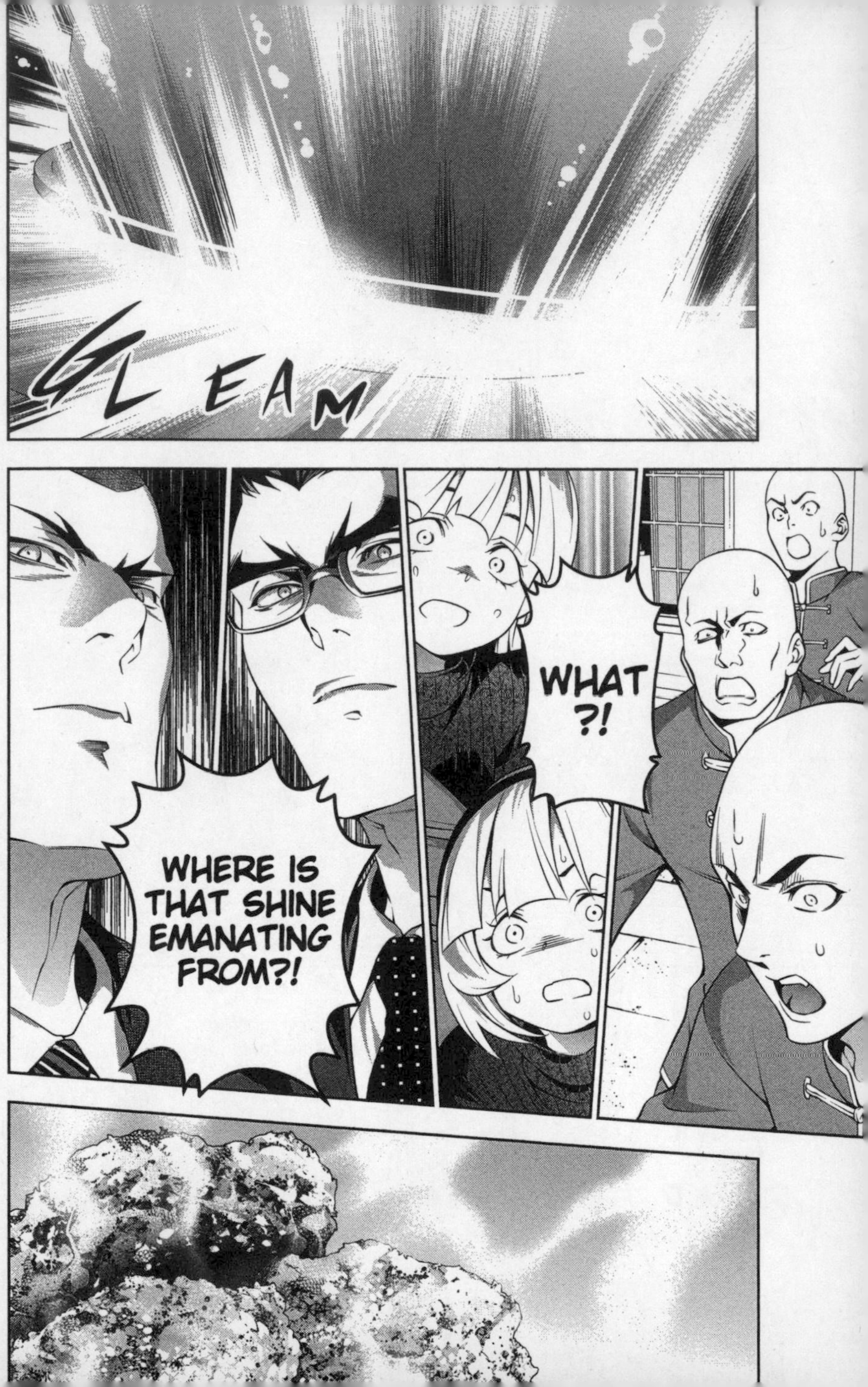
GLEAM
WHAT?!
WHERE IS THAT SHINE EMANATING FROM?!

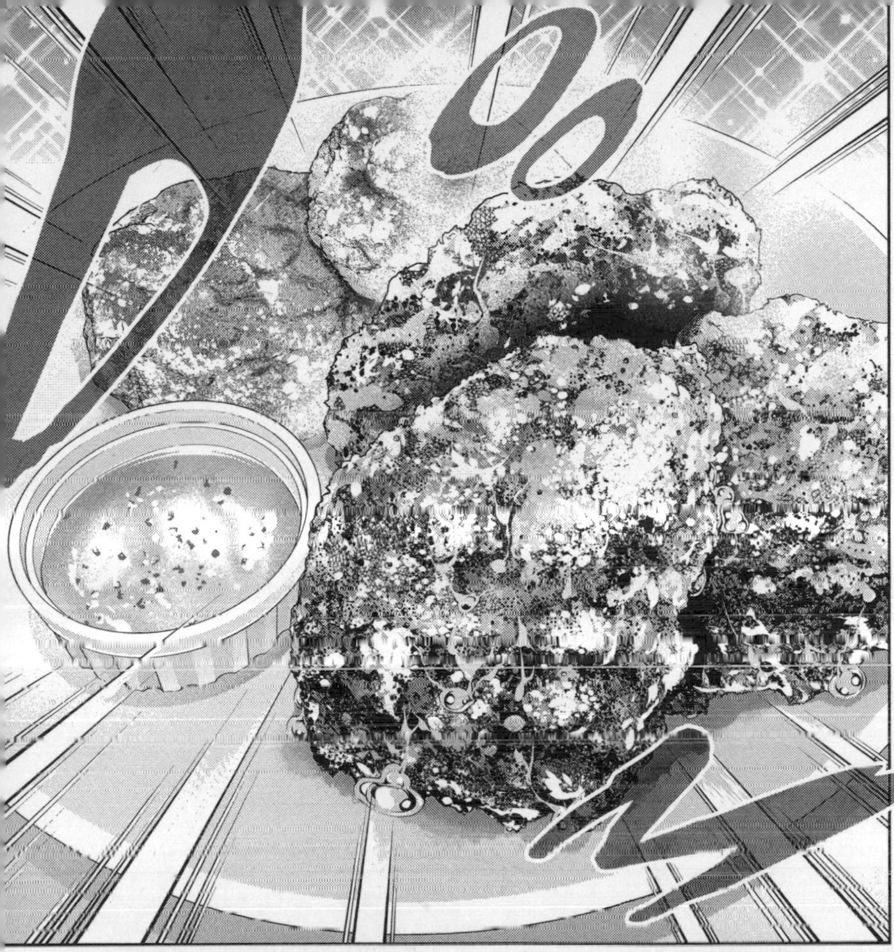

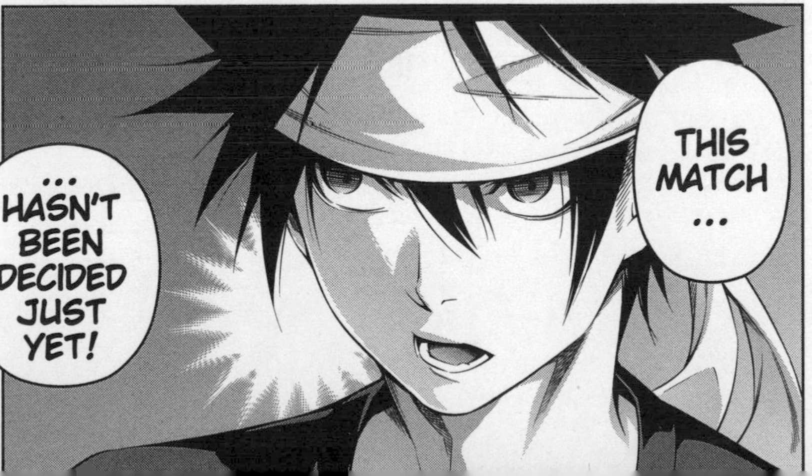
THIS MATCH ...
... HASN'T BEEN DECIDED JUST YET!

NAKIRI FATHER & SON
EYEBROW COMPARISON

YES!
THEY'RE
ALIKE!

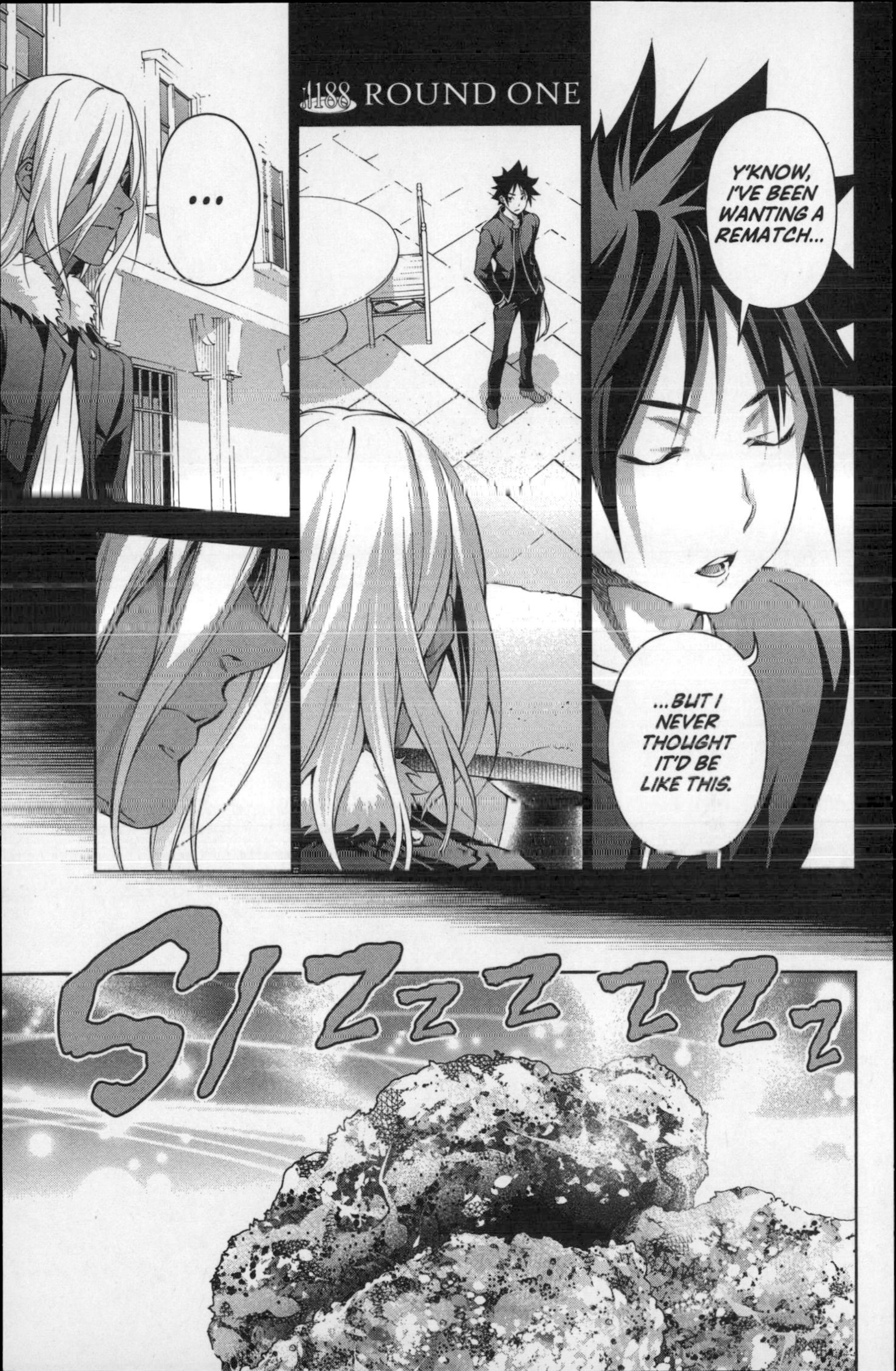
188 ROUND ONE
Y'KNOW, I'VE BEEN WANTING A REMATCH...
...BUT I NEVER THOUGHT IT'D BE LIKE THIS.
...
SIZZZZZZZz

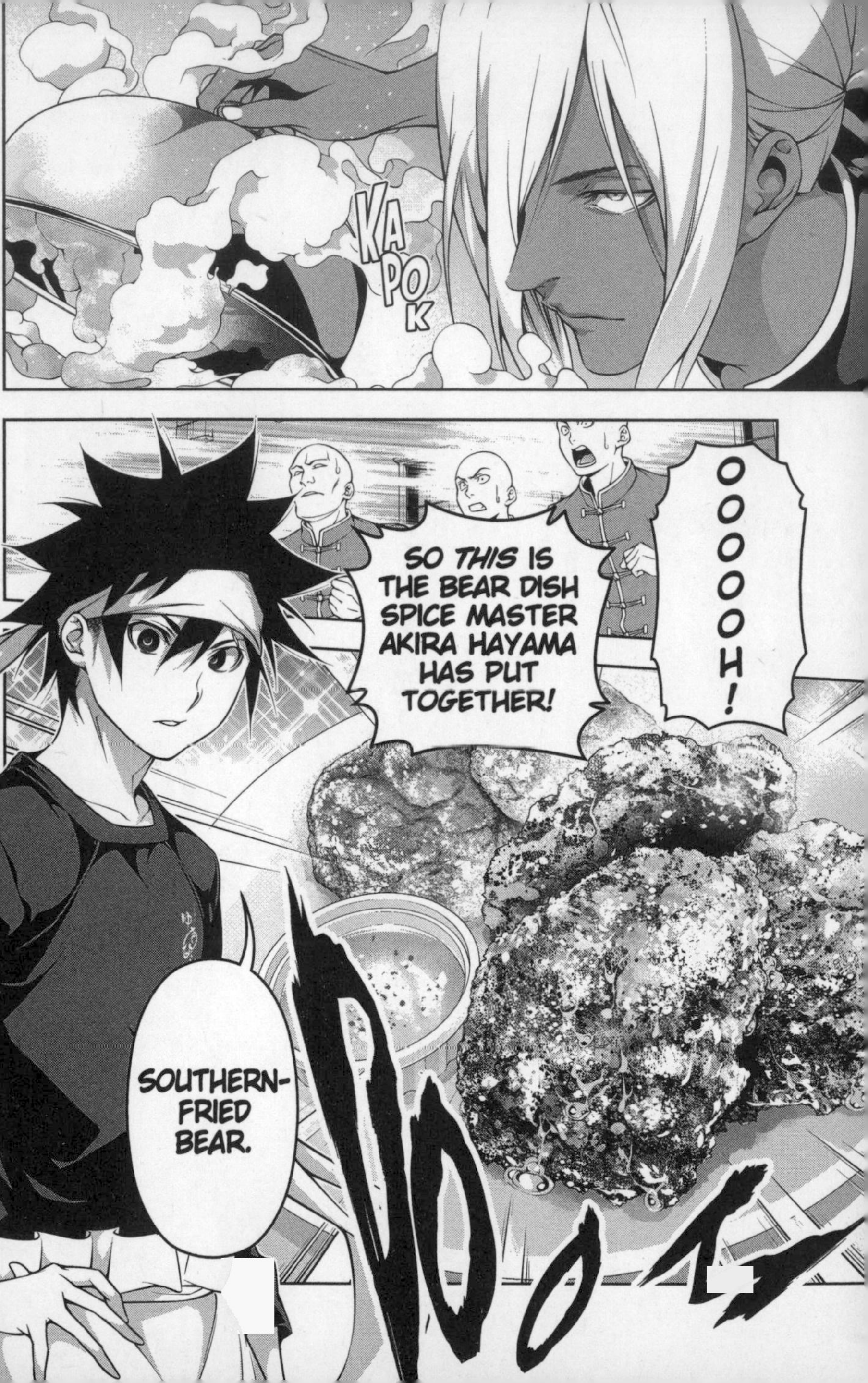
KAPOK
OOOOOOH!
SO THIS IS THE BEAR DISH SPICE MASTER AKIRA HAYAMA HAS PUT TOGETHER!
SOUTHERN-FRIED BEAR.

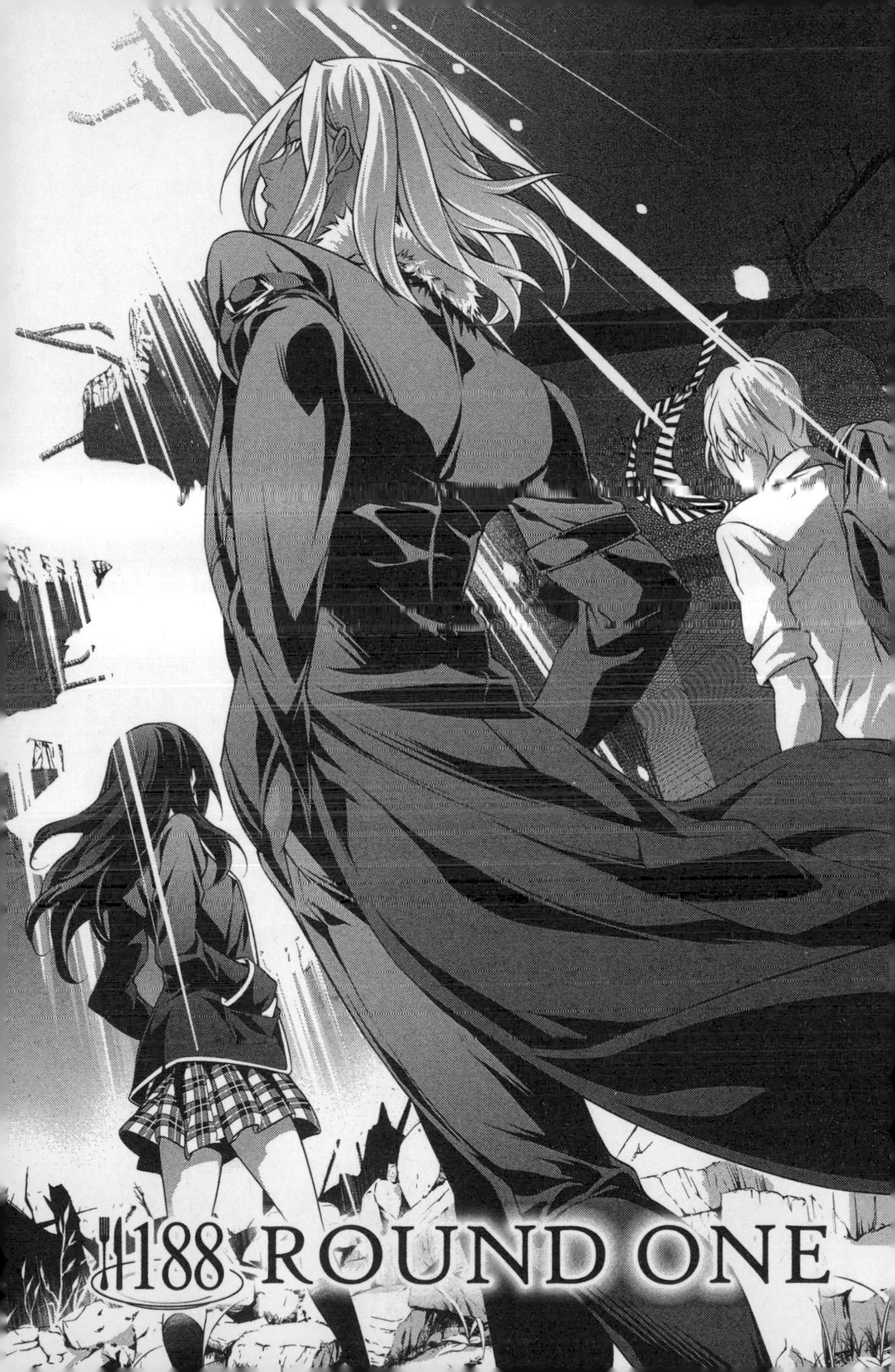
#188 ROUND ONE

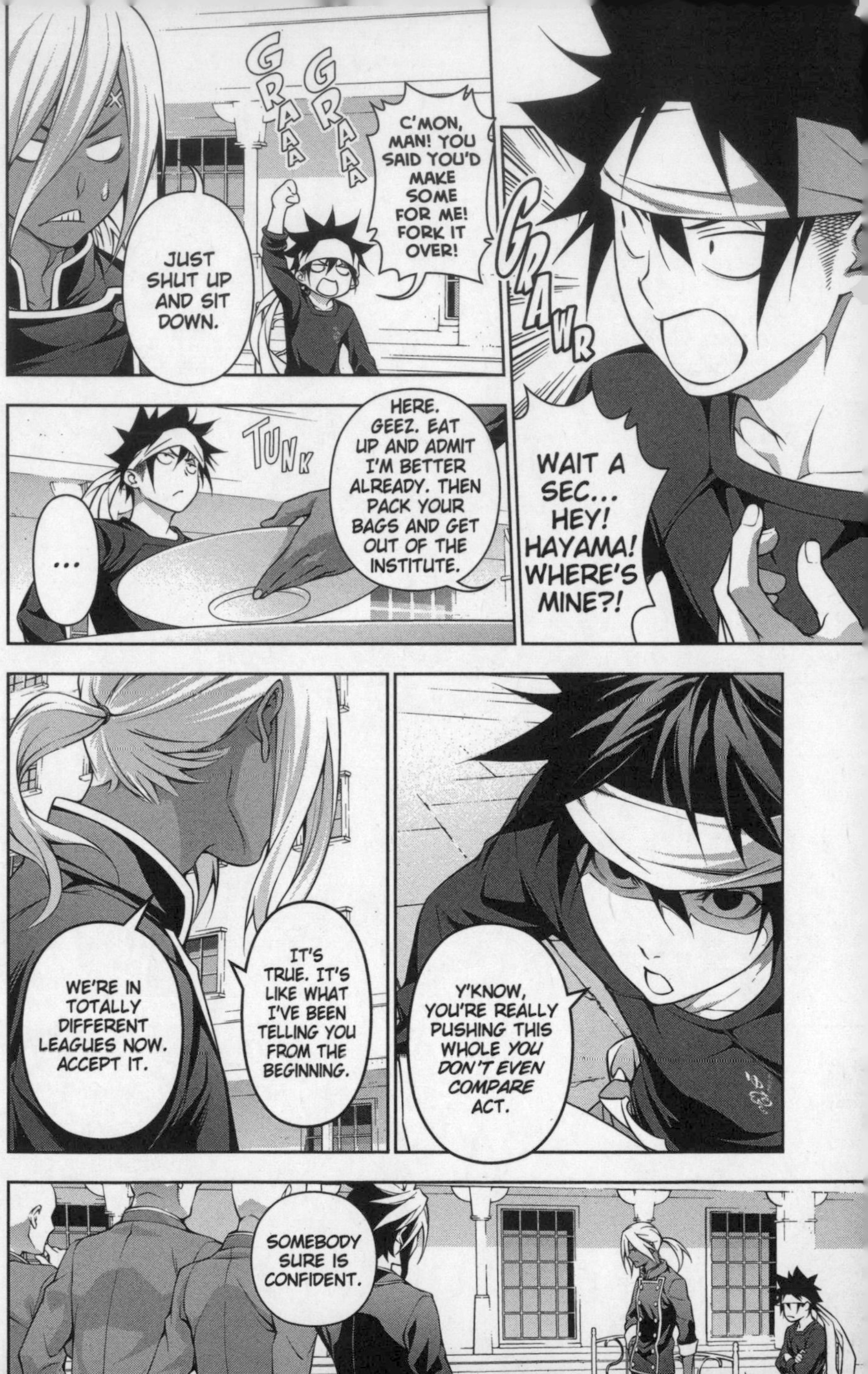
GRAWR
WAIT A SEC... HEY! HAYAMA! WHERE'S MINE?!
GRAAA
GRAAA
C'MON, MAN! YOU SAID YOU'D MAKE SOME FOR ME! FORK IT OVER!
JUST SHUT UP AND SIT DOWN.
TUNK
HERE. GEEZ. EAT UP AND ADMIT I'M BETTER ALREADY. THEN PACK YOUR BAGS AND GET OUT OF THE INSTITUTE.
...
Y'KNOW, YOU'RE REALLY PUSHING THIS WHOLE *YOU DON'T EVEN COMPARE* ACT.
IT'S TRUE. IT'S LIKE WHAT I'VE BEEN TELLING YOU FROM THE BEGINNING.
WE'RE IN TOTALLY DIFFERENT LEAGUES NOW. ACCEPT IT.
SOMEBODY SURE IS CONFIDENT.

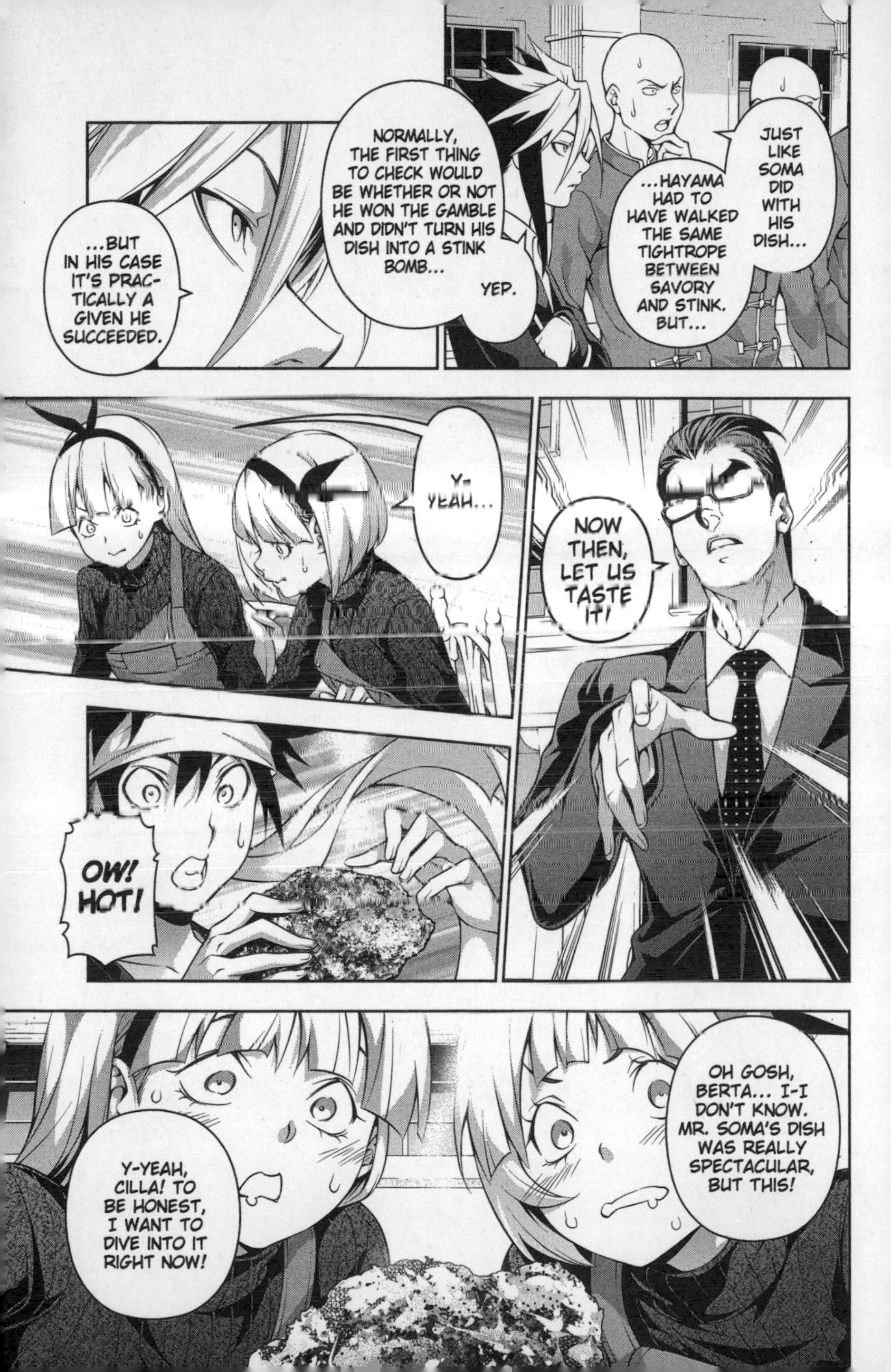
JUST LIKE SOMA DID WITH HIS DISH...
...HAYAMA HAD TO HAVE WALKED THE SAME TIGHTROPE BETWEEN SAVORY AND STINK. BUT...
NORMALLY, THE FIRST THING TO CHECK WOULD BE WHETHER OR NOT HE WON THE GAMBLE AND DIDN'T TURN HIS DISH INTO A STINK BOMB...
YEP.
...BUT IN HIS CASE IT'S PRACTICALLY A GIVEN HE SUCCEEDED.
NOW THEN, LET US TASTE IT!
Y-YEAH...
OW! HOT!
OH GOSH, BERTA... I-I DON'T KNOW. MR. SOMA'S DISH WAS REALLY SPECTACULAR, BUT THIS!
Y-YEAH, CILLA! TO BE HONEST, I WANT TO DIVE INTO IT RIGHT NOW!

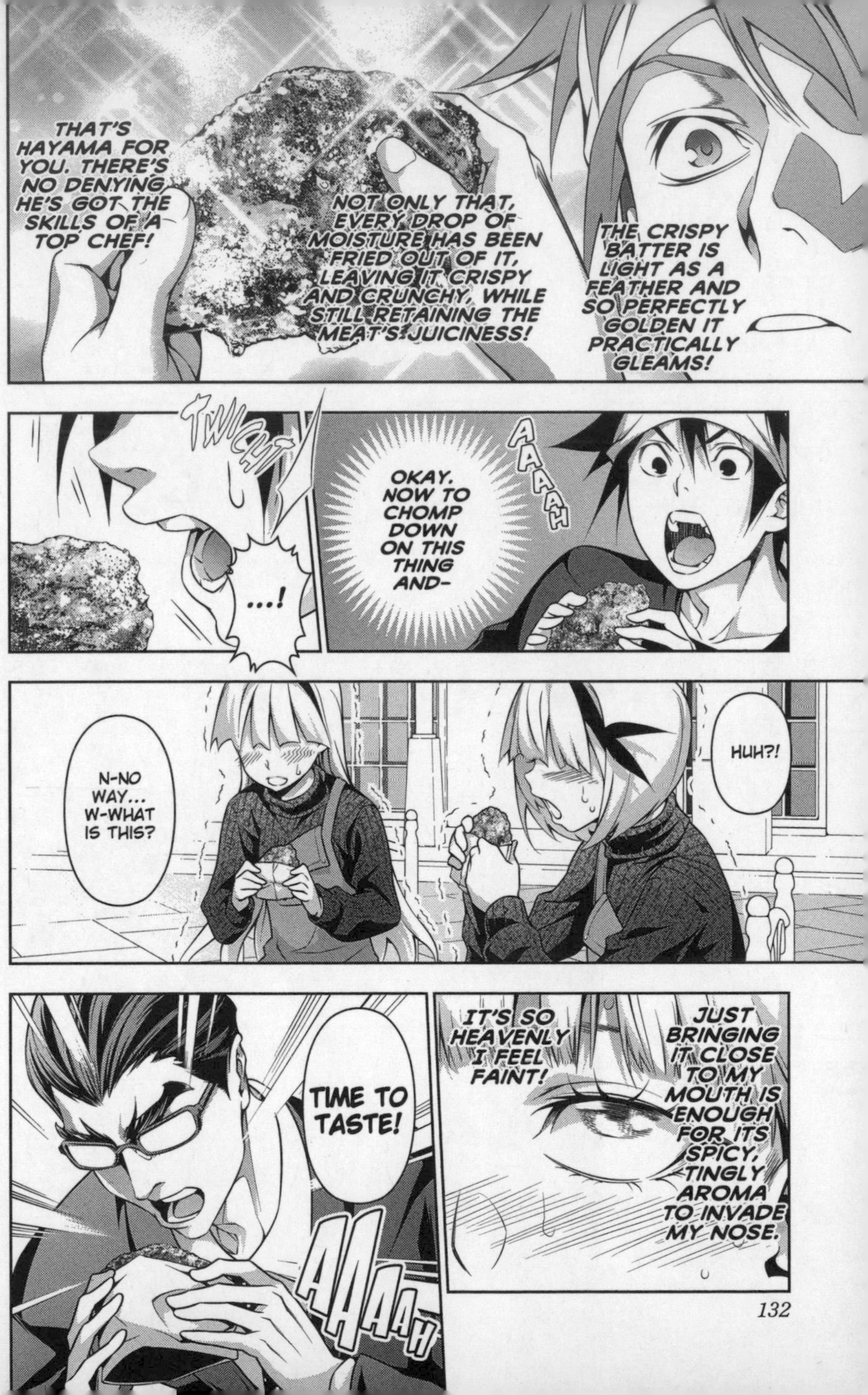
THE CRISPY BATTER IS LIGHT AS A FEATHER AND SO PERFECTLY GOLDEN IT PRACTICALLY GLEAMS!
NOT ONLY THAT, EVERY DROP OF MOISTURE HAS BEEN FRIED OUT OF IT, LEAVING IT CRISPY AND CRUNCHY, WHILE STILL RETAINING THE MEAT'S JUICINESS!
THAT'S HAYAMA FOR YOU. THERE'S NO DENYING HE'S GOT THE SKILLS OF A TOP CHEF!
AAAAH
OKAY. NOW TO CHOMP DOWN ON THIS THING AND-
TWITCH
...!
HUH?!
N-NO WAY... W-WHAT IS THIS?
JUST BRINGING IT CLOSE TO MY MOUTH IS ENOUGH FOR ITS SPICY, TINGLY AROMA TO INVADE MY NOSE.
IT'S SO HEAVENLY I FEEL FAINT!
TIME TO TASTE!
AAAAAH

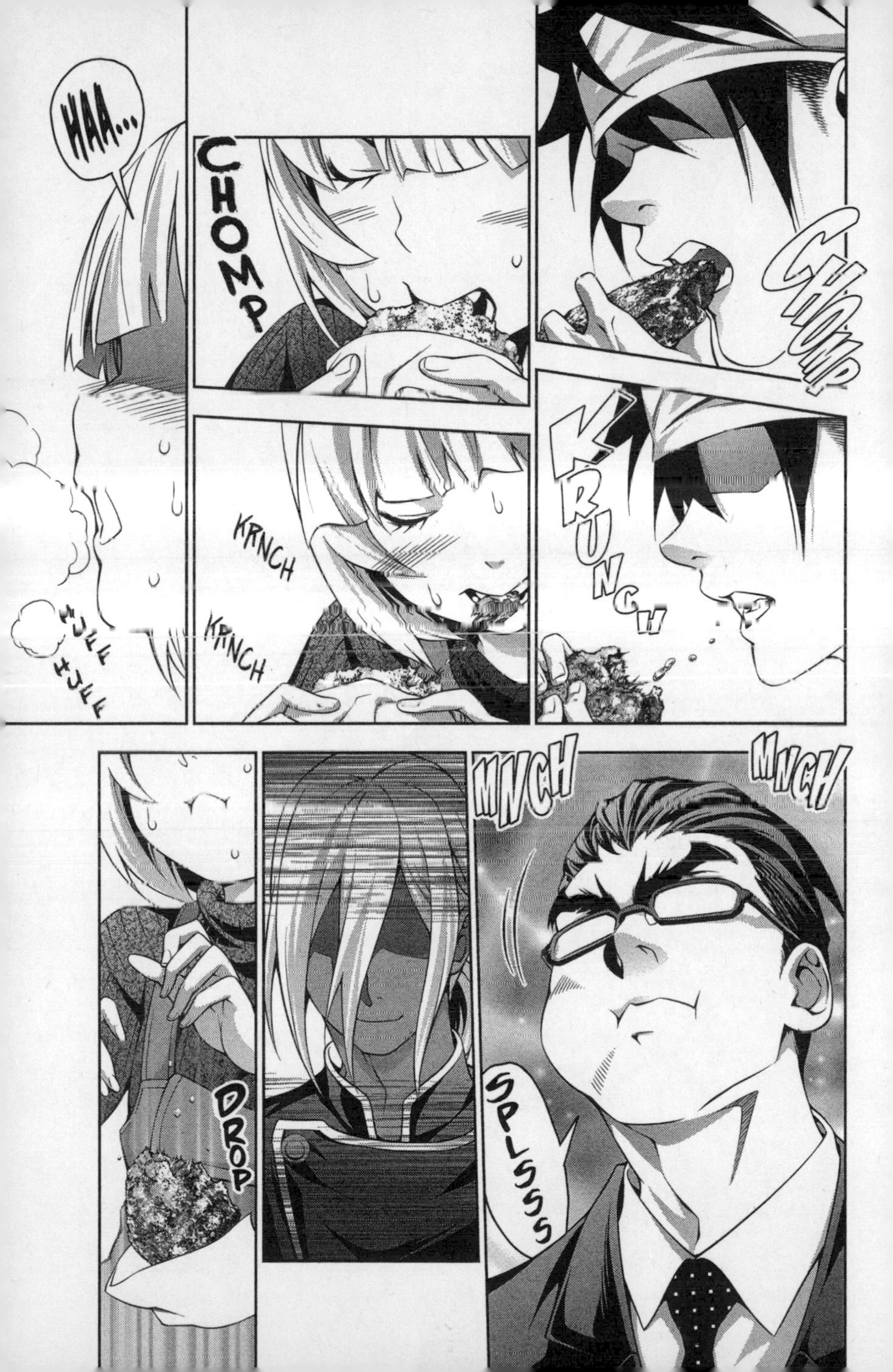
CHOMP
KRUNCH
CHOMP
KRNCH
KRNCH
HAA...
HUFF
HUFF
MNCH
MNCH
SPLSSS
DROP

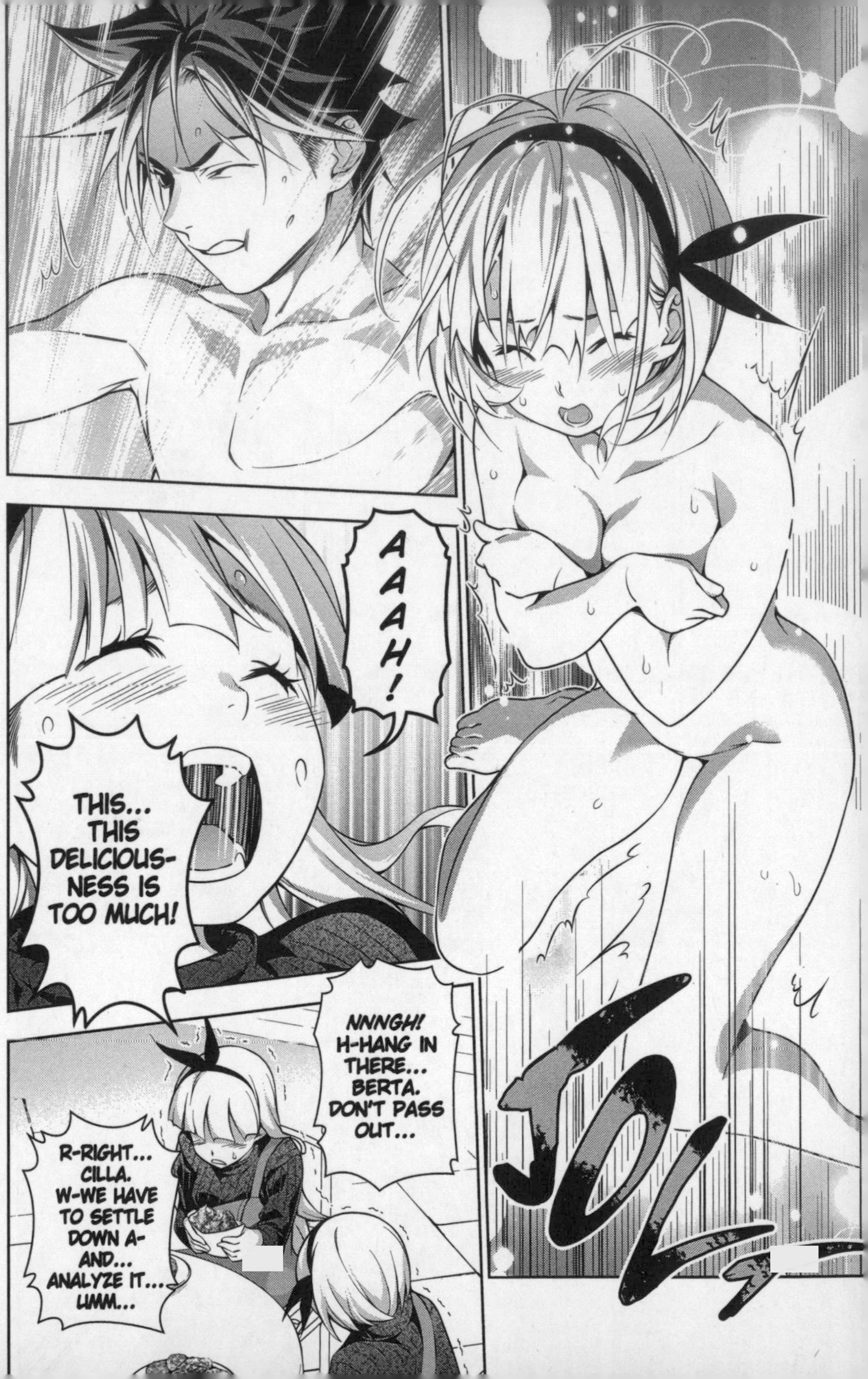
AAAH!
THIS... THIS DELICIOUSNESS IS TOO MUCH!
NNNGH! H-HANG IN THERE... BERTA. DON'T PASS OUT...
R-RIGHT... CILLA. W-WE HAVE TO SETTLE DOWN A-AND... ANALYZE IT... UMM...

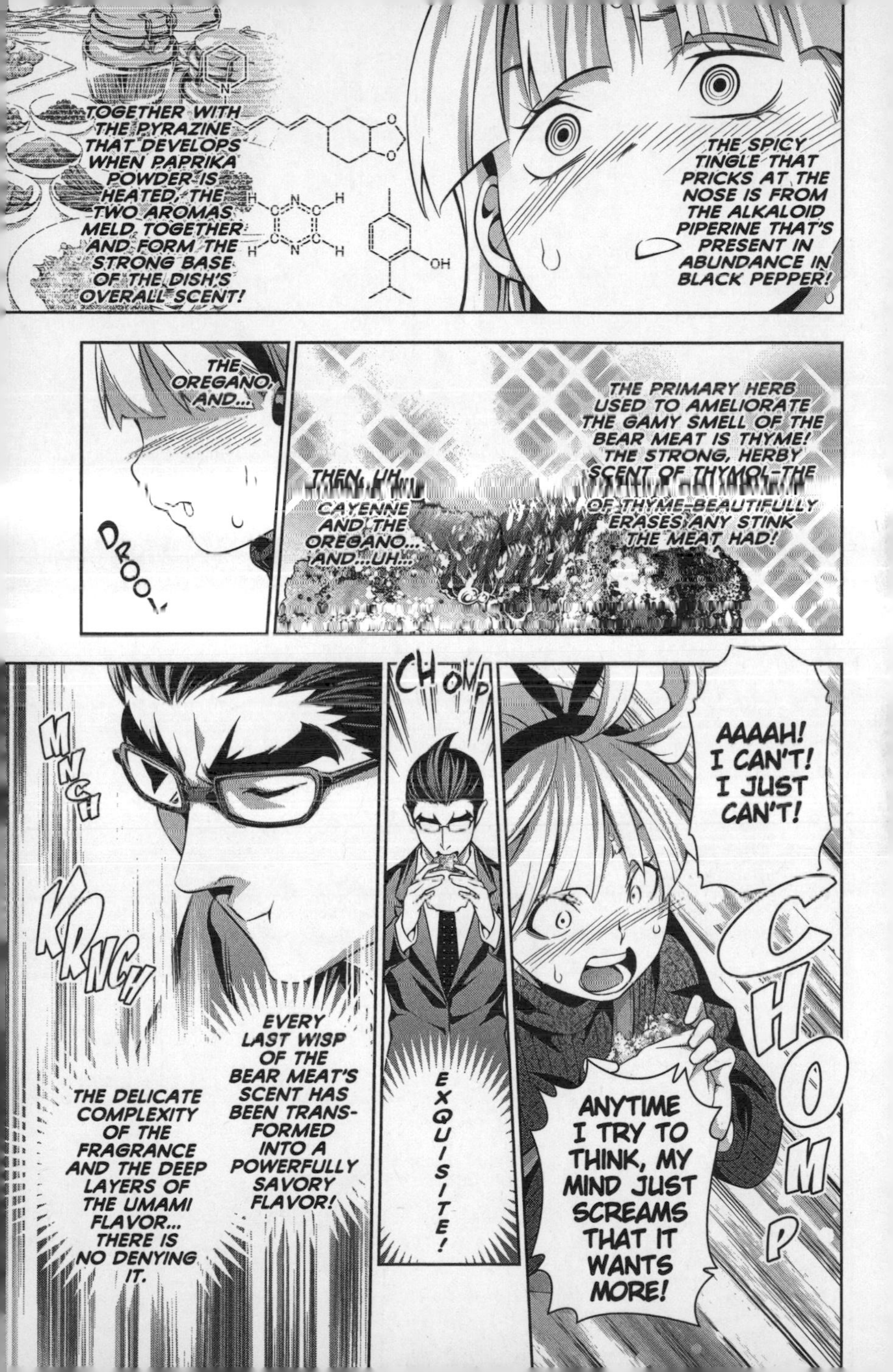
THE SPICY TINGLE THAT PRICKS AT THE NOSE IS FROM THE ALKALOID PIPERINE THAT'S PRESENT IN ABUNDANCE IN BLACK PEPPER!
TOGETHER WITH THE PYRAZINE THAT DEVELOPS WHEN PAPRIKA POWDER IS HEATED, THE TWO AROMAS MELD TOGETHER AND FORM THE STRONG BASE OF THE DISH'S OVERALL SCENT!
THE PRIMARY HERB USED TO AMELIORATE THE GAMY SMELL OF THE BEAR MEAT IS THYME! THE STRONG, HERBY SCENT OF THYMOL—THE
OF THYME—BEAUTIFULLY ERASES ANY STINK THE MEAT HAD!
THEN, UH
CAYENNE AND THE OREGANO... AND...UH...
THE OREGANO, AND...
DROOL
AAAAH! I CAN'T! I JUST CAN'T!
CHOMP
ANYTIME I TRY TO THINK, MY MIND JUST SCREAMS THAT IT WANTS MORE!
CHOMP
EXQUISITE!
MNCH
KRNCH
EVERY LAST WISP OF THE BEAR MEAT'S SCENT HAS BEEN TRANS-FORMED INTO A POWERFULLY SAVORY FLAVOR!
THE DELICATE COMPLEXITY OF THE FRAGRANCE AND THE DEEP LAYERS OF THE UMAMI FLAVOR... THERE IS NO DENYING IT.

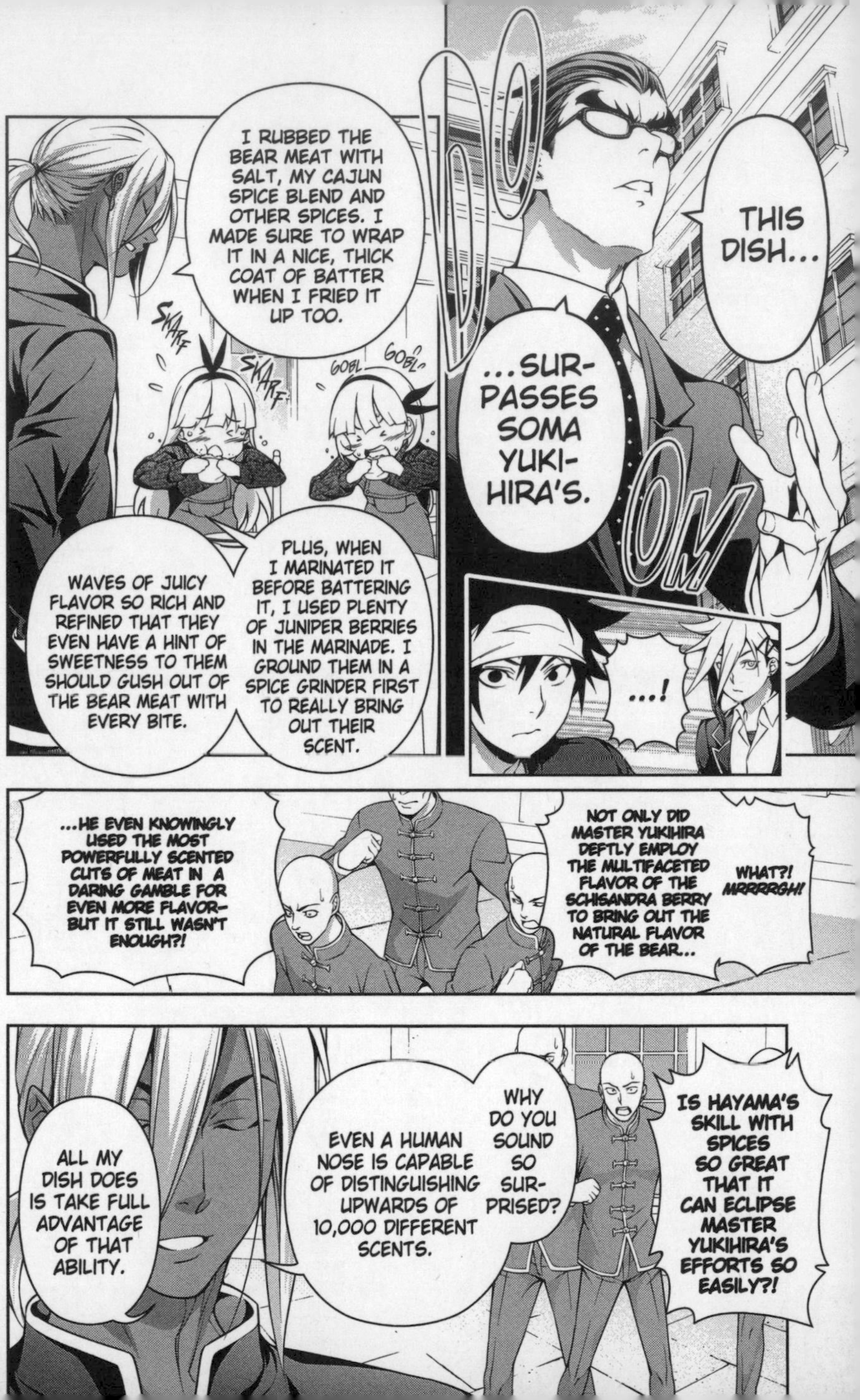
THIS DISH...
...SURPASSES SOMA YUKIHIRA'S.
...!
I RUBBED THE BEAR MEAT WITH SALT, MY CAJUN SPICE BLEND AND OTHER SPICES. I MADE SURE TO WRAP IT IN A NICE, THICK COAT OF BATTER WHEN I FRIED IT UP TOO.
SKARF
SKARF
GOBL
GOBL
PLUS, WHEN I MARINATED IT BEFORE BATTERING IT, I USED PLENTY OF JUNIPER BERRIES IN THE MARINADE. I GROUND THEM IN A SPICE GRINDER FIRST TO REALLY BRING OUT THEIR SCENT.
WAVES OF JUICY FLAVOR SO RICH AND REFINED THAT THEY EVEN HAVE A HINT OF SWEETNESS TO THEM SHOULD GUSH OUT OF THE BEAR MEAT WITH EVERY BITE.
WHAT?! MRRRRGH!
NOT ONLY DID MASTER YUKIHIRA DEFTLY EMPLOY THE MULTIFACETED FLAVOR OF THE SCHISANDRA BERRY TO BRING OUT THE NATURAL FLAVOR OF THE BEAR...
...HE EVEN KNOWINGLY USED THE MOST POWERFULLY SCENTED CUTS OF MEAT IN A DARING GAMBLE FOR EVEN MORE FLAVOR-BUT IT STILL WASN'T ENOUGH?!
IS HAYAMA'S SKILL WITH SPICES SO GREAT THAT IT CAN ECLIPSE MASTER YUKIHIRA'S EFFORTS SO EASILY?!
WHY DO YOU SOUND SO SURPRISED?
EVEN A HUMAN NOSE IS CAPABLE OF DISTINGUISHING UPWARDS OF 10,000 DIFFERENT SCENTS.
ALL MY DISH DOES IS TAKE FULL ADVANTAGE OF THAT ABILITY.

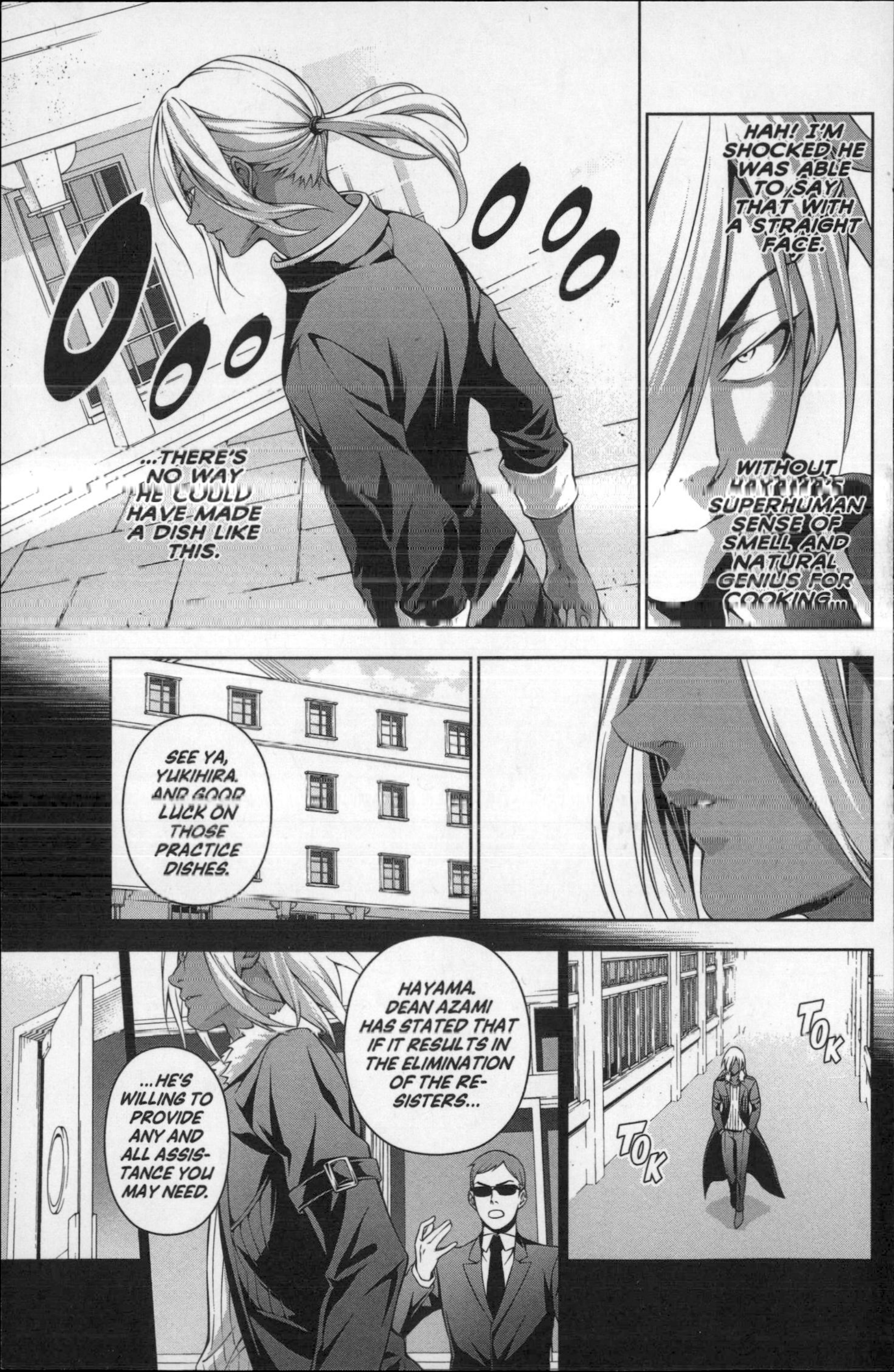
HAH! I'M SHOCKED HE WAS ABLE TO SAY THAT WITH A STRAIGHT FACE.
WITHOUT HAYAMA'S SUPERHUMAN SENSE OF SMELL AND NATURAL GENIUS FOR COOKING...
...THERE'S NO WAY HE COULD HAVE MADE A DISH LIKE THIS.
SEE YA, YUKIHIRA. AND GOOD LUCK ON THOSE PRACTICE DISHES.
TOK
TOK
HAYAMA. DEAN AZAMI HAS STATED THAT IF IT RESULTS IN THE ELIMINATION OF THE RE-SISTERS...
...HE'S WILLING TO PROVIDE ANY AND ALL ASSIS-TANCE YOU MAY NEED.

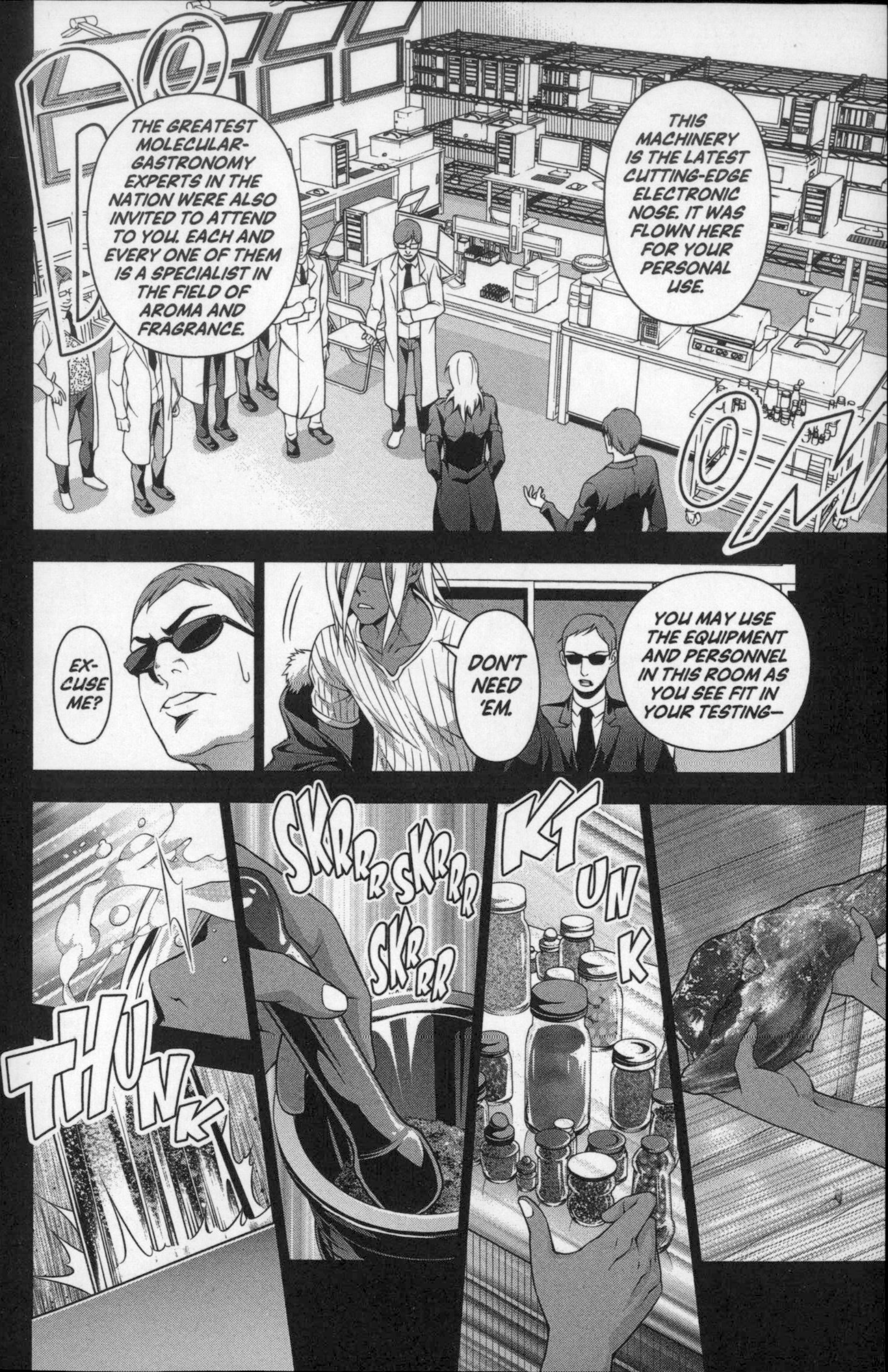

THIS MACHINERY IS THE LATEST CUTTING-EDGE ELECTRONIC NOSE. IT WAS FLOWN HERE FOR YOUR PERSONAL USE.
THE GREATEST MOLECULAR-GASTRONOMY EXPERTS IN THE NATION WERE ALSO INVITED TO ATTEND TO YOU. EACH AND EVERY ONE OF THEM IS A SPECIALIST IN THE FIELD OF AROMA AND FRAGRANCE.
YOU MAY USE THE EQUIPMENT AND PERSONNEL IN THIS ROOM AS YOU SEE FIT IN YOUR TESTING—
DON'T NEED 'EM.
EX-CUSE ME?
KTUNK
SKRRRR SKRRRR SKRRRR
THUNK

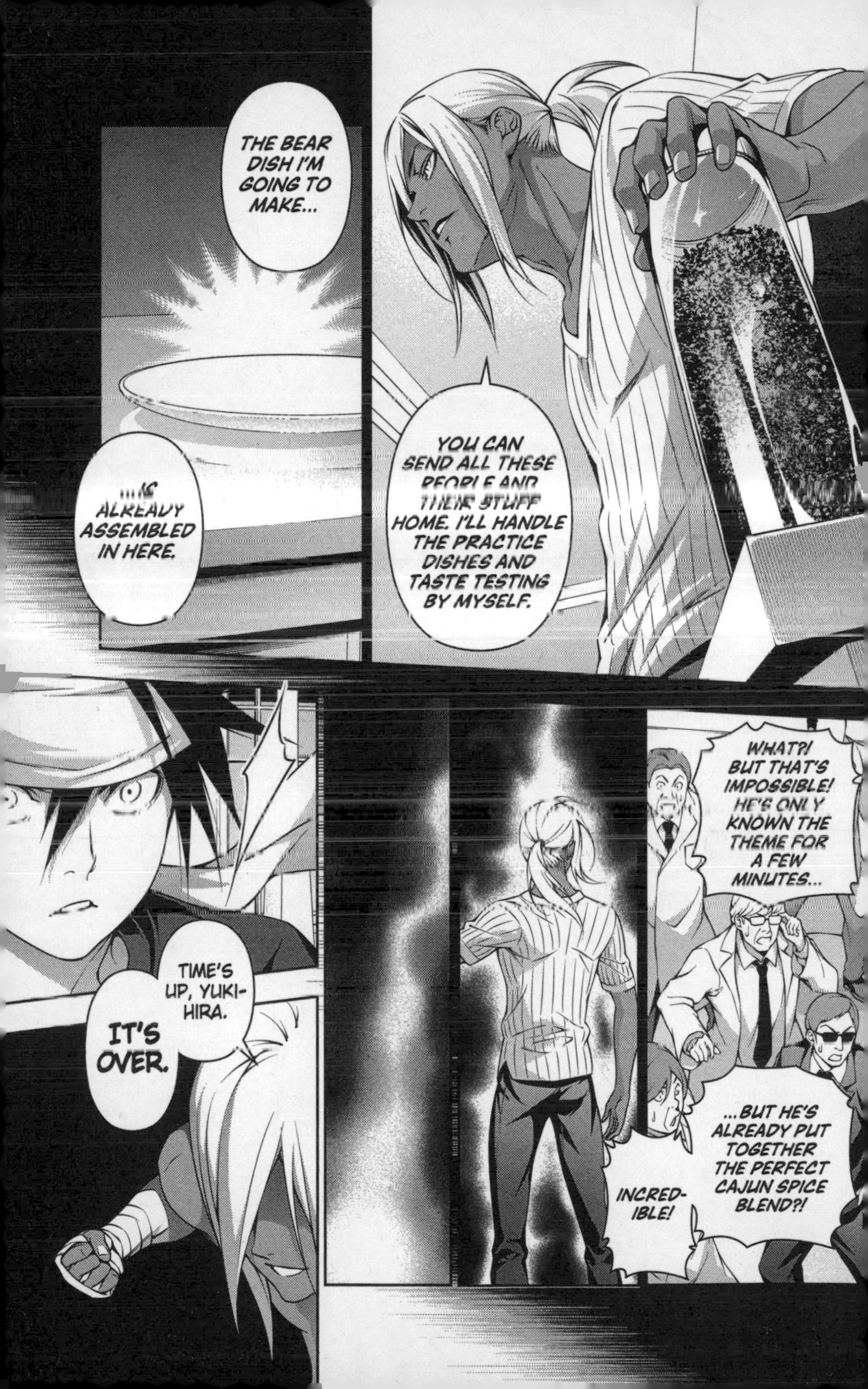
YOU CAN SEND ALL THESE PEOPLE AND THEIR STUFF HOME. I'LL HANDLE THE PRACTICE DISHES AND TASTE TESTING BY MYSELF.
THE BEAR DISH I'M GOING TO MAKE...
IS ALREADY ASSEMBLED IN HERE.
WHAT?! BUT THAT'S IMPOSSIBLE! HE'S ONLY KNOWN THE THEME FOR A FEW MINUTES...
...BUT HE'S ALREADY PUT TOGETHER THE PERFECT CAJUN SPICE BLEND?!
INCRED-IBLE!
TIME'S UP, YUKI-HIRA.
IT'S OVER.

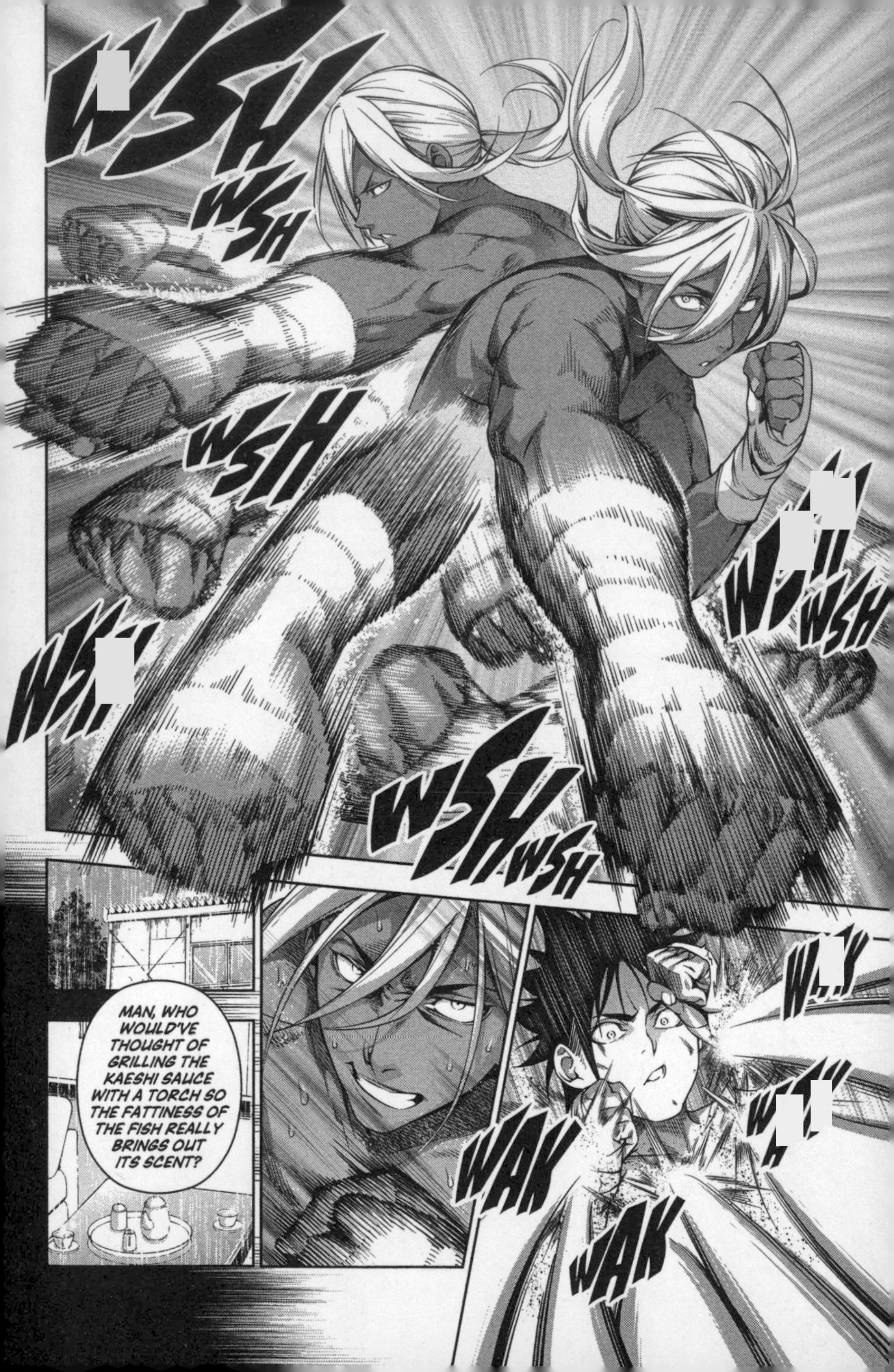
WSH
WSH
WSH
WSH
WSH
WSH
WAK
WAK
MAN, WHO WOULD'VE THOUGHT OF GRILLING THE KAESHI SAUCE WITH A TORCH SO THE FATTINESS OF THE FISH REALLY BRINGS OUT ITS SCENT?

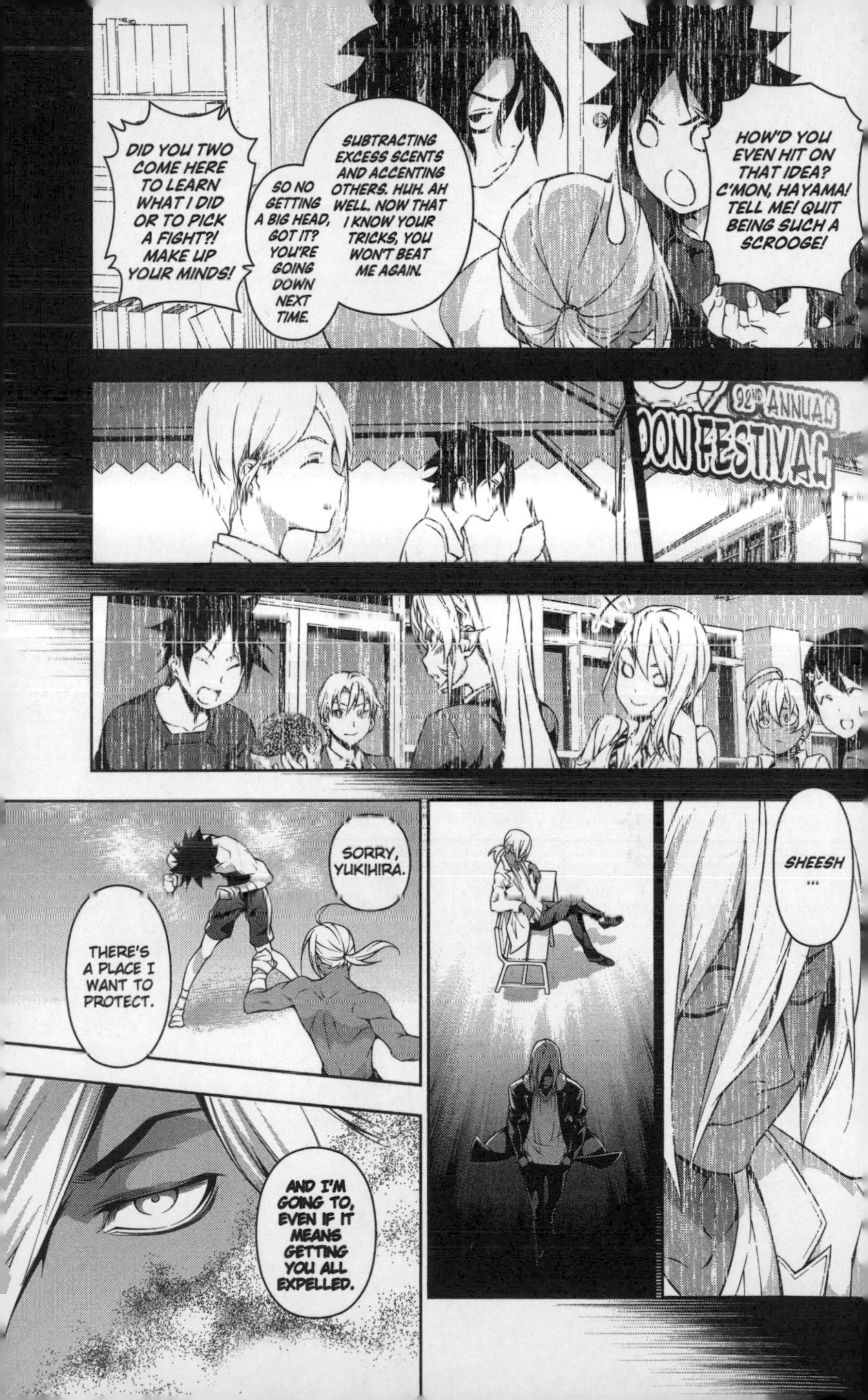
HOW'D YOU EVEN HIT ON THAT IDEA? C'MON, HAYAMA! TELL ME! QUIT BEING SUCH A SCROOGE!
SUBTRACTING EXCESS SCENTS AND ACCENTING OTHERS. HUH. AH WELL. NOW THAT I KNOW YOUR TRICKS, YOU WON'T BEAT ME AGAIN.
SO NO GETTING A BIG HEAD, GOT IT? YOU'RE GOING DOWN NEXT TIME.
DID YOU TWO COME HERE TO LEARN WHAT I DID OR TO PICK A FIGHT?! MAKE UP YOUR MINDS!
22ND ANNUAL
OON FESTIVAL
SHEESH ...
SORRY, YUKIHIRA.
THERE'S A PLACE I WANT TO PROTECT.
AND I'M GOING TO, EVEN IF IT MEANS GETTING YOU ALL EXPELLED.

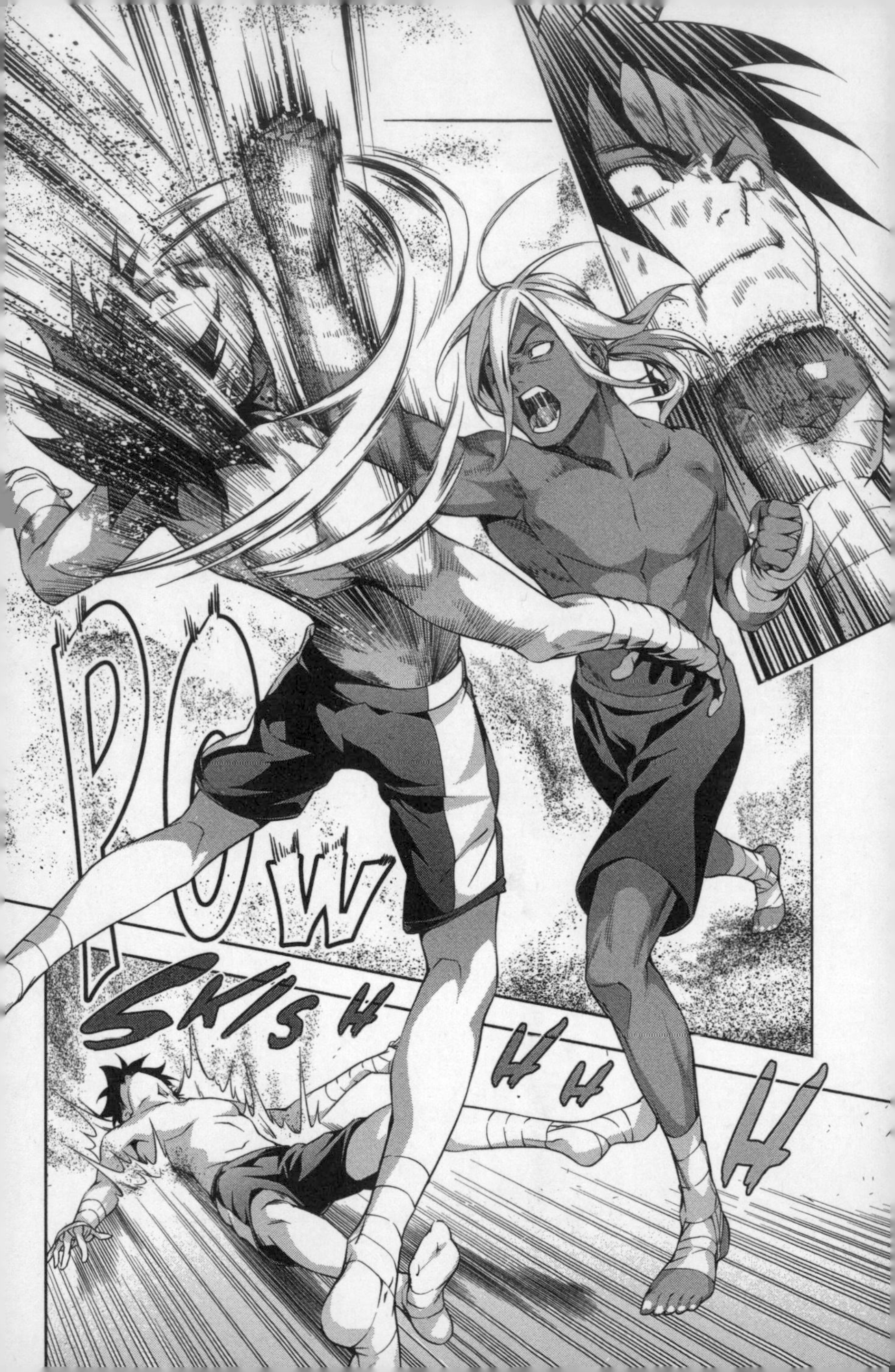
POW
SKISHHHHH

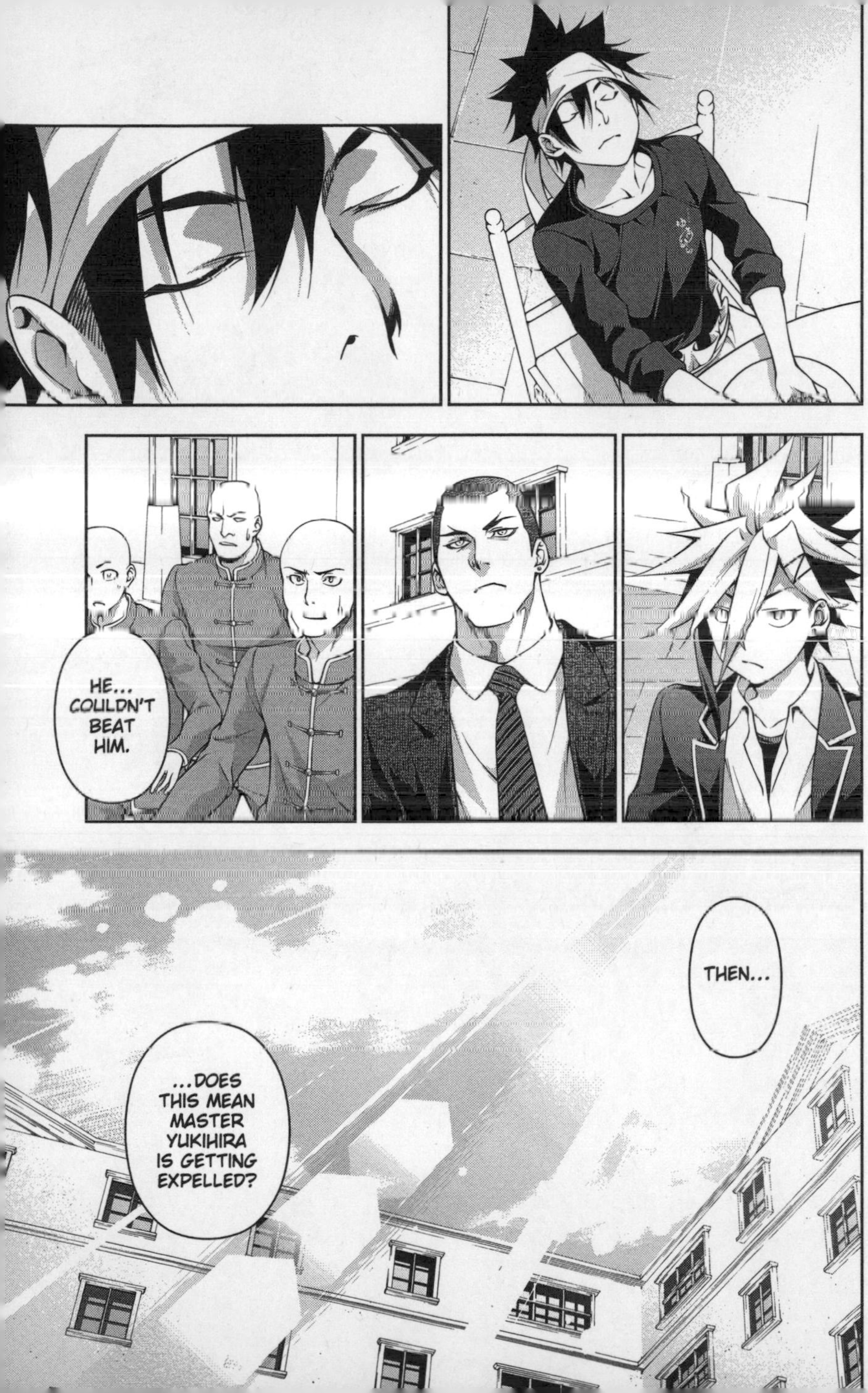
HE... COULDN'T BEAT HIM.
THEN...
...DOES THIS MEAN MASTER YUKIHIRA IS GETTING EXPELLED?

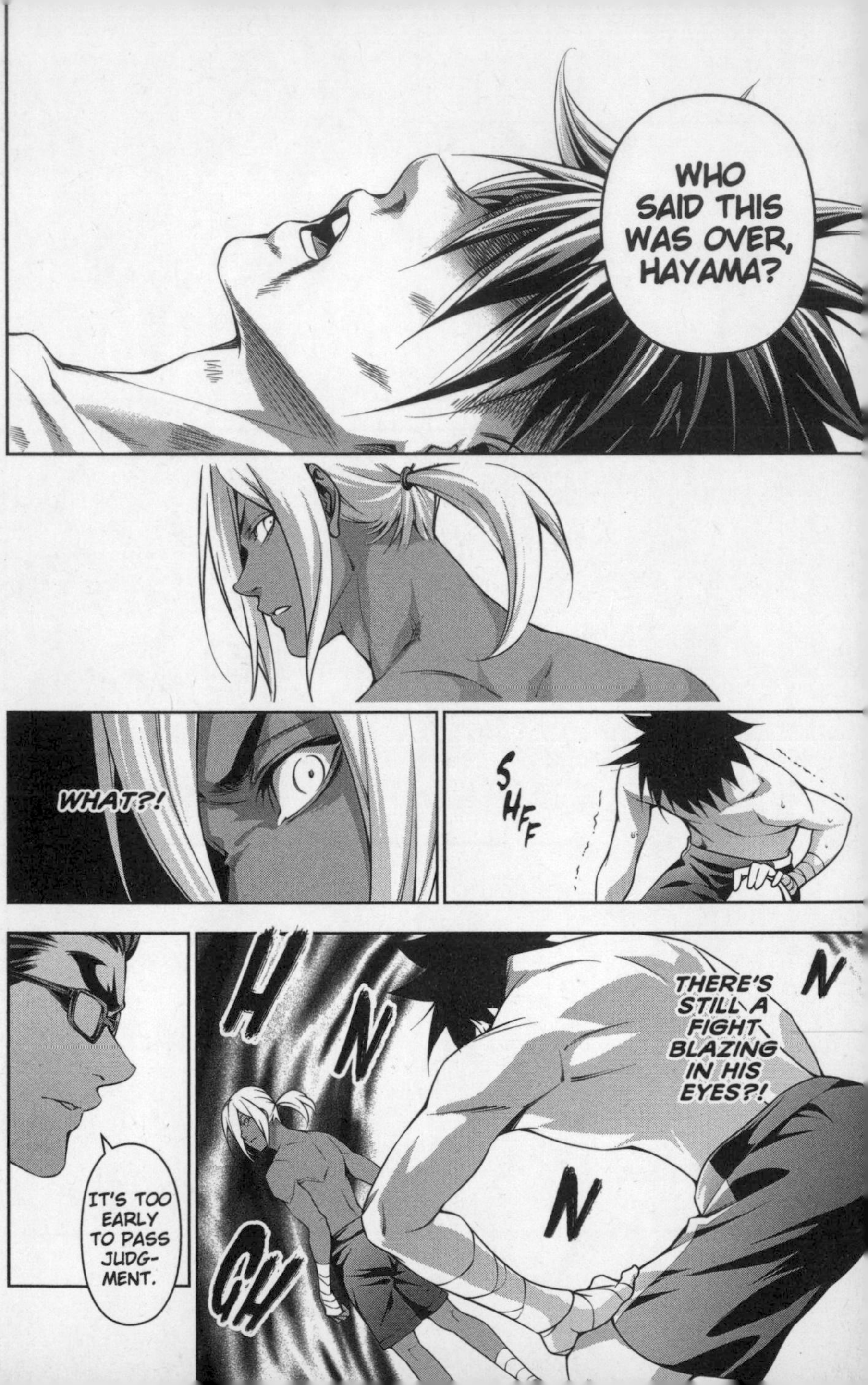

WHO SAID THIS WAS OVER, HAYAMA?
SHFF
WHAT?!
THERE'S STILL A FIGHT BLAZING IN HIS EYES?!
HNNNGH
IT'S TOO EARLY TO PASS JUDG-MENT.

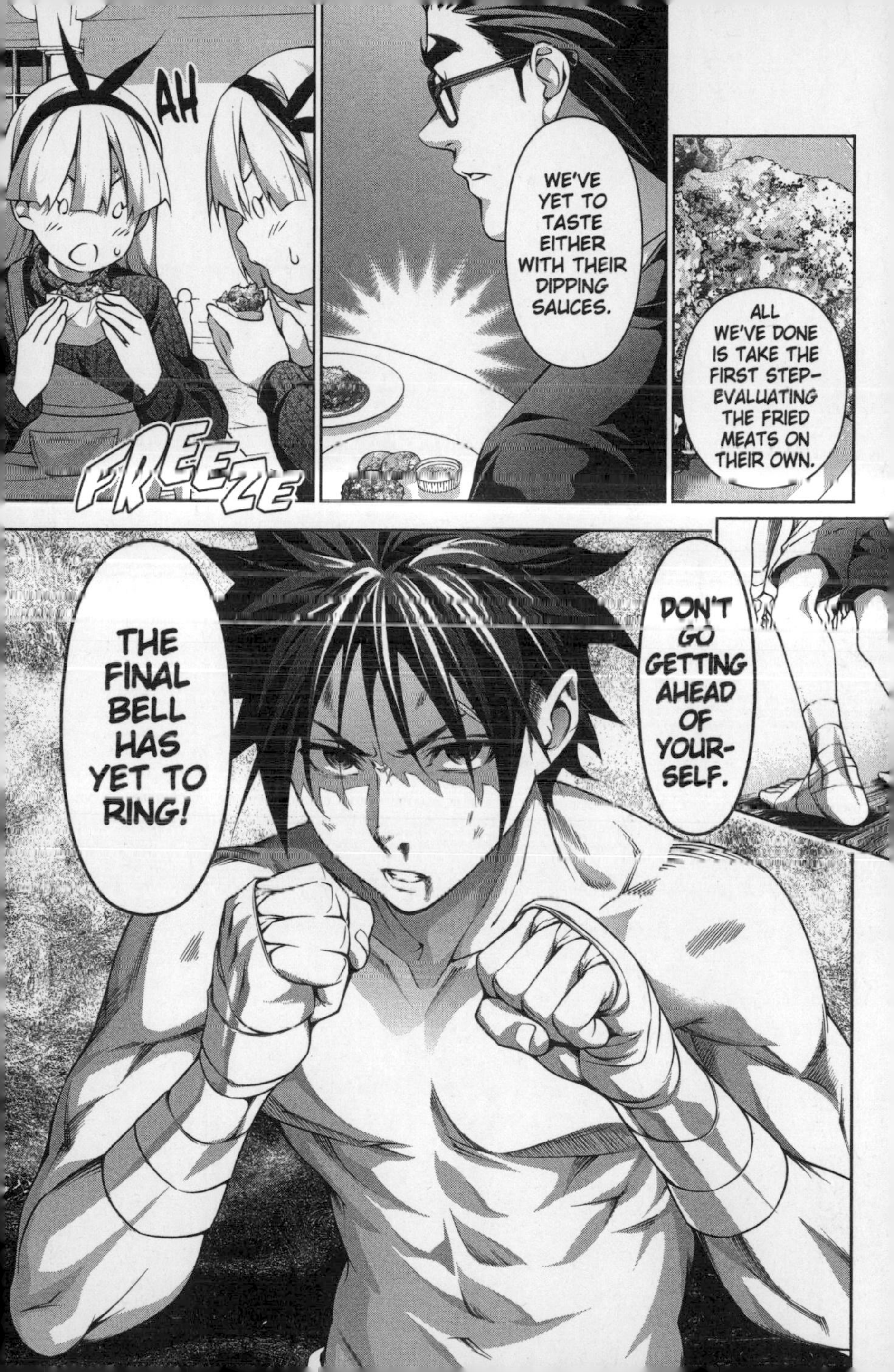
ALL WE'VE DONE IS TAKE THE FIRST STEP—EVALUATING THE FRIED MEATS ON THEIR OWN.
WE'VE YET TO TASTE EITHER WITH THEIR DIPPING SAUCES.
AH
FREEZE
DON'T GO GETTING AHEAD OF YOURSELF.
THE FINAL BELL HAS YET TO RING!

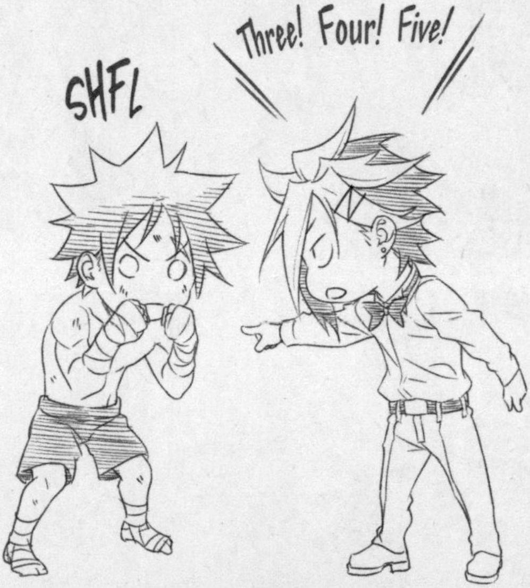
Three! Four! Five!
SHFL

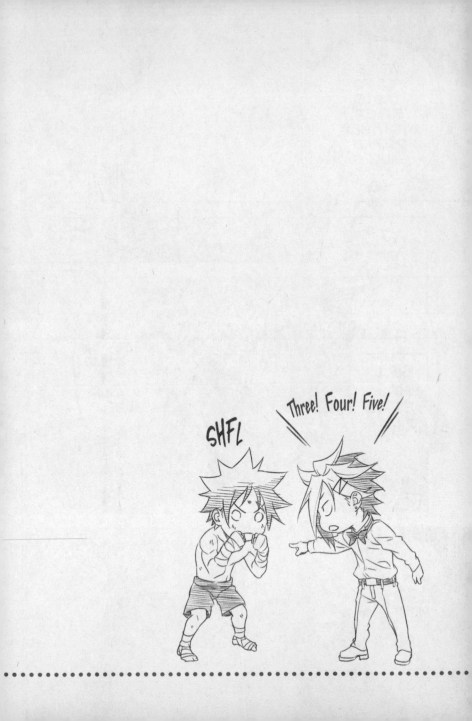

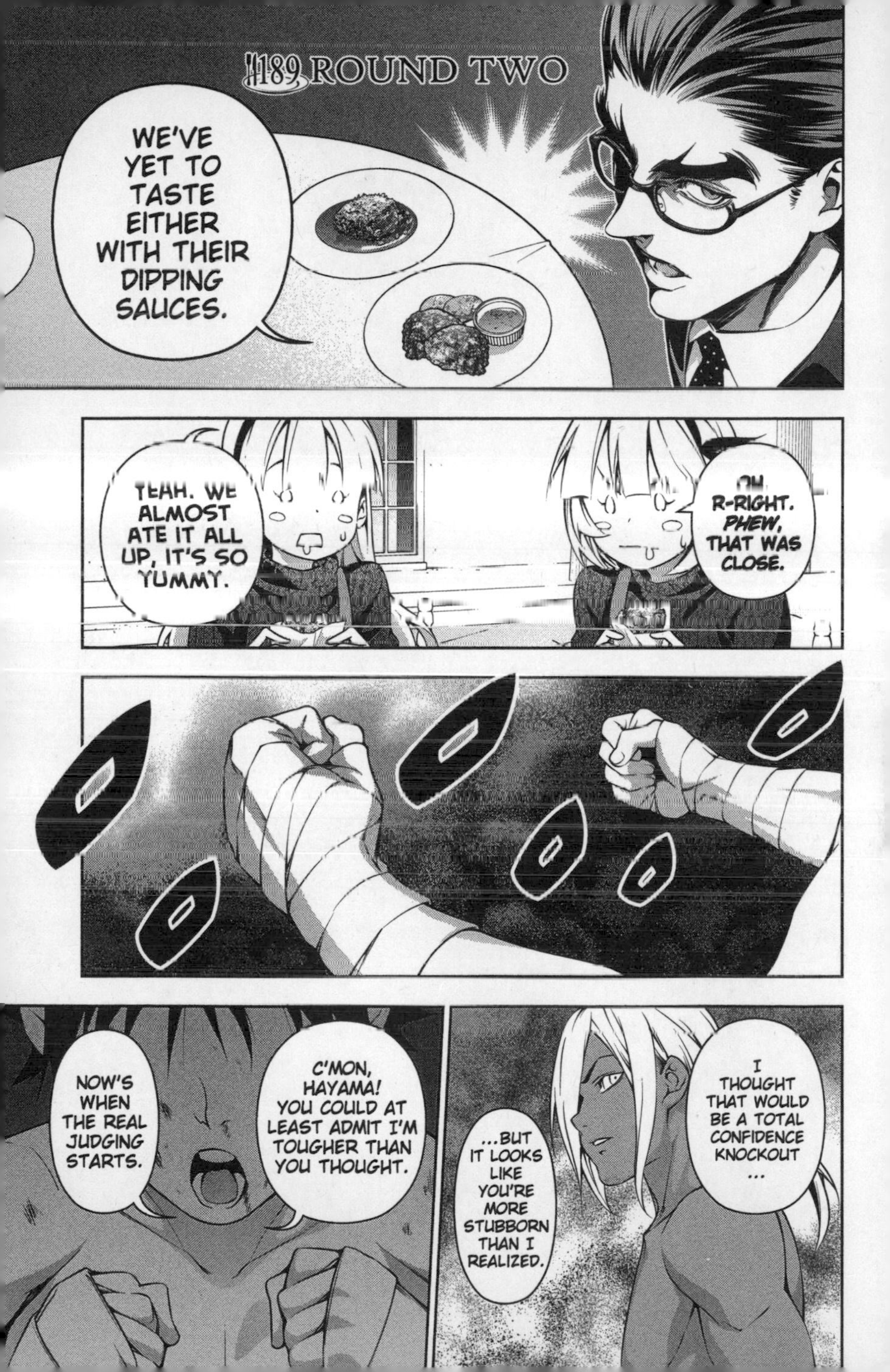
#189 ROUND TWO
WE'VE YET TO TASTE EITHER WITH THEIR DIPPING SAUCES.
OH, R-RIGHT. *PHEW*, THAT WAS CLOSE.
YEAH. WE ALMOST ATE IT ALL UP, IT'S SO YUMMY.
I THOUGHT THAT WOULD BE A TOTAL CONFIDENCE KNOCKOUT...
...BUT IT LOOKS LIKE YOU'RE MORE STUBBORN THAN I REALIZED.
C'MON, HAYAMA! YOU COULD AT LEAST ADMIT I'M TOUGHER THAN YOU THOUGHT.
NOW'S WHEN THE REAL JUDGING STARTS.

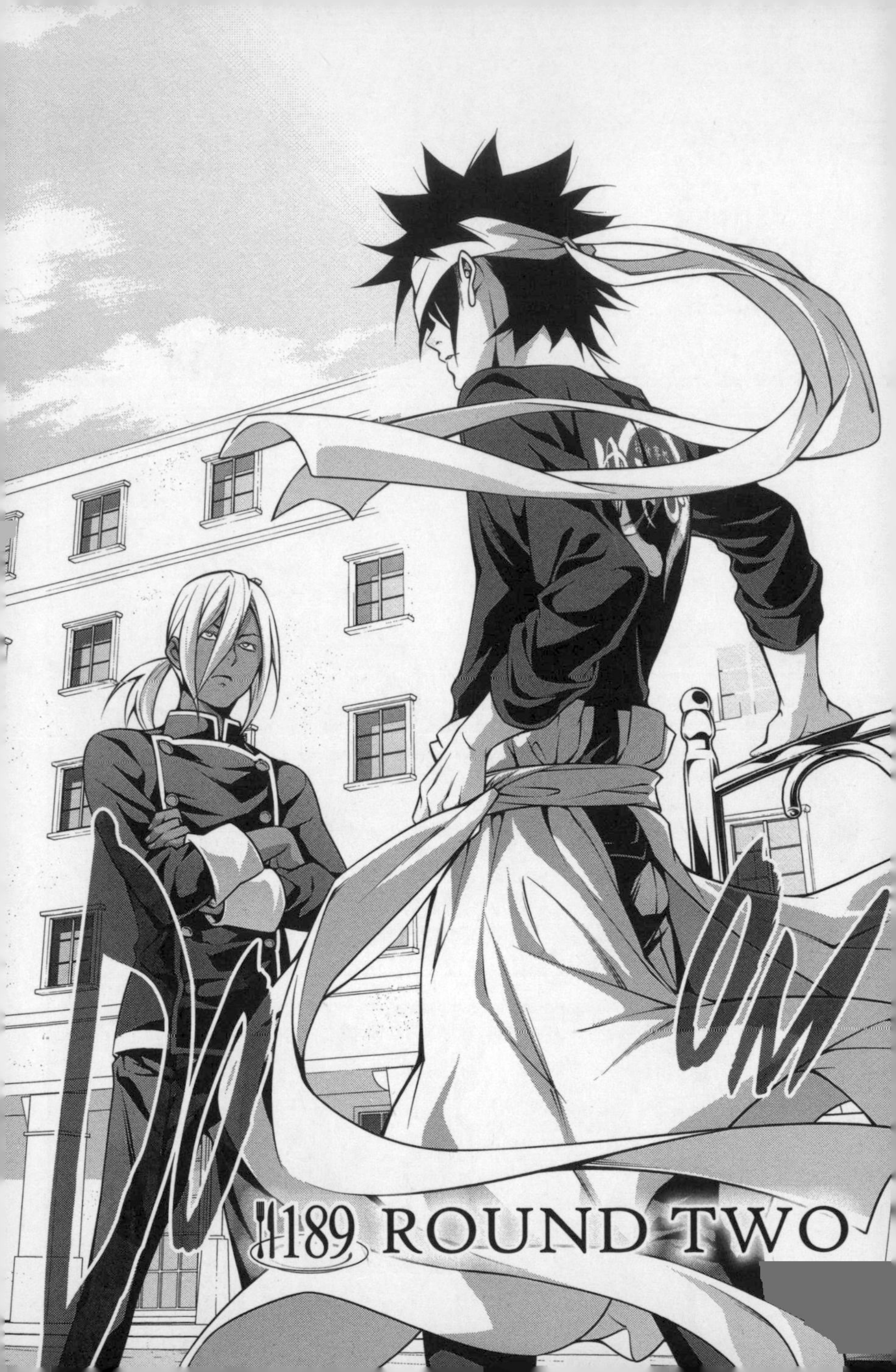

189 ROUND TWO

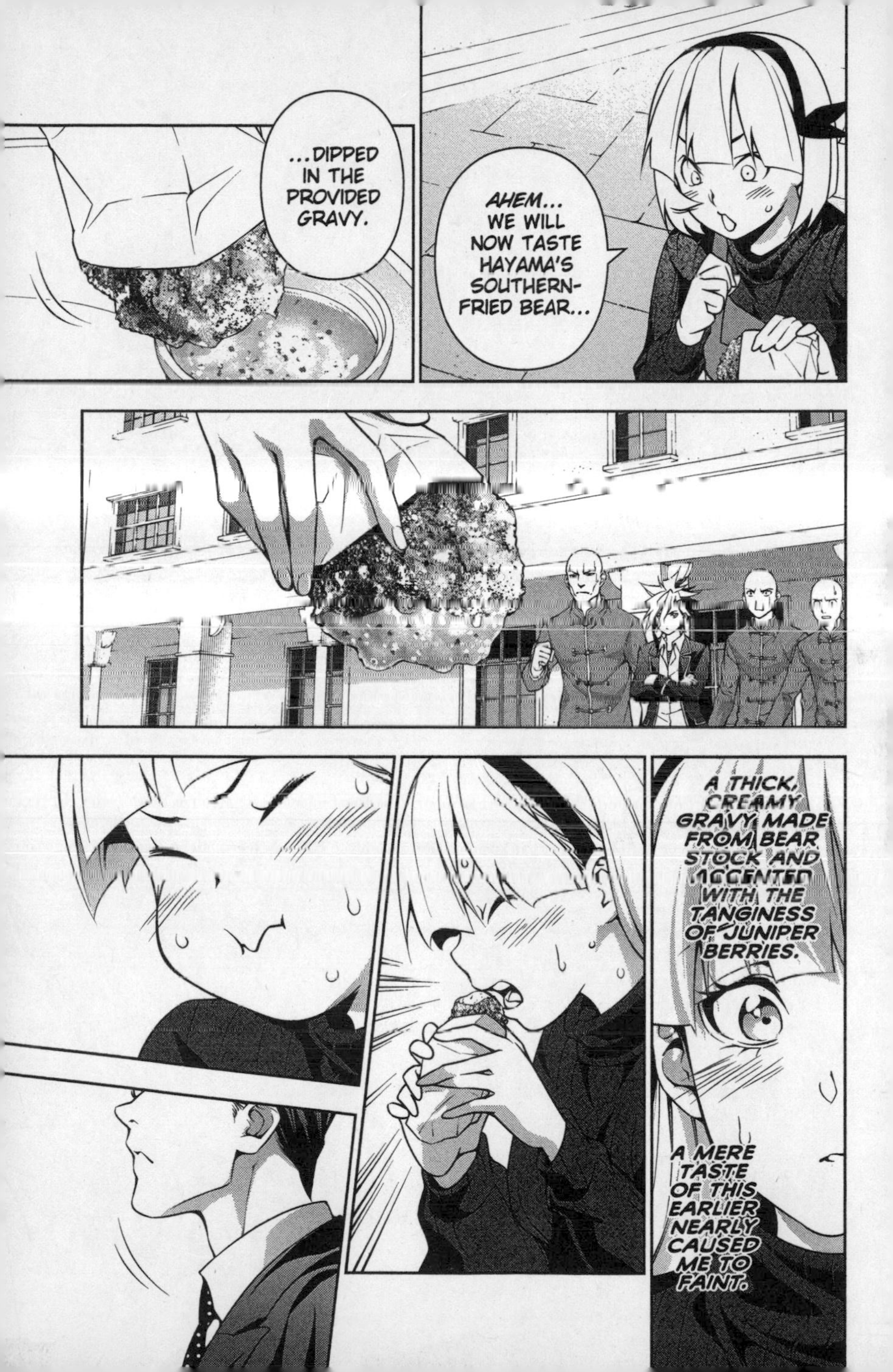
AHEM... WE WILL NOW TASTE HAYAMA'S SOUTHERN-FRIED BEAR...
...DIPPED IN THE PROVIDED GRAVY.
A THICK, CREAMY GRAVY MADE FROM BEAR STOCK AND ACCENTED WITH THE TANGINESS OF JUNIPER BERRIES.
A MERE TASTE OF THIS EARLIER NEARLY CAUSED ME TO FAINT.

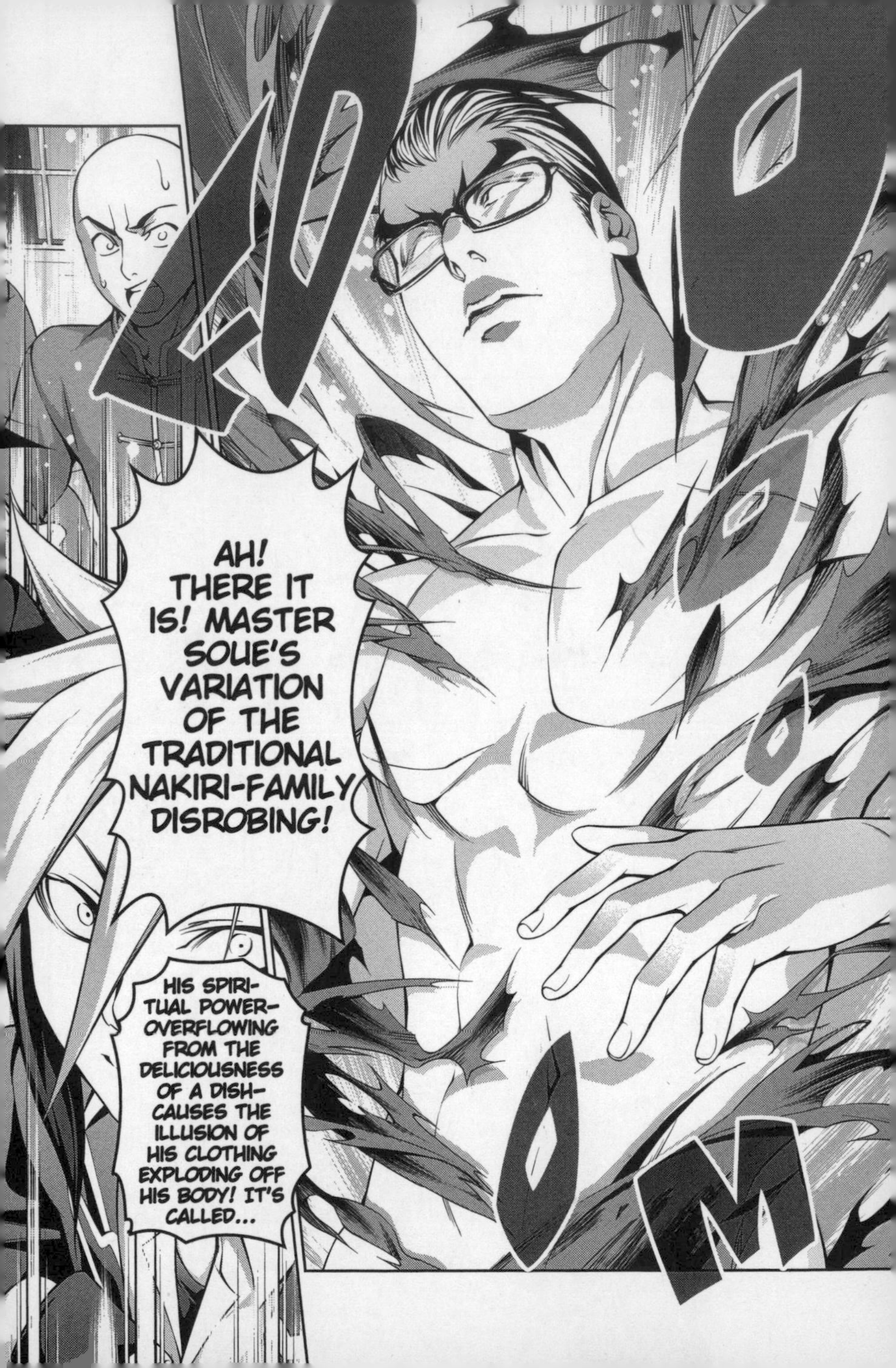
AH! THERE IT IS! MASTER SOUE'S VARIATION OF THE TRADITIONAL NAKIRI-FAMILY DISROBING!
HIS SPIRITUAL POWER—OVERFLOWING FROM THE DELICIOUSNESS OF A DISH—CAUSES THE ILLUSION OF HIS CLOTHING EXPLODING OFF HIS BODY! IT'S CALLED...

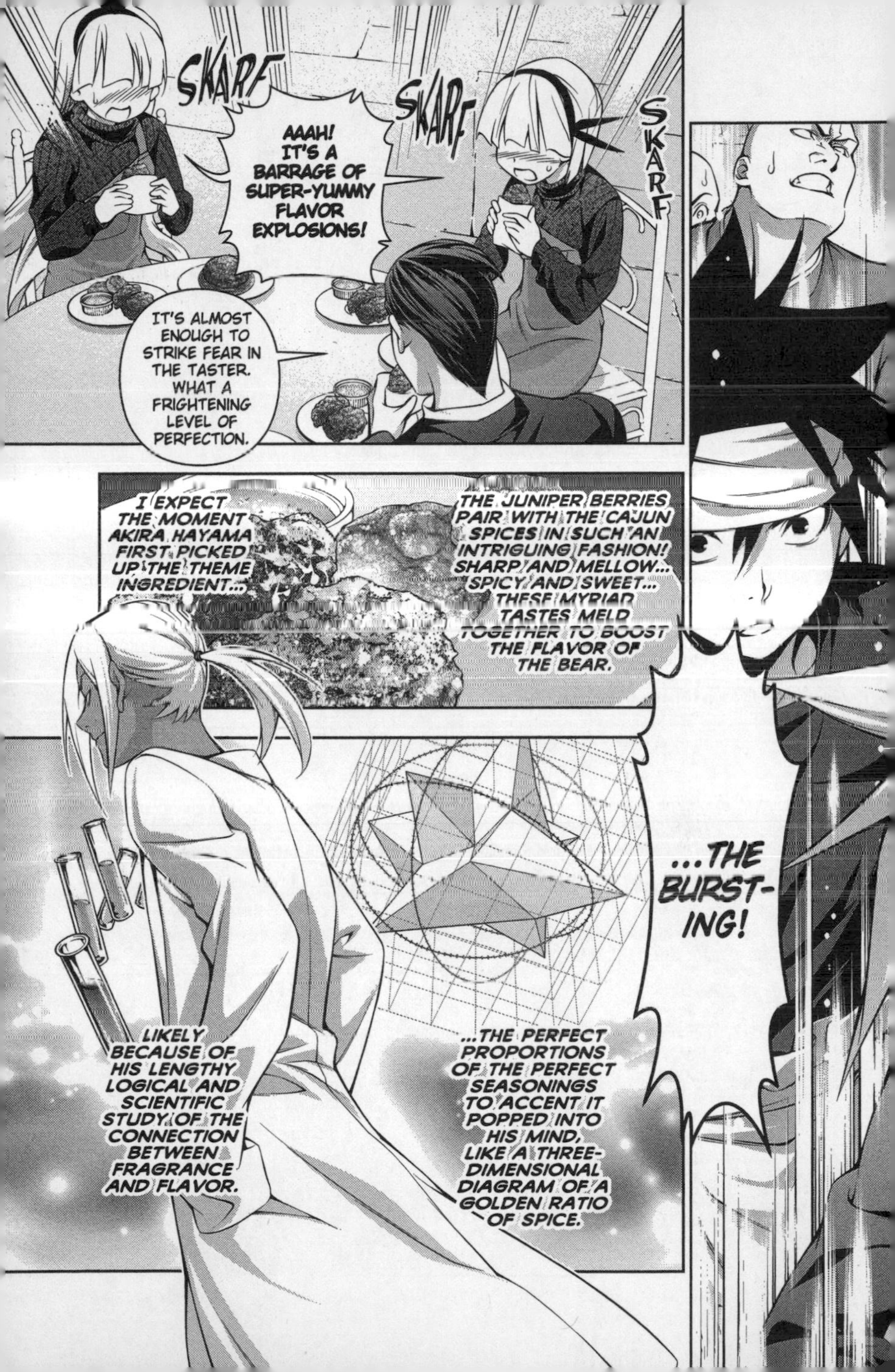
SKARF
SKARF
SKARF
AAAH! IT'S A BARRAGE OF SUPER-YUMMY FLAVOR EXPLOSIONS!
IT'S ALMOST ENOUGH TO STRIKE FEAR IN THE TASTER. WHAT A FRIGHTENING LEVEL OF PERFECTION.
...THE BURSTING!
THE JUNIPER BERRIES PAIR WITH THE CAJUN SPICES IN SUCH AN INTRIGUING FASHION! SHARP AND MELLOW... SPICY AND SWEET... THESE MYRIAD TASTES MELD TOGETHER TO BOOST THE FLAVOR OF THE BEAR.
I EXPECT THE MOMENT AKIRA HAYAMA FIRST PICKED UP THE THEME INGREDIENT...
...THE PERFECT PROPORTIONS OF THE PERFECT SEASONINGS TO ACCENT IT POPPED INTO HIS MIND, LIKE A THREE-DIMENSIONAL DIAGRAM OF A GOLDEN RATIO OF SPICE.
LIKELY BECAUSE OF HIS LENGTHY LOGICAL AND SCIENTIFIC STUDY OF THE CONNECTION BETWEEN FRAGRANCE AND FLAVOR.

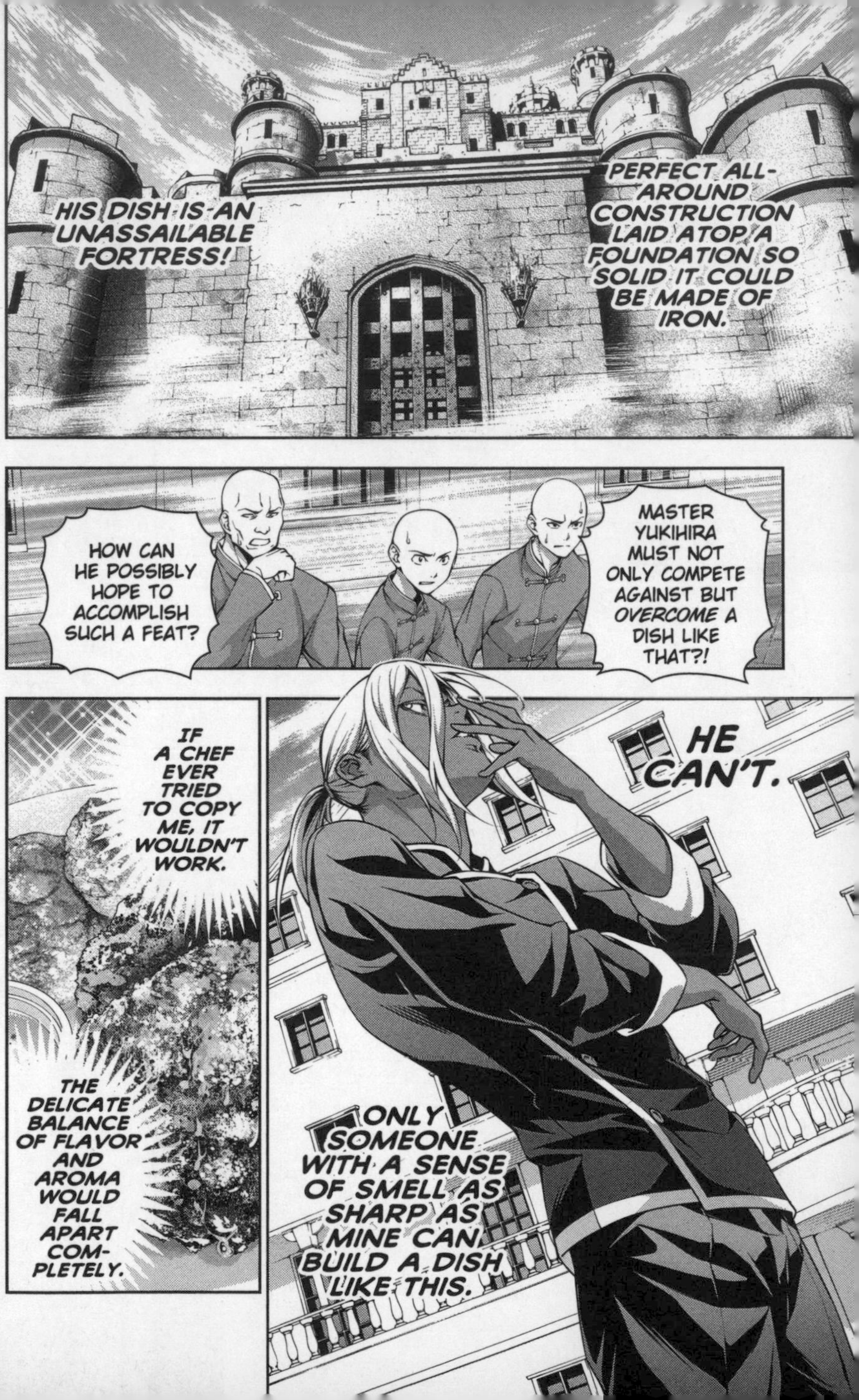
PERFECT ALL-AROUND CONSTRUCTION LAID ATOP A FOUNDATION SO SOLID IT COULD BE MADE OF IRON.
HIS DISH IS AN UNASSAILABLE FORTRESS!
MASTER YUKIHIRA MUST NOT ONLY COMPETE AGAINST BUT OVERCOME A DISH LIKE THAT?!
HOW CAN HE POSSIBLY HOPE TO ACCOMPLISH SUCH A FEAT?
HE CAN'T.
ONLY SOMEONE WITH A SENSE OF SMELL AS SHARP AS MINE CAN BUILD A DISH LIKE THIS.
IF A CHEF EVER TRIED TO COPY ME, IT WOULDN'T WORK.
THE DELICATE BALANCE OF FLAVOR AND AROMA WOULD FALL APART COM-PLETELY.

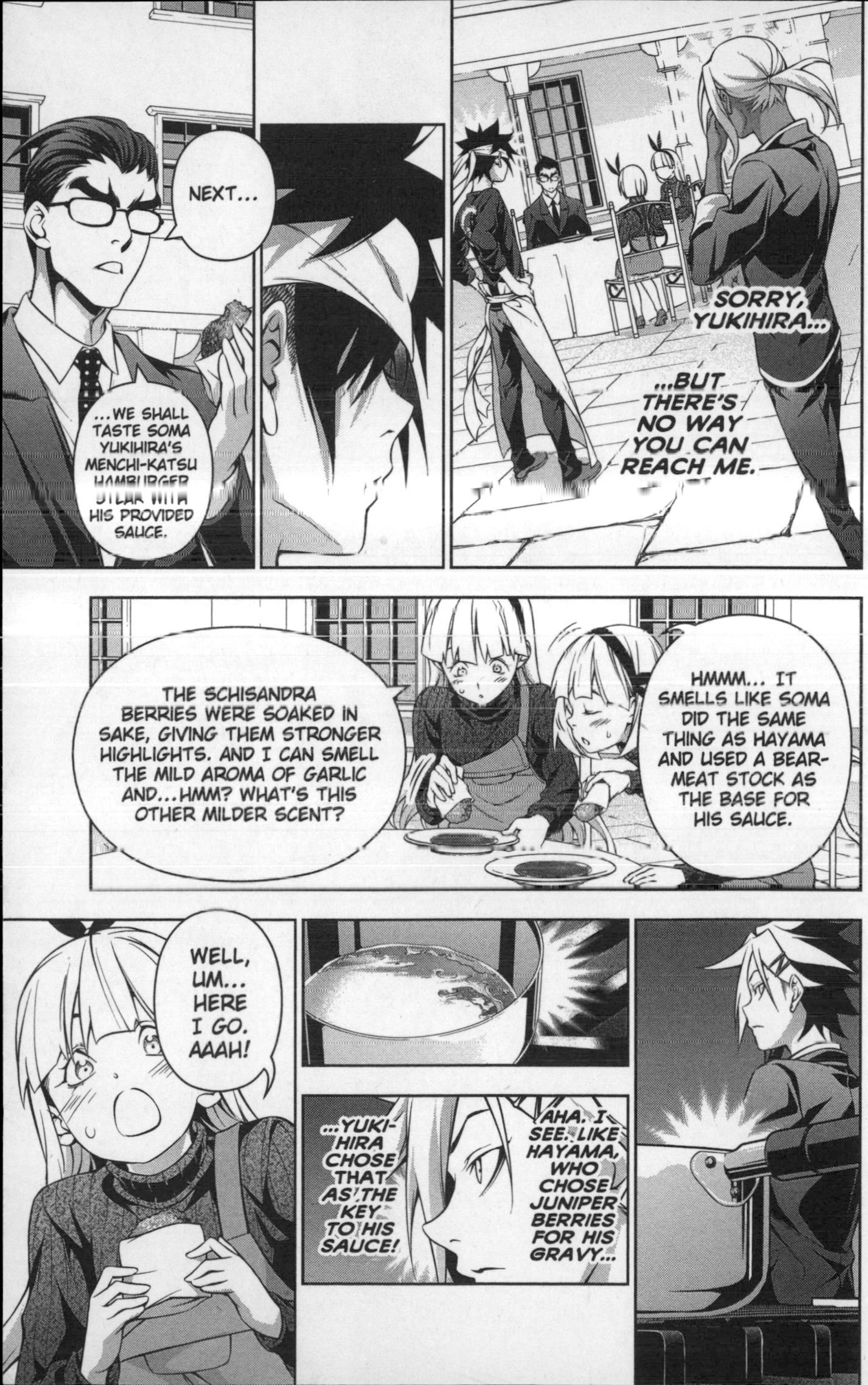
SORRY, YUKIHIRA...
...BUT THERE'S NO WAY YOU CAN REACH ME.
NEXT...
...WE SHALL TASTE SOMA YUKIHIRA'S MENCHI-KATSU HAMBURGER STEAK WITH HIS PROVIDED SAUCE.
HMMM... IT SMELLS LIKE SOMA DID THE SAME THING AS HAYAMA AND USED A BEAR-MEAT STOCK AS THE BASE FOR HIS SAUCE.
THE SCHISANDRA BERRIES WERE SOAKED IN SAKE, GIVING THEM STRONGER HIGHLIGHTS. AND I CAN SMELL THE MILD AROMA OF GARLIC AND...HMM? WHAT'S THIS OTHER MILDER SCENT?
AHA. I SEE. LIKE HAYAMA, WHO CHOSE JUNIPER BERRIES FOR HIS GRAVY...
...YUKIHIRA CHOSE THAT AS THE KEY TO HIS SAUCE!
WELL, UM... HERE I GO. AAAH!

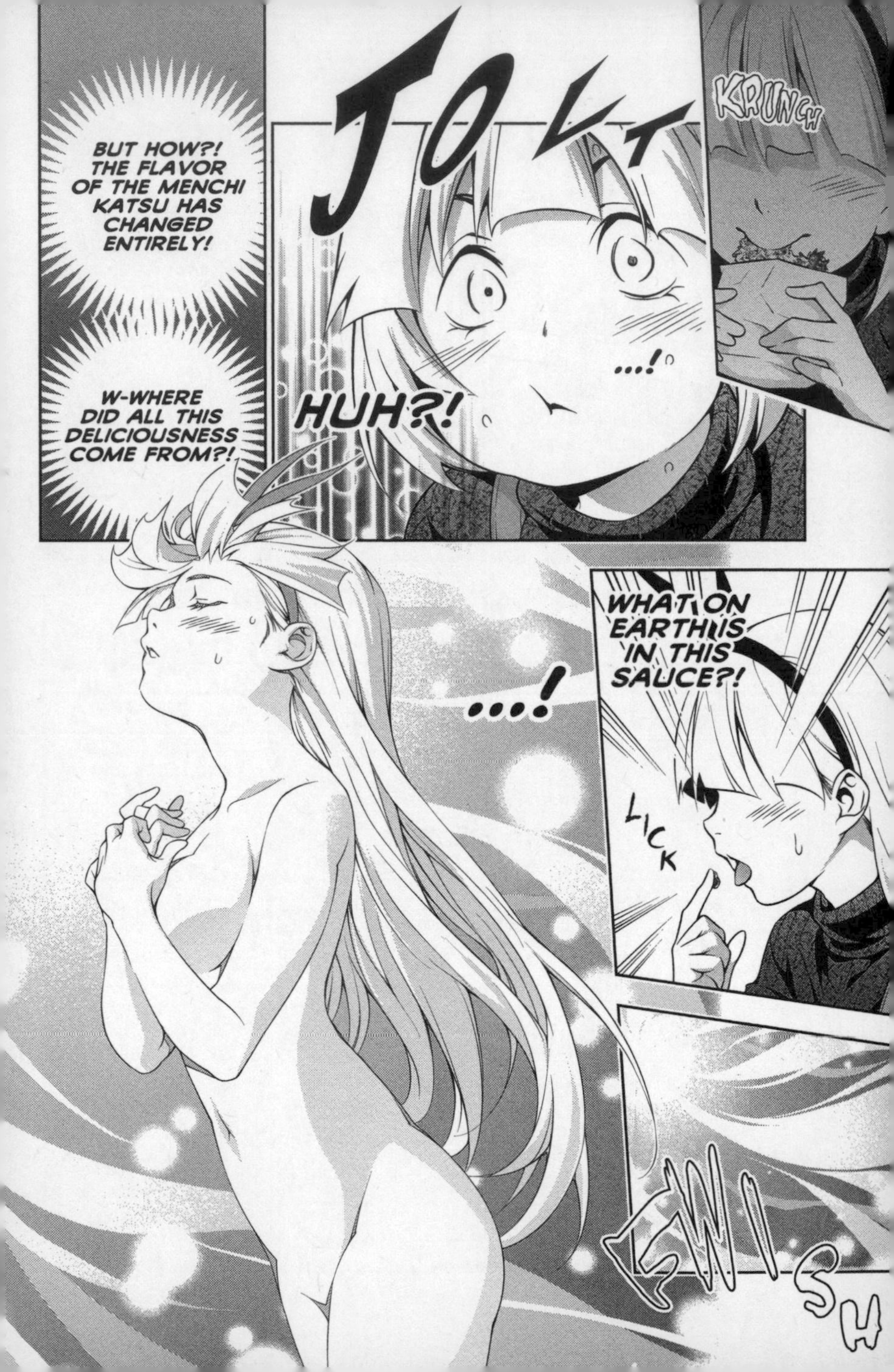
KRUNCH
JOLT
...!
HUH?!
BUT HOW?! THE FLAVOR OF THE MENCHI KATSU HAS CHANGED ENTIRELY!
W-WHERE DID ALL THIS DELICIOUSNESS COME FROM?!
WHAT ON EARTH IS IN THIS SAUCE?!
LICK
FWISH
...!

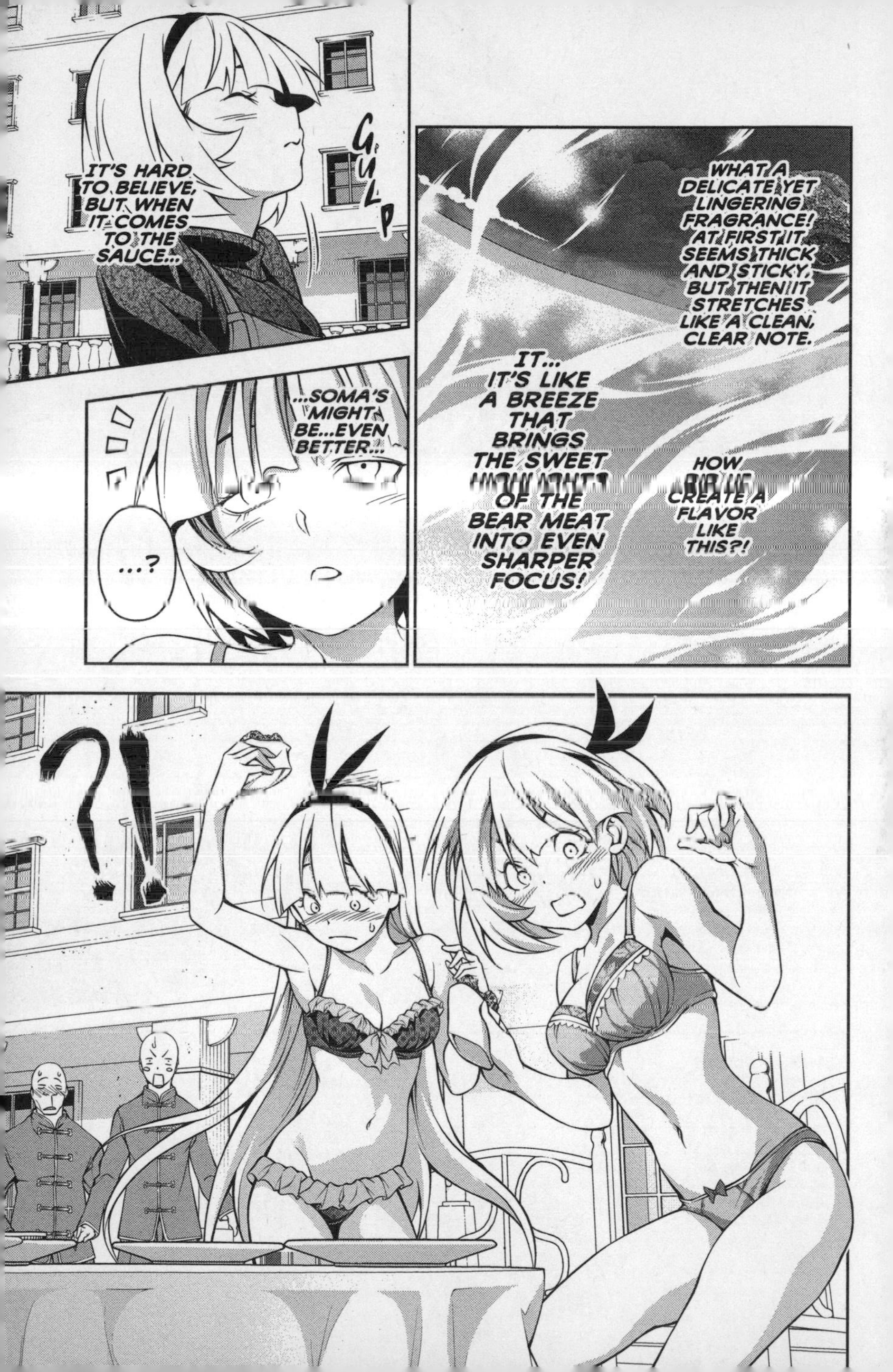
IT'S HARD TO BELIEVE, BUT WHEN IT COMES TO THE SAUCE...
GULP
...SOMA'S MIGHT BE...EVEN BETTER...
...?
WHAT A DELICATE YET LINGERING FRAGRANCE! AT FIRST IT SEEMS THICK AND STICKY, BUT THEN IT STRETCHES LIKE A CLEAN, CLEAR NOTE.
IT... IT'S LIKE A BREEZE THAT BRINGS THE SWEET OF THE BEAR MEAT INTO EVEN SHARPER FOCUS!
HOW CREATE A FLAVOR LIKE THIS?!
?!

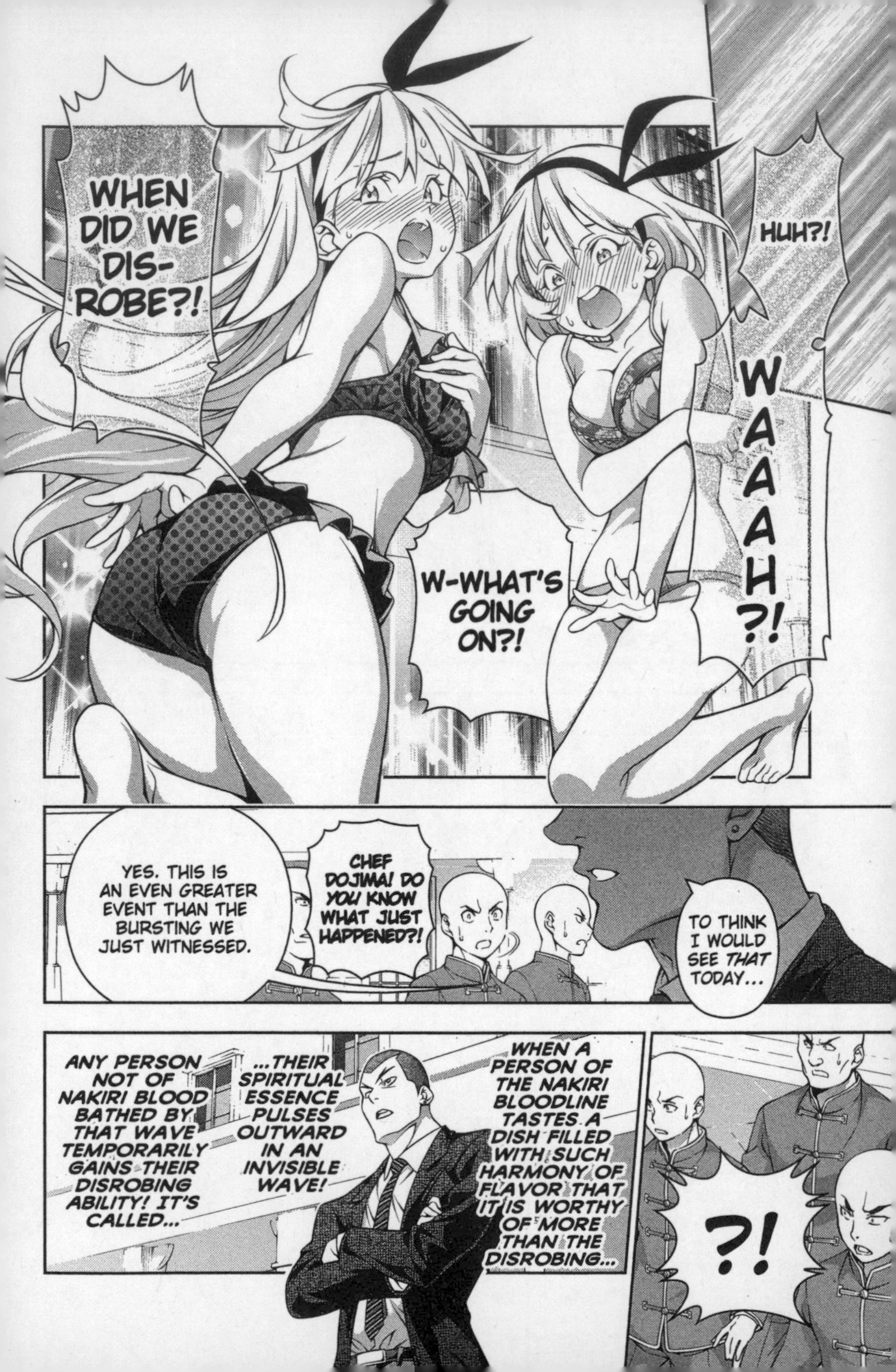
HUH?!
WAAAAH?!
WHEN DID WE DIS-ROBE?!
W-WHAT'S GOING ON?!
TO THINK I WOULD SEE *THAT* TODAY...
CHEF DOJIMA! DO YOU KNOW WHAT JUST HAPPENED?!
YES. THIS IS AN EVEN GREATER EVENT THAN THE BURSTING WE JUST WITNESSED.
?!
WHEN A PERSON OF THE NAKIRI BLOODLINE TASTES A DISH FILLED WITH SUCH HARMONY OF FLAVOR THAT IT IS WORTHY OF MORE THAN THE DISROBING...
...THEIR SPIRITUAL ESSENCE PULSES OUTWARD IN AN INVISIBLE WAVE!
ANY PERSON NOT OF NAKIRI BLOOD BATHED BY THAT WAVE TEMPORARILY GAINS THEIR DISROBING ABILITY! IT'S CALLED...

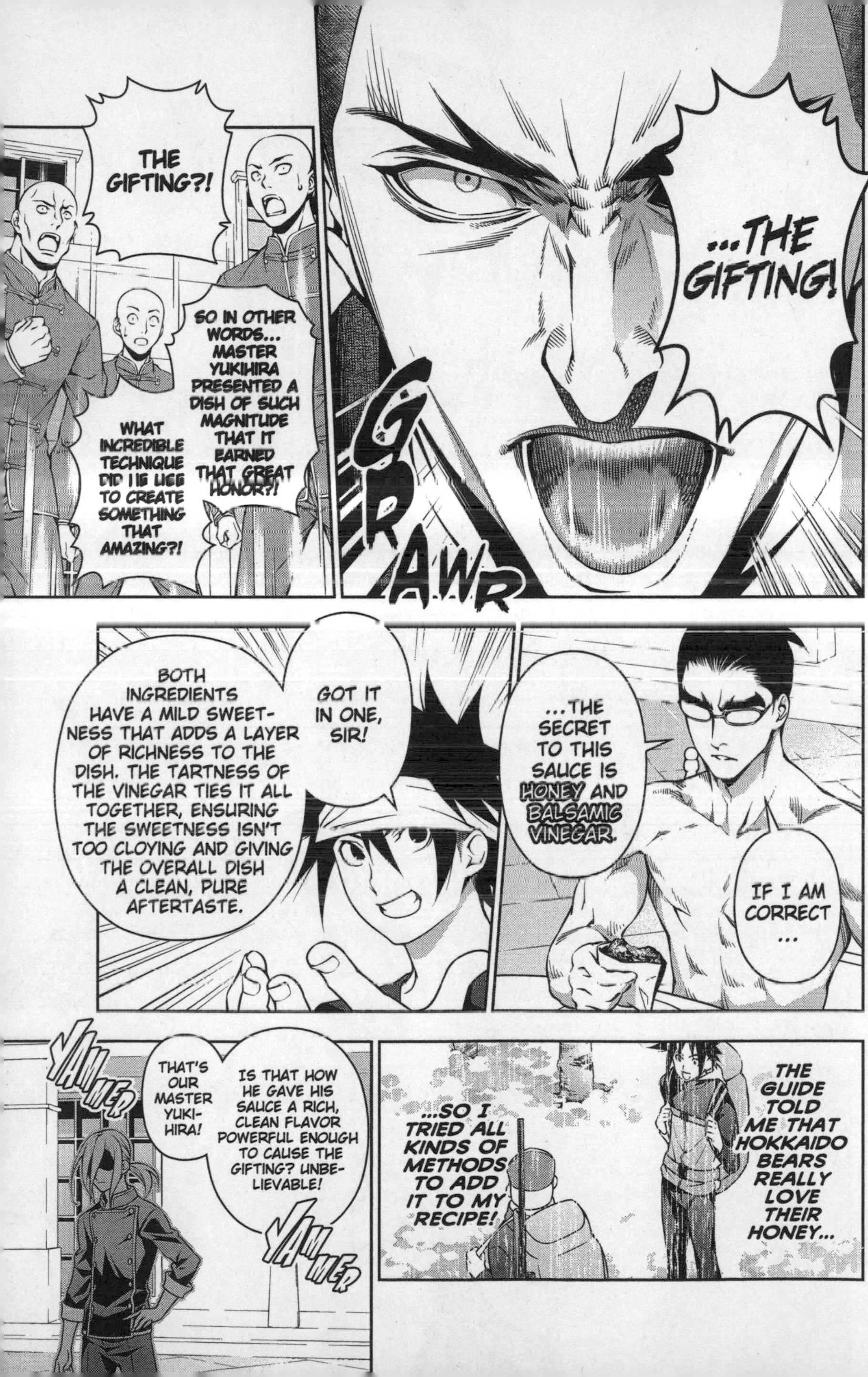
...THE GIFTING!
GRAWR
THE GIFTING?!
SO IN OTHER WORDS... MASTER YUKIHIRA PRESENTED A DISH OF SUCH MAGNITUDE THAT IT EARNED THAT GREAT HONOR?!
WHAT INCREDIBLE TECHNIQUE DID HE USE TO CREATE SOMETHING THAT AMAZING?!
IF I AM CORRECT ...
...THE SECRET TO THIS SAUCE IS HONEY AND BALSAMIC VINEGAR.
GOT IT IN ONE, SIR!
BOTH INGREDIENTS HAVE A MILD SWEETNESS THAT ADDS A LAYER OF RICHNESS TO THE DISH. THE TARTNESS OF THE VINEGAR TIES IT ALL TOGETHER, ENSURING THE SWEETNESS ISN'T TOO CLOYING AND GIVING THE OVERALL DISH A CLEAN, PURE AFTERTASTE.
THE GUIDE TOLD ME THAT HOKKAIDO BEARS REALLY LOVE THEIR HONEY...
...SO I TRIED ALL KINDS OF METHODS TO ADD IT TO MY RECIPE!
IS THAT HOW HE GAVE HIS SAUCE A RICH, CLEAN FLAVOR POWERFUL ENOUGH TO CAUSE THE GIFTING? UNBELIEVABLE!
THAT'S OUR MASTER YUKIHIRA!
YAMMER
YAMMER

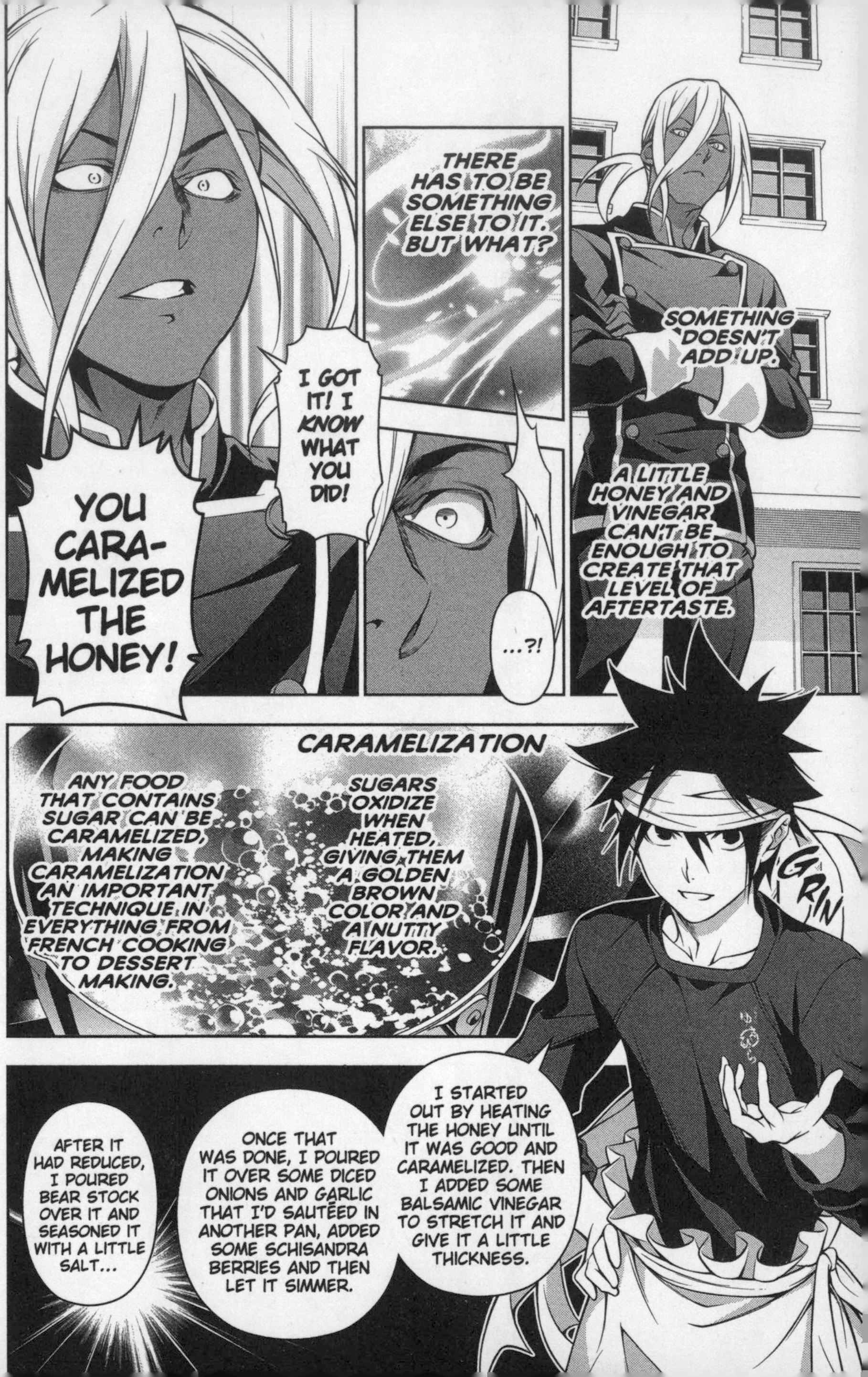
SOMETHING DOESN'T ADD UP.
A LITTLE HONEY AND VINEGAR CAN'T BE ENOUGH TO CREATE THAT LEVEL OF AFTERTASTE.
THERE HAS TO BE SOMETHING ELSE TO IT. BUT WHAT?
...?!
I GOT IT! I *KNOW* WHAT YOU DID!
YOU CARAMELIZED THE HONEY!
CARAMELIZATION
SUGARS OXIDIZE WHEN HEATED, GIVING THEM A GOLDEN BROWN COLOR AND A NUTTY FLAVOR.
ANY FOOD THAT CONTAINS SUGAR CAN BE CARAMELIZED, MAKING CARAMELIZATION AN IMPORTANT TECHNIQUE IN EVERYTHING FROM FRENCH COOKING TO DESSERT MAKING.
GRIN
I STARTED OUT BY HEATING THE HONEY UNTIL IT WAS GOOD AND CARAMELIZED. THEN I ADDED SOME BALSAMIC VINEGAR TO STRETCH IT AND GIVE IT A LITTLE THICKNESS.
ONCE THAT WAS DONE, I POURED IT OVER SOME DICED ONIONS AND GARLIC THAT I'D SAUTÉED IN ANOTHER PAN, ADDED SOME SCHISANDRA BERRIES AND THEN LET IT SIMMER.
AFTER IT HAD REDUCED, I POURED BEAR STOCK OVER IT AND SEASONED IT WITH A LITTLE SALT...

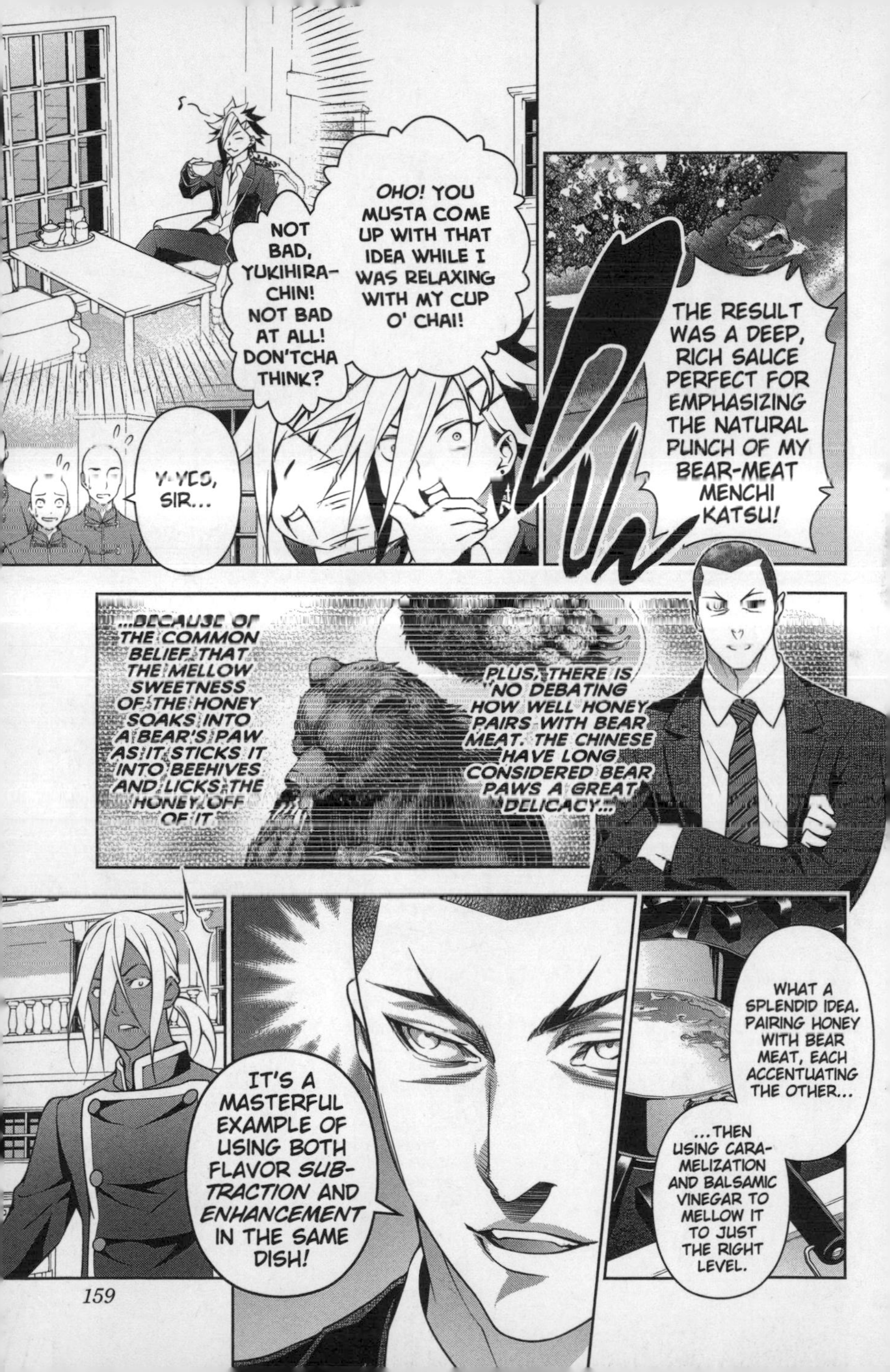
THE RESULT WAS A DEEP, RICH SAUCE PERFECT FOR EMPHASIZING THE NATURAL PUNCH OF MY BEAR-MEAT MENCHI KATSU!
OHO! YOU MUSTA COME UP WITH THAT IDEA WHILE I WAS RELAXING WITH MY CUP O' CHAI!
NOT BAD, YUKIHIRA-CHIN! NOT BAD AT ALL! DON'TCHA THINK?
Y-YES, SIR...
PLUS, THERE IS NO DEBATING HOW WELL HONEY PAIRS WITH BEAR MEAT. THE CHINESE HAVE LONG CONSIDERED BEAR PAWS A GREAT DELICACY...
...BECAUSE OF THE COMMON BELIEF THAT THE MELLOW SWEETNESS OF THE HONEY SOAKS INTO A BEAR'S PAW AS IT STICKS IT INTO BEEHIVES AND LICKS THE HONEY OFF OF IT.
WHAT A SPLENDID IDEA. PAIRING HONEY WITH BEAR MEAT, EACH ACCENTUATING THE OTHER...
...THEN USING CARA-MELIZATION AND BALSAMIC VINEGAR TO MELLOW IT TO JUST THE RIGHT LEVEL.
IT'S A MASTERFUL EXAMPLE OF USING BOTH FLAVOR *SUB-TRACTION* AND *ENHANCEMENT* IN THE SAME DISH!

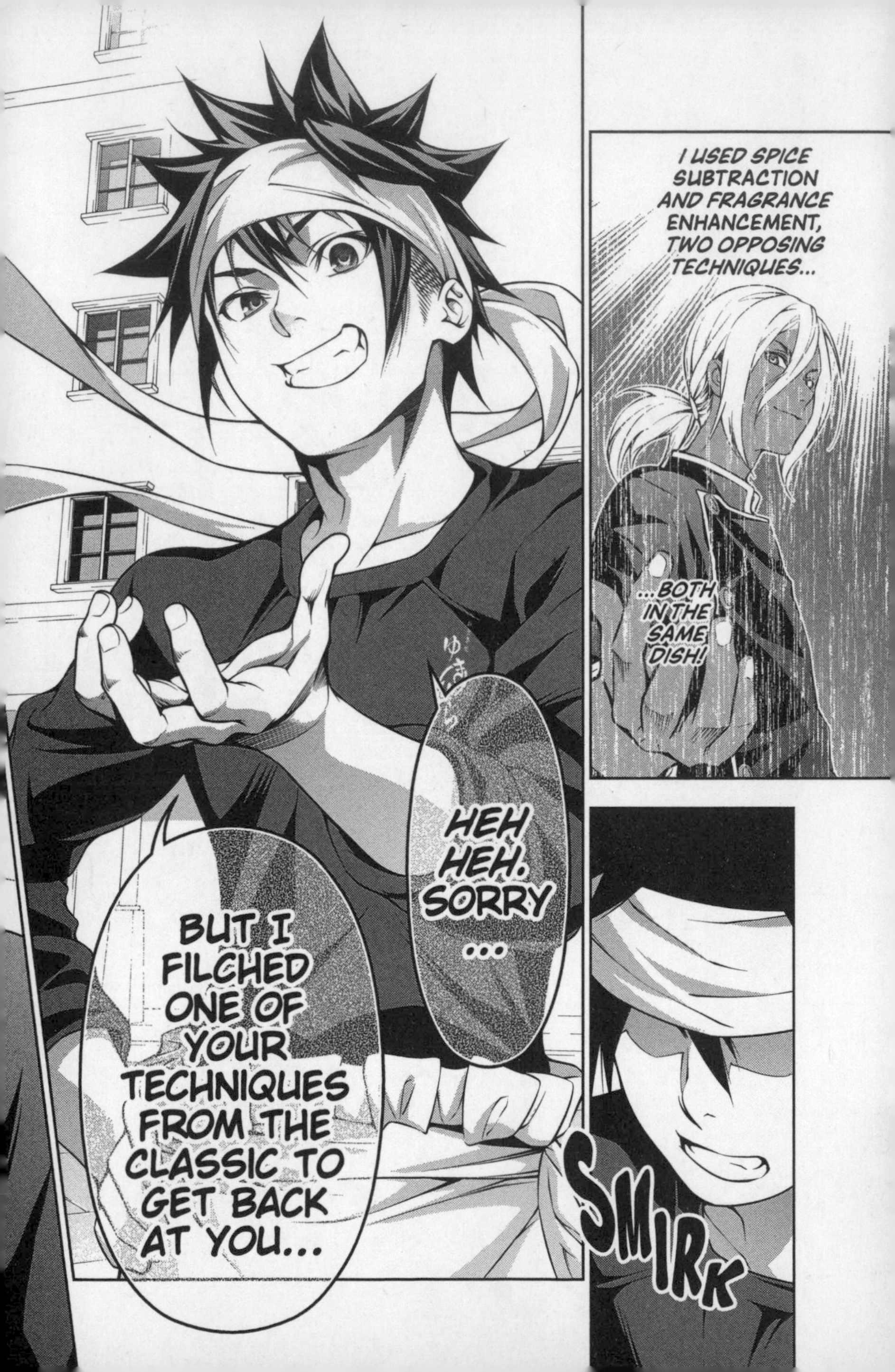
I USED SPICE SUBTRACTION AND FRAGRANCE ENHANCEMENT, TWO OPPOSING TECHNIQUES...
...BOTH IN THE SAME DISH!
SMIRK
HEH HEH. SORRY...
BUT I FILCHED ONE OF YOUR TECHNIQUES FROM THE CLASSIC TO GET BACK AT YOU...

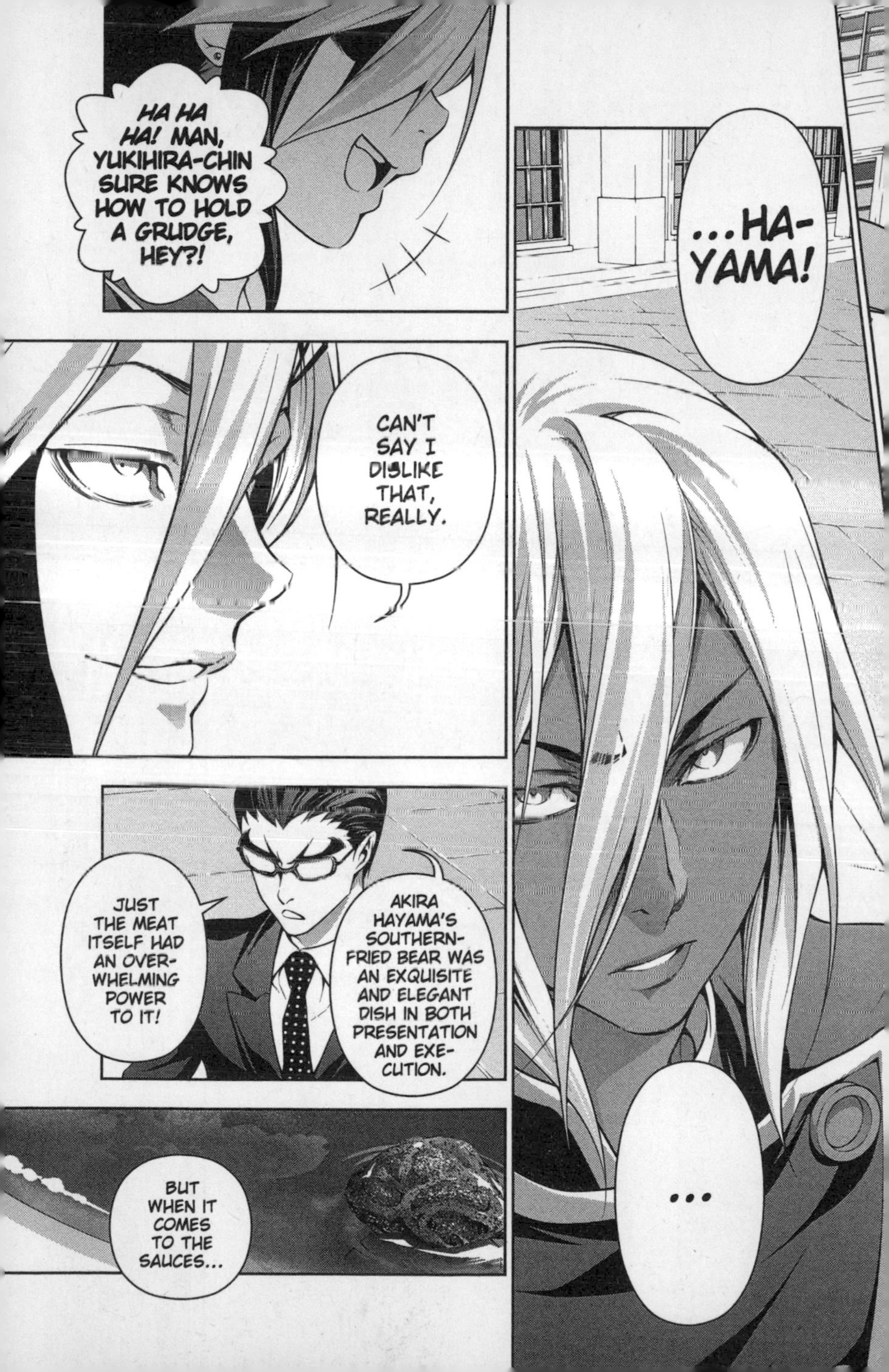
...HA-YAMA!
...
HA HA HA! MAN, YUKIHIRA-CHIN SURE KNOWS HOW TO HOLD A GRUDGE, HEY?!
CAN'T SAY I DISLIKE THAT, REALLY.
AKIRA HAYAMA'S SOUTHERN-FRIED BEAR WAS AN EXQUISITE AND ELEGANT DISH IN BOTH PRESENTATION AND EXECUTION.
JUST THE MEAT ITSELF HAD AN OVERWHELMING POWER TO IT!
BUT WHEN IT COMES TO THE SAUCES...

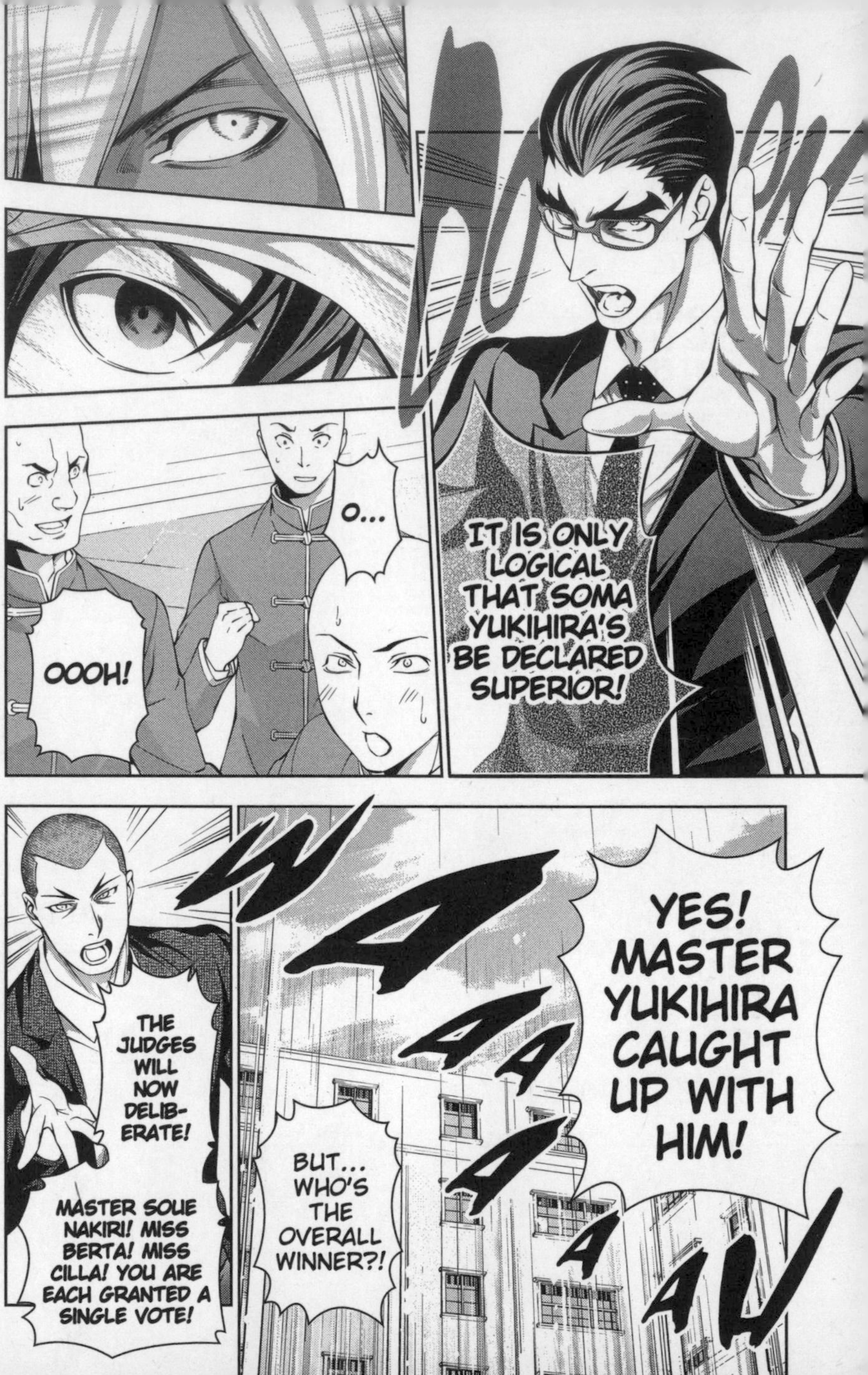
IT IS ONLY LOGICAL THAT SOMA YUKIHIRA'S BE DECLARED SUPERIOR!
O...
OOOH!
YES! MASTER YUKIHIRA CAUGHT UP WITH HIM!
BUT... WHO'S THE OVERALL WINNER?!
THE JUDGES WILL NOW DELIB-ERATE!
MASTER SOUE NAKIRI! MISS BERTA! MISS CILLA! YOU ARE EACH GRANTED A SINGLE VOTE!

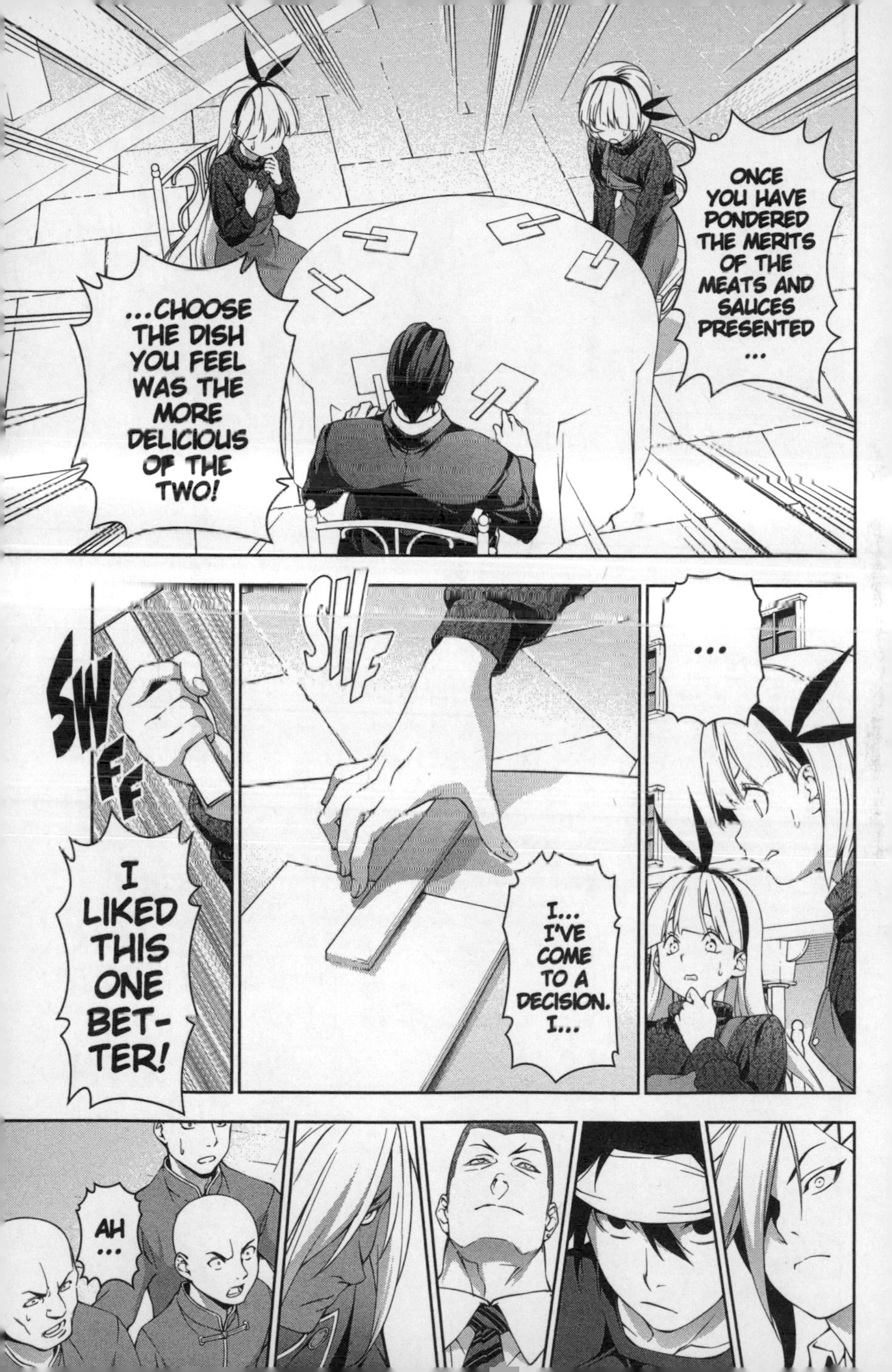
ONCE YOU HAVE PONDERED THE MERITS OF THE MEATS AND SAUCES PRESENTED...
...CHOOSE THE DISH YOU FEEL WAS THE MORE DELICIOUS OF THE TWO!
...
SHF
I... I'VE COME TO A DECISION. I...
SWFF
I LIKED THIS ONE BET-TER!
AH...

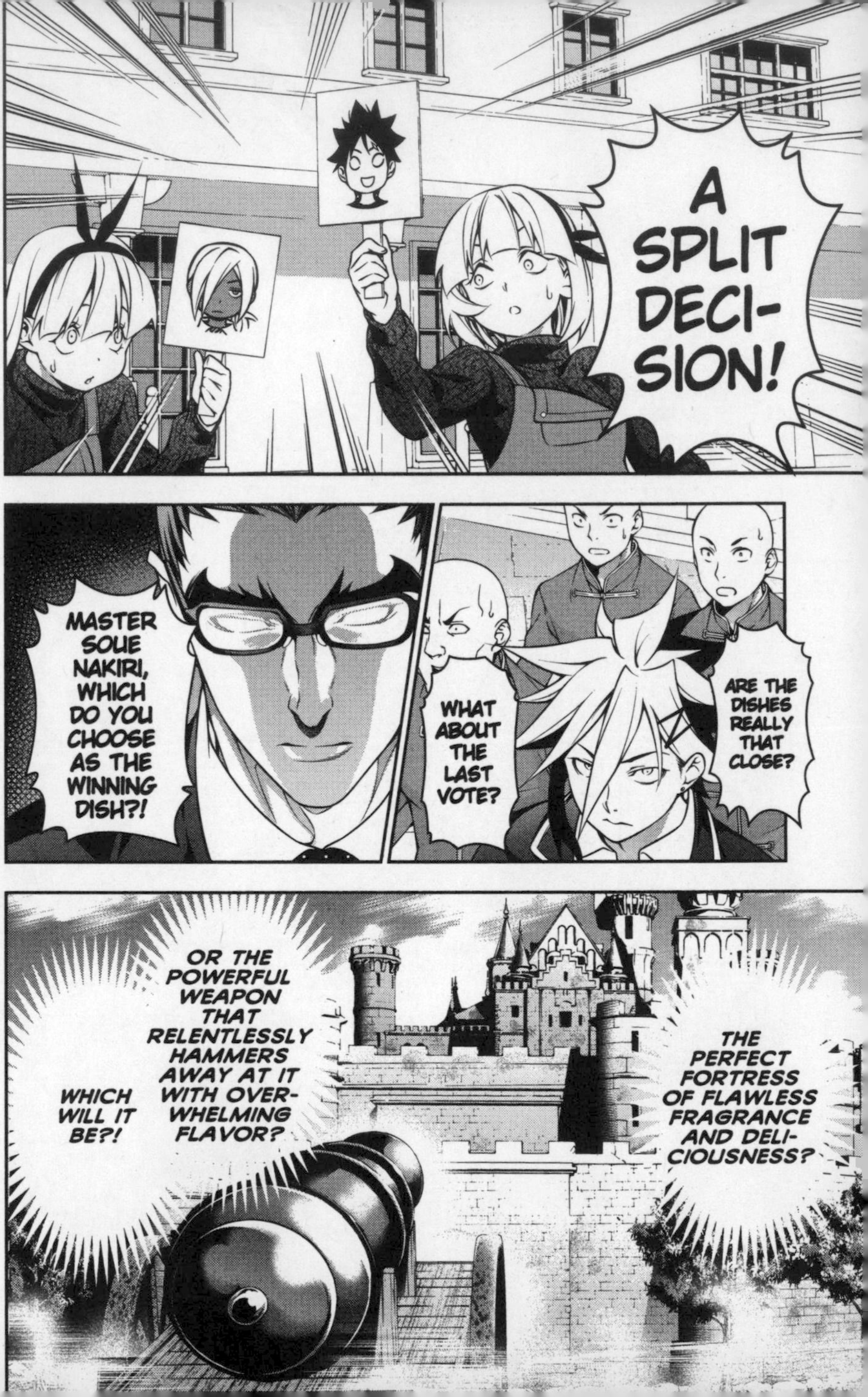
A SPLIT DECISION!
ARE THE DISHES REALLY THAT CLOSE?
WHAT ABOUT THE LAST VOTE?
MASTER SOUE NAKIRI, WHICH DO YOU CHOOSE AS THE WINNING DISH?!
THE PERFECT FORTRESS OF FLAWLESS FRAGRANCE AND DELICIOUSNESS?
OR THE POWERFUL WEAPON THAT RELENTLESSLY HAMMERS AWAY AT IT WITH OVERWHELMING FLAVOR?
WHICH WILL IT BE?!

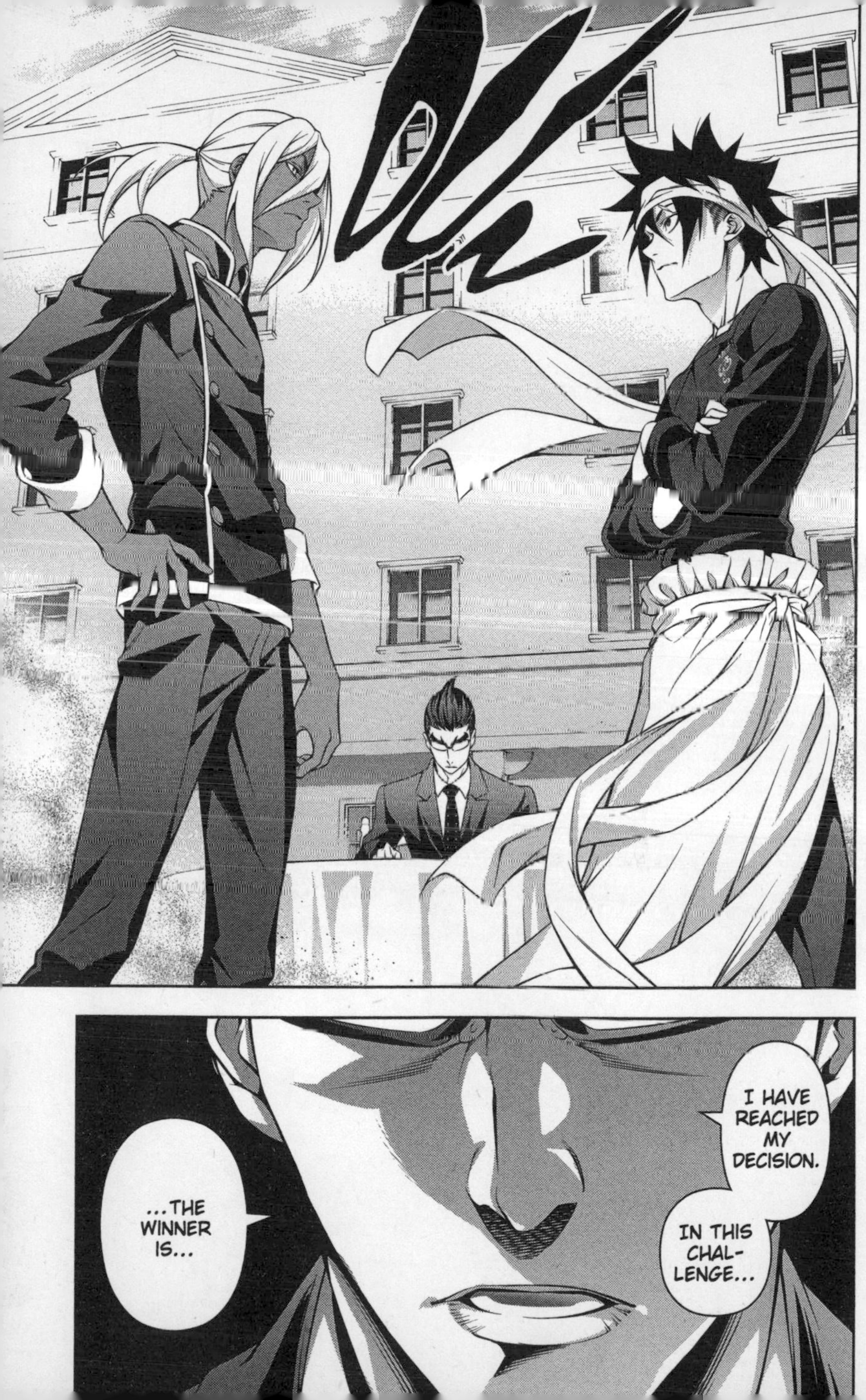
I HAVE REACHED MY DECISION.
IN THIS CHAL-LENGE...
...THE WINNER IS...

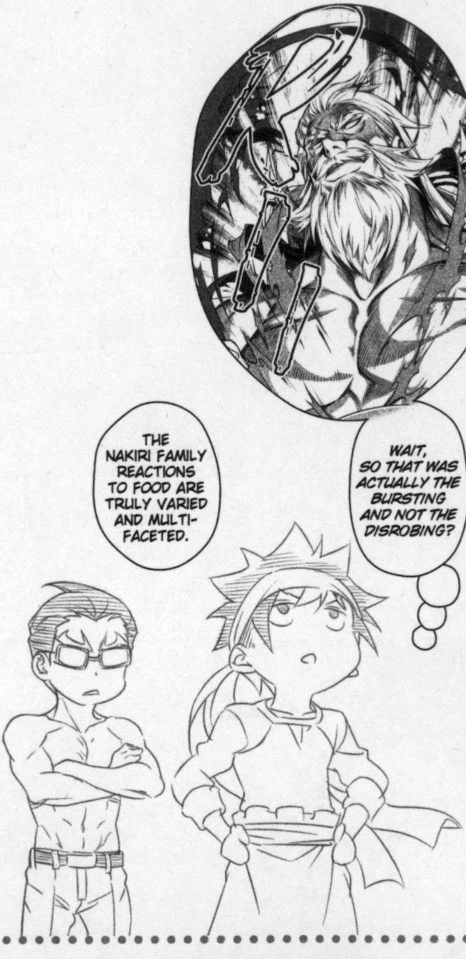
WAIT, SO THAT WAS ACTUALLY THE BURSTING AND NOT THE DISROBING?
THE NAKIRI FAMILY REACTIONS TO FOOD ARE TRULY VARIED AND MULTI-FACETED.

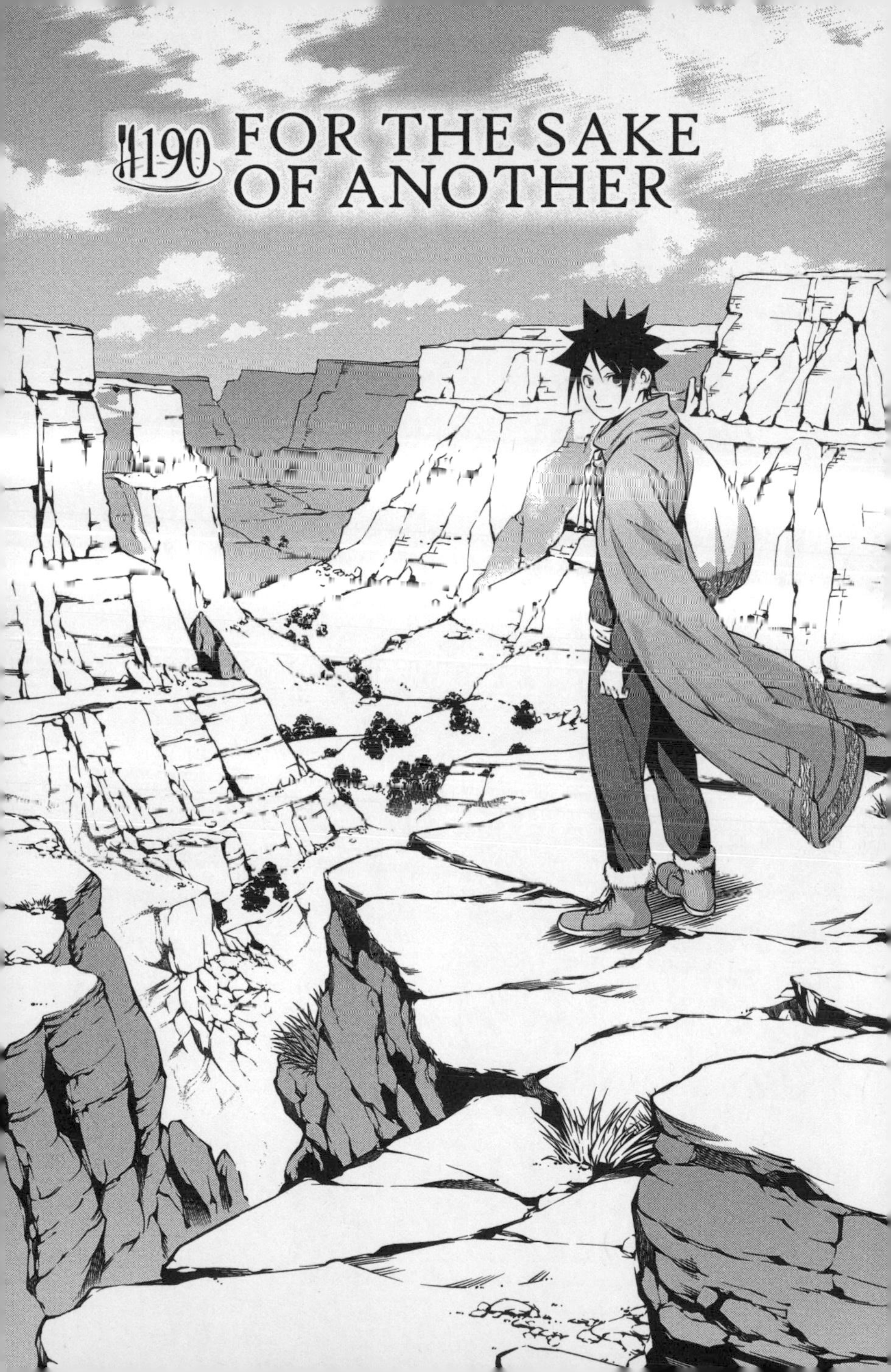
190
FOR THE SAKE OF ANOTHER

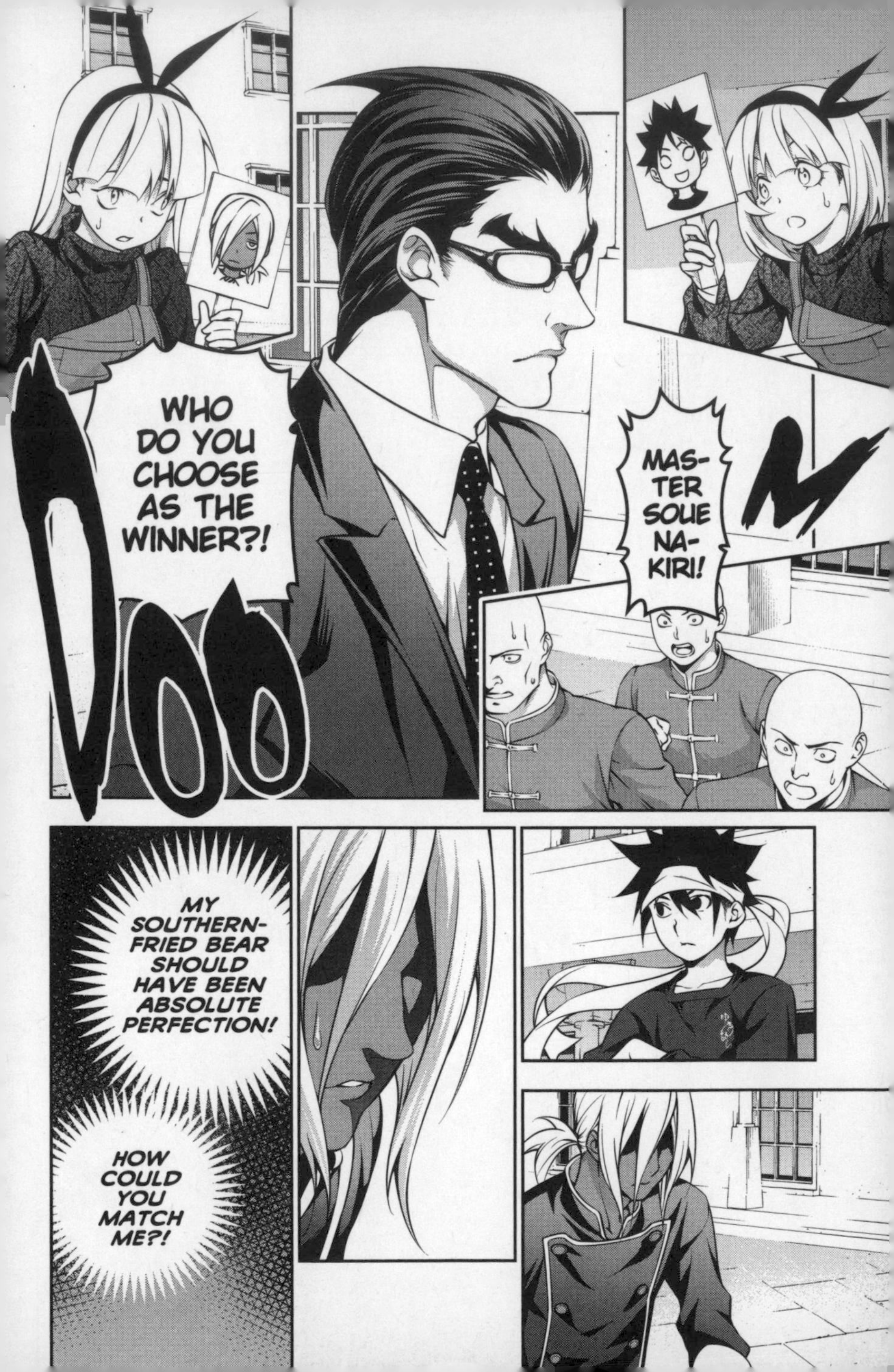
WHO DO YOU CHOOSE AS THE WINNER?!
DOO
MAS-TER SOUE NA-KIRI!
M
MY SOUTHERN-FRIED BEAR SHOULD HAVE BEEN ABSOLUTE PERFECTION!
HOW COULD YOU MATCH ME?!

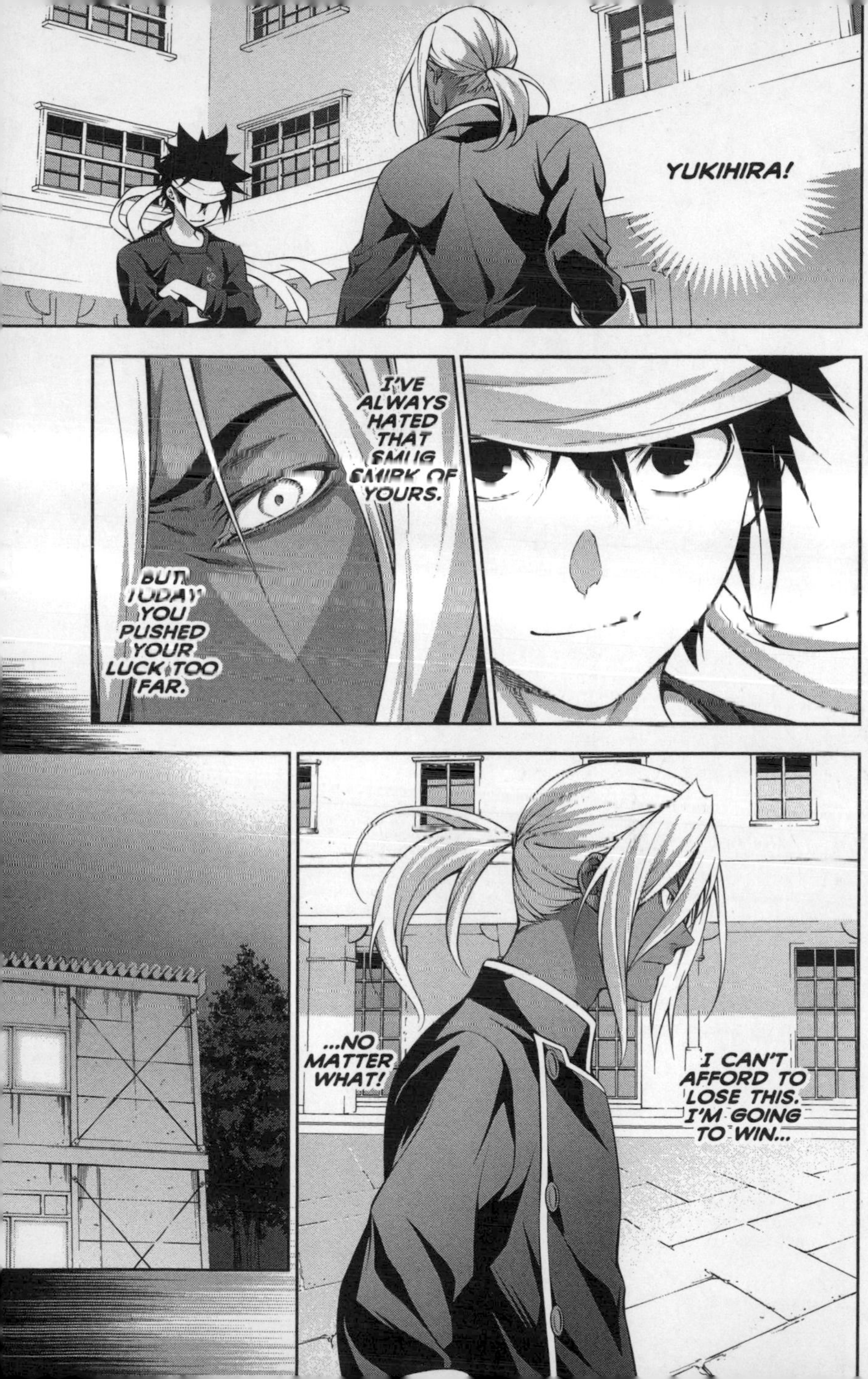
YUKIHIRA!
I'VE ALWAYS HATED THAT SMUG SMIRK OF YOURS.
BUT TODAY YOU PUSHED YOUR LUCK TOO FAR.
I CAN'T AFFORD TO LOSE THIS. I'M GOING TO WIN...
...NO MATTER WHAT!

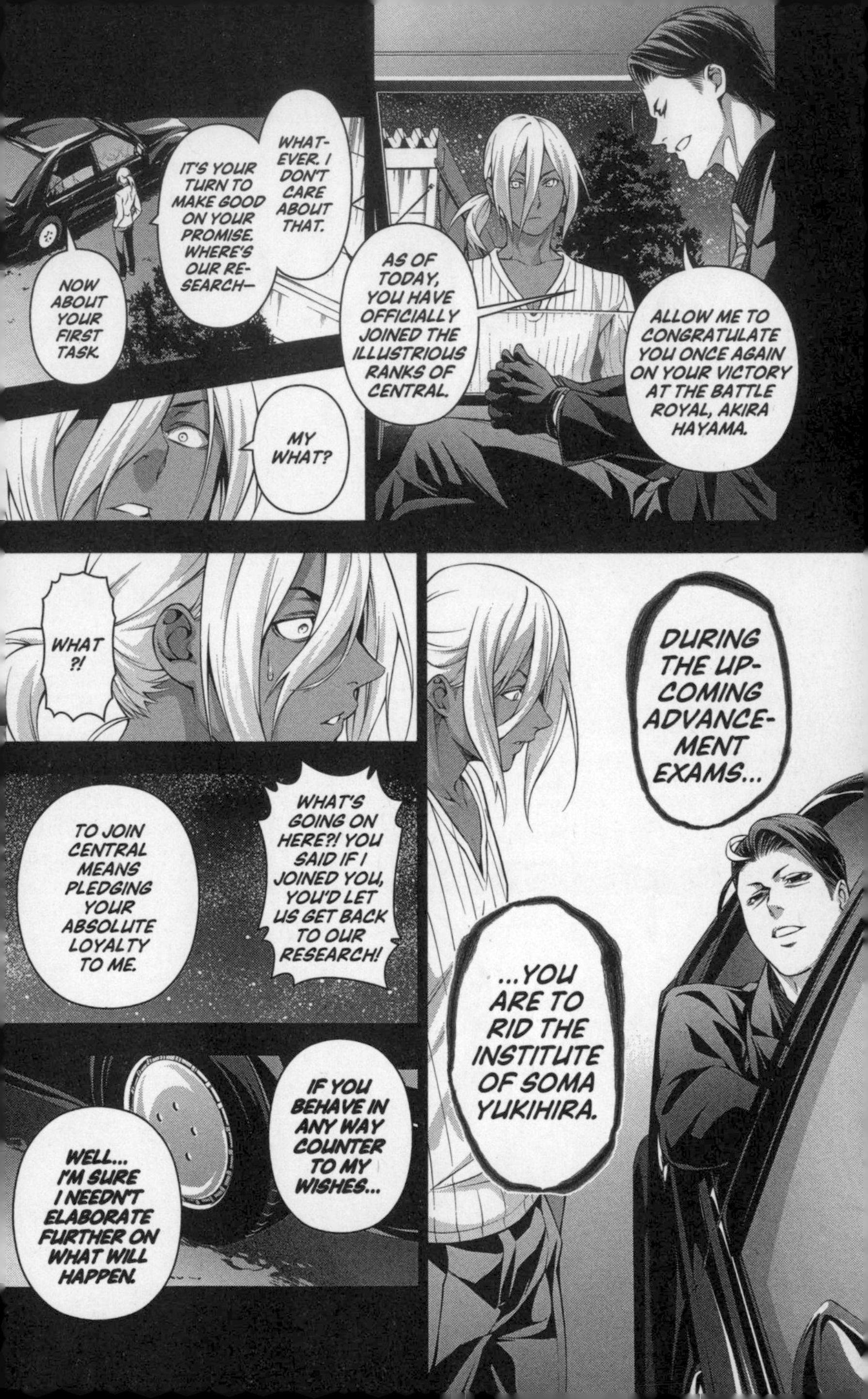
ALLOW ME TO CONGRATULATE YOU ONCE AGAIN ON YOUR VICTORY AT THE BATTLE ROYAL, AKIRA HAYAMA.
AS OF TODAY, YOU HAVE OFFICIALLY JOINED THE ILLUSTRIOUS RANKS OF CENTRAL.
WHAT-EVER. I DON'T CARE ABOUT THAT.
IT'S YOUR TURN TO MAKE GOOD ON YOUR PROMISE. WHERE'S OUR RE-SEARCH—
NOW ABOUT YOUR FIRST TASK.
MY WHAT?
DURING THE UP-COMING ADVANCE-MENT EXAMS...
...YOU ARE TO RID THE INSTITUTE OF SOMA YUKIHIRA.
WHAT ?!
WHAT'S GOING ON HERE?! YOU SAID IF I JOINED YOU, YOU'D LET US GET BACK TO OUR RESEARCH!
TO JOIN CENTRAL MEANS PLEDGING YOUR ABSOLUTE LOYALTY TO ME.
IF YOU BEHAVE IN ANY WAY COUNTER TO MY WISHES...
WELL... I'M SURE I NEEDN'T ELABORATE FURTHER ON WHAT WILL HAPPEN.

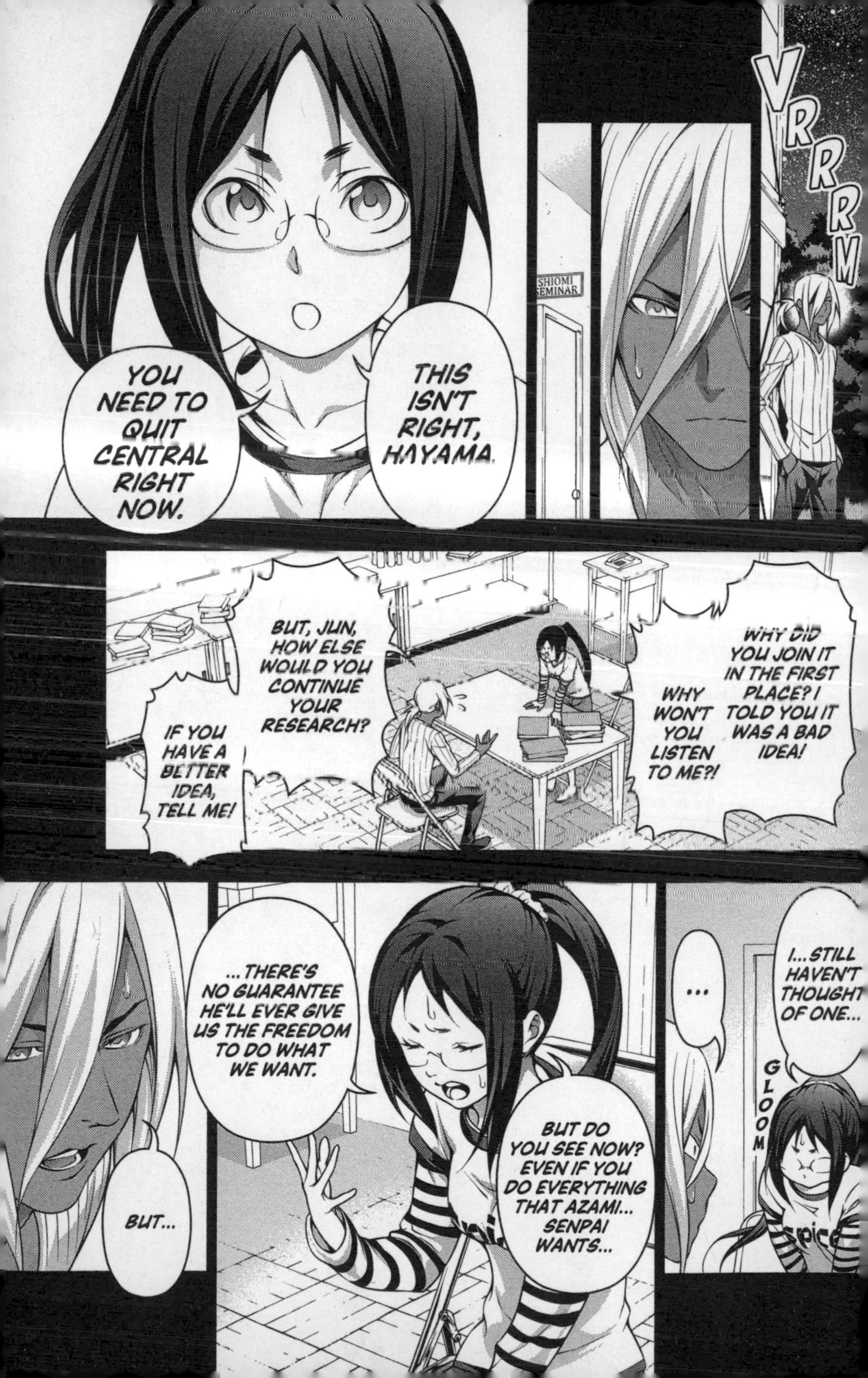
VRRRM
SHIOMI SEMINAR
THIS ISN'T RIGHT, HAYAMA.
YOU NEED TO QUIT CENTRAL RIGHT NOW.
WHY DID YOU JOIN IT IN THE FIRST PLACE? I TOLD YOU IT WAS A BAD IDEA!
WHY WON'T YOU LISTEN TO ME?!
BUT, JUN, HOW ELSE WOULD YOU CONTINUE YOUR RESEARCH?
IF YOU HAVE A BETTER IDEA, TELL ME!
I... STILL HAVEN'T THOUGHT OF ONE...
...
GLOOM
BUT DO YOU SEE NOW? EVEN IF YOU DO EVERYTHING THAT AZAMI... SENPAI WANTS...
...THERE'S NO GUARANTEE HE'LL EVER GIVE US THE FREEDOM TO DO WHAT WE WANT.
BUT...

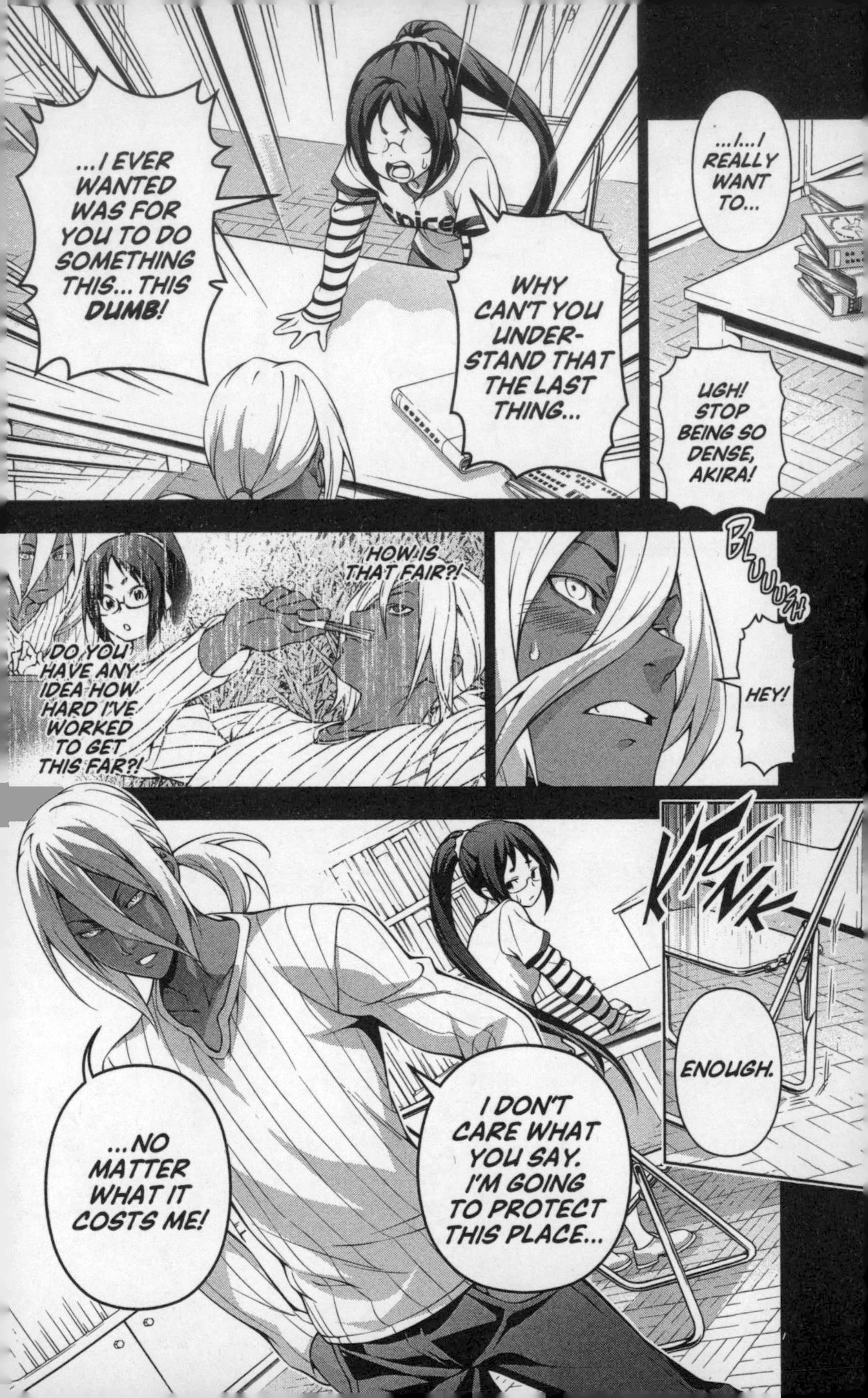
...I...I REALLY WANT TO...
UGH! STOP BEING SO DENSE, AKIRA!
WHY CAN'T YOU UNDER-STAND THAT THE LAST THING...
...I EVER WANTED WAS FOR YOU TO DO SOMETHING THIS... THIS DUMB!
BLUUUSH
HEY!
HOW IS THAT FAIR?!
DO YOU HAVE ANY IDEA HOW HARD I'VE WORKED TO GET THIS FAR?!
KTUNK
ENOUGH.
I DON'T CARE WHAT YOU SAY. I'M GOING TO PROTECT THIS PLACE...
...NO MATTER WHAT IT COSTS ME!

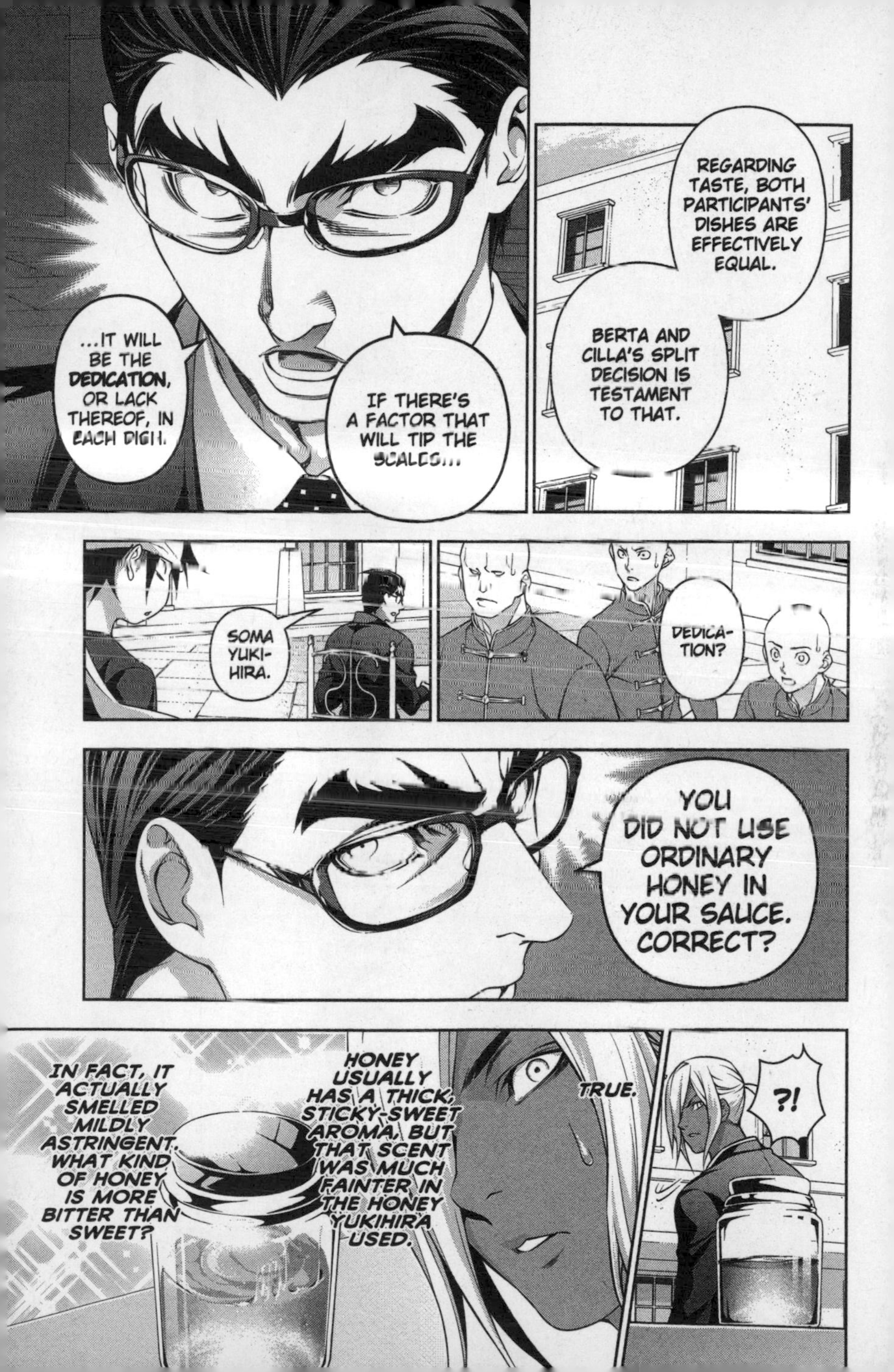
REGARDING TASTE, BOTH PARTICIPANTS' DISHES ARE EFFECTIVELY EQUAL.
BERTA AND CILLA'S SPLIT DECISION IS TESTAMENT TO THAT.
IF THERE'S A FACTOR THAT WILL TIP THE SCALES...
...IT WILL BE THE DEDICATION, OR LACK THEREOF, IN EACH DISH.
DEDICATION?
SOMA YUKIHIRA.
YOU DID NOT USE ORDINARY HONEY IN YOUR SAUCE. CORRECT?
?!
TRUE.
HONEY USUALLY HAS A THICK, STICKY-SWEET AROMA, BUT THAT SCENT WAS MUCH FAINTER IN THE HONEY YUKIHIRA USED.
IN FACT, IT ACTUALLY SMELLED MILDLY ASTRINGENT. WHAT KIND OF HONEY IS MORE BITTER THAN SWEET?

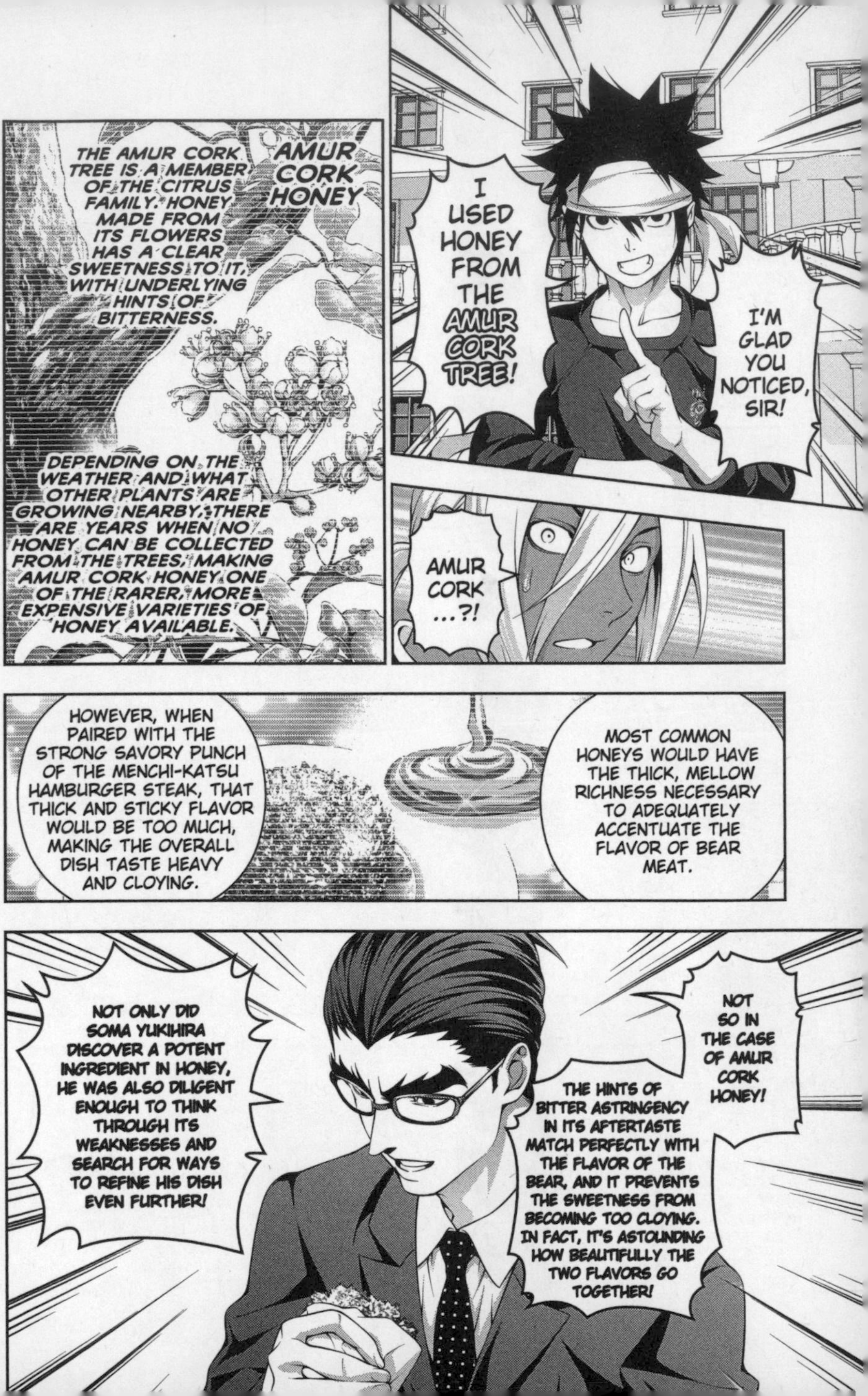
I USED HONEY FROM THE AMUR CORK TREE!
I'M GLAD YOU NOTICED, SIR!
AMUR CORK ...?!
AMUR CORK HONEY
THE AMUR CORK TREE IS A MEMBER OF THE CITRUS FAMILY. HONEY MADE FROM ITS FLOWERS HAS A CLEAR SWEETNESS TO IT, WITH UNDERLYING HINTS OF BITTERNESS.
DEPENDING ON THE WEATHER AND WHAT OTHER PLANTS ARE GROWING NEARBY, THERE ARE YEARS WHEN NO HONEY CAN BE COLLECTED FROM THE TREES, MAKING AMUR CORK HONEY ONE OF THE RARER, MORE EXPENSIVE VARIETIES OF HONEY AVAILABLE.
MOST COMMON HONEYS WOULD HAVE THE THICK, MELLOW RICHNESS NECESSARY TO ADEQUATELY ACCENTUATE THE FLAVOR OF BEAR MEAT.
HOWEVER, WHEN PAIRED WITH THE STRONG SAVORY PUNCH OF THE MENCHI-KATSU HAMBURGER STEAK, THAT THICK AND STICKY FLAVOR WOULD BE TOO MUCH, MAKING THE OVERALL DISH TASTE HEAVY AND CLOYING.
NOT SO IN THE CASE OF AMUR CORK HONEY!
THE HINTS OF BITTER ASTRINGENCY IN ITS AFTERTASTE MATCH PERFECTLY WITH THE FLAVOR OF THE BEAR, AND IT PREVENTS THE SWEETNESS FROM BECOMING TOO CLOYING. IN FACT, IT'S ASTOUNDING HOW BEAUTIFULLY THE TWO FLAVORS GO TOGETHER!
NOT ONLY DID SOMA YUKIHIRA DISCOVER A POTENT INGREDIENT IN HONEY, HE WAS ALSO DILIGENT ENOUGH TO THINK THROUGH ITS WEAKNESSES AND SEARCH FOR WAYS TO REFINE HIS DISH EVEN FURTHER!

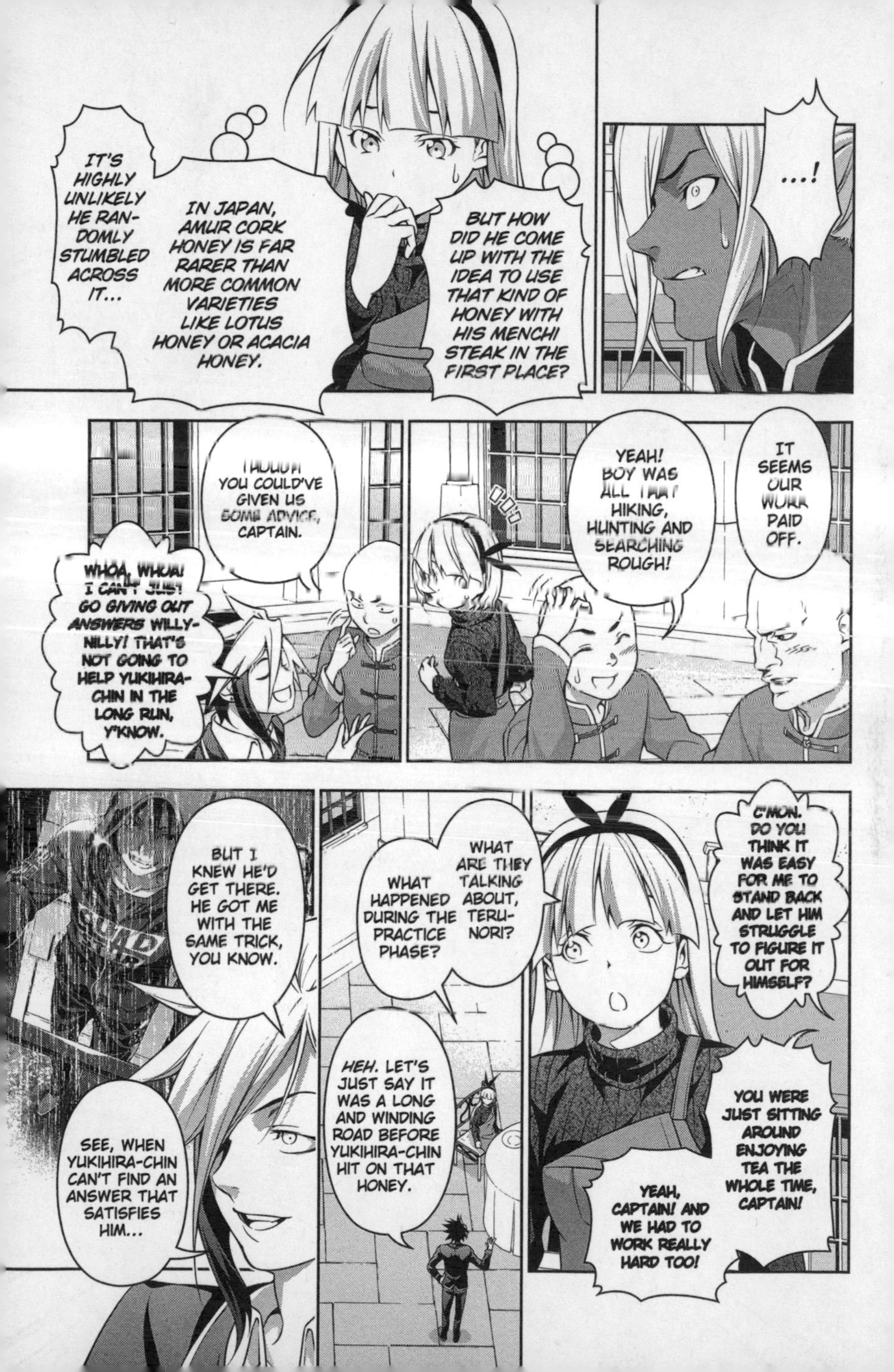
...!
BUT HOW DID HE COME UP WITH THE IDEA TO USE THAT KIND OF HONEY WITH HIS MENCHI STEAK IN THE FIRST PLACE?
IN JAPAN, AMUR CORK HONEY IS FAR RARER THAN MORE COMMON VARIETIES LIKE LOTUS HONEY OR ACACIA HONEY.
IT'S HIGHLY UNLIKELY HE RANDOMLY STUMBLED ACROSS IT...
IT SEEMS OUR WORK PAID OFF.
YEAH! BOY WAS ALL THAT HIKING, HUNTING AND SEARCHING ROUGH!
THOUGH YOU COULD'VE GIVEN US SOME ADVICE, CAPTAIN.
WHOA, WHOA! I CAN'T JUST GO GIVING OUT ANSWERS WILLY-NILLY! THAT'S NOT GOING TO HELP YUKIHIRA-CHIN IN THE LONG RUN, Y'KNOW.
C'MON. DO YOU THINK IT WAS EASY FOR ME TO STAND BACK AND LET HIM STRUGGLE TO FIGURE IT OUT FOR HIMSELF?
YOU WERE JUST SITTING AROUND ENJOYING TEA THE WHOLE TIME, CAPTAIN!
YEAH, CAPTAIN! AND WE HAD TO WORK REALLY HARD TOO!
WHAT ARE THEY TALKING ABOUT, TERUNORI?
WHAT HAPPENED DURING THE PRACTICE PHASE?
HEH. LET'S JUST SAY IT WAS A LONG AND WINDING ROAD BEFORE YUKIHIRA-CHIN HIT ON THAT HONEY.
BUT I KNEW HE'D GET THERE. HE GOT ME WITH THE SAME TRICK, YOU KNOW.
SEE, WHEN YUKIHIRA-CHIN CAN'T FIND AN ANSWER THAT SATISFIES HIM...

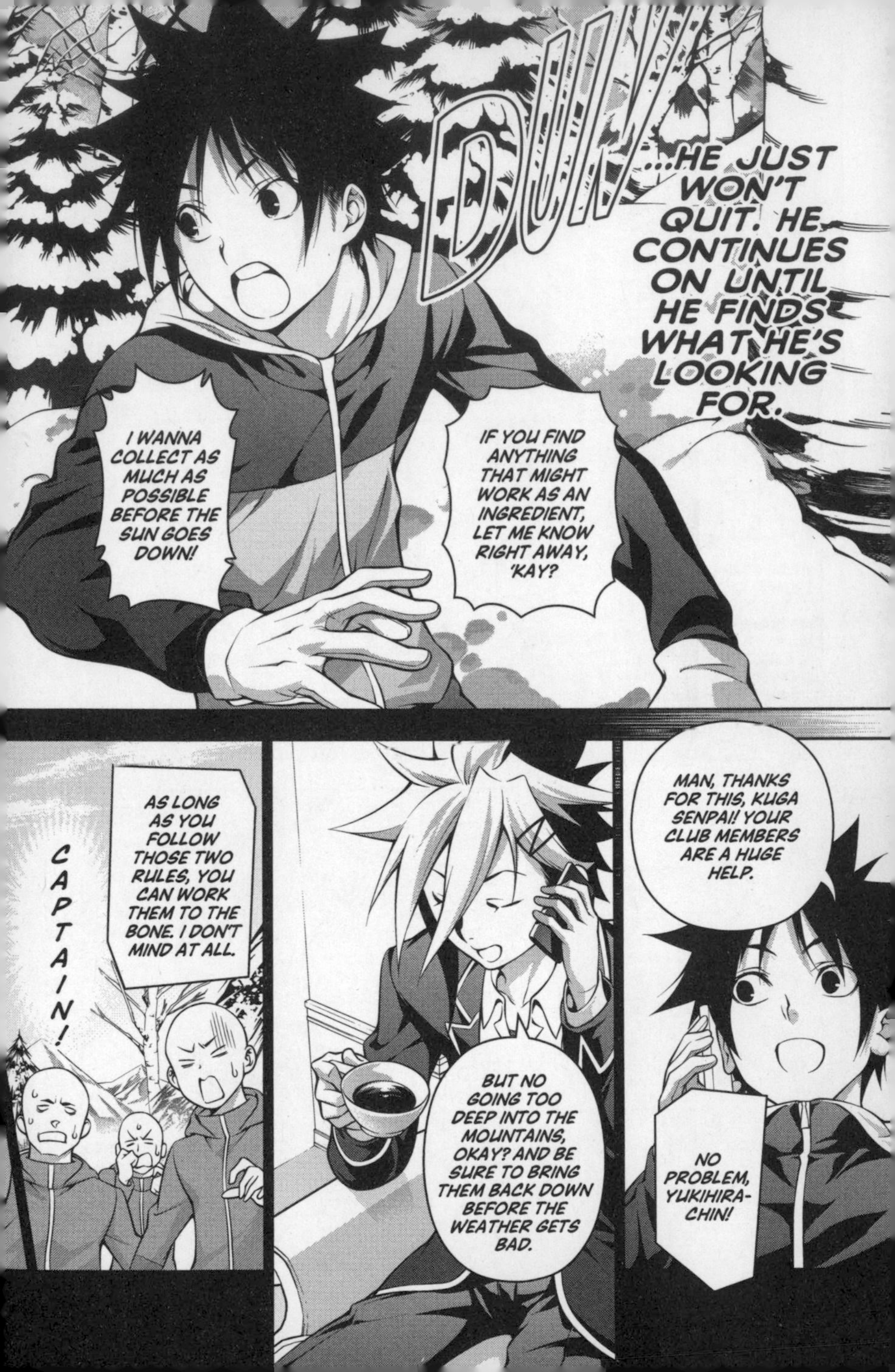
DUN
...HE JUST WON'T QUIT. HE CONTINUES ON UNTIL HE FINDS WHAT HE'S LOOKING FOR.
IF YOU FIND ANYTHING THAT MIGHT WORK AS AN INGREDIENT, LET ME KNOW RIGHT AWAY, 'KAY?
I WANNA COLLECT AS MUCH AS POSSIBLE BEFORE THE SUN GOES DOWN!
MAN, THANKS FOR THIS, KUGA SENPAI! YOUR CLUB MEMBERS ARE A HUGE HELP.
NO PROBLEM, YUKIHIRA-CHIN!
BUT NO GOING TOO DEEP INTO THE MOUNTAINS, OKAY? AND BE SURE TO BRING THEM BACK DOWN BEFORE THE WEATHER GETS BAD.
AS LONG AS YOU FOLLOW THOSE TWO RULES, YOU CAN WORK THEM TO THE BONE. I DON'T MIND AT ALL.
CAPTAIN!

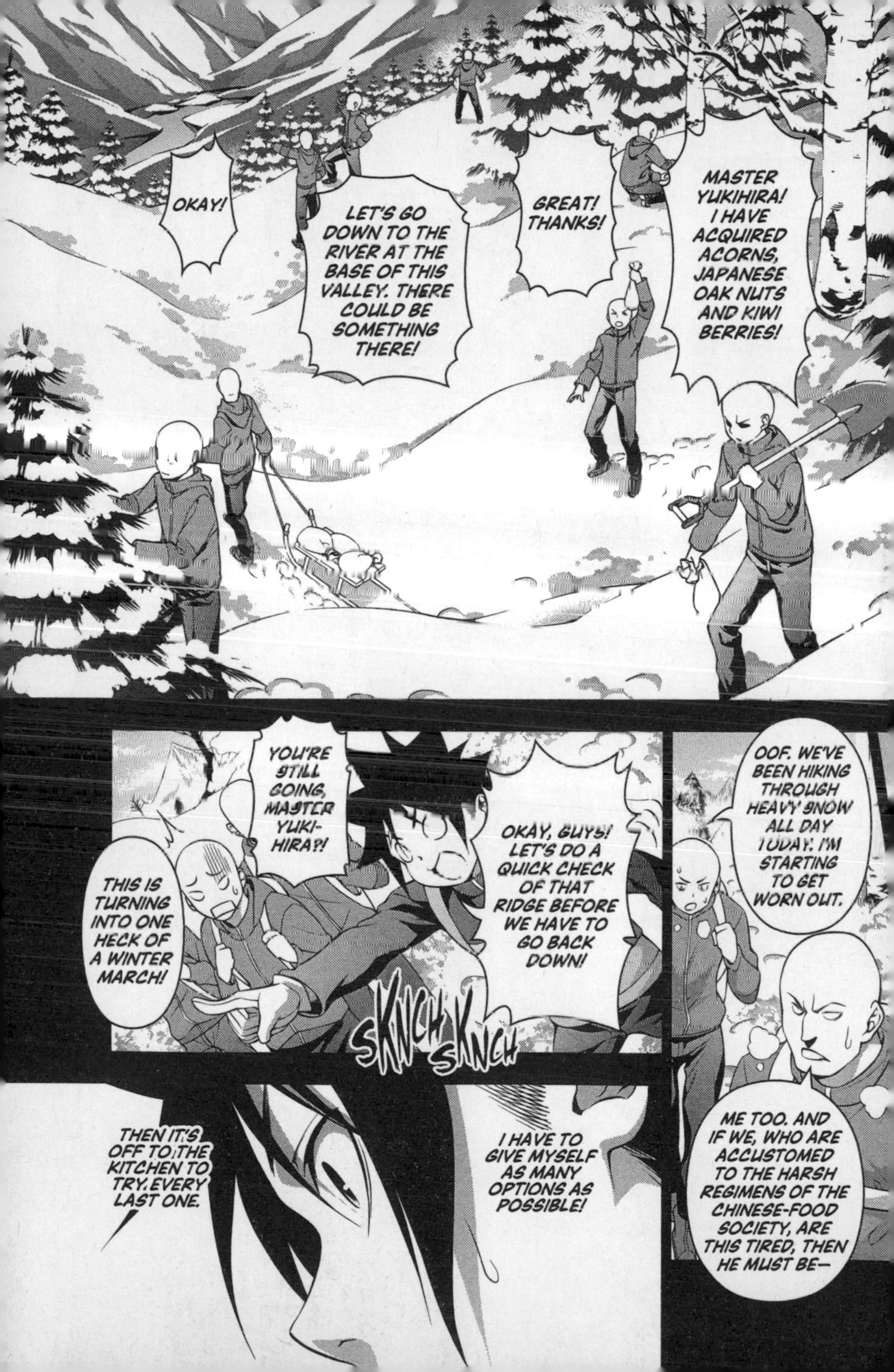
MASTER YUKIHIRA! I HAVE ACQUIRED ACORNS, JAPANESE OAK NUTS AND KIWI BERRIES!
GREAT! THANKS!
LET'S GO DOWN TO THE RIVER AT THE BASE OF THIS VALLEY. THERE COULD BE SOMETHING THERE!
OKAY!
OOF. WE'VE BEEN HIKING THROUGH HEAVY SNOW ALL DAY TODAY. I'M STARTING TO GET WORN OUT.
ME TOO. AND IF WE, WHO ARE ACCUSTOMED TO THE HARSH REGIMENS OF THE CHINESE-FOOD SOCIETY, ARE THIS TIRED, THEN HE MUST BE—
OKAY, GUYS! LET'S DO A QUICK CHECK OF THAT RIDGE BEFORE WE HAVE TO GO BACK DOWN!
YOU'RE STILL GOING, MASTER YUKIHIRA?!
THIS IS TURNING INTO ONE HECK OF A WINTER MARCH!
SKNCH SKNCH
I HAVE TO GIVE MYSELF AS MANY OPTIONS AS POSSIBLE!
THEN IT'S OFF TO THE KITCHEN TO TRY. EVERY LAST ONE.

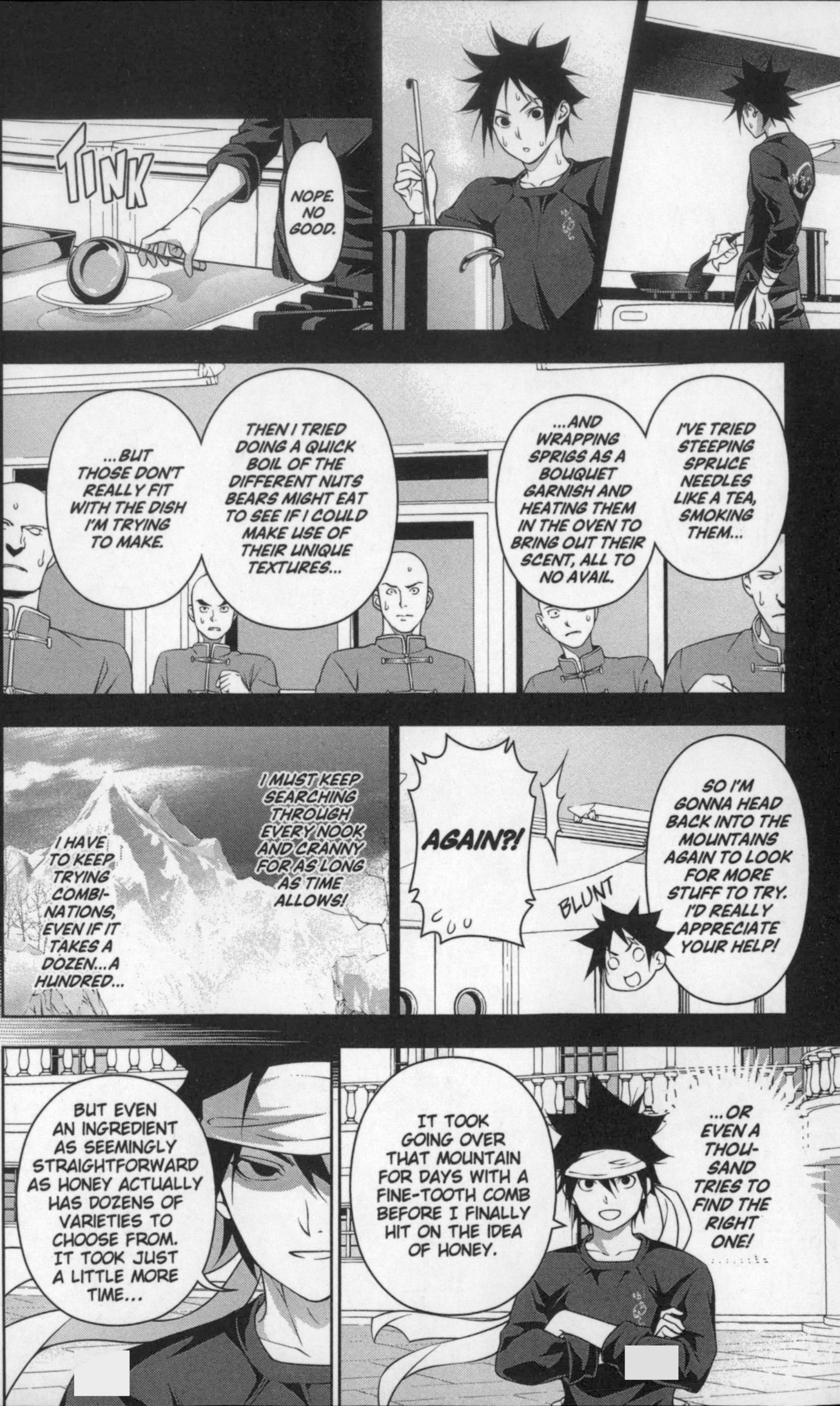
NOPE. NO GOOD.
TINK
I'VE TRIED STEEPING SPRUCE NEEDLES LIKE A TEA, SMOKING THEM...
...AND WRAPPING SPRIGS AS A BOUQUET GARNISH AND HEATING THEM IN THE OVEN TO BRING OUT THEIR SCENT, ALL TO NO AVAIL.
THEN I TRIED DOING A QUICK BOIL OF THE DIFFERENT NUTS BEARS MIGHT EAT TO SEE IF I COULD MAKE USE OF THEIR UNIQUE TEXTURES...
...BUT THOSE DON'T REALLY FIT WITH THE DISH I'M TRYING TO MAKE.
SO I'M GONNA HEAD BACK INTO THE MOUNTAINS AGAIN TO LOOK FOR MORE STUFF TO TRY. I'D REALLY APPRECIATE YOUR HELP!
AGAIN?!
BLUNT
I MUST KEEP SEARCHING THROUGH EVERY NOOK AND CRANNY FOR AS LONG AS TIME ALLOWS!
I HAVE TO KEEP TRYING COMBI-NATIONS, EVEN IF IT TAKES A DOZEN...A HUNDRED...
...OR EVEN A THOU-SAND TRIES TO FIND THE RIGHT ONE!
IT TOOK GOING OVER THAT MOUNTAIN FOR DAYS WITH A FINE-TOOTH COMB BEFORE I FINALLY HIT ON THE IDEA OF HONEY.
BUT EVEN AN INGREDIENT AS SEEMINGLY STRAIGHTFORWARD AS HONEY ACTUALLY HAS DOZENS OF VARIETIES TO CHOOSE FROM. IT TOOK JUST A LITTLE MORE TIME...

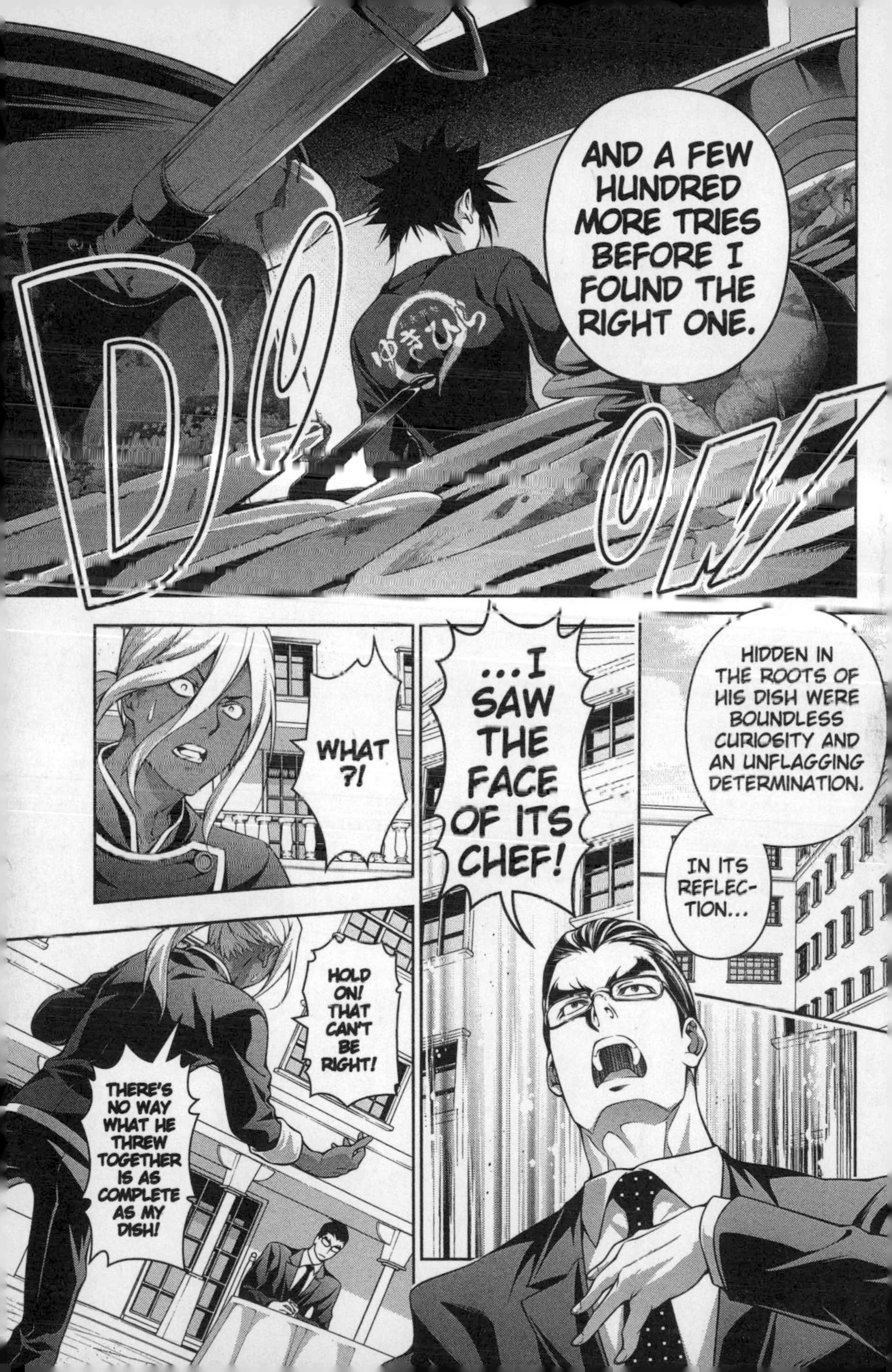
AND A FEW HUNDRED MORE TRIES BEFORE I FOUND THE RIGHT ONE.
DOOM
HIDDEN IN THE ROOTS OF HIS DISH WERE BOUNDLESS CURIOSITY AND AN UNFLAGGING DETERMINATION.
IN ITS REFLECTION...
...I SAW THE FACE OF ITS CHEF!
WHAT?!
HOLD ON! THAT CAN'T BE RIGHT!
THERE'S NO WAY WHAT HE THREW TOGETHER IS AS COMPLETE AS MY DISH!

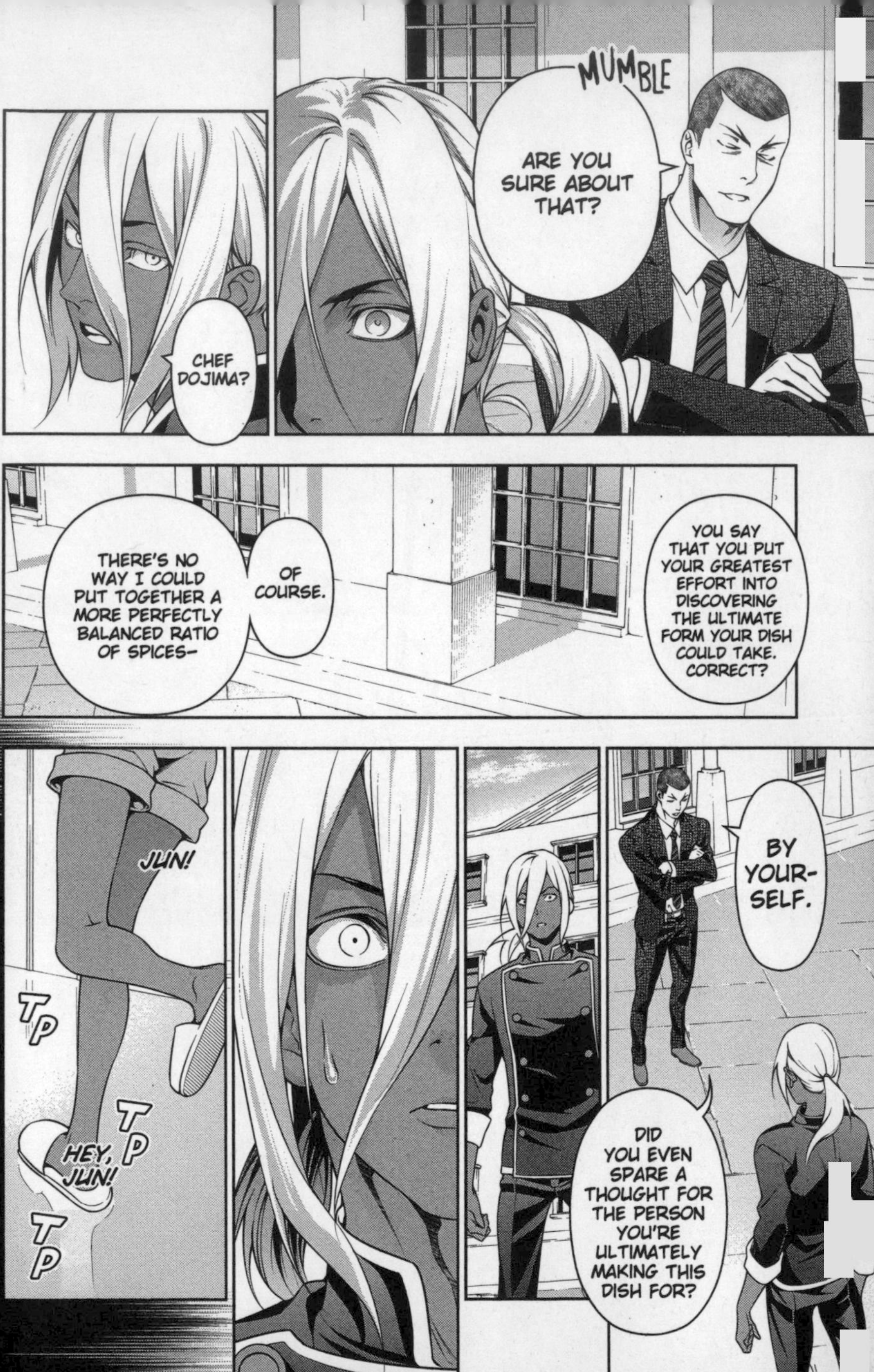
MUMBLE
ARE YOU SURE ABOUT THAT?
CHEF DOJIMA?
YOU SAY THAT YOU PUT YOUR GREATEST EFFORT INTO DISCOVERING THE ULTIMATE FORM YOUR DISH COULD TAKE. CORRECT?
OF COURSE.
THERE'S NO WAY I COULD PUT TOGETHER A MORE PERFECTLY BALANCED RATIO OF SPICES-
BY YOUR-SELF.
DID YOU EVEN SPARE A THOUGHT FOR THE PERSON YOU'RE ULTIMATELY MAKING THIS DISH FOR?
JUN!
TP
TP
HEY, JUN!
TP

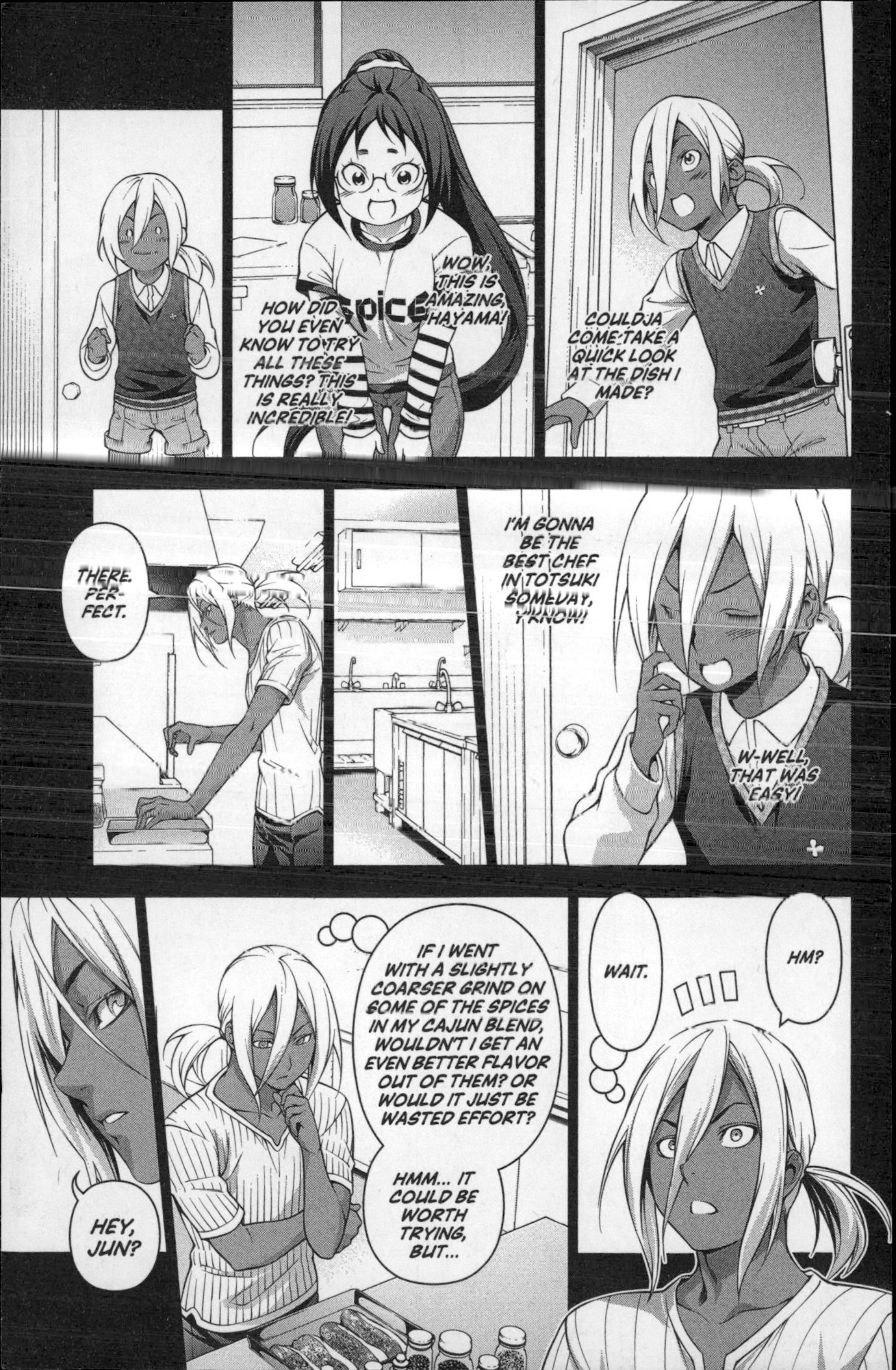
COULDJA COME TAKE A QUICK LOOK AT THE DISH I MADE?
WOW, THIS IS AMAZING, HAYAMA!
Spice
HOW DID YOU EVEN KNOW TO TRY ALL THESE THINGS? THIS IS REALLY INCREDIBLE!
W-WELL, THAT WAS EASY!
I'M GONNA BE THE BEST CHEF IN TOTSUKI SOMEDAY, Y'KNOW!
THERE. PER-FECT.
HM?
WAIT.
IF I WENT WITH A SLIGHTLY COARSER GRIND ON SOME OF THE SPICES IN MY CAJUN BLEND, WOULDN'T I GET AN EVEN BETTER FLAVOR OUT OF THEM? OR WOULD IT JUST BE WASTED EFFORT?
HMM... IT COULD BE WORTH TRYING, BUT...
HEY, JUN?

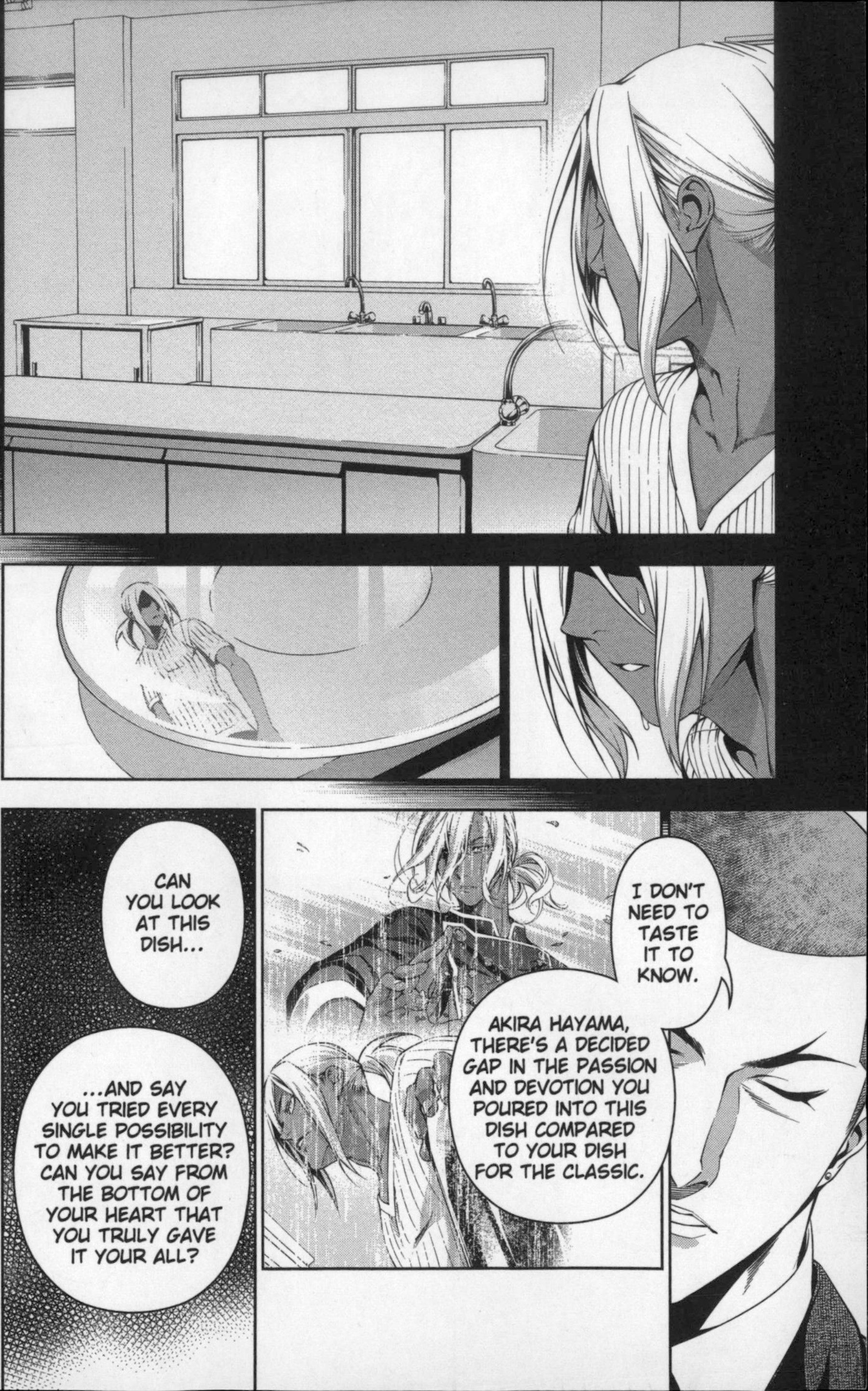
I DON'T NEED TO TASTE IT TO KNOW.
AKIRA HAYAMA, THERE'S A DECIDED GAP IN THE PASSION AND DEVOTION YOU POURED INTO THIS DISH COMPARED TO YOUR DISH FOR THE CLASSIC.
CAN YOU LOOK AT THIS DISH...
...AND SAY YOU TRIED EVERY SINGLE POSSIBILITY TO MAKE IT BETTER? CAN YOU SAY FROM THE BOTTOM OF YOUR HEART THAT YOU TRULY GAVE IT YOUR ALL?

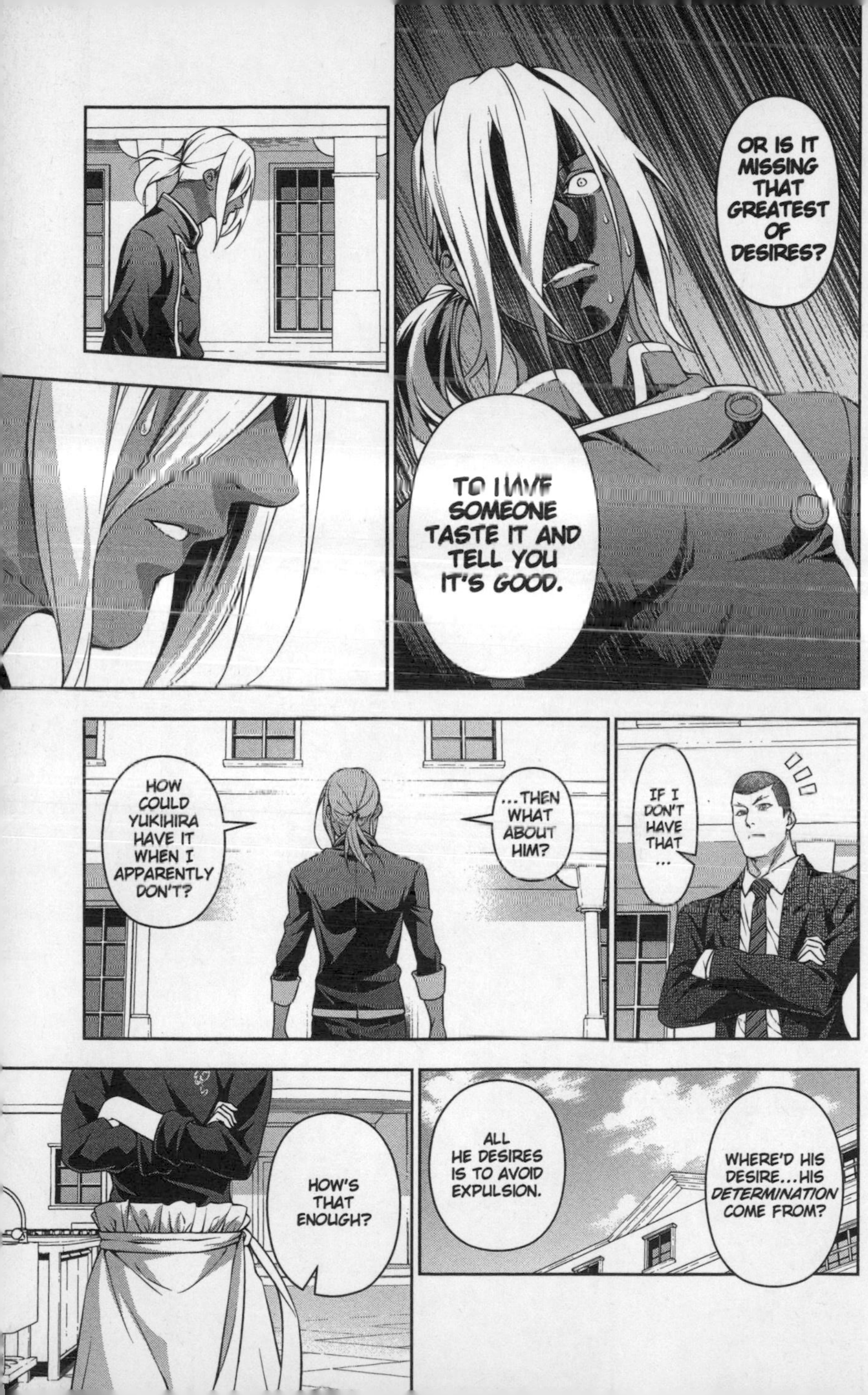
OR IS IT MISSING THAT GREATEST OF DESIRES?
TO HAVE SOMEONE TASTE IT AND TELL YOU IT'S GOOD.
IF I DON'T HAVE THAT ...
...THEN WHAT ABOUT HIM?
HOW COULD YUKIHIRA HAVE IT WHEN I APPARENTLY DON'T?
WHERE'D HIS DESIRE...HIS *DETERMINATION* COME FROM?
ALL HE DESIRES IS TO AVOID EXPULSION.
HOW'S THAT ENOUGH?

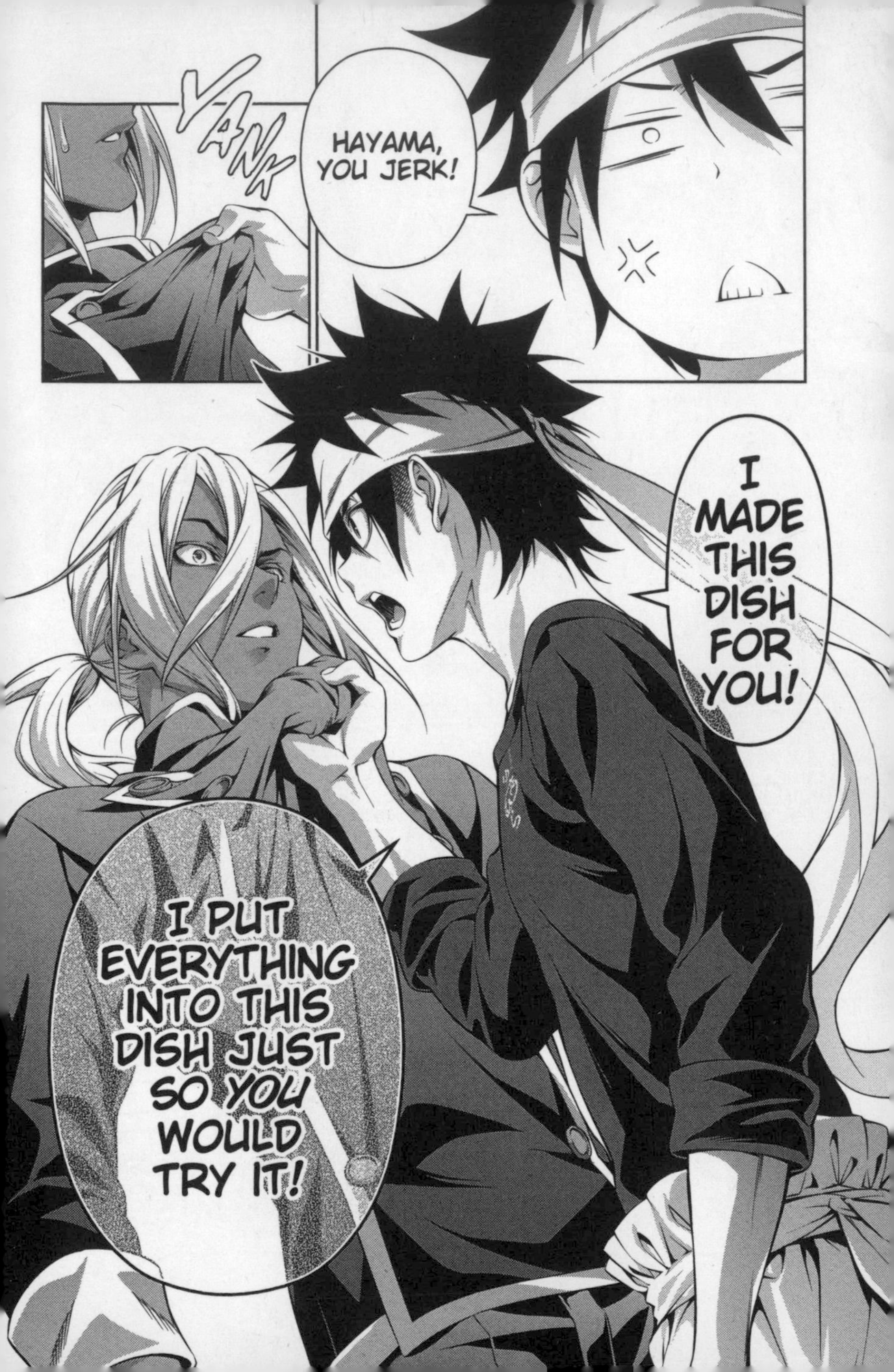
HAYAMA, YOU JERK!
YANK
I MADE THIS DISH FOR YOU!
I PUT EVERYTHING INTO THIS DISH JUST SO YOU WOULD TRY IT!

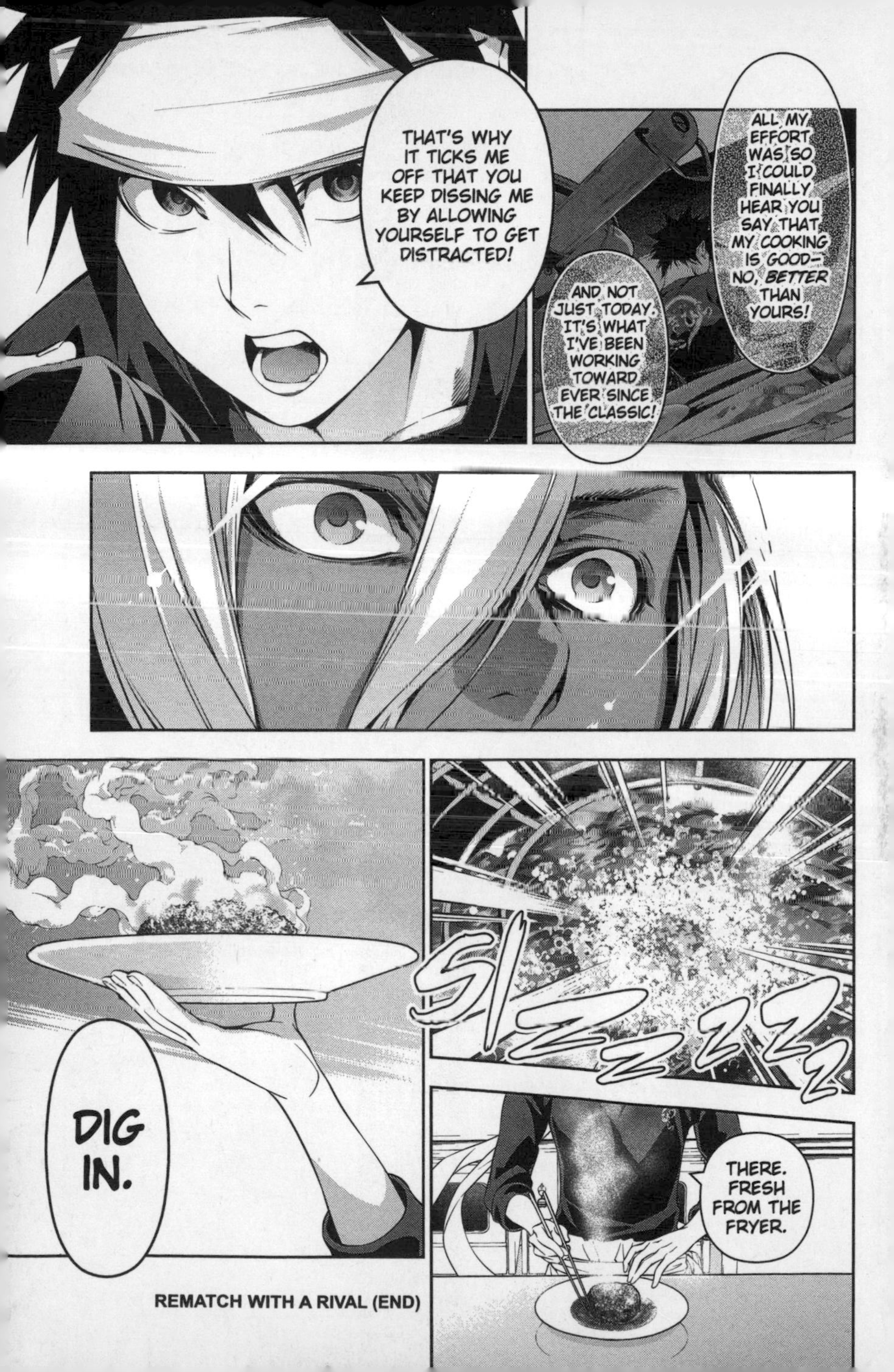
ALL MY EFFORT WAS SO I COULD FINALLY HEAR YOU SAY THAT MY COOKING IS GOOD— NO, *BETTER* THAN YOURS!
AND NOT JUST TODAY. IT'S WHAT I'VE BEEN WORKING TOWARD EVER SINCE THE CLASSIC!
THAT'S WHY IT TICKS ME OFF THAT YOU KEEP DISSING ME BY ALLOWING YOURSELF TO GET DISTRACTED!
SIZZZZZZ
THERE. FRESH FROM THE FRYER.
DIG IN.

REMATCH WITH A RIVAL (END)

ARTIST: YUTO TSUKUDA RECIPE BY: YUKI MORISAKI

VOLUME 22
SPECIAL SUPPLEMENT!

PRACTICAL RECIPE #1

HAYAMA'S FRIED CHICKEN

~W/ CREAMY JUNIPER BERRY GRAVY~

<<EASY FAMILY VERSION>>

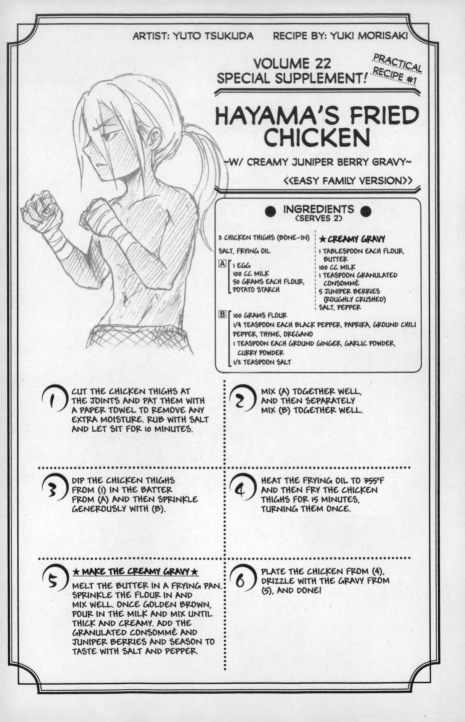

● INGREDIENTS ●
(SERVES 2)

2 CHICKEN THIGHS (BONE-IN)

SALT, FRYING OIL

[A]
- 1 EGG
- 100 CC MILK
- 50 GRAMS EACH FLOUR, POTATO STARCH

★ CREAMY GRAVY
- 1 TABLESPOON EACH FLOUR, BUTTER
- 100 CC MILK
- 1 TEASPOON GRANULATED CONSOMMÉ
- 5 JUNIPER BERRIES (ROUGHLY CRUSHED)
- SALT, PEPPER

[B]
- 100 GRAMS FLOUR
- 1/4 TEASPOON EACH BLACK PEPPER, PAPRIKA, GROUND CHILI PEPPER, THYME, OREGANO
- 1 TEASPOON EACH GROUND GINGER, GARLIC POWDER, CURRY POWDER
- 1/2 TEASPOON SALT

1. CUT THE CHICKEN THIGHS AT THE JOINTS AND PAT THEM WITH A PAPER TOWEL TO REMOVE ANY EXTRA MOISTURE. RUB WITH SALT AND LET SIT FOR 10 MINUTES.
2. MIX (A) TOGETHER WELL, AND THEN SEPARATELY MIX (B) TOGETHER WELL.
3. DIP THE CHICKEN THIGHS FROM (1) IN THE BATTER FROM (A) AND THEN SPRINKLE GENEROUSLY WITH (B).
4. HEAT THE FRYING OIL TO 355°F AND THEN FRY THE CHICKEN THIGHS FOR 15 MINUTES, TURNING THEM ONCE.
5. **★ MAKE THE CREAMY GRAVY ★**
   MELT THE BUTTER IN A FRYING PAN. SPRINKLE THE FLOUR IN AND MIX WELL. ONCE GOLDEN BROWN, POUR IN THE MILK AND MIX UNTIL THICK AND CREAMY. ADD THE GRANULATED CONSOMMÉ AND JUNIPER BERRIES AND SEASON TO TASTE WITH SALT AND PEPPER.
6. PLATE THE CHICKEN FROM (4), DRIZZLE WITH THE GRAVY FROM (5), AND DONE!

VOLUME 22 SPECIAL SUPPLEMENT!

PRACTICAL RECIPE #2

SOMA'S MENCHI KATSU HAMBURGER STEAK

~W/ HONEY SAUCE~

<<EASY FAMILY VERSION>>

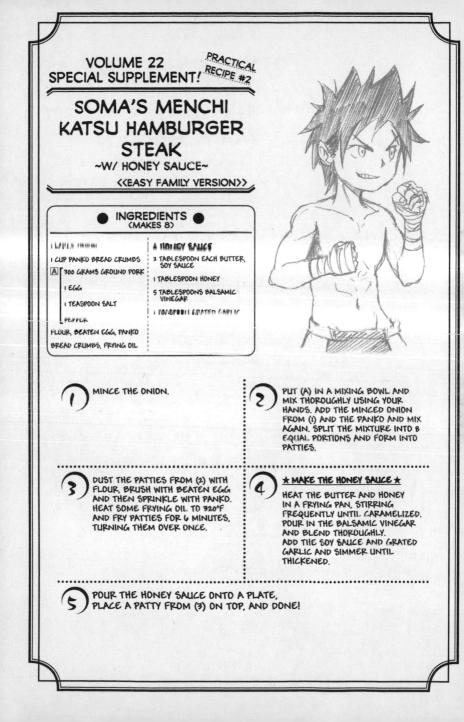

● INGREDIENTS ●
(MAKES 8)

1 LARGE ONION

1 CUP PANKO BREAD CRUMBS

A
- 300 GRAMS GROUND PORK
- 1 EGG
- 1 TEASPOON SALT
- PEPPER

FLOUR, BEATEN EGG, PANKO BREAD CRUMBS, FRYING OIL

★ HONEY SAUCE

2 TABLESPOON EACH BUTTER, SOY SAUCE

1 TABLESPOON HONEY

5 TABLESPOONS BALSAMIC VINEGAR

1 TEASPOON GRATED GARLIC

1. MINCE THE ONION.

2. PUT (A) IN A MIXING BOWL AND MIX THOROUGHLY USING YOUR HANDS. ADD THE MINCED ONION FROM (1) AND THE PANKO AND MIX AGAIN. SPLIT THE MIXTURE INTO 8 EQUAL PORTIONS AND FORM INTO PATTIES.

3. DUST THE PATTIES FROM (2) WITH FLOUR, BRUSH WITH BEATEN EGG AND THEN SPRINKLE WITH PANKO. HEAT SOME FRYING OIL TO 320°F AND FRY PATTIES FOR 6 MINUTES, TURNING THEM OVER ONCE.

4. ★ MAKE THE HONEY SAUCE ★

   HEAT THE BUTTER AND HONEY IN A FRYING PAN, STIRRING FREQUENTLY UNTIL CARAMELIZED. POUR IN THE BALSAMIC VINEGAR AND BLEND THOROUGHLY.
   ADD THE SOY SAUCE AND GRATED GARLIC AND SIMMER UNTIL THICKENED.

5. POUR THE HONEY SAUCE ONTO A PLATE, PLACE A PATTY FROM (3) ON TOP, AND DONE!

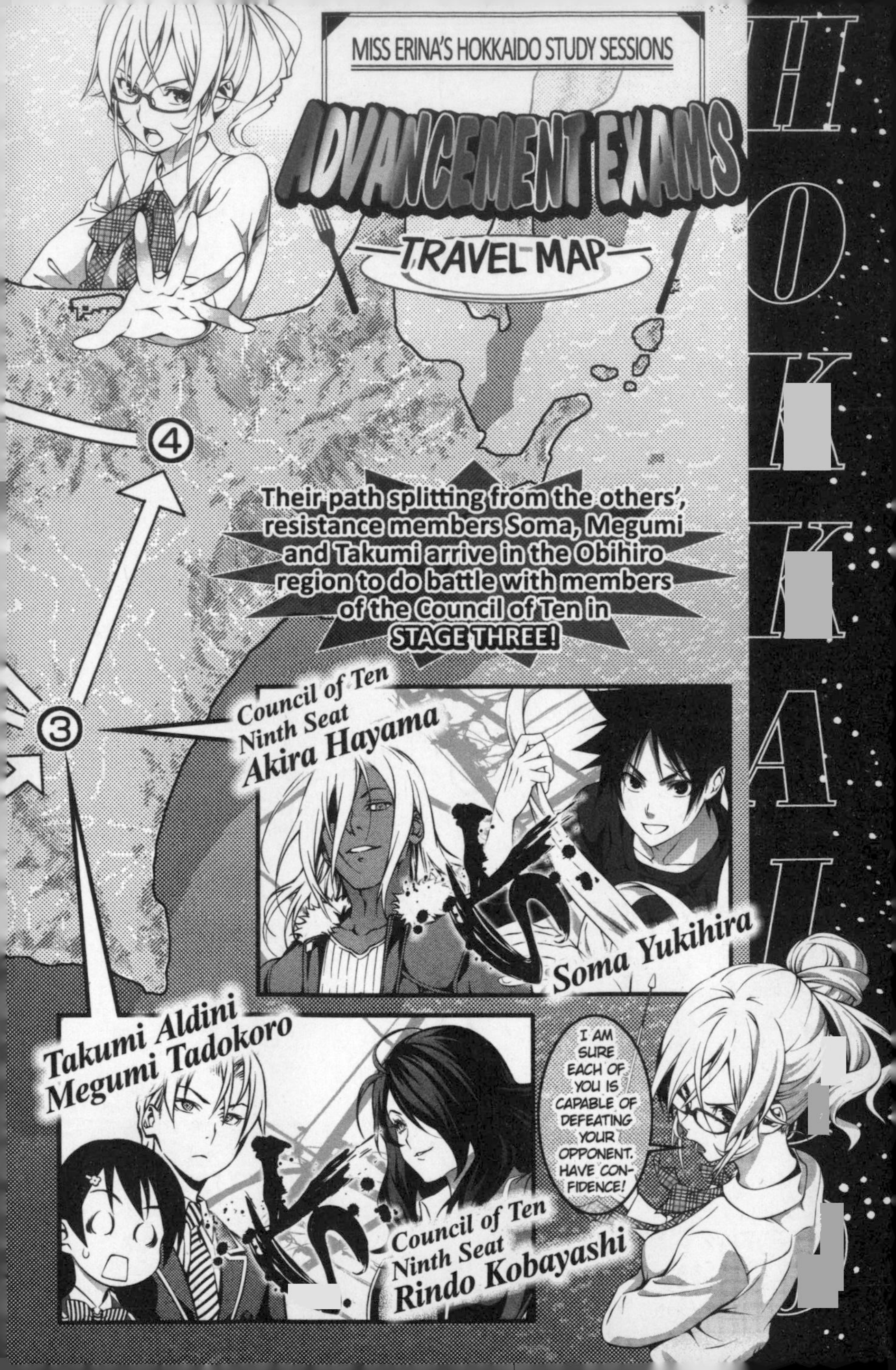
MISS ERINA'S HOKKAIDO STUDY SESSIONS
ADVANCEMENT EXAMS
TRAVEL MAP
④
Their path splitting from the others', resistance members Soma, Megumi and Takumi arrive in the Obihiro region to do battle with members of the Council of Ten in STAGE THREE!
③
Council of Ten Ninth Seat Akira Hayama
Soma Yukihira
Takumi Aldini
Megumi Tadokoro
I AM SURE EACH OF YOU IS CAPABLE OF DEFEATING YOUR OPPONENT. HAVE CONFIDENCE!
Council of Ten Ninth Seat Rindo Kobayashi

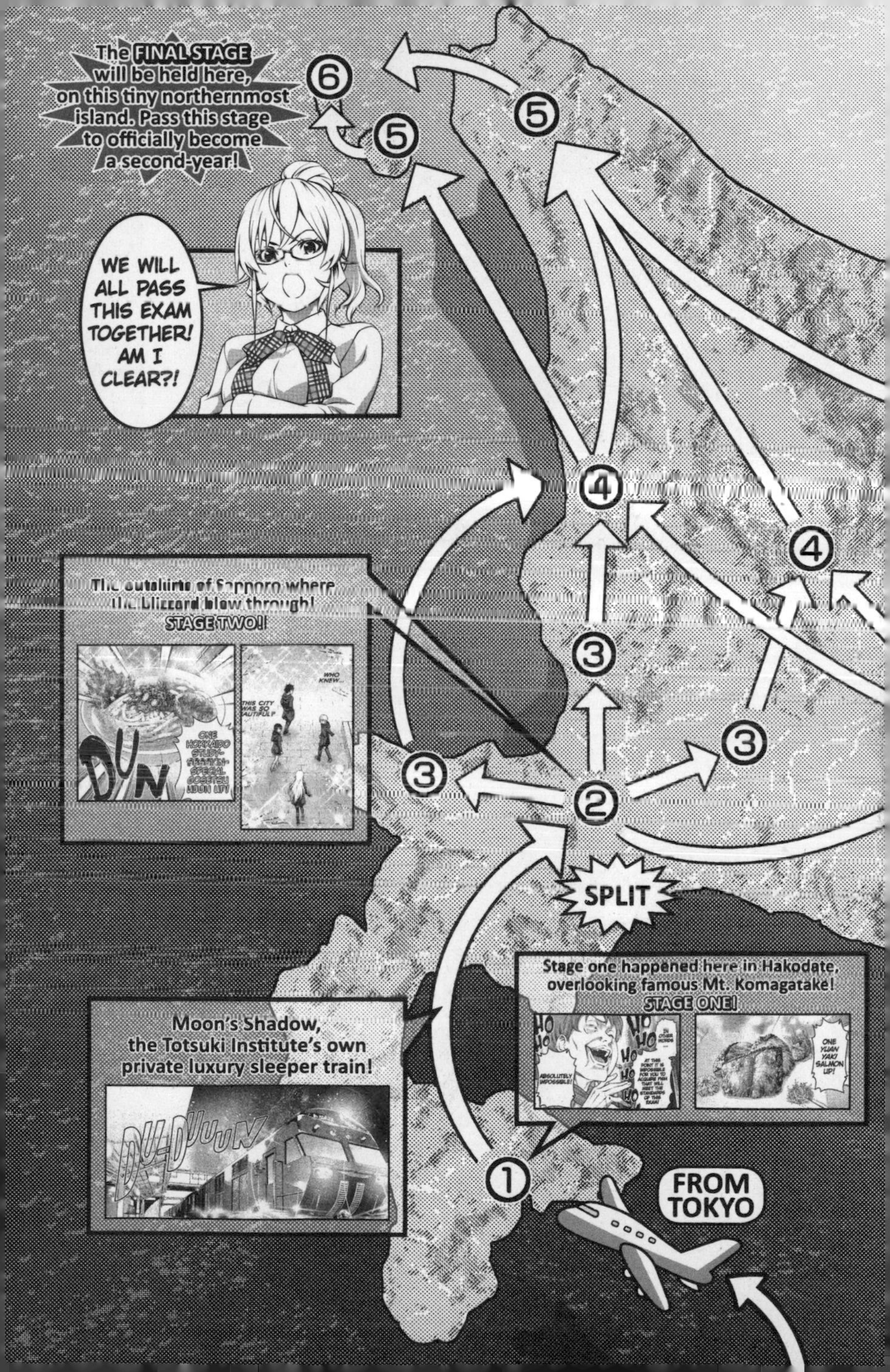

The FINAL STAGE will be held here, on this tiny northernmost island. Pass this stage to officially become a second-year!
⑥
⑤
⑤
WE WILL ALL PASS THIS EXAM TOGETHER! AM I CLEAR?!
④
④
The outskirts of Sapporo where the blizzard blew through!
STAGE TWO!!
WHO KNEW...
THIS CITY WAS SO BEAUTIFUL?
DUN
ONE HOKKAIDO STUDY-
SPECIAL GOSETSU UDON UP!
③
③
③
②
SPLIT
Stage one happened here in Hakodate, overlooking famous Mt. Komagatake!
STAGE ONE!
ONE YUAN YAKI SALMON UP!
IN OTHER WORDS...
AT THIS POINT IT IS IMPOSSIBLE FOR YOU TO ACQUIRE FISH THAT WILL MEET THE STANDARDS OF THIS EXAM!
HO HO HO HO HO HO HO
ABSOLUTELY IMPOSSIBLE!
Moon's Shadow, the Totsuki Institute's own private luxury sleeper train!
DU-DUUUN
①
FROM TOKYO

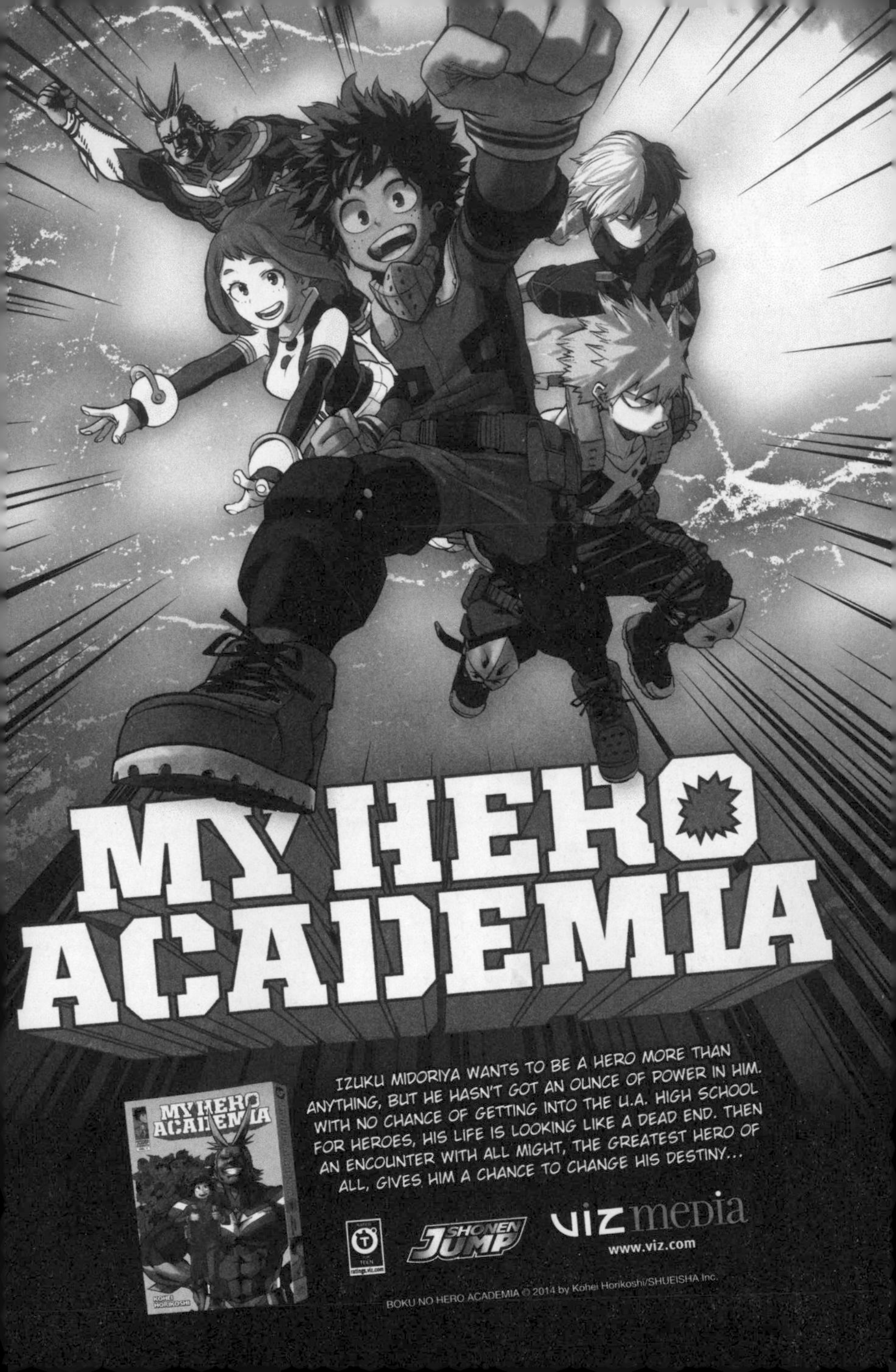
MY HERO ACADEMIA
IZUKU MIDORIYA WANTS TO BE A HERO MORE THAN ANYTHING, BUT HE HASN'T GOT AN OUNCE OF POWER IN HIM. WITH NO CHANCE OF GETTING INTO THE U.A. HIGH SCHOOL FOR HEROES, HIS LIFE IS LOOKING LIKE A DEAD END. THEN AN ENCOUNTER WITH ALL MIGHT, THE GREATEST HERO OF ALL, GIVES HIM A CHANCE TO CHANGE HIS DESTINY…
MY HERO ACADEMIA
KOHEI HORIKOSHI
TEEN
ratings.viz.com
SHONEN JUMP
viz media
www.viz.com
BOKU NO HERO ACADEMIA © 2014 by Kohei Horikoshi/SHUEISHA Inc.

You're Reading in the Wrong Direction!!

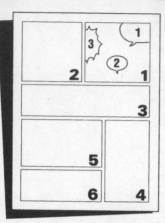

Whoops! Guess what? You're starting at the wrong end of the comic!

...It's true! In keeping with the original Japanese format, **Food Wars!** is meant to be read from right to left, starting in the upper-right corner.

Unlike English, which is read from left to right, Japanese is read from right to left, meaning that action, sound effects and word-balloon order are completely reversed... something which can make readers unfamiliar with Japanese feel pretty backwards themselves. For this reason, manga or Japanese comics published in the U.S. in English have sometimes been published "flopped"—that is, printed in exact reverse order, as though seen from the other side of a mirror.

By flopping pages, U.S. publishers can avoid confusing readers, but the compromise is not without its downside. For one thing, a character in a flopped manga series who once wore in the original Japanese version a T-shirt emblazoned with "M A Y" (as in "the merry month of") now wears one which reads "Y A M"! Additionally, many manga creators in Japan are themselves unhappy with the process, as some feel the mirror-imaging of their art skews their original intentions.

We are proud to bring you Yuto Tsukuda and Shun Saeki's **Food Wars!** in the original unflopped format.

For now, though, turn to the other side of the book and let the adventure begin...!

—Editor